Their Lives and Times
Women in Newfoundland and Labrador: A Collage

Their Lives and Times

Women in Newfoundland and Labrador: A Collage

Carmelita McGrath, Barbara Neis, Marilyn Porter, editors

Killick Press
St. John's, Newfoundland
1995

© 1995

Appreciation is expressed to *The Canada Council* for publication assistance.

The publisher acknowledges the financial contribution of the *Department of Tourism and Culture, Government of Newfoundland and Labrador,* which has helped make this publication possible.

The support of the Government of Canada and the Province of Newfoundland, through the *Canada/Newfoundland COOPERATION Agreement on Cultural Industries,* is gratefully acknowledged.

∝ Printed on acid-free paper

Cover design: Beth Oberholtzer

Published by
KILLICK PRESS
an imprint of CREATIVE BOOK PUBLISHING
a division of 10366 Newfoundland Limited
a Robinson-Blackmore Printing & Publishing associated company
P.O. Box 8660, St. John's, Newfoundland A1B 3T7

Printed in Canada by:
ROBINSON-BLACKMORE PRINTING & PUBLISHING

Canadian Cataloguing in Publication Data

Main entry under title:

Their lives and times

Includes bibliographical references.

ISBN 1-895387-42-6

1. Women — Newfoundland — History. 2. Women — Newfoundland — Social conditions. 3. Feminism — Newfoundland — History. I. McGrath, Carmelita. II. Neis, Barbara, 1952- III. Porter Marilyn, 1942-

    ⁀ N48T43 1995   305.4'09718   C95-950143-6

Table of Contents

Preface

WHEN SHE HAD WORKED ALL NIGHT HEADING COD Kitty would "wash down the splitting table, and get upon it, would put up her skirts, and dance an Irish jig to her own singing" (Devine, 1990: 21).

This collage brings together pieces of work that have sought to capture women's experience in Newfoundland and Labrador. The title, *Their Lives and Times*, plays on the double meaning of *Times* (historical and celebratory). Central themes in the collage include oppression, drudgery, resistance and joy. Kitty, a turn of the century fish header, is perhaps an appropriate symbol for these diverse themes.

When a few feminists began working on the history and sociology of women in Newfoundland and Labrador in 1980, there was very little previous work to draw on and few other feminist scholars with whom to compare notes. Surely, we thought, the history of women in Newfoundland and Labrador could not have been so thoroughly neglected? It had been, of course. But the next decade saw a surge of major new work by both scholars and creative writers that brought women into the forefront.

It was in this atmosphere of enthusiasm for the project of recapturing and understanding women's experience that we started work on this book—an attempt to bring together previously published material with unpublished work, to place academic papers alongside poems and stories. There are many ways of understanding and expressing reality; only a combination of them can do justice to the richness of women's lives. Many of you will find pieces by writers familiar to you, and others by writers new to you.

The editors had known each other before we began to collaborate on this book. Barbara and Marilyn work in the same university department. This, however, didn't necessarily mean that the chance to work together on an enjoyable project came easily or often. Too often, feminists whistle past each other in hallways, too busy with myriad chores to dwell on the really important things. Marilyn and Carmelita had worked together before, but on a very different project, and in a different working relationship. Unlike the other project, Carmelita's involvement with this one grew out of her work as a writer and editor within the writing community in Newfoundland. Her approach was to view literary work as another "way of knowing": experience recorded and reflected and, taken a step further, distilled into art. Her participation meant that we could turn away from the confines of academic writing and expertise and embrace a variety of literary expressions.

The editors of this book had long since defined ourselves as "feminist," and, indeed, had met each other in the feminist community in St. John's. We also knew that the object of the book was to bring together "feminist" pieces and to contribute to a "feminist" understanding of women's lives in Newfoundland and Labrador. But what is this "feminism"? Is it the same for everyone? Can it be defined? Is it the "F" word we are supposed to avoid? And if it is, why don't we?

There have been many attempts to define feminism—both friendly and unfriendly. One 'Feminist Dictionary' gives eleven separate (and often conflicting) accounts. Feminism is many and various. We believe that at its core, feminism is about being interested in the situation of women and committed to improving it. We also believe that feminism includes all women, and certainly all those with enough interest in the subject to pick up a book like this!

The papers in this book, especially the more "academic" ones, are rooted in and shaped by particular theories about how the world works, about how to do research, and how to interpret its results. When you read it, it will be helpful to know something of the different contexts in which its contents were framed. Differences are most clearly illustrated in the academic papers, but some of the same shifts in interests and methods are also evident in the creative writing.

Hilda Murray (1979), Greta Hussey (this volume) and others writing in the 1970s did not use the word "feminism" nor did they explicitly use the theory that was being developed by feminist scholars. They seemed primarily to want to write about women's lives, to somehow arrest the near invisibility of women's experience. It was enough to describe how things really were. And, at the time, Hilda Murray's account of women's work in Elliston and Greta Hussey's description of her life in a Labrador fishing station were revolutionary because no one had previously written about such experiences. At last women readers could recognize *themselves* as opposed to having to make do with identifying with descriptions of *men's* lives. The underlying theory of both these works and others of the same period was that women did, indeed, contribute to the household economy, and through that to the economy of the province and region.

The 1970s had seen the emergence of several distinct strands of feminist interpretation. These included a "liberal" strand that tended to seek equality with men and to ascribe women's subordination to discrimination and to individual men's lack of education about the rights of women, and the "radical" strand that saw the world as polarized on sex lines and took a more militant approach to the problem of women's subordination. Both these approaches produced their own agendas for both action and research, but academic feminism, at least in Canada and the UK, was dominated by feminists who derived their basic framework from Marx's work. They added gender to their analysis of class relations, and they focused on the economic and political structures of capitalism as the source of women's subordination. This meant that they took a particular interest in economic conditions and in the economic structure of particular industries (such as the fishery). Much marxist-feminist attention at this time was taken up with efforts to understand and evaluate women's economic contributions to the household, especially in terms of their unpaid work—housework, childcare and other subsistence activities. It was also important for marxist-feminist writers to see the experience of Newfoundland women in the context of a marxist interpretation of similar situations, such as those of fishing communities in Nova Scotia and in Norway. Ellen Antler, Marilyn Porter and Barbara Neis situated their work in this framework for many years. Others, such as Linda Christiansen-Ruffman and Dona Davis brought other ideas and priorities to their work.

One of the striking things about marxist-feminist work is the way in which feminism forced the scholars involved to mount challenges to both the form and the substance of established marxist scholarship. This can be seen in the explicit challenges to male marxist scholars' conclusions and to the broader focus we chose. For example, both Porter (1985) and Neis (Doin' Time) took seriously women's forms of political organization in a way that would have been unrecognizable to male marxists.

We made the family, household and the community foci for understanding how things worked in Newfoundland. All this was necessary and apposite. It moved the feminist project forward. But the next generation of work has infinitely expanded both the foci of interest and the approaches used to understand them.

Earlier scholars, especially those who had not been brought up in Newfoundland, tended to focus on the "difference" of life in the outports, and to study them in that light. The newer generation of writers, more of whom were brought up in Newfoundland, is less romantic and more inclined to be interested in lives that reflect their own experience. For these feminists, creating a shared identity and understanding became more important. Rural to urban mobility was a fact in the lives of Newfoundlanders, as, indeed, it was for those who went on to graduate work. A growing interest in the circumstances of urban life was a natural outcome of this migration and is reflected in Cecilia Benoit's description of the urbanization of Stephenville and Linda Parsons' discussion of women's lives in Labrador City. Nancy Forestell's piece on working- class women in St. John's reflects the more recent influence of feminist social history on scholarly work in the province.

We can see shifts in the topics that attract the interest of feminists in the work of both academic and creative writers. Much of this is because of the pioneering work done to uncover the darker side of family and community life. Violence against women and children, child sexual abuse, incest and sexual harassment are among the issues that have come to light over the past few years. Only now is there sufficient recognition that such things happen to enable some serious research to take place. In the 1980s it would not have occurred to most researchers to ask about such things. Not only were such topics not central to their theoretical frameworks, but if a researcher had asked, she would have met with blank, and even hostile, rebuttal. Within the terms of the nostalgic idyll of rural Newfoundland that still prevailed, such things were literally "unheard of." It took the traumas of the Mount Cashel investigation and the series of cases against Catholic priests and brothers and other, escalating revelations of long-buried pain to demonstrate that Newfoundland was not a unique, pastoral heaven, but a participant in the consequences of a sexist, patriarchal and violent culture. There has been an upsurge of writing that attempts to uncover and understand these issues.

More particularly, the issue of choice or lack of it, or of the constitution of the subjective, became more important than the economic context that framed it. Increasingly, writers preferred to discuss intimate relationships and the nature of the individual psyche rather than the nuts and bolts of material life that had preoccupied their predecessors. This trend draws together the work of academic and creative writers; now, both are looking at the same set of topics, using different methods. Indeed, one of the most exciting developments in feminist work recently has been the upwelling of research in disciplines that used to be more removed from the research frontline. New theories and approaches in these disciplines have meant that young scholars working on feminist interpretations of the lives of New-foundland women are just as likely to be trained in textual criticism as in fieldwork.

New writers are challenging the feminist and nonfeminist traditions in which they have been brought up. The first generation of feminist graduate students from the province are bringing to their writing on Newfoundland women insights from new and different theoretical perspectives. Several of the contributors to this collage have, for example, drawn on the writings of Dorothy Smith in identifying new research questions and developing new analytical frameworks. Smith has been most valuable in concentrating the growing feminist dissatisfaction with the treatment of feminist theory within the established disciplines, and for making a space for a distinctive "sociology for women" (Smith, 1987). Her original ideas drew on both marxism and a theory known as "ethnomethodology." The latter corrected the marxist bias towards macro-analysis and an exclusive concentration on the economic sphere, by highlighting the sociology of the everyday and developing detailed, qualitative methodologies to enable us to examine aspects of our everyday lives. Linked with another strand of inquiry, discourse analysis, Smith's work provided a complex and sensitive means that aided feminists' search for a theory and methodologies that did justice to the invisible, the personal and the supposedly unimportant parts of our lives. Her influence is evident in the contributions by Linda Cullum, Glenys George, Robin Whitaker and Jane Robinson.

If there is one theory that dominates much of the new writing, it is the one known variously as "post-modernism," "post-structuralism" or (in the narrower textual criticism context) "de-constructionism." Post-modernism began and was developed mainly by male scholars. Many feminists argue (as they did about marxism) that it is inappropriate and potentially misleading to try to "fit" feminist theory to an existing "male" theory. They point to the overwhelming number of males involved in post-modern writing and to the heavy sexist bias of much of it. More extreme opposition holds that post-modernism is inherently and inescapably anti-feminist. Its adherents, on the other hand, especially those in literature, film studies and psychoanalysis, say that post-modernism's rejection of any overarching "correct" approach, any absolute, universal theory, enables them to dethrone the establishment "dead white men" who have dominated western thought for so long. By opening up space, new voices can be heard, including those of First Nations women, lesbians, disabled women and others. The liberating, anti-establishment, de-constructive verve of post-modernists is, indeed, refreshing, and you will find that the writers in this book, like Robin Whitaker, who espouse it, are able to use it to pry open new areas and interpretations for women. Nevertheless, it seems more adapted to textual criticism and to breaking into new areas of enquiry than to political analysis and action. This flies in the face of one of the fundamental tenets of feminist scholarship, which is to understand women's experience in order to improve it.

The fishery is so important in Newfoundland that despite profound shifts in feminist foci, much work continues to focus on it. Included in this book are several papers by scholars who have recently examined aspects of women and the fishery using a wider variety of approaches and methods than was common earlier. Miriam Wright, for example, uses official texts and illustrations to demonstrate underlying sexism in federal fisheries policies; Victoria Silk describes her own experience as a fisher and analyzes why it was so difficult; Jane Robinson looks at the gender-biased administration of government assistance to Trepassey after the closure of its fish plant in the early days of the current fisheries crisis; Dona Davis discusses some of the impacts of the collapse of the cod stocks on women in a fishing community. Barbara Neis (1994) has addressed related questions elsewhere. In response to the crisis, women in the fishery have recently begun, once again, to tell their own stories, extending the tradition of Greta Hussey (Educational Planning and Design Associates, 1994). We look forward to future publications of this kind. Because of its continuing importance to Newfoundland women, the fishery—or lack of it— will continue to be an important strand in research and writing on Newfoundland and Labrador. However, the methods by which we study it and the interpretations we make will shift as new scholars and writers take new approaches.

Despite the greatly enlarged agenda of more recent feminist writing, there is still much unexplored terrain. In editing this book, we have learned to listen a little more carefully to some voices that have been silenced for too long. First Nations women are an obvious example. We still have few accounts about and by First Nations women. We have tried to encourage more work in this area with our opening and closing collages of historical accounts and a sample of quotes from the Innu Nation's *Gathering Voices*. Other groups are also absent either as subjects or as writers. There is little here that addresses the issues of older and younger women. There is nothing on disability, the lesbian experience, or the lives of Franco-New-foundland women. Some geographical areas, including the Northern Peninsula and northern Labrador, hardly feature in the book.

In terms of creative work, only a few pieces from a very large and varied body of new work are included. We have deliberately included selections that were written in the same time period as the academic pieces. It would be interesting to see an anthology of women's creative writing that illustrated the shifts that have occurred in these women's work since it first began to appear.

It is simply not possible to collect in one book all that now exists on women in Newfoundland and Labrador, but the present collection represents some of the variety of interests and approaches that women have developed to understand and express their experience. Each reader will be able to assemble a powerful list of what is missing from this book. Our hope is that some will feel impelled to create further collections that will better represent the issues they identify with. The end of this book is a beginning.

Acknowledgements

THE EDITORS would like to thank the following individuals and organizations whose intellectual and practical support helped to see this project to its conclusion: Annette Carter and Denise Porter of Memorial University; Memorial University of Newfoundland; the Provincial Archives of Newfoundland and Labrador; the Federal/Provincial Cooperation Agreement on Cultural Industries.

For permission to reprint published works, we are grateful to: ISER Books for works by Bonnie McCay and Barbara Neis; *Newfoundland History 1986: Proceedings of the First Historical Society Conference* for work by Roberta Buchanan; Peter Penashue of the Innu Nation for "Gathering Voices"; AMS Press, Inc. for work by Anauta and Heluiz Washburne. Also: excerpts from books by Mary Dalton, Bernice Morgan and Helen Porter appear courtesy of Breakwater Books; works by Nancy Forestell and Marilyn Porter are reprinted with the permission of the editor of *Labour/Le Travail*, 24 (Fall 1989) and 15 (Spring 1985). © Committee on Canadian Labour History.

We would also like to the thank the contributors to this book for their work and patience throughout its long gestation period. Our publisher, Don Morgan at Killick Press, had confidence in a new kind of enterprise. Barbara and Marilyn would especially like to thank Carmelita for many cups of coffee, for reminding us that sometimes we have to "kill our darlings" to achieve a better book and for all of her extra work editing the final manuscript. Carmelita would like to express appreciation to Marilyn and Barbara for their vision and staying power, and to Ken and Leah for their support.

A Collage Within a Collage:
Original Traces of First Nations Women

Barbara Neis

Introduction

In 1997, the Newfoundland government will celebrate the 500th anniversary of the arrival of John Cabot. Although by no means the first European presence in the region, this arrival symbolizes the initiation of European colonization. European women were to become an integral part of that colonization process. However, just as the history of the region does not begin with European contact, the arrival of European women did not mark the beginning of women's presence in the area. On the contrary, Newfoundland and Labrador had already been home to a succession of peoples. Some of these appear to have disappeared prior to the arrival of the Europeans; others, including Innu, Inuit, Beothuk and Micmac met the Europeans when they arrived. One people, the Beothuk, disappeared as a result of the onslaught of disease, hunger and violence that came with white settlement. The ranks of others were decimated, but some survived.

We have decided to open this anthology with a loosely analyzed collage of historical and other documents highlighting key features of the early colonization lives of First Nations women. Our intent is to remind our readers that Newfoundland and Labrador were not "untracked wildernesses" prior to the arrival of Europeans, and that there is a need to document in more detail these women's lives and experiences. We would also like our readers to critically reflect on plans to "celebrate" historical events that had catastrophic consequences for First Nations people.

The voices of First Nations women are rarely heard in documents from the first years of European colonization. Portrayals of these women are generally constructed from the perspective of contemporary and current men of European descent. These portrayals probably tell us as much about male European imaginings as they do about First Nations women and gender relations among these peoples (Francis, 1992). Archaeological and anthropological accounts have added somewhat to our understanding, but even these do not provide a clear picture of the pre- and early contact lives of First Nations women. In some cases, women's power can be interpreted through the crafts they left behind. In others, their rage is detectable in descriptions of their "sulkiness" or "bad-tempered" response to capture.

The Beothuk

The Maritime Archaic and palaeo Eskimo people were the predecessors of the Beothuk on the island of Newfoundland. While the origins of the Beothuk remain obscure, they seem to have had cultural links to Algonkians, including the Innu of Quebec-Labrador (Armitage, 1991). From 800 A.D. to 1500, the Beothuk appear to have had the island of Newfoundland to themselves. They lived in migratory bands of 30-50 spread across much of the island. The total estimated population was somewhere between 1200 and 500 (Marshall, 1989; Pastore, 1992). After 1500 A.D., an influx of Europeans from England, France, Spain and Portugal, and the increased presence of the Micmac along the southwest coast, worked to gradually limit the territory occupied by the Beothuk. By the end of the 17th century they were concentrated in a region extending from Bonavista Bay perhaps as far north as Hare Bay. Encroachments on their remaining territory increased with settlement and the establishment of salmon fishery/fur enterprises on the rivers in the region. Conflict escalated as European and Beothuk competition for the same resources deepened. Shawnadithit, the last known surviving Beothuk, was captured in 1823 and died in St. John's in 1829. Around this time her people became extinct.

Much of the existing literature concentrates on the role of European settlers in the demise of the Beothuk. Scholarly accounts have challenged the all too common presentation of Newfoundland settlers as peculiarly violent and uncaring in their treatment of them (see, for example, Budgell, 1992). There appears to have been relatively little contact between Europeans and Beothuk during the first 300 years although "the records suggest that Beothuk were captured or otherwise wronged, that the Indians, on their part, indulged in pilfering gear and tools, and that relations were precarious" (Marshall, 1989: 13). Aggression on the part of some English settlers is substantiated by the historical record, particularly for the period after the mid-18th century when conflict over resources peaked.

Because there was little formalized trade between Europeans and the Beothuk and no missionaries or other literate whites spent time among them, virtually nothing is known about the internal workings of Beothuk society (Pastore, personal communication). Pre-contact gender relations and the impact of contact on those relations remain obscure. There are no gender analyses of existing material on the Beothuk or white-Beothuk relations. The following discussion does not provide such an analysis but rather uses some passages taken from existing documents to point to themes that could be pursued.

Ironically, while written history in Western culture is dominated by the thoughts and activities of men, this is less true of existing eye-witness accounts of Beothuk lives and Beothuk-European contacts. Aside from the accounts of observers like Cormack and archaeological evidence, much of what is known about the Beothuk was learned from two women, Demasduit and Shanawdithit. Demasduit was captured in 1819. Pursued by starvation, isolation and illness, Shanawdithit surrendered with her mother and sister in 1823. These women provided information on Beothuk language, food, housing and on Beothuk-white contact. Their behaviour during captivity was used as a basis for assessing gender and family relations among the Beothuk. Although this information came from Beothuk women, it was largely elicited, selected and interpreted by English men. Men also documented, in diverse forms, the events that led to their capture. (Howley, 1974).

The capture of Demasduit figures strongly in Howley's summary description of the "Status of the Red Indian Women."

Amongst the Beothuks the women seem to have been held in greater esteem and been treated more in accordance with civilized notions of what is due to the weaker sex, than was usual amongst savage peoples. At least we are led to infer as much from several facts contained in the foregoing references and traditions.

There are two or three instances recorded, where when surprised by the whites, the women had recourse to appealing to their enemies' sympathy or better nature, by laying bare their bosoms, thus disclosing their sex, in the vain hope of turning aside their enmity. I look upon this fact as clearly indicating that such an appeal would be considered amongst themselves as one calculated to ward off the threatened blow. Then again we have the noble example of affection displayed by poor Nonos-a-ba-sut, husband of Mary March, who did not hesitate to face his enemies and brave death itself, in the endeavour to rescue his wife from the despoilers' hands. There is the further example of filial affection displayed by the Indian boy August, who said if he could come across the ruffian who shot his mother, he would wreak vengeance upon him.

In the tradition about the Carbonear white women captives, we are told that these women were treated with every consideration by the Indians, and that they observed that their own women were also well treated by the sterner sex, in that respect, fully as well as amongst civilized beings.

Mr. Peyton informed me, that when conveying Mary March out to the sea coast, they drew her on a sled. She seemed to demand and expect kindly treatment at their hands. She would sit upon the sled, put out her feet and intimate by signs she wanted someone to lace up her moccasins, and in many other ways seemed to look upon such little services as a matter of course. Both she and Nancy during their sojourn among the white people, looked for and expected as their right such small attentions, and resented anything approaching rough, harsh or unseemly conduct on the part of the fishermen" (1974: 261-262).

Howley's account dichotomizes savage and civilized. Our sympathy for the Beothuk is elicited on the basis of the extent to which Beothuk women and gender relations among the Beothuk approximate accepted European, bourgeois standards for female behaviour. Howley's attempt to distance the Beothuk from other First Nations peoples suggests their claim to humanity depends upon proof of their distance from a more common "savagery." Other, less sympathetic accounts of the Beothuk located them firmly in the dark, "primitive" category of ignoble savage 'waiting to be civilized.' As argued by Richard Budgell, neither portrait serves them well because "[t]he conception of the primitive...dooms the primitive group to changing, or perishing, as much as does the [more flattering] conception of savage" (1992: 10).

Peyton remarked upon Demasduit's apparent expectation that she should be treated kindly and with respect. That this should be remarkable implies that some other behaviour was anticipated. Assessment of the behaviour of Demasduit and Shanawdithit after their capture takes no account of their status as captives. If Demasduit expected her male captors to lace up her moccasins, perhaps this had more to do with passive resistance to removal from her people than with expectations about appropriate male treatment of females. Accounts of the time seem to imply that captured Beothuk women enjoyed the comforts of western society. The description of Demasduit's life with Rev. Mr. Leigh of Twillingate both reflects this assumption and offers evidence that challenges it (Howley, 1974: 127-129).

3

A cursory examination of the documents and Howley's summary of the material suggests that a eurocentric male gaze shaped the nature of the information provided and its interpretation. There is evidence for this in the discussions of the detailed maps and pictures drawn by Shanawdithit. In these discussions, much is made of Shanawdithit's ability to draw easily and capture in minute detail the "the entire River Exploits from the tide water to Red Indian Lake and the greater part of the Lake... Every fall, rapid, or other feature is given with extraordinary minuteness" (Howley, 1974: 242). It is worth reflecting on why it should be surprising that a Beothuk woman would have intimate knowledge of the river system on which her people depended and should be able to communicate that knowledge. Beneath such surprise is a basic process of dehumanization according to which aboriginal peoples are assumed to be incapable of certain kinds of human knowing and expression. In the European mind of the 18th and 19th centuries, land was fundamentally associated with private property; ownership was associated with agriculture; and agriculture was evidence of humanity (Chamberlin, 1975). From this perspective, the Beothuk, like other First Nations people, were ineligible for sovereign owner-ship and control of their lands.

Eurocentric male culture might also partly account for the limited information about Beothuk culture that was collected from these women. Rowe puzzles over why Shawnadithit, "this handsome, vivacious, intelligent young woman was allowed to remain an obscure servant in John Peyton's kitchen, warding off the approaches of some of the more loutish fishermen, at times lapsing into fits of melancholy, at others showing flashes of her talent and craftsmanship, and fre-quently demonstrating a rich and lively sense of humour"(1977: 79-80). If men and not women had been captured after interest in and concern for the Beothuk had developed, would these men have been left to work as servants for years before some attempt was made to elicit information about their culture?

The drawings elicited by Cormack are Shanawdithit's but the writing on the drawings is Cormack's. Would Shanawdithit have highlighted different things in her drawings? Was information elicited from Shanawdithit and Demasduit that has not made it into the historical record? Did men like Cormack see women as appropriate purveyors of information? Were they comfortable asking them about their culture?

More recent accounts of the Beothuk have not always broken free from the white, male assumptions of earlier writers. Fardy (1988) describes a sexual division of labour that appears to be absolute in terms of clear boundaries between men's and women's work and that implies women's responsibility for children. While it is probable that there was a sexual division of labour, it may not have taken the form described by Fardy and may have been rather fluid, as in the case of the Inuit (see below).

Rowe argues that accounts of the time suggest that "most of Peyton's and Hamilton's contemporaries, and even subsequent students, such as Howley, saw little reprehensible in the abduction of this wife and mother, and in the killing of her husband when he attempted to do what any white man would have been expected to do in similar circumstances" (1977: 69). While the critique is an important one and points to racist assumptions that limited opposition to such abductions, Rowe's use of the terms "wife," "mother" and "husband" invites us to equate gender relations among the Beothuk with those of current, middle-class western society. Elsewhere he argues that "[q]uite clearly, monogamy and family living were practised, children enjoyed parental care and affection, and wives did not suffer the abuse so often found in primitive societies" (1977: 132). Leaving aside Rowe's association of First Nations with the abuse of women, it is improbable that the equation he constructs between gender and familial relations among the Beothuk and our own society is valid. During her captivity, Demasduit is reported to have stolen some blue material from which she fashioned 16 pairs of moccasins. Apparently, 16 people shared her mamateek. This sits uneasily with the implicit model of a nuclear family with male household head that such notions as "wife" and "mother" elicit.

Rowe (1977: 55ff) also argues that it is "highly improbable there was a romantic entanglement" between a third Beothuk woman and her captors because this woman is referred to as "old" or "middle-aged" in eye-witness accounts. Rowe's assumption that older or middle-aged women were unlikely to be the target of sexual assaults is questionable. In the current context sexual violence is related more to availability and vulnerability than to the victim's age or appearance.

The lacunae in existing knowledge on Beothuk gender relations seem to have contributed to a process of blending fact and fiction. As argued recently by Mary Dalton, "[t]he literary works about the Beothuks, full of expressions of empathy and sympathy and awe and guilt, nonetheless exclude and deny them...the Newfoundland literature about the Beothuks treats the Indian as emblem: the Noble Savage, the spirit of Nature, the past, the timeless, death, the source of wound for the European colonizers... We write shadow Indians, who serve us beyond the grave" (1992: 144).

Micmac

Newfoundland was the most easterly part of the territory of the Micmac nation. This extended from eastern Quebec through the Maritime provinces and Newfoundland. There is no agreement on when the Micmac began to visit Newfoundland but there is clear evidence they were familiar with the island when Europeans first encountered them in the 1600s (Anger, 1988: 37). Unlike the Beothuk, the Micmac rapidly developed trade and other relations with white settlers in addition to adopting their religious beliefs. The Micmac allied with the French and combined their adopted Roman Catholicism with some of their traditional beliefs (Anger, 1988: 74). Their first permanent settlements were in the Codroy Valley and Bay St. George but as white settlement increased in these areas, they shifted towards unsettled areas along the south coast. Hunting, gathering and trapping territories spread across the southern half of the island and extended into the northern half before the extinction of the Beothuk. The Beothuk appear to have feared or at least avoided the Micmac.

In the twentieth century, schooling in English and "social pressures against 'speaking Indian'" meant young Micmac people lost their language. The Micmac underwent a "long period of loss of cultural identity" (Anger, 1988: 75; 2). The Micmacs of Conne River are currently the only First Nations people in Newfoundland and Labrador to be officially registered under the Indian Act. This happened in 1984. Little has been done regarding the question of registration for other Micmac who live on the west coast and in central Newfoundland. As with other native peoples, little progress has been made on land claims.

There exist no feminist accounts of either the history of Micmac women in Newfoundland or of their current lives. Pastore (1978) describes traditional male and female clothing, arguing that:

> The making and ornamenting of this clothing was a task performed only by women. In common with many other Indian people, Micmac women did one sort of work, the men another. While comparisons of this sort are risky, it would appear as if the women worked harder and longer than the men. In addition to making all the clothing, they had to cook and preserve food, carry game from the site of the kill back to the wigwams, move and set up camp, and care for the children. Spared from this drudgery, the males hunted, fished, made weapons and other implements, and did the fighting and governing (1978: 3).

This description assumes that "governing" was controlled by men but the meaning of this term within Micmac culture is not explored. Elsewhere, Pastore points out that Micmac shamans, some of them women, had considerable power (1978: 6), and Anger (1988: 75) argues that chiefs were drawn from particular families but "decisions were reached by consensus of the village rather than by decree of the chief." She also argues that kinship structures, the broad organizational basis for Micmac culture, were "loosely organised" and "kinship was reckoned on both the mother's and father's side." Some of the historical documents on the Micmac collected by Dorothy Anger provide interesting clues about gender relations among the Micmac and about women's lives and experiences. The Earl of Dunraven's description of the Joe family of Halls Bay, for example, tells us that women had a detailed knowledge of the woods and had similar skills to men.

> We tried hard to obtain the services of some able-bodied Joe, but they were all bent on going into the woods to hunt beaver on their own account, and nothing would induce any of the men to take service with us. We might have had our pick of the women, and we regretted afterwards that we had not engaged a couple of girls. They are just as well acquainted with the country as the men; they can paddle a canoe and do all that a man can, except carry loads, and are able to fulfil certain duties that a man cannot—for instance, they can cook, tan hides, and wash and mend clothes (Anger, 1988: 29-30).

Anger (1988: 78-80) also reproduces two strikingly different accounts of the physical and social structure of Micmac wigwams. The first presents a picture of social relations that are rigidly hierarchical with men and older people at the top. This does not fit with the description of "traditional" gender relations among the

Micmac but may have become characteristic of some households in the post-contact period. The second description reveals the racist assumptions of its author including his belief that the product of European and native liaisons could only be degenerates.

> The wigwam is a curious structure... The fire occupies the centre. On each side is the *kamigwom* [qamikuom]. There sit, on the one side of the fire, the master and mistress; and, on the other, the old people, when there are old people in the family; and the young women, when there are young women, and no old people. The wife has her place next the door, and by her side sits her lord. You will never see a woman setting *above* her husband — for towards the back part of the camp, the *kuktakumuk* [kitaqamuk], is *up*. This is the place of honour. To this place visiters and strangers, when received with a cordial welcome, are invited to come....
>
> The inmates of the "camp" have their appropriate postures as well as places. The men sit cross-legged, like the Orientals. The women sit with their feet twisted round to one side, one under the other. The younger children sit with their feet extended in front. To each of these postures an appropriate word is applied...

And in the second account:

> August 15 [1833]...I spent part of the day drawing, and then visited the wigwams of the Indians across the bay [at Seal Rocks]. We found them, as I expected, all lying down pell-mell in their wigwams, and a strong mixture of blood was perceptible in their skins, shape, and deportment: some were almost white, and sorry I am to say, that the nearer they were to our nobler race the filthier and the lazier they were. The women and children were particularly disgusting in this respect. Some of the women were making baskets, and others came in from collecting a fruit called here the baked apple... and when burnt a little it tastes exactly like a roasted apple. The children were catching lobsters and eels, of which there are a great many in the bay,... The young Indians found them by wading to their knees in eel grass.

The Innu

The native people of the Quebec-Labrador peninsula with perhaps the longest history have been variously called the Montagnais, Naskapi, Montagnais-Naskapi and East Cree. They call themselves "Innu." The ancestors of the Innu moved into the area more than 2,000 years ago. They hunted caribou in the winter and moved to coastal areas to hunt seals and other marine mammals in the spring and summer. For most of the Innu, this reliance on land- and marine-based animals and plants was disrupted by the arrival of the Thule Inuit about 500 years ago. They blocked the coast and forced the Innu to confine their hunting to deeper bays and river mouths. The Innu's first contact with Europeans may have been with the Norse. Eriksson describes conflict with *skraelings* in the Lake Melville area. Subsequent contact occurred with the French and, from the early 1540s, with Basque whalers in the Strait of Belle Isle. On the latter occasion, contact is reported to have been friendly (Armitage, 1991: 15ff).

Karen Anderson describes the social division of labour that is believed to have existed among the Montagnais (Innu):

The social division of labour... assigned different economic tasks to men and to women. Women transported the game that men killed, gathered wood, made household articles, skinned and prepared hides, caught fish and hunted small animals, made canoes and set up tents... The men hunted and waged war. Marriages were sometimes polygamous and tribal leaders often had more than one wife, they claimed, to help with the extra tasks that such an office required...

The largest unit of production, consumption and residence among the Montagnais was the extended family. During the winter the tribe broke up into small bands, the members of which comprised several nuclear families. About ten to twenty persons lived together for the entire winter in conical lodges that served as a base camp from which the men left to hunt. Residence rules were flexible and people moved on the basis of personal choice and the need to keep a balance in the working group between young and old, men and women... Ideally, though, a man resided with his wife's kin after marriage...

Divorce and remarriage between man and woman was relatively simple if they had no children. Remarriage became more difficult for widows and widowers. The relatives of a deceased man or woman did not look favourably on the remarriage of their kin's surviving spouse until three years after their kin's death. A man who remarried before, without the permission of his former spouse's kin, was held in contempt, while a woman who thus married could expect to see her new husband "plundered" *(1991: 102; 77-78).*

Southern Quebec Innu (often referred to as Montagnais) had early and intense contact with the French. Initially, these Innu had an advantage over the Europeans who were competing for furs. They acted as so-called "middle men" between the French and Innu in hinterland areas like Labrador and James Bay. It is unknown whether or not there ever existed a people commonly referred to as the Naskapi that was distinct from the Montagnais. However, José Mailhot's analysis of the history of the term "Naskapi" suggests that it quickly came to refer to non-Christianized Innu less influenced by European culture. By the twentieth century when adventurers like the Hubbards went seeking the Naskapi, Mailhot argues, they had become "an image of what we ourselves are not; an image of the Other Person, from whom at all costs we seek to distance ourselves... This *Naskapi* is the product of our old fascination with the leather clothes worn by the Indians: the symbol of the real *Savage*, and the figure par excellence of northeastern museology" (1986: 411).

Mina Hubbard's *A Woman's Way Through Unknown Labrador* offers us a rare glimpse of the "Montagnais" and "Naskapi" women in northern Labrador, as seen through the eyes of an American, middle-class woman explorer. In the summer of 1905, Mina Hubbard and her crew journeyed from Northwest River to Ungava Bay. She completed an exploratory trip undertaken two years earlier by her husband who had died in the attempt. Mina Hubbard's regular references to Indian campsites and portage routes make it evident that the Labrador she was charting was "unknown" only to Europeans and Americans. She encounters some of the Innu who used these trails only well into her journey, at a lake she names Resolution Lake. Her first encounter is with a camp she describes as Montagnais. She describes the women's clothing and their manner:

> We were greeted with much hand-shaking, and their number was gradually swelled from the camp on the hill. They displayed not the least sign of shyness or embarrassment, being altogether at their ease. Their clothing was of a quite civilised fashion, the dresses being of woollen goods of various colours made with plain blouse and skirt, while on their feet they wore moccasins of dressed deerskin... They were not scrupulously clean, but were not dirtier than hundreds of thousands to be found well within the borders of civilisation, and all, even the little children, wore the crucifix... Children played about quietly, or clung to their mothers' skirts, as they watched the strangers with curious interest and the mothers were evidently happy in their motherhood as mothers everywhere.
>
> "We are poor," said one, "and we live among the trees, but we have our children."
>
> The camp consisted of two wigwams, one a large oblong and the other round. They were covered with dressed deer-skins drawn tight over the poles, blackened round the opening at the top by the smoke of the fires, which are built in the centre within. I was not invited to go into the wigwams, but through the opening which served as doorway in front of one of them I had a glimpse of the interior... Except for their children they were poor indeed now, for there was not a taste of sugar, tea, or tobacco at the camp. They rarely have flour, which with them is not one of the necessities of life. They were living on what fish they could catch while the hunters were away, and were not having the best success with their fishing. They did not know of the presence of the caribou so near them... While I wandered over the hillside a little, keeping a wary eye on the dogs, the women devoted their attentions to the men (1983: 157-162).

This description contrasts with Hubbard's account of the so-called Naskapi (Nascaupee) or barren-ground Innu camped a short distance further on. Hubbard presents the Naskapi women as poorer and less civilized than their Montagnais counterparts — true "Savages."

> Meanwhile the old women had gathered about me begging for tobacco. I did not know, of course, what it was they wanted, and when the coveted tobacco did not appear they began to complain bitterly, "She is not giving us any tobacco. See, she does not want to give us any tobacco..."
>
> Here the younger women and the children were waiting, and some of them had donned their best attire for the occasion of the strangers' visit. Their dresses were of cotton and woollen goods. Few wore skin clothes, and those who did had on a rather long skin shirt with hood attached, but under the shirt were numerous cloth garments... One young woman appeared in a gorgeous purple dress, and on her head the black and red "tuque" with beaded band worn by most of the Montagnais women, and I wondered if she had come to the Nascaupee camp the bride of one of its braves. There was about her an air of conscious difference from the others, but this was unrecognised by them. The faces here were not bright and happy looking as at the Montagnais camp. Nearly all were sad and wistful. The old women seemed the brightest of all and were apparently important people in the camp. Even the little children's faces were sad and old in expression as if they

too realised something of the cares of wilderness life... Seeing a young mother with her babe in her arms standing among the group, near one of the wigwams, I stepped towards her, and touching the little bundle I spoke to her of her child and she held it so that I might see its face. It was a very young baby, born only the day before, I learned later, and the mother herself looked little more than a child. Her face was pale, and she looked weak and sick. Though she held her child towards me there was no lighting up of the face, no sign of responsive interest...As they stood about during the last minutes of our stay, the chief's arm was thrown across his little daughter's shoulders as she leaned confidingly against him. While the parting words were being exchanged he was engaged in a somewhat absent-minded but none the less successful, examination of her head. Many of the others were similarly occupied. There was no evidence of their being conscious that there was anything extraordinary in what they were doing, nor any attempt at concealing it. Apparently it was as much a matter of course as eating *(Ibid.: 174-180)*.

Innu women and women of other Algonkian-speaking peoples living in the tundra and open woodland areas of the Quebec-Labrador peninsula were excellent craftswomen. Elaborate painted caribou coats that have survived from the period 1700-1930 illustrate both their skill and the central role women played in the cultural life of their communities. Dorothy Burnham has studied the surviving caribou coats. In the introduction to her book, *To Please the Caribou*, she explains how they were produced and their importance to Innu culture.

As time went on, contact with Europeans, and especially with the fur traders, generated great and continuing changes, but in the northeast the caribou hunt remained an essential form of life support, and every means of ensuring a successful hunt, both mundane and magical, was undertaken. Hunting had to be approached with careful preparation, part of which was the making and wearing of a painted caribou-skin coat, both for the hunt itself and for a special feast that might be held beforehand.

Dreaming and drumming — reaching out for guidance to the spirit world — were very important in this culture. The men received instructions in their dreams about the motifs that would give them power when put on their hunting equip-ment, and the women then carried out the work, although it is not known how this partnership, combining the man's dream with the woman's creativity, was worked out. The motifs that were acceptable for use were not many... When the decoration of the coats is carefully analyzed it seems likely that one or perhaps two main motifs were dictated by the man, while the rest was left up to the woman. The rhythms of the way the motifs are used are reminiscent of music. The layout used for the patterning is traditional and well defined. A theme is stated in the bottom border or at centre back, variations are played on that theme, a secondary theme may be introduced on the collar or to the sides, and then these main themes are decorated with lesser motifs, imaginatively varied and repeated to enrich the whole.

When the painted coats, with their elaborate designs, are considered in the context of the nomadic life of the caribou-hunting people, it seems a miracle that, in spite of the well-recognized craft skills of many native women, this painting could be done without even a smooth drawing surface. What did the makers lay the skin on when they drew those firm and fine lines? This is not craft work on a small scale, it is a major art creation. It must not be forgotten that life largely depended on the success of the hunt. Hunting was a "holy" occupation, and these coats could be considered to be holy vestments, one of the ritual elements that would ensure the success of the hunt. The hunters believed that the Lord of the Caribou would send the animals out from the Magical Mountain where they were believed to live, and that the caribou would be pleased to give themselves to the hunters. The hunters would treat the slain caribou in a correct manner, so that their spirits could return to the Magical Mountain and be released again for a future hunt. This extreme simplification of a very complex set of beliefs and observances gives some indication of the reason for expending the time and effort necessary to create one of these special coats.

As is true of so much of the skilled work done by native women in all parts of Canada, the best of it seems to date back to a time when the Christian missionaries had not yet managed to impose the concept of one man-one woman. In earlier days, not only could a good hunter afford to support more than one wife, he needed more than one to do the work of a good hunter's camp. Where there were several wives, one with special skills could be released from cooking, caring for the children, chopping the firewood, and other chores, so that she could withdraw for however long it took to pain the coat that would ensure her husband's success on the next caribou hunt (Burnham, 1992: 1-3).

There are no known cases of Innu women becoming shamans. However, the Innu believed that women acquired power through handling the animals their male relatives killed. Their power increased as they aged and in some cases, they are reported to have acquired enough power to kill a shaman in psychic battles in dreams and shaking tents (Armitage, 1992). Women also participated in the communal *mukushan* caribou ceremony. Georg Henriksen observed the *mukushan* ceremony during his stay among the Naskapi of Davis Inlet. He describes a largely male-dominated ceremony with women's role limited to preparation of the tent and consumption of the caribou broth (1973: 36-37). Anauta, an Inuit woman who observed a *mukushan* ceremony at Fort Chimo earlier in the twentieth century, describes a ceremony in which women seem to have been more direct participants (Washburne and Anauta, 1940).

By the early 17th century, the Quebec Innu had lost their role as intermediaries between the French and hinterland groups. Local food and fur resources were depleted and they were debilitated by the effects of illness and disease making them more dependent on the French. This dependence was accompanied by conversion to Christianity (Armitage, 1991). Anderson (1991) maintains that within three decades of the arrival of the French among the Montagnais of New France, fundamental changes had occurred in gender relations. By the mid-17th century, she claims, many women had already been "subdued, rendered docile and obedient" (1991: 4).

The impact of colonization, settlement and Christianization on gender relations among the more distant Innu has not been studied. Changes in Innu culture were, however, slower in Labrador. By the early 20th century the effects of disease and European encroachment through settlement, competition for resources, and resource management policies led to growing dependence on relief payments as well as hunger and starvation among the Labrador Innu. These trends were exacerbated by the collapse of fur prices and a decline in local caribou populations.

The tensions and alcoholism associated with Innu abandonment of their nomadic lives and settlement in Davis Inlet are well-documented in Henriksen's work (1973). His analysis focuses, however, mainly on male hunting activities and the contrast between sources of prestige in the "country" and in Davis Inlet. The precise impact of settlement on gender relations and on relations between women is not clear in Henriksen's account.

Recent efforts to "gather the voices of the Innu" have, however, allowed us to create a collage of words from Innu women today that captures some of their understandings about the factors that have contributed to the pain and suffering experienced by many Innu people in recent years. This collage can be found at the end of the book.

The Inuit

As with other First Nations in Newfoundland and Labrador, there exists neither a detailed study of pre-colonial Inuit gender relations, nor a study of the changes these relations have undergone in the intervening years. The earliest Eskimos in the Canadian Arctic are generally referred to as "Palaeo-Eskimos." Archaeological evidence shows that some Palaeo-Eskimos inhabited parts of northern Labrador between 4,000 and 3,500 years ago. The next traces of Palaeo-Eskimo culture, those of the Groswater Eskimos, can be found around the entire Newfoundland and Labrador coasts. These date from about 2,600 to 2,100 years ago when they "appear to have vanished without a trace" (Tuck and Pastore, 1985: 70). The next Inuit culture was that of the Dorset Eskimos whose cultural history was similar to that of the Groswater in that they spread rapidly around the island, appear to have thrived, but eventually disappeared from the Newfoundland coast between 500 and 800 A.D. The current Eskimos, the Thule Eskimos or Inuit, arrived in Labrador around 500 years ago (Tuck, 1976).

Inuit lived in southern Labrador during the early period of European contact. Conflicts with Europeans and perhaps with Labrador Innu contributed to their eventual disappearance from this area (Ben-Dor, 1966). In northern Labrador, the 18th century arrival of the Moravian Mission provided the basis for peace as well as for protection of some aspects of Inuit culture. Protection was also encouraged by European dependence. During the 19th century, Northern Labrador European traders frequently married Inuit women and adopted many Inuit tools and practices. These settlers hunted, fished, trapped, and traded with the Inuit for furs. Relations with the Inuit were relatively good. However, "[d]espite the dependence of first-generation Settler men on Inuit, their letters home reveal a strong European consciousness and a reluctance to discuss their unions with Inuit women" (Kennedy, 1982: 23). In some cases, English traders took Inuit back to England with them. John Steffler's fictionalized account of George Cartwright's diaries provides a particularly tragic account of one such voyage. A young Inuit woman, Caubvick, contracts smallpox in England. Although she recovers, her hair separates from her skull and Cartwright has to remove it.

> When he was done, he asked Caubvick to give him her hair so he could throw it into the sea. She sprang to her feet, bald, skeletal, dropping her blanket, the bright pink scars of the smallpox dotting her body. She raved through the cabin with frightening energy, clutching her hair in her hands. It was hers, she said, hers, she would lock it in her trunk. And she did, while Cartwright looked on. Shaking, falling with the ship's gentle roll, she found the key in her clothes under the bed, opened her trunk, and folded her hair inside.
> He couldn't have stopped her.
> He knew that for some reason, if he had thrown her hair into the sea, she would have thrown herself in after it (Steffler, 1992: 239).

Cartwright knows the hair is filled with disease and will put her people at risk but he does not take it from her. He later discovers the bones of the members of her community. All had perished from smallpox.

By the mid-19th century, "Settlers" (people of mixed Inuit and white ancestry) appear to have begun to separate themselves socially from the Inuit. It is worth reflecting on how the Inuit mothers of these Settlers must have felt about this growing separation from their own families and culture. Roberta Buchanan's discussion of the autobiography of Lydia Campbell, in this volume, provides some insights. A comparison of Settler and Inuit activities from Makkovik in the 1960s suggests that Settler men were much more likely than the Inuit to pursue hunting, fishing and trapping activities without their wives and children (Ben-Dor, 1966: 41-46).

The Moravian Mission encouraged the Inuit to settle for prolonged periods. It also provided schools, religious instruction and encouragement to hunt and trap for trade rather than only for subsistence. The Moravians were opposed to the religious beliefs and practices of the Inuit and encouraged the transition from communal sod houses to single-family wooden buildings heated with wood (Kennedy, 1982: 18).

Relatively little research appears to have addressed the impact of the Moravian Missions on Inuit gender relations and Inuit women in particular. An important exception is the work of Carol Brice-Bennett (1981) which includes an analysis of a religious awakening that began in 1804 on the northern Labrador coast. Drawing primarily on Moravian records, Brice-Bennett argues that Inuit women played a central role in the adoption of Christianity by Labrador Inuit.

> Women were among the most active participants in the awakening; they played a prominent role throughout the episode. The Nain missionaries noted in 1799 that, in general, women were more determined to abide by the faith than men. All the key players in the drama that unfolded at Hopedale and later at Nain and Okak were women: the young widow who was the first true convert and her three friends, the grandmother who brought her sinful granddaughter to the mis-

sionaries, the three women who wept at the scripture class in Nain, the Nain women who influenced the Okak women...

The Inuit response to Christianity and the Moravian presence was largely determined by the ability of Inuit society to sustain conflict and by the kinds of conflict that occurred within the traditional social order. These aspects of Inuit society will be examined briefly, with emphasis on the status of women, to explain the advantages Christianity and affiliation with the mission stations offered women and consequently the prominent role played by them during the awakening. Religious enthusiasm is a redressive strategy used by women in many cultures to counteract social tensions that derive from their sexual and political inequality. These tensions are often related to perceived threats to their position resulting from social and economic changes.

Taylor's (1974) research on Inuit society in the early contact period indicates that authority and leadership patterns were weak and ill-defined such that social or economic conflict could not be sustained above the level of household or extended family units. The most common disputes within households were between husbands and wives, and conflict at the community (seasonal camp) or local (regional) group level occurred mainly as a result of sexual jealousies and wife-stealing. Taylor found a low adult male-female ratio in the structure of the 1776-7 Inuit population and a high incidence of polygynous marriages. However, although polygyny was the desired goal of Inuit males, the demand for additional wives was greater than could be supplied by the sex-ratio imbalance. This situation would appear to have enhanced the position of women in Inuit society: they were a valued commodity, sought after and a source of prestige to men. However, in reality women were used as pawns in relationships between men; they could expect little stability or security from marriage and lacked influence and authority within their society. In his study of Greenlandic Inuit, Crantz (1820) remarked that all adult women lived a life of slavery and, from the age of twenty until their death, their life was marked by a series of anxieties, wretchedness, and toil. The situation of Labrador Inuit women was not much different.

Women had no choice in marriage; their spouses were selected for them when they were born or in infancy. They were usually married between the age of ten and fourteen. Women could easily lose their spouse, through murder or divorce, or find their status threatened by the introduction of an additional wife. The only recourse a woman had when she objected to a decision made by her husband was to run away but women were usually forced to return to their husbands and the punishment for running away was often quite severe. A second recourse women may have used was to encourage men to abduct them from unhappy marital relationships. Wife 'stealing' occurred frequently and often led to murder (of the male) and revenge killings. Taylor (1974) does not examine, and information may not be available on, whether or not women played an active role in their abduction. When a man died, his brother(s) had a stronger claim to his possessions than his widow. If he did not have any surviving brothers and had been married polygynously, his possessions were divided among his widows and this sometimes caused disputes between them. A young woman usually returned to her family when her husband died and her father or brother arranged the next marriage. Older women appear to have been left to fend for themselves.

Taylor (1974) believes the number of adult males in the early contact Inuit population was reduced because of the frequent conflict that occurred among Inuit and between Inuit and European fishermen and traders along the south coast... Scheffel (1980), however, considers that hunting accidents were more important than violence in reducing the male population and adds that a low male-female ratio continued into the 19th century. Whatever the cause of the continuing disproportion between adult males and females, the effects were felt most by women and contributed to the overall instability and insecurity of Inuit society. Reductions in the adult male population meant that there were fewer productive hunters available to support family or household units and consequently more unproductive members, widows and their children, who were dependent on relatives and friends for their support until, and unless, another marriage could be arranged. Young widows had no difficulty remarrying, and were often pursued by men who already had one or more wives, but old widows were less attractive and unlikely to find a spouse.

... A large number of widows were among the early converts at Okak and probably also at Nain and Hopedale as well. As the population at the mission stations grew in the 19th century, the proportion of widows in the congregations increased; largely because of the effects of disease rather than from immigration. The mission stations tended to attract people who were unable to provide for themselves and who would have found it difficult to obtain elsewhere the regular and assured support offered by mission charity: widows and their children, orphans, the aged and infirm. As Scheffel (1980) notes, "it is not surprising that they were among the most willing converts."

In addition to providing material assistance to their dependent converts, the missionaries offered another form of social security that would have directly appealed to Inuit women. The Moravians advanced a religion that included strict rules governing sexual relationships and penalties for their infraction. They stressed fidelity in marital relations and objected to wife-exchange and pre-marital sexual relations. Inuit women may have seen the Moravian's rules on marriage and sexual relations as a means to decrease tension within households, stabilize social relations, and thus a way to bring an end to the uncertainty and conflict which factionalized their society. The rules enhanced women's position and gave them a security that was lacking in traditional Inuit society...

Polygyny was a source of male prestige in traditional Inuit society but it was a drawback and limited a man's status in the congregations of the Moravian communities. By discouraging polygyny and stressing marital fidelity, the missionaries were advancing the model of their own stable nuclear families but they were also undermining traditional areas of Inuit male privilege. The missionaries were so concerned that their female converts should not be forced into polygynous marriages or contract a marriage with an unbaptized male that they interceded and influenced the choice of a suitable spouse. By trying to preserve the social and religious integrity of their converts, they assumed a function which was traditionally the prerogative of male kin and thereby further eroded male authority and dominance. The missionaries not only introduced an element of choice in the selection of marriage partners but they also provided women with the option of not marrying. The mission stations offered women sanctuary; they were places women could safely reside and depend on support from the missionaries without being married if they so chose...By defending the position of their female converts and providing the option of not marrying, the missionaries enabled women to have more independence and status than they could have achieved in traditional Inuit society... The Moravian social code forced men and women to reexamine the behaviour and attitudes which had been accepted or tolerated in Inuit community life.

The missionaries' wives were active in the community and met with Inuit women at private speakings and in congregational meetings. They were the first European women with whom the Inuit became familiar and their example must have impressed Inuit women. The Moravian wives were a model and Inuit women may have attempted to emulate their peaceful and co-operative family relations, independence, confidence, and the active role they played within the community...

The awakening was a conversion crisis, a critical turning point, that endorsed social and moral changes in Inuit society. It is questionable whether the episode was a specifically religious experience in the sense that, although Inuit embraced the Moravian belief system, Christianity may have been primarily a vehicle for obtaining social changes and for relieving the anxieties and conflict that had built up as a result of Inuit contact with European culture and, more particularly, contact with the Moravian missionaries.

The Moravians encouraged the Inuktitut language, and their schools emphasized training for traditional occupations. In contrast, the government schools established after 1950 showed no such sensitivity to Inuit culture or economy. Perhaps as a consequence, they had a more marginal influence on Inuit lives (Brantenburg, 1977).

In the 1950s, Inuit residents of Nutak and Hebron were resettled against their wishes to Hopedale, Nain and Makkovik. Carol Brice-Bennett is currently documenting the processes that led to this resettlement and its tragic consequences for the families involved. As with the Innu, settlement and particularly resettlement were accompanied by increased alcoholism, poverty and violence among the Inuit.

In contrast to Crantz' (1820) dreary and rigid assessment of the lives of Inuit women, Jean Briggs argues on the basis of her detailed research among the Inuit of Chantry Inlet in the Eastern Arctic that women's lives prior to settlement were diverse. She comments:

[a]s I think about the Eskimo women I know, what strikes me most vividly is the variety of their lives. There are women whose lives seem full of satisfaction and others for whom frustration is certainly the most salient fact of life. Some women are busy, others have little to do; some take an active part in the male world of hunting and traveling, others are wholly occupied at home with children and other family members to care for; some rule the household (including their husbands) with a vigorous hand and voice, others are docilely obedient to husband, mother, mother-in-law, or older sister. There are "good" marriages and "bad" marriages and they are good and bad for a variety of reasons. It is impossible to generalize about the quality of a "typical" Eskimo woman's life without doing violence to the realities of individual lives (1974: 261).

Briggs goes on to argue that despite past practices of female infanticide among some groups, there was little evidence that boys were "more desired or loved than girls" (Ibid: 267). Inuit girls and boys learned aspects of their adult roles from a very young age. Boys and girls tended to play separately, but this was not always the case. In addition,

[s]ome girls retain a taste for vigorous outdoor activity all their lives and some boys prefer sedentary pursuits to active hunting and traveling, but in general, by the time they are physically mature, each sex is fully occupied with its own work and a person has little time to indulge any taste he may have for the way of life of the other sex...[But] [t]here are exceptions to this rule too, however, since Eskimos are pragmatic people. There is nothing holy to them about the sexual division of labour; neither is there, in their view, anything inherent in the nature of either sex that makes it incapable of doing some of the jobs that the other sex ordinarily does. So if a family is short of daughters, a son —often the eldest son — may be brought up to help his mother....Similarly, if a family has only daughters, a father may decide to bring up one or two daughters as hunters, so that they can help him and also so that, if anything should happen to him, the family will not be left without a provider...Such girls will go hunting with their fathers from the time they are small. To be sure, they also learn female skills, and eventually they marry and have children, but the masculine training they have received may show itself... in a tendency to be somewhat bossy toward their husbands.

Orphans of either sex also, of necessity, tend to acquire the skills of both sexes—partly in self-defense because they have no one to take care of them and partly because they tend to become camp slaveys, at the beck and call of anyone of either sex who needs a job done (Ibid: 270-271).

Another way to describe the pattern outlined by Briggs is to suggest that among the Inuit, there was a "gendered, not a sexual, division of labour" (Bodenhorn, 1990: 60) in the sense that although specific tasks were ideally assigned to men and women, there appears to have been no assumption that either sex was congenitally incapable of carrying out the tasks of the other. Work rather than biological sex alone appears to have been gender-defining (Guemple, 1986: 12). This distinction between biological sex and gender is reflected in Inuit religious beliefs according to which "men can be reborn as women, and women as men" as well as in the fact that both men and women can act as shamans because shamans must be able to transcend gendered divisions (Oosten, 1986: 128; Ben-Dor, 1966: 69-70). These patterns and beliefs are evident in the following excerpt from the autobiography of Anauta, an Inuit woman. *Land of the Good Shadows,* co-written with Heluiz Washburne, shows the pragmatism of Inuit traditional practice alluded to by Jean Briggs as well as the religious beliefs that sustained it. Anauta was born female but was raised as a male by a woman who was not her mother. The Moravian missionaries may well have discouraged practices such as this. Constraints on gender fluidity would, in turn, have limited the subsistence options of households headed by widows and with female daughters.

from

Land of the Good Shadows The Life Story of Anauta, an Eskimo Woman

Anauta and Heluiz Washburne

Anauta was born on Baffin Island but spent part of her adult life in northern Labrador. Her autobiography, first published in 1940, was co-authored with Heluiz Chandler Washburne who met Anauta after she moved to the United States in later life. The short excerpt here describes Anauta's early childhood and adoption by Oomiálik, the widow who named her and raised her to replace the son who died the night Anauta was born (pp. 13-19).

EARLY CHILDHOOD

Y ORGKE AND ALEA were old friends of Oomiálik's. She had seen them several times each year when she traveled down the coast to hunt seal or replenish her supply of ammunition and tobacco. Now that her son's spirit had been reborn in the body of their daughter, a new bond was established between them. Alea allowed Oomiálik to care for the baby, realizing that in doing so the old woman's grief was assuaged. Many times Oomiálik would sit crooning to the little one in her arms, "Ami-lang, Anauta, once you were a big strong man. You took care of your mother and hunted for her. Now she must hunt for you again and train you to be brave and good as you were before."

She took an especial pleasure in giving Anauta her daily snowbath. Bringing in a pile of clean snow in the front of her coat, she would rub the naked kicking body with handful after cold handful. And when Anauta screamed and chattered and her lips turned blue, Oomiálik only laughed, knowing this was the first thing an Eskimo had to learn. It was a matter of necessity as well as cleanliness. If an Eskimo neglected this vigorous snowbath which stimulated and brought up the circulation, he would be cold and miserable all day, and no amount of furs would keep him warm.

Sometimes, when Oomiálik went hunting for the day, she slipped Anauta up under her fur coat into the loose pocket on her back, where she could feel the small body lying next to hers as she ran along beside the dogs. Supported by the belt around Oomiálik's waist and protected by the sample hood that hung over her, the baby was warm and happy. When Anauta was weaned, and could be fed on finely pounded frozen meat, Oomiálik took her farther from home, for a day and a sleep perhaps. At last came the time when several moons elapsed between Anauta's visits to her "mother-far-away," as Alea was called.

Even in those early days Oomiálik began talking to the little girl whose face peered over her shoulder, building in Anauta's mind the pattern she must never forget, of Anauta-the-man, for whom she had been named, and whose example she must follow.

As Oomiálik traveled about she ran into old friends: funny, fat, bowlegged

Ikkerra perhaps, with his wife Petseolak and their brood of homely children; Aulamah and his daughter Supeali; or the brothers Shemegak and Tuklavik, each with their two wives and children. Occasionally she would join one of these families and travel with them for a day or two, for wherever she went people welcomed her. She was a wise, kind presence in their homes. Soon everyone knew that the little girl she carried in her hood was her son, Anauta, come back.

As soon as Anauta was able to walk, Oomiálik fashioned her a pair of snowshoes made from branches of the dwarf willow bushes and strips of rawhide, and with infinite patience taught her to use them. Confining her own long strides to the smallest ones she could take, she would break the path, and when Anauta tipped over, would pick her up and encourage her with words of confidence. "Anauta would not cry. You did this when you were here before. You can do it again. Try once more."

Even after Anauta had learned to walk quite well she loved to ride in Oomiálik's hood. And Oomiálik humored her, seeming not to notice when Anauta, playing with her, unstrapped her belt. This accomplished Anauta would squeeze up under the loosened coat and tuck her feet down into the pocket. It was warm and comfortable standing there with the commodious hood held about her like a tent. As they ran along, the runner of the sledgem[1] squeaking on the hard snow, the dogs waving plumy tails and pulling eagerly, Oomiálik would tell her stories of her previous life — of her courageous exploits — pointing out the places where they had occurred. One of Anauta's earliest memories is of riding so, and hearing Oomiálik say, "When you lived before, Anauta, you were a brave man. Do you remember the time you were nearly killed by the bear over there on the cliff?" Anauta knew that Oomiálik wanted her to remember; so, to please her, she pretended. "Um-humm," she said, nodding her head so vigorously she almost convinced herself. Then Oomiálik chuckled in satisfaction.

The day finally came when Anauta, jumping to squeeze herself down in the pocket which she had outgrown, jumped once too often and tipped Oomiálik over into the snow. "You must come out now, and dress in boy's clothes, and be a man," said Oomiálik. After that Anauta had to walk and run all day beside the sledge. When she thought she could not go another step, Oomiálik would tell her to climb on the komotik. But she was not allowed this luxury long. Soon Oomiálik would hold out her hand and she must hop off and run on again. And so Anauta grew strong and swift of foot...

Another early memory of Anauta's was Oomiálik's care that she be modest. Sometimes when she had removed her boots and was sitting on the furs and wiggling her toes happily, she would look up to find Oomiálik's disapproving eyes fixed upon her. "Anauta, your feet are not to look at. They are a part of your body and not for people to see naked." When preparing for bed she must quickly hide them from view under the furs.

In all their traveling around, Anauta was seldom far from Oomiálik's side, running with her, or riding the sledge when she went to hunt caribou, to set traps, or to spear fish through the holes chopped in the deep ice of the frozen lakes. And on all occasions Oomiálik taught her to be useful, preparing the bait for the traps, or carrying away the buckets of loose ice. She let Anauta hold her rifle and pull the trigger. She taught her to throw the bird spear, first at a mark, later at herons and gulls on the wing. She instructed her in the training and handling of her own team of puppies. Bringing down a block of ice to be melted for drinking-water was one of Anauta's first tasks. During the long winter evenings Oomiálik would make the small harness for the puppies, showing Anauta how they were patterned exactly after those of the full grown dogs.

Oomiálik was determined that Anauta must be skilled in all the things an Eskimo should know. Most necessary, of course, was the building of a substantial snowhouse. Many times Anauta had watched Oomiálik make their igloo, and had helped her, standing on the outside and filling in the chinks between the snow-blocks as Oomiálik laid them. But she had to be able to make a snowhouse of her own and this Oomiálik proceeded to teach her. Drawing a circle on the snow, to mark the size of her snowhouse, she instructed Anauta to do the same. "It's a bad house builder," she said scornfully, "who can't get enough snow-blocks from inside of his circle to build his igloo. You must never come out of your house until it is finished." That was lesson number one. Step by step Oomiálik showed her what she must do...

That first snowhouse of Anauta's took her practically all day to build, but finally it was completed to the last detail — a real igloo just large enough for herself. Oomiálik's broad shoulders would not even go through the doorway. Many times thereafter Anauta made such small houses, and one of her pleasantest memories today is of "playing house" with Angmak and Supeali, borrowing furs and lamps to furnish their igloos, imitating the behavior and conversation of their elders, as children do the world over...

1   These Sledges, or komotiks, as the Eskimos called them, were fifteen to twenty feet long, with whalebone runners to make them slick. The usual team was twelve dogs.

dead Indians

Mary Dalton

dead Indians are safer—
in poems, museums,
archaeo-
logical pamphlets,
bone pendants and ochre—
lament, monographs,
no threat to our order

weeping walrus
we mourn the Beothuk
close the sky in
on Labrador Innu
the land wired
and caribou fled

Women, the Migratory Fishery and Settlement

As with First Nations women, the lives of European women associated with the migratory fishery and early settlement remain largely undocumented. Existing historical accounts generally begin with women of English or Irish descent who migrated to Newfoundland and Labrador. Also of interest are the women of these and other origins left behind in Europe whose lives and labour were shaped by the fishery economy. Some would have been wives of migrant fishery workers; others mothers, perhaps partly dependent on support from their sons; still others would have been young, single women working in fishery-related industries in England, Ireland, Portugal or France.

Seasonal male absence and the risk of widowhood or abandonment seem to have been enduring features of the lives of the women left behind. An examination of Poor Law removal orders in Poole by Gordon Handcock highlights these vulnerabilities:

> Many mariners employed by merchants and traders brought their wives and families into Poole and rented rooms. Others married local girls. Normally men employed on monthly wages made arrangements with merchants to allow regular payments to their families. Frequently, however, seamen were drowned, became unemployed, failed to return, neglected their families, or came home penniless. For these and other reasons, their dependents were forced to seek parish relief and subject themselves, if suspected of being illegal residents, to a settlement examination. In many of the removal orders of married women, it was noted that the husband was "gone from her and now abroad beyond the sea," or "hath deserted her and is now abroad by sea," which then, almost invariably, meant the overseas fishery
>
> ...Over 68 percent of removals from Poole involved a married woman, widow, or single female as the principal person. In the twenty-nine removals related to unmarried females, five were asserted to be pregnant presumably by transient seamen; single females were scrutinized carefully by local authorities as potential problems should they bear illegitimate children who might become chargeable to the parish. Removals to Poole tended to have the same characteristic features as those from the port and consisted principally of single females and married females or widows and the families of mariners being returned home (1989: 199).

The sons of widows and abandoned women may well have made up some of the "less than" 10% of servants indentured from the Dorset region (Handcock: 193). Handcock has found only one case of a female from Dorsetshire being bound as a parish apprentice to a master in Newfoundland from Dorsetshire during the late 18th century. Most were apprenticed as domestics in Dorset, "a trade known as 'housewifery' "(1989: 302).

The women left behind would have provided support for return migrants. If fortunate, these return migrants came back in good health and with money to spare at the end of the fishing season. Some, however, would have been injured and ill.

Return migrants also included "children who had been sent home for schooling, orphans returned to the care of relatives, wives and widows of English-born males, grandchildren, nephews, and nieces of the head of household..."(Handcock, 1989: 198).

Detailed research could tell us more about the economic and social lives of the women left behind. It might, for example, provide clues regarding whether, as in other fishery economies, responsibility for child-rearing in a context of male absence meant that the mother became "the exemplar and mediator of class relations to the child... Practice in the home shapes expectations as to what is 'normal' domestic practice and what the proper fields of activity are for men and women" (Lummis, 1985: 119-120). Their histories could broaden our understanding of the forces shaping both gender and class relations in the emergent Newfoundland economy.

Paul O'Neill's 1980 lecture to the Newfoundland Historical Society, "Jezebels and the Just: Women in Newfoundland 1500-1800," seems to have been one of the first attempts to discuss women's presence in Newfoundland during early settlement. A series of portraits of women, as its title suggests, this paper divides them into categories resembling those of angel and whore, a 19th century Victorian categorization that has been critiqued by feminist scholars. In O'Neill's paper, the categories used are "poor angishores" or "hard tickets" and "princesses". O'Neill contrasts the life of "worthy Mistress Anne Mason" wife of John Mason, governor of John Guy's plantation in Cupids, with that of "the equally unworthy" Mistress Maria Cobham, common-law wife of a pirate, and the life of Eleanor Power, "probably a washerwoman or maid-of-all work" who, O'Neill claims, was "the first woman to be hanged for murder in English Canada" (1980: 16). This approach to biographical history can be contrasted with Buchanan's treatment (in this volume) of women's autobiography. Her paper uses the autobiographies of three Labrador women to explore alternative notions of history as public, objective events and private, subjective, individual experience.

Recent research challenges previous estimates of the female population in Newfoundland in the 17th century. Men outnumbered women in the period of early settlement, but less than was thought when Porter (this volume) wrote her paper. It is now known that women played a central role in the operation of the 17th century Avalon fishing economy (Pope, 1992; Kealey, 1993). Some research has examined early settlement, the sexual division of labour, and the development of laws affecting women (Cullum et al, 1993; Cadigan, 1991 and this volume; Handcock, 1989, Porter, this volume).

Women who lived in Newfoundland during the early 1800s were generally wives who migrated as part of a nuclear family, servants, or native-born women. Those who migrated as wives tended to be married to members of the middle and upper classes (Handcock, 1989: 249). In contrast, single female migrants tended to be domestics from poorer households. More of them may also have been Irish. These different migratory patterns point to the need to consider class and ethnic differences between women as factors shaping women's history from the early years of settlement. We know of no research in this area.

Peter Pope's detailed study of the 18th century South Avalon Planters tells us that "Edward Wynne suggested in a letter of 1621 from Ferryland, that 'women would bee necessary heere for many respects'" (1992: 306). Those who came engaged in a range of activities from 'brewing to baking'; livestock husbandry to work in the fishery. Women's labour contributed to the prosperity of households. Pope finds that women's presence correlates with larger herds of cattle and with pigs in planter households. He also argues that the wives and daughters of planters were "curiously" prominent as planters in their own right in the 17th century fishery. The plantations of widows who did not remarry were among the largest, suggesting that these women may have had the financial means to remain single, and may have wanted to avoid the loss of control over their assets that remarriage might entail (Pope, 1992: 311). Echoing feminist writers on women in the fishery (see Porter this volume), Pope maintains that, planters wives were "at least as fully in economic power as women anywhere in the seventeenth century. In other words, they were powerful relative to their sisters elsewhere, in a century in which women were powerful, relative to their great-granddaughters" (1992: 306-307).

As early as 1804, women and children were active as members of the "shore crew" in many areas. Fishing families that migrated to the temporarily vacant French or Treaty shore were described in the following way by one contemporary observer: "The activity of these industrious people is so great that their women, even in advanced pregnancy, rather than stay at home, take midwives with them on this expedition..." (quoted in McLintock, 1941: 99).

Young women servants and the daughters of migrants were more likely to remain as settlers than their male counterparts in the 18th and early 19th centuries. Younger, locally-born women marrying older, migrant men and living matrilocally was the dominant pattern. In contrast, native-born men tended to marry out of their communities, and most migrant males returned to Europe or left for elsewhere in the Americas. This pattern partly reflects the relative shortage of women in the colony. Local marriages for migrant females might have been encouraged by policies designed to restrict ships' masters from landing poor, (particularly Irish) women in the colony who might then "become Chargable to the inhabitants" and corrupt the men (Cullum et al, 1993: 71; Handcock, 1989: 92). Single women who became pregnant could be removed.

Handcock treats the period of matrilocality and male outmigration in Trinity Bay in the late 18th and early 19th centuries as a transition phase from an unsettled to a settled area with a "consolidated, stable population" in the form of a "traditional" "patrilineal-patrilocal society" (1989: 142). However, he does not show that the households out of which fishing servants came were either patrilocal or "tradition-al." In a context of prolonged male-absence and probable high marital instability due to the risk of death and desertion, it is quite possible that many of these households were matrilocal and, as in some other fishing economies, women provided the basis for local communities (Nadel-Klein and Davis, 1988; Cole,

24

1991). By treating patrilocality, patrilineality and, by extension, patriarchy, as simple evolutionary outcomes of gender parity, Handcock misses the possibility that local settlement and inheritance structures, like those in England at the time, were the focus of struggle the outcome of which was neither inevitable nor necessarily homogenous. In geography, as in anthropology, the purpose of feminist research is "to provoke some radical rethinking of long-accepted...'truths', and to open up new areas of investigation" (Nadel-Klein and Davis, 1988: 1). In the Newfoundland and Labrador migrant and emergent settler fisheries, as in other fishery economies, gender and patriarchy are perhaps better depicted "not as fixed categories, but as dynamic processes in the act of formation" (Howell and Twomey, 1991: 9).

Insights into these processes can be found in the recently published *Pursuing Equality* which "breaks the silence" on the dynamic political and legal history of women in Newfoundland and Labrador in the 19th and 20th centuries (Kealey, 1993).

However, the lives and experiences of urban and upper-class women in the 19th century need more research.

Women's involvement with collective action is another important gap. Recent contributions to the social history of 19th century Newfoundland have challenged the dominant view that the "plebeian" classes were largely passive. Linda Little's 1984 M.A. thesis on plebeian collective action in Harbour Grace and Carbonear, 1830-1840, for example, documents a wide range of methods from night visits to anonymous notes, mass meetings and riots used to "manoeuvre within the bounds set by the ruling class"(Little, 1984). As she reminds us, her account deals mainly with the actions of men, largely because historical documents have primarily recorded the activities of men. It should be noted, however, that the sex (not to speak of the sexual orientation) of unapprehended anonymous authors and disguised and masked mummers is uncertain. And if, as history tells us, protesting men dressed as women, it is conceivable that protesting women dressed as men. At any rate, women's involvement in 19th century plebeian collective action is another unwritten chapter of their history.

An additional piece of unwritten political history, this time from the early twentieth century fishery, is that of women's involvement in the Fishermen's Protective Union (FPU), a major cooperative movement and political party that developed in Newfoundland in 1908. In her early research on the FPU, Neis (1980) found that the organization of fishery work was different on the northeast coast, where the movement was successful, from other regions where it failed. She argued that this work organization enhanced the ability of northeast coast fishermen to organize against merchant domination despite the opposition of the clerical elite. Another important regional difference was the greater extent of women's direct involvement in fish processing on the northeast coast in contrast to other regions. However, neither this nor women's participation in the movement receive attention in the thesis. Other scholarly writings on the FPU have also failed to address women's involvement. It is likely that few of the women directly involved in the

FPU are still living. Because women's history is not easily accessed through historical documents written by men, we must accept that gender bias in research has meant that much of that history has been——and will continue to be——lost, in a province where resources for documenting women's history remain thin. Despite the loss, a women's history of the FPU can and ought to be written.

An issue of interest that might throw some light on women and the FPU was a public controversy about women's involvement in the so-called Labrador floater fishery that erupted around the turn of the century. Nina Patey (n.d.) has provided a preliminary overview of women's involvement in this fishery and some dimensions of the controversy. Every year, schooners from many parts of the northeast coast journeyed to Labrador to set cod traps. Most vessels carried one or two women who were responsible for cooking and other tasks on the Labrador, most of them unmarried. Often hired by the skipper's wife, girls could be as young as 11 but most were 15 to 30. The controversy over the employment of women in this fishery had four elements: the impact of the voyages and working conditions on their health; the influence on their decorum and femininity of "the constant company of men"; concern about "opportunities for immorality" and "loss of chastity"; and fears about the contagious effects these women might have on the fabric of Newfoundland society (Patey: 12). Opposition to their employment seems to have been particularly strong among the clergy. Governor McCullum and Sir Wilfred Grenfell, Patey argues, "[i]n true Victorian fashion…concentrated their efforts on the scourging of iniquity and immorality" rather than attempting to improve the wages and working and living conditions of these women (Patey: 22). They ignored the impact prohibition of employment would have on the incomes of these women and their families. The underlying processes that produced this public controversy, with its focus on regulating women's morality by limiting their work opportunities, deserve further research.

Sean Cadigan's paper, in this volume, adds a new and interesting wrinkle to fishery women's legal and political history in the nineteenth century. Excerpts from Bernice Morgan's *Random Passage* and Greta Hussey's *Our Life on Lear's Room* provide us with a sense of the texture of women's lives in fishing communities during the 19th and early 20th centuries. Carmelita McGrath's poem, "Annie, Telling Stories," picks up on women's pride in accomplishments made amidst the fatigue of constant work. Ellen Antler's 1977 paper, "Women's Work in Newfoundland Fishing Families" was the first academic paper to systematically examine women's economic contribution to the household saltfishery. Marilyn Porter's "She Was the Skipper of the Shore Crew" was the second; we include Porter's in this volume, as it focuses more on early settlement.

from the novel
Random Passage

Bernice Morgan

*This excerpt portrays women's summer work in a recently established settlement on
the French Shore in the early 19th century.*

In THE SHORT TIME before the fish are expected to strike in, the women begin to
clear a space to grow potatoes. Meg and Jennie Andrews, along with Sarah and
Annie Vincent and Mary Bundle, spend the best part of each day working in the
spot where Josh cut last year's firewood. It is a narrow, fairly flat strip of rocky soil
between the wooded area and the outcropping—the place from which the children
had looked down at the empty Cape and been so afraid. Not a promising location
for a garden, but almost the only one possible in a land newly emerged from eons
beneath glaciers.

The women have established a routine from which they seldom vary. Each
morning, when the most necessary household chores are done, the babies fed, the
day's water hauled from the pond, the pot of salt fish set to simmer over the banked
fire, they pack Sarah's wooden chest.

This container, half the size of a coffin, a seaman's trunk for generations of Gill
men, was taken by Sarah as a blanket box when she left Pinchards Island to marry
Josh. Into the bottom of this chest the women fold a thick quilt, on top of which they
put an iron pot filled with hot coals, a kettle, food, extra clothing and whatever else
they can fit in.

They have scrounged an unlikely collection of tools, things the men can spare
from more important work: a blunt axe, a pick, the long iron rod Josh found tangled
in his net last summer, a shovel, a length of rope and several brin bags. Meg carries
as many tools as she can, Jenny and Mary carry the chest between them by its rope
handles, and Annie trails behind with a baby in each arm. Meg's two-year-old
Willie usually runs ahead of the women, who make slow progress up the twisting
path to the clearing.

Upon reaching what they call the garden—although it is nothing but rocks and
tree stumps—they start a fire with the hot coals, piling on blasty boughs until it
crackles and sends a shimmer of heat up into the cool morning air. They wrap
Mary's baby Fannie and Charlie Vincent in warmed quilts and lay them toe to toe
inside the now empty chest. The women take great satisfaction in this efficient
arrangement, which was worked out by Mary Bundle.

"For all Mary's quiet, she's not stunned. She got some good head for figurin'
things out," Mary heard Sarah tell Meg Andrews one day. The description pleases
Mary, who takes pride in her ability to figure things out—a skill she has noticed
most people lack.

Work in the garden is back-breaking. Hour after hour the women pry rocks up
out of the hard earth and carry them to a loose stone wall they are building between
the garden and the cliff edge. Sarah, the only one with any experience at growing
things, says that the coldest winds come in from the sea, that if they lay their garden

crosswise between the line of trees and the rock wall it will be protected. The women often have to tie a rope around the larger boulders and, using the iron rod as a lever, push and pull until they come loose. Then they roll and drag the big rocks over to the pile they hope will become a wall. Sometimes it takes most of a day to move just one rock. Two rocks withstand their best efforts and finally, after days of sweat and strain, they conclude that these are the tip of the cliff that must lie just below the shallow soil.

The women pile roots and underbrush onto the fire that grows as the day progresses. Their faces become ingrained with smoke and soot, their fingernails tear and split, blisters rise, break and bleed until their hands grow as hard and calloused as the men's. During the first weeks arms and shoulders pain constantly. Jennie has to sit sometimes, resting her head on her knees, waiting for the pounding behind her eyes to pass.

When the sun sinks to the tops of the spruce trees, they stop work. Gathering up tools and children, they trudge home to get supper before the men return. The women are bone weary. The sea chest, heavy as lead, bumps against their legs. Willie cries to be carried and they move stiffly back through the last light, walking on their own long shadows that proceed them down the steep path.

For all that, the women love working on the garden. It is exhilarating to be outside, to smell the earth, to feel the air on your face and the warmth of sun between your shoulder blades. At midday they always take a spell, sit on the ground eating bread with cups of black tea and the salt fish that has been roasting all morning on flat stones near the fire. Taking time to look around at what they have done, they talk quietly, become female again, tidying their hair, rubbing aching limbs. Mary and Sarah nurse their babies.

Sitting by the fire with the smell of burning boughs, tea and roasted fish filling the air, the babies fed and quiet, with Willie curled in his grandmother's lap, with winter over and gone and their garden coming to shape around them, they talk, get to know each other, begin to love each other.

Jennie speaks of the flat on Monk Street, of Mrs. Thorp's bread and pie shop, of the cart and of old Bones, the horse. She says nothing of why they left these things to come to the Cape.

Sarah tells about her grandmother Loveys, who was the first woman along the coast.

"Borned three children, Nan did, without another woman to help her. Saw two of them die, one soon as it was born and one scalded to death when it was three. Mother were the oldest and she said Nan was never the same after. Had it hard, poor mortals. Sometimes no one even knew they was here—and sometimes they didn't want anyone to know—they was that scared of being caught and dragged back to England for something they done. Me own grandfather jumped ship from an English man o' war. He'd been pressed, so the first time they come ashore to take on water he ran off. The boys was half-starved and beat for the least thing. He had no use for the navy, or for the English come to that."

Sarah shakes her head. "Tis only the last few year it's been fit to live along this coast. We got things easy now compared to them times."

During these exchanges, Mary Bundle sits rocking Fanny and says not a word but she feels the contentment. There by the fire they all feel happy, satisfied that they are doing something worthwhile, something unlike cooking and cleaning: something that will last.

When they go back to the work, standing stiffly because their muscles hurt, Jennie Andrews often grumbles that Lavinia should be helping, "instead of gallivantin' with the young ones."

"Still and all, she takes the youngsters off our hands so's we only got Willie to keep an eye on," Meg always says. How would they talk, discuss women's problems, with young maids around? Having them there would spoil the lovely peace, the feeling of completeness.

Spring has separated the people on the Cape into three distinct groups. At night, bone tired, they come together only to eat supper and fall into bed. The long nights of story-telling have stopped for the present.

* * *

In the garden, now a half-cleared triangle, the hastily planted potatoes are abandoned to their fate. Each day the men make three or four trips to the fishing ground along the shoals offshore and the women must spend every waking minute down on the flakes gutting and splitting fish. When the *Charlotte Gosse* comes in, there is even more work. Fish landed from the schooner has been just lightly salted. The women must finish curing it: spread it on the flakes each day, turn it, stack it, put it inside if it looks like rain or cover it with bark on clear nights to protect it from the damp.

Jennie Andrews smiles now to think of herself asking to buy food from Thomas Hutchings. As she works, she thinks of what she has learned in the past eight months: how to clear rocks from ground, how to slide a knife through a cod, flicking its guts into the barrel at the end of the table, how much salt to spread on fish, when to turn them. She has learned that the food they will have next winter will depend upon these things, upon the credit they can build with Caleb Gosse, upon how much fish the men catch and how much the women make. It is a formula she now understands completely.

At fifty-two, Jennie is the oldest person on the Cape and although every bone in her body pains, although her hands crack and bleed and her legs swell so that she can no longer lace her boots, she works as hard as any of the women. Not only must the Andrews family earn food for the next winter, they must settle up for the food they ate last winter, for the gear Ned and Ben are using, for the salt. Even, God forbid, should Thomas Hutchings request it, pay for the use of the store and the flakes.

Lavinia, Lizzie and Annie, "the young maidens," Sarah calls them, take turns away from the flakes to haul water and cook for the men who have mug-ups between trips. They bring endless kettles of tea to the women, who drink it still half bent over the drying cod; by then it is painful to stand straight. They all work like beasts. Even the small girls, Jane, Patience and Emma, fetch and carry, tend babies, shoo goats away from the flakes, or stand with boughs waving at the hordes of flies that would make the precious fish maggoty with eggs. Day after day, the men heave fish up onto the wharf until every inch of flake is covered and the remaining cod must be spread out on rocks.

Not even in the long days of midsummer is there time to do everything. Thomas makes lighted torches soaked in cod oil, fixing them to the ends of the flake and they work on, far into the night, cutting, scooping, scraping, until they can no longer lift their arms. Some nights none of the adults go to bed, but drop, still wearing the gut-spattered, salt-encrusted clothing, wherever sleep overtakes them, waking a few hours later to begin again.

July and August blur into a haze of weariness. The women, who had become so close while clearing the garden, are silent, and when they do speak, are gruff, as if salt has laid a crust on their throats. There is no laughter, no easy talk. Words require energy they cannot spare. With their slow deliberate movements, their red rimmed eyes, their hair caked with dirt, they look like trolls newly come into the light from some underground cave.

Days pass without husbands and wives exchanging a word, and mothers barely notice the existence of their children. One night Meg wakes, staring into the dark, her heart pounding. She cannot remember seeing Willie all day. She sits up and feels around. The child is not lying in his usual place beside her and Ben. Suddenly she is sure her son is drowned. She thinks how easily he could have slipped off the edge of the wharf or fallen between the cracks—disappeared. Who would notice? The sound of the sea would not change, the gulls would go on screeching, his mother would continue to spread fish as the little body was swept into the undertow and carried out to sea.

Meg's hands shake and she has to swallow the bile that rises in her mouth. She crawls about, finds one of the torches, lights it and looks around at her family, sleeping, just as they had in the fishing store, on boughs and quilts. She steps carefully between them, bending to hold the light near each face.

She finds her son, dirty-faced and smiling like a cherub. He is sound asleep, squashed between his sister Lizzie and his Aunt Lavinia. Meg straightens, tears of tiredness and relief spilling down her face.

Holding the flickering light higher, she studies her family, strewn like dead people about the floor. She notes the look of grey exhaustion on Jennie's face, the tight lines that never relax, even in sleep, around the mouths of the men. She remembers Hazel and wonders who will be next to die. Then she shakes herself. Pushing away the black despair, she lies down for the hour or so left until dawn. Before sleep overtakes her she whispers a prayer to the God who lived in the grey stone church in Weymouth—the God she hopes has kept track of them and still knows where they are.

The next day Meg knots a length of rope to the straps of Willie's overalls and ties the other end around her own waist. It is an awkward arrangement that annoys both the mother and child, but it gives Meg some peace of mind and it continues until summer is over.

Annie, Telling Stories

(for my grandmother, Annie O'Rourke)

Carmelita McGrath

When her hat wore out,
she turned it backwards,
pinned the brim with a cabbage rose
of secondhand organza;
when that didn't work, she turned
the hat inside out, revelling
in the new felt, the wear and tear
hidden in her hair.

When she needed coloured wool,
she boiled some moss; after
you feed and shear and card and spin
and ball, what's a little extra effort, after all?

When her daughter had first Communion,
waiting upstairs were the old lace curtains—
ready to become a veil. Annie bleached and starched,
and then, pinned and tucked, and sewed
the pleating when she got it right—add a crown
of lily-of-the-valley, and you look
as good as anyone.

But it was someone else who told me
how Annie would tie a rope around her waist,
one summer when she'd come home
from the flakes to see to dinner;
there just wasn't enough time. One end was tied
to the baby's cradle, she'd knead the bread and rock
him with the rhythms of her labour, two actions
simultaneous, without interruption.

"She Was Skipper of the Shore-Crew": Notes on the History of the Sexual Division of Labour in Newfoundland

Marilyn Porter

This article first appeared in Labour/ Le Travail *in 1985. Some of the notes and references have been updated, but it is, essentially, unrevised. It represents a strand of feminist analysis and awareness that was current in the early 1980s. As readers of this book will realize, newer feminist scholarship operates from different assumptions and uses different theoretical frameworks.*

OUR CURRENT INADEQUATE KNOWLEDGE of the generation and maintenance of the sexual division of labour has generally limited the discussion either to broad generalizations or to extrapolation based on highly specific examples. What we do know suggests that there is a tension between the remarkable consistency of the *general* lines of the sexual division of labour and the degree of variation that prevents the establishment of "universal" rules. Within the broad patriarchal relations of dominance and subordination, there is almost infinite variation in both gender relations and the sexual division of labour. Nor is the pattern fixed in any single society. Sexual divisions are constructed, negotiated, and endlessly challenged. Work by anthropologists and sociologists has focused on ways in which patriarchal relations operate through the institutions of marriage and the family and in relation to capitalist productive relations. Historians have contributed a growing body of detailed studies which show subordination mediated through family patterns, economic and technological organization, religious and political ideology, and many other factors.

Newfoundland rural outports are maritime communities, dominated economically and ideologically by fishing. While fishing is no longer the mainstay of the province's economy, it is the mainstay (together with fishing-related government transfer payments) of the 900-plus outports scattered along the 6,000 miles of island coastline and the Labrador coast that is, of the rural population.[1] Despite an offshore fishery and the increasing numbers of long-liners and small privately owned trawlers (some 800), which can venture further from their home ports, most outports are still dominated by a traditional inshore fishery carried out in small boats (usually crewed by male agnates) operating close to their home ports. A few exceptional women fish, and many more process fish in plants or provide supplementary services.[2] But by and large, the traditionally rigid sexual division of labour is unbreached. In addition, physical conditions in the outports are tough, and "male" activities such as hunting and woodcutting still play a large part in the rural economy. In short, the ethos of "fishermen" is a rugged *male* identity, and it is clamped firmly over the image of outport life.

This association of maritime communities with a rigid and extreme sexual division of labour is a commonplace of anthropological literature, yet studying gender relations and the sexual division of labour in Newfoundland rural communities raises certain problems. Rigid and extreme sexual divisions have been traditionally interpreted as giving rise to oppressive male dominance. J. Tunstall gave a classic account of the negative consequences of seafaring domestic relations among the Hull fishermen and similar tendencies have been reported from Aberdeen and San Diego. J. Zulaika, writing about Portuguese fishermen, describes similar manifestations but makes some interesting and sensitive comments on the relationship between the demands of a tough seaman identity and its expression in sexual relations. Male anthropologists working in Newfoundland with this implicit understanding have stressed women's heavy work load, male authority in the family, male-biased inheritance rules, and the practice of exogamy.[3]

Yet it is not quite like that. Feminist studies[4] have found outport women to be relatively independent, politically and economically, and to be in possession of a vibrant and positive women's culture. In puzzling this apparent contradiction in previous papers, I have focused on a number of countervailing forces, of which the women's considerable economic leverage deriving from their continued share in the fishery seemed to me the most salient. However, it is also noticeable that all of the studies of male oppression associated with maritime activities have been based on communities where men are at sea for considerable periods of time. This is not true of most Newfoundland fishermen, and is certainly not true of the traditional inshore cod fishery. P. Thompson,(1983) working in Scotland, has argued forcibly that the considerable variations in gender and family relations between Scottish communities are associated with different patterns of childrearing practices and economic adaptations. In this essay, I have approached the problem more circuitously: to see if it is possible, by using historical material, to clarify how current gender relations and sexual divisions of labour arose. A number of caveats have to be entered.

There is a considerable quantity of material on the early history of Newfoundland (from the sixteenth to the eighteenth century), but no serious work has been done on women in this period, and we are left with tantalizing glimpses, extrapolation, and plain guesswork about the lives of the early female settlers. All that we can be sure about is that women *did* come from the times of the earliest settlements, both as wives and daughters, and as single women who came as servants. Inevitably all their lives were both hard and hard working, and there are indications that certain traditions and divisions of labour that are current on the island today originated then. But the argument that follows is based on the more certain evidence of demography and patterns of settlement, until we reach the better-documented nineteenth and twentieth centuries.

The island of Newfoundland has always been characterized by considerable variation in climate and geography, which dictates variations in fishing patterns and strategies. There are also variations relating to the relative strengths of different denominations and sects in different areas, and to the origins of the first settlers and subsequent arrivals. All this has consequences for gender relations and the sexual division of labour, but because of the paucity of the material on women we cannot, as yet, make province-wide generalizations. I have, therefore, indicated which area

34

of the island each piece of evidence relates to and how far it can be taken to be generally applicable. Most evidence comes from the northeast coast, and can only be applied with caution to the south coast, the southern shore, or the northern peninsula.

Nevertheless, I would argue that it is only by taking a larger perspective that we may be able to understand the current negotiation of gender relations.

"Soe long as there comes noe women they are not fixed:" Settlement, Expansion, and Permanence

Although European fishermen from England, France, the Basque Country, Portugal, and Spain were exploiting the bountiful supplies of cod over the Grand Banks in the summer months by the end of the fifteenth century, if not earlier, there was no attempt at permanent settlement until 1610 when the London and Bristol Company of the Colonization of Newfoundland established a settlement of 40 men at Cupids, Conception Bay. Manifestly women were needed to establish a settlement and in August 1611, sixteen women arrived, and by March 1613 the first recorded child was born.[5] Apart from that we know little of who they were, why they came, or what their lives were like save that in the prevailing conditions there was no room for slackers of either sex. The story is repeated for the Welsh settlements at Renews (1618), and Calvert's more successful venture at Ferryland (1620). Throughout it is arguable that tough and hard working though the women were, it was less relevant to the development of their economic independence and mutual respect than their role in settlement as such.

A signal feature of settlement in Newfoundland up to the end of the eighteenth century was the demographic sexual imbalance and the effect the absence of women had on the speed and success of settlement. There was a huge preponderance of men on the island, especially in summer when the seasonal migrants (wholly men) far outnumbered the winter residents. Small groups of men (and a very few families) wintered over for one or two seasons. Even among the permanent residents the number of male apprentices and servants far outnumbered the imported women. Significant as they were, the servant girls were in no way sufficient to produce a balanced population. It produced problems of order in St. John's[6] and prevented further settlement on the frontiers. As a naval captain put it succinctly in 1684, "soe long as there comes noe women they are not fixed." This situation was a double-edged sword to the authorities. Those on the ground complained bitterly about disorder "for the permanent growth of a colonial population every single man who is sent out in excess of the number of single women is absolutely useless."[7] On the other hand, the English government did not want growth of the colony and was reluctant to admit that it had grown as much as it had, in which case the answer was simple: restrict the number of women immigrants. While there seems to be no evidence that this measure was ever tried, it does seem to have been on the agenda for some time.[8]

In any event, the pattern of a large summer (male) migration and a much smaller resident population continued through the eighteenth century, and so did the friction between them. In 1675, 1,200 people wintered on the island; by 1730 it was 3,500; by 1750 it was 7,300, and by 1753 it had risen twofold to 12,000. The proportion of women at the beginning of the century was only 10 per cent (instead of a "normal" 25 per cent) and children only accounted for 25 per cent (instead of 50 per cent). By the end of the century these proportions had risen to 13 per cent and 33 per cent respectively and they climbed to normal proportions a few years later. As G. Head put it, "the wintering population was approaching normal characteristics and no longer contained an overwhelming mass of single male labourers. With women and children the attachment to the island was firmer."

The necessity of women to settlement was clear, but the growth in the number of women had another important consequence. The "planters" (established fishermen with their own boats) ceased to import large numbers of "youngsters" (servants from Europe) and relied instead on their families. It is likely, given the tradition of active female involvement, that wives had always helped out on shore at peak times, but evidence suggests that the heyday of family production began in the late eighteenth century.

I will examine the Newfoundland family fishery in more detail below, but first I want to complete the record of women's more basic contribution to the colony as sexual partners and founders of families. Bonavista Bay and Trinity Bay had scattered settlements in the eighteenth century (of 450-900 and 1,500 respectively in 1772) and a few pioneers had already moved north to Notre Dame Bay and Fogo. On the south coast, settlement was centered on St. Jacques, Fortune, and Grand Bank at the east end, and on Port aux Basques in the west, and these gradually extended to meet at Burgeo and Ramea, although the total resident population of the south coast continued to be small (about 600 in 1763).

By the beginning of the nineteenth century, new settlements were established not by new immigration from England but by families moving to a "summer station" on a less frequented stretch of the coast as far as the northern peninsula, and later Labrador. If the family was happy, they might well settle there. Those families then had children and the ensuing marriageable girls attracted further settlement. In one example, on the extreme northwest tip of the island, a tiny group of Englishmen in a merchant's employment survived until the Watts family arrived, with two sons and two daughters. One daughter married William Buckle in the late 1890s and they founded the Buckle family that spreads across Labrador to this day. The other daughter, Mary, married a naval deserter, Alexander Duncan, who changed his name to his mother's maiden name of Gould. They had three sons (from whom are descended the numerous and powerful Goulds of the Flowers Cove/Port au Choix area) and nine daughters "who grew into beautiful girls" providing a sudden bonus supply of eligible wives for the young English settlers. These couples spread along the coast from Eddie's Cove to St. Margaret's Bay, populating all the coves.(Firestone, 1978:23)

The demographic contribution of women to settlement has been recognized by contemporary authorities and spelt out in academic studies, although the feminist implications have not been. But the economic contribution of "the skipper of the shore crew" has been more slowly recognized. It is to her that we now turn.

Women's Work in the Fishing Settlements

The best documented area is the northeast coast and much of the discussion that follows is taken from there. The situation, for example, on the south coast where the trap fishery never developed, was significantly different. Moreover, the evidence is too sparse for any legitimate conclusions to be drawn as to whether the consequences of women's different roles in the fishing economy were as great as might be expected. At this point, all I am attempting is a description of the sexual division of labour as it developed, especially on the northeast coast, together with certain congruences with women's position as observed today.

A further caveat needs to be entered when collapsing such a long period as that between the beginning of the nineteenth century and Confederation (1949). Clearly there were profound technical changes (such as the introduction of the cod trap, and of engines), social changes (such as the rise and fall of the Fishermen's Protective Union in the early twentieth century). Nevertheless it seems that the essential pattern of the sexual division of labour did remain relatively constant, and in this discussion I shall stress that continuity. It is in this context that I am using material such as Greta Hussey's autobiography to illustrate patterns that existed long before. It should, however, be reiterated that the context in which they occurred was changing.

The outport communities were always (up to the influx of federal money in 1949) on the brink of survival. A bad year could push whole settlements into starvation or emigration. I stress this because it was women who, as always, had the prime responsibility for feeding, cleaning, and caring for themselves, the men and the children. It would have been hard in those wild conditions even in prosperity: in poverty it was an enormous task.

A complication that affected many families was a pattern of transhumance. Families who lived out on the exposed headlands would often "winter in" the head of the bay where there was more shelter and more wood. They lived in "tilts," crude shacks which, nonetheless, women had to make habitable. Conversely, many families lived "at home" in the winter but moved in the summer to "summer stations" or "outside" to fish. These places were often hundreds of miles away "on the Labrador." Greta Hussey describes her mother packing everything the family might need in "the Labrador box" for four or more months. They took "pots, pans, dishes, cooking gear and most of the rough grub that we lived on, such as salt beef, dried peas, dried beans, hard bread, sugar, butter and salt pork"(Hussey, 1981:5).

The range of domestic activities Newfoundland women undertook as a matter of course accords closely with descriptions given of the lives of rural women in the nineteenth and early twentieth centuries in other parts of America and Europe.[9] Feeding the family included most of the care of the animals a few cows, sheep, goats, horses, and later chickens, who needed hay and roots to help them survive the winter. The garden was a major responsibility. Men usually did the actual digging, but women cleared or "picked" the ground of stones, planted and weeded it, and defended it against animals. Then they gathered the vegetables and dried them or preserved them (sometimes in salt) in a root cellar, as they are recorded as doing in Edward Winne's letter from Ferryland in 1622.[10] They practised rotation of crops and despised shop-bought seed because "the flies would eat it." Besides, a woman was considered lazy "if she did not grow her own seeds" (Murray, 1979:18).

If the family kept cows or goats, then the wife made butter. A major food gathering activity was berry picking, and while men sometimes did this, it was primarily the task of the women and children. Most of them relished the opportunity to get out on the barrens and the marshes. Blueberries, partridge berries, the succulent bake apples, marsh berries, currants and cranberries, raspberries and blackberries were all gathered on different parts of the island. Many of them were sold, and a family might well provide itself with its winter supplies of flour, margarine, sugar, molasses, beef, and pork with its "berrynote." In passing we should note that this is, in effect, a cash contribution to the family income. The rest were bottled or "jammed down." And so we enter the kitchen. The Newfoundland housewife was honour-bound to set a meal before any member of the family (or visitor) the moment they entered the house. Like many of the practices noted here, it survives today. Everyone had at least four meals a day, and in summer it often rose to seven or eight—a man's light snack in the early morning, breakfast about 7:30-8:00, a mug-up at 10:30-11:00, dinner at 12:00-1:00 p.m., mug-up at 3:30-4:00, tea at 5:30-6:00 p.m. and a mug-up before bedtime at 10:30-11:00 p.m. "Mug-ups" consisted of tea, bread and butter, and "relish," leftover fish or home-made jam, and the last meal of the day, "the night-lunch," was often quite substantial. Main meals, not surprisingly, revolved around fish and potatoes, but salt pork, salt beef, figgy duff and pease pudding, thick soups and dumplings were common. Game-meat or birds were a coveted extra. A glance at any traditional Newfoundland cookbook will show that housewives stressed quantity and weight above all else, but they were ingenious in ringing the changes on limited ingredients.

Bread-making was both a major chore and a woman's pride: "The knowledge of breadmaking was one skill all marriageable girls were expected to possess" and little girls would stand on chairs to make the "barm" or dough. Most housewives baked at least once a day; large families needed two bakings (Murray, 1979:121). Before commercial yeast was introduced in the 1920s, women grew their own hops. Greta Hussey made her own yeast from hops and raw potato because she was dissatisfied with the bread made from shop-bought yeast. In times of dire poverty women would mix potatoes with the flour to eke it out.

Men's suits always seem to have been bought when possible, but most other clothes were homemade. It was another task made more obviously complicated by poverty. Coats had to be "turned," flour sacks had to be transformed into pillow cases, aprons, and tablecloths, and in the poorer families, into dresses and shirts brightened by embroidery. "The coloured thread was inexpensive and with a bit of skill and a few hours work, plain flour sacking was made very attractive" (Murray,

1979:29). Quilting was less developed than it was in the United States, but hooking mats developed into a folk art (Pocius, 1979:92,365). This developed because the women covered bare floor with mats of brin "hooked" with pictures or designs using any brightly coloured rags they could find, thus saving the last scraps of an old garment. The results fetch high prices today and are an enduring testimony to the skill and resourcefulness of Newfoundland housewives.

Some women made sails or "twine" for the nets but such work is usually conspicuous by its absence in women's tasks—a sign and a symbol of the separation of worlds that began exactly at the shoreline, or landwash. Some women could card and spin wool straight from the sheep; all women could knit, and the list of garments that had to be turned out is staggering. Murray cites "knitted petticoats, long stockings, vamps (ankle-length socks), corsocks (balaclavas), mittens, cuffs, gloves, vests, long johns and sweaters." In addition, there was the mending, a much less attractive task and one heartily hated by the young cooks who went on the Labrador fishery (Hussey, 1981:44).

Washing started with carrying water and splitting wood—both women's tasks. Before the 1930s, they made their own soap from rotten cod livers and wood ash. They took care to "blue" and bleach their whites—and even after scrubbing boards were introduced, some women would not use them because they were "hard on the clothes." The production of a faultless line of washing was another indication of a woman's pride. Even today there is a correct order in which to hang clothes on the line that newcomers flout at their peril.

Health was another female concern, and most women knew some folk remedies but the real skill resided with the midwives. Two or three women in each com munity won the confidence of the women with their skill and patience, at a time when doctors were frequently unavailable. Their work needs a separate account.[1]

Houses gradually became more complex (and larger) but some features endured (and still endure today). They were made of wood by the men of the family. A man's pride rested on his ability to build his own boat and house as surely as the woman's did in her "domestic" skills. The central room was the kitchen in which virtually all family activity took place, and in which the many visitors were received. Houses were kept spotless. They were repainted or repapered inside at least once a year and the kitchen was done spring and fall including repainting the floor linoleum. Hussey records repapering their Labrador house with newspaper or religious tracts each year when they arrived. Floors and steps were scrubbed daily. Mats and bedding were aired. One of the heaviest and least popular jobs was washing the heavy winter bed covers when summer eventually released them. Lamps were trimmed and polished, stoves polished. There is an endless list of such recurring tasks.

The enormous extent and weight of the work, as well as the variety of the skills and the standards of excellence the women maintained are impressive, but they are not unique. What marks out the Newfoundland women was that into this crowded schedule came the fishing. The timing and length of the fishing season varied around the coast as did the species pursued and the methods used. The south coast, for instance, could pursue a winter fishery free of ice. Its proximity to the Grand

Banks also made it a natural headquarters for the banking schooners. On the northeast coast, the seal hunt was an important part of the economy. Herring were important on the south and west coasts. Shellfish were increasingly caught, and lobster-canning factories were established on the northern peninsula in the nineteenth century.

But these were all supplementary to the inshore pursuit of "King Cod." In most parts of the island, cod came inshore in pursuit of caplin in early summer and remained until fall. The traditional English approach had always focused on this catch, taken from small boats first with hook and line, and later in cod traps. Boats were under pressure to catch as much as possible in the short season—up to five boatloads a day. The crews did not have time to deal with the much more complex and time-consuming operation of drying the fish onshore. While the shore operation never became "women's work" the way baking was, it did become an area in which women developed skills and expertise. Above all, in the context of the full-fledged trap fishery it involved considerable authority as the "skipper," that is the fisherman's wife, had charge of the whole process, including the hiring and supervision of labour.

The fish, each one of which could weigh up to ten pounds or more, were processed along an assembly line. Each load was pitchforked up onto the stage. There the "cut throat" began the operation, the "header" removed the head and guts, and the "splitter" (the most skillful operator) removed the backbone. The fish were then washed and the "salter" put them in layers into barrels of salt. After a few weeks, the fish were "made." First they were washed and then carried out to the flakes where they were dried and stacked. It was an operation calling for timing and experience to spread the fish out at the correct time and then build stacks of the right size so that the fish stayed in perfect condition throughout the process:[12]

> It was first taken up with a small fish placed over a large one, both back up. Care had to be taken with the big "ickle" fish when taking them up for the first time, especially if it were a Saturday. Sunday might be hot and the big ones might sunburn if left unshielded. Next evening we put four fish together, head and tails. Then small "faggots," then larger "faggots" [that is rectangular piles nicely rounded on the top]. When the fish dried hard they were put in a big round pile (Murray, 1979:16).

While this process was carried out by all fishing families, the degree of division of labour and the timing varied according to whether the crew was a hand-lining crew or a trap crew. It was immensely hard work. Wilson reports one woman saying "If I had but two hours sleep in 24, I could stand the week's labor; but to do without rest for nearly a week is too much for my strength" (Wilson :212). This was in addition to women's usual work, which at this time of year included the preparation and clearing of seven meals a day for the equally exhausted fishermen. Luckily this intensity only lasted for two to three months with a gradual tailing off in the fall.

40

Economy and Authority:
"The Woman was more than 50 per cent"

Not surprisingly, male writers largely failed to recognize the strategic importance of women's economic contribution to the fishery until Ellen Antler made a serious effort to estimate the cash value of the women's contribution to the fishery. She argued that the drying of the fish added $2,400 to the value of the season's catch in Labrador, $1,500-2,000 in Conception Bay. Other writers have tried to put monetary or proportional values on the total amount that women's work contributed to the family income. Alexander reckoned it was at least half. But to most outside authorities, this was an invisible reality. The economic unit was the family, and the head of that unit was the fisherman. Combined with ideological pre-eminence of the fisherman as a catcher of fish, it has helped to obscure not only the real contribution of women but also our understanding of the sexual division of labour in the outports.

Josiah Hobbs, who gave the title to Hilda Murray's book, was not alone in his estimation that "the woman was more than 50 per cent.... I should say, a woman, in a fisherman's work, was half the procedure." Whenever they are asked, Newfoundland men unhesitatingly credit women with at least half the work of the family. There is an air of something like awe in the folklore descriptions older men give of the women of their youth.

The handling of what little cash actually passed in outport families reflects this trust. Women handled the "berry money," as we have seen. They also bartered the occasional dry fish for something they needed at the store. The end of the season reckoning when the fish were "shipped," that is sold to the local fish merchant, was in the hands of the man, but when he had "settled up" he gave this money to his wife (Murray, 1979:24). Money earned "away" was passed to the wife and all household transactions were handled by her. Contemporary evidence bears this out. Dona Davis working on the south coast records women handling all the domestic finances, referring major decisions to their husbands as a formality to rubber stamp their approval. Furthermore, they consider wages that they earn "theirs to spend as they see fit" (Davis, 1983:101).

All this suggested that women had earned, and been granted, a place in the economic unit of the family as nearly equal partners. Yet, much evidence from studies done elswhere on the handling of family budgets suggests that while women often "manage" money, this does not necessarily imply real control. This suspicion is reinforced in Newfoundland by the fact that whatever arrangements were made within the family, external economic relations were carried out by, or in the name of, men.

There is, in addition, the tradition of male-dominated fishing communities, the "authoritarianism" of Newfoundland fathers and the extreme sexual division of labour. Both historically and in contemporary Newfoundland there are particular difficulties in establishing the dimensions of "power" and its relation to "authority." The pervasive egalitarian ethic and the consequent avoidance of authority in outport communities have often been remarked on. Coupled with a stress on individualism (which is interpreted as individual families) this means that there is virtually no possibility for leadership or the exercise of power within the community. Even minor success is penalized, but on the other hand, if an individual or a family (or a community) feels wronged, then voluble public protest is in order. When we look at the distribution of power in Newfoundland it is also important to remember that prior to Confederation, outport communities, in common with rural communities elsewhere, were not only politically powerless but economically marginal, with each individual family equally exploited by merchant interests.

Some writers suggest that women (partly because of their stronger status) are less susceptible to the egalitarian ethic. In a previous paper, I pointed to one way which women had found of deferring to the ethic but escaping its consequences. Dona Davis, who worked in a community that was not characterized by exogamy, found women powerful in defence of their families and their own positions in the house, but less effective in public associations and penalized if they trespassed into the male sphere. Even today it makes little sense to talk of either men or women having power in a situation when the communities themselves have such a minimal public voice.

Patriarchal assumptions permeate nineteenth-century accounts and later anthropological work. Faris, for instance, simply states "In a fishing community one might reasonably expect a sharp division of labour along sexual lines, and Cat Harbour is certainly no exception," going on to observe that virilocal residence and exogamy reinforce such divisions. Faris has been criticized for this assumption on a number of grounds. Stiles (1972) and Davis, who worked on the south coast, which never operated the trap fishery in family units as on the northeast coast, both point to much closer and more reciprocal husband/wife relationships. Regional differences are certainly important, but here I want, rather, to stress Faris's dubious assumption that the people of Cat Harbour, especially the women, gave priority to men's work in the same way that Faris himself does.

Both Firestone and Faris produce some evidence for what they see as extreme male authority in the home. It is worth quoting the passage in which Firestone states:

> The family is patriarchal. Decisions pertaining to family activities are ultimately those of the father... and plans of a group of brothers working under their fathers are finalized by him. In the house the woman gets a drink for her husband from the water barrel or food on demand.... The man tells his wife to do whatever it is that he wants in a matter of fact way neither a command nor a request and she complies (Firestone, 1978:77).

He concludes "there is no question as to the man's authority nor to the woman's subordination." He cites as corroborative evidence a woman saying "it is best when the wife does what the husband wants." But in the very next quotation we hear a woman saying "a good woman here is one who is obedient and doesn't try to tell the man what to do....at least the men would say that." Thus, even on the evidence

Firestone gives us, there are some contradictions. Firstly, economic decisions relating to the fishing crew might well have been taken by the skipper without infringing on the way in which domestic decisions were taken. Secondly, the apparent servitude of women in the matter of providing food applies not just to the men of the house, but to everyone, including female visitors. I suggest that rather than reflecting subordination, it arises out of poverty and the extreme skill needed to produce sufficient food and drink. It has become part of the housewife's pride that she can, and does, supply what is necessary. When I see it today, I do not notice subjugation, but rather a sense of quiet confidence in the women's control of the kitchen and the house. Thirdly, it is hard for a feminist to escape intimations of connivance in the last quotation. She was, after all, talking to a man, Firestone, who would, she assumed, also "say that."

A more overt example of patriarchal practice is that of remuneration within the family for women's work in the shore crew. Women who were hired from outside the family were paid, but while the sons who fished received a share (or more likely a part share) of the voyage, the daughters who worked on shore got nothing. On the other hand, girls who worked outside the home did not have to contribute to the household, whereas boys did (Firestone, 1978:42). Again it was part of the economic structure organized around a patrilocal fishing crew. As Faris's unsympathetic male informant puts it, "Maids leave, so why should they get anything." What we see here seems to reflect an awkward transition from the time that a household is dependent on a daughter's labour to the time when another household is dependent on her labour as a wife. At this level, the Newfoundland situation seems to confirm the stress that Levi Strauss and his followers put on "the exchange of women" as fundamental to the social organization of male dominance. Yet, as Mackintosh has pointed out in connection with Meillassoux's arguments, because he regarded female subordination as a fact and not a problem, he slipped into illegitimate theoretical assertions that confused the relations of human reproduction with the process of the reproduction of the whole society, and this led to a deduction of social relations from production relations (1977:121). Mackintosh, rightly, insists that we "should seek rather to grasp the way in which specific forms of these oppressions operate, how they are maintained and reinforced, how they are overthrown or why they are not overthrown," and this brings us back to the women of Newfoundland and the problem of an extreme sexual division of labour.

In many ways, this seems to be the crux. Partly because it is so expected in a maritime society, both male and female writers have tended to take it for granted. There are, and probably always have been, exceptions, but the sexual division of labour in the outports is now and always has been both pronounced and rigid. There are clearly and geographically limited spheres of activity. Lists of "men's tasks" and "women's tasks" hardly overlap at all. Social, cultural, and political life is largely carried out in single sex groups. Responsibilities within the household are quite separate. The problem lies in assessing what the consequences of this are, and this is compounded by the primacy accorded to the male activity of fishing. Because of the patriarchal structure of the wider society from which the outports come and in which they continue to be embedded, this carried with it (and still carries) various overt indications of dominance over the female spheres.

As the material under discussion has indicated, however, the extreme sexual division of labour in Newfoundland communities has been combined with women's vital and acknowledged economic contributions to the household economy, with the tradition of their vital role in settlement and with an ideology of egalitarianism. One consequence of this has been that women express their autonomy, control, and authority within "separate spheres." These spheres are not coterminous with the usual delineations of "public" and "private." Indeed, the whole concept rests on the interrelationship and interdependence of men's and women's economic efforts in both the household and the fishery. Rather there are various physical boundaries, which, together with the sexual division of labour, allow women both the physical and ideological space they need. One of these is the shoreline, or "landwash." Men controlled the fishery at sea; women the fishery on shore. I would suggest that the acceptance of that boundary in such matters as women not going in the boats, or even making the nets, reinforces their control of the shorework and its importance in the recognition of their economic cooperation. Even more important was women's control of the house and everything in it, including the kitchen. The distinction between "public" and "private" in New-foundland outports did not happen between "outside" and "inside" but between the kitchen, which was public, and the rest of the house, which was private. The kitchen was not just an extension of the community, but in effective terms, the centre of it. No one knocked at a kitchen door. Anyone could come and go as they pleased—but were forbidden to pass into the "private" areas of the house. Only "strangers" or those in authority knocked (and sometimes entered by another door). In the absence of community meeting places, the kitchens were the places in which the community met, that is, publicly interacted, held discussions, and came to decisions. Even where alternatives were available, the absence of any effective heating except the kitchen stove would not encourage much conversation to take place there.[13] In this context it is vital that the kitchen was readily and obviously acknowledged to be the women's domain. It was impossible to exclude them in those circumstances. Present-day observation shows male conversation being carefully monitored by the women who often disguise their interest behind ceaselessly working hands. Coupled with the egalitarian ethic, it helps to explain the much-noticed practice of "waiting-on-men." In this way, the women can easily intervene in the men's conversation without apparently leaving their own sphere and thus can exert a correct authority of their own.

In assessing this somewhat contradictory material, the most useful comparison is with the material gathered in Scottish fishing communities by P. Thompson. The crux of his argument is that the very different gender relations and economic attitudes (past and present) in Buckie, Lewis, Aberdeen, and Shetland are inextricably linked. In particular, the "moral order" of a community, its interpretation of religion, its child-rearing practices, and its attitudes to gender affects its ability to adapt and survive in different economic conditions. Regional differences have also played a complicating part in the study of Newfoundland, although it would be hard to find such overall contrasts as there are in Scotland. However, the parallels, especially the social practices described in Buckie and Shetland, are illuminating. Shetland represents the high point in both gender relations and economic success, perhaps exemplified by positive handling of oil activity. The situation of women there is characterized by a degree of economic involvement and genuine equality, a lack of male authority in the home, sexual freedom, and political and intellectual energy, which it would be hard to equal in Newfoundland. Nevertheless, some similarities with Shetland support the argument that women's economic participation in the fishery and the non-authoritarian domestic relations in Newfoundland are integrally connected.

In Buckie, which Thompson characterizes as "the moral order of free enterprise," individualism, a greater separation of gender spheres, greater male authority, and a more deferential religious observance, create a more immediately recognizable comparison with Newfoundland. The most notable contrast is that, in the absence of an egalitarian imperative, highly capitalized Buckie boats are among the most successful fishing enterprises in Britain. As in Newfoundland, however, Buckie women have asserted control over their own sphere, and the house operates similarly as the centre of a warm and egalitarian community—"Strangers knock, friends come in." It was an open-door community; and as today, food was always offered to a visitor—"the table was always laid for anyone who came in" (Thompson, 1983:250).

Too much can be made of these comparisons, but they help to set the material presented here in context. While Newfoundland outports are not unique and their experience is parallelled elsewhere, they operate in a specific historical, economic, and ideological situation and aspects of these may vary from community to community, making generalization even within Newfoundland difficult. The eventual gender relations and sexual division of labour will be the result of complex interaction of economic and ideological forces, not least of which will be women's active participation in their own lives.

What I want to suggest here is that women in Newfoundland—at least the wives of fishermen, that is the owners of boats (and that is a considerable caveat), have used their vital roles in initial settlement and in the fish-producing economy not to destroy the sexual division of labour but to establish its boundaries in such a way as to confirm their control over at least their own spheres. Inheritance did not matter if a woman gained a "woman's sphere" by marriage; nor did the ownership of a share if she controlled the household budget. Nor, and this is also important, did either matter in conditions of bare survival, when there was no surplus to be appropriated.

Conclusion

We can speak of "traditional outport life" at least in the sense that the outlines of the sexual divisions of labour and the basis for the negotiation of gender and power come into sharpest focus at the end of the eighteenth century with the establishment of the Planter's household unit with its inshore fishing crew and shore crew as the key unit in the fishing economy. And these outlines remain until the demise of sun-dried fish as a product in the 1950s and the access of modern goods, services, cash, and opportunities in the heady post-Confederation days after 1949. Much of what is evident today is rooted in that long experience, but the precise connections still need to specified. Here I have restricted myself to an examination of the context of the male domination of the fishery in which the signal fact of women's contribution as both settlers and shore crew serve to alert us that women were in a position to negotiate actively in the formation and development of the relations of production. In its turn, this forces a reconsideration of the consequences of the sexual division of labour and its relationship with other areas of women's interest.

We are still a long way from a wholly adequate theory of the subordination of women. But the route lies through careful examination of the evidence of different women's lives. The fishing communities of Newfoundland offer a perspective that sharpens our view of certain aspects of the sexual division of labour, and, I hope, contributes to the gradual filling out of the complex picture of negotiation and adaptation that constitutes the reality of gender divisions.

1   When this article was written the fishery had already declined to the point where it contributed only 12% of the net value of production and employed only 13% of the labour force. But it was still the most socially significant sector of the economy and few people foresaw the complete collapse of its role as the mainstay of rural Newfoundland and Labrador.

2   Estimates vary, but there are probably not more than a couple of dozen full-time fisherwomen. Nearly all of them do it because of unusual family circumstances, for example, a family of daughters with no close male relatives to take over the boat and gear. A few wives fish with their husbands in the smaller crews; more since a change in the UIC regulations in 1981 made this a more profitable adaptation. For a discussion of the experience of one female fisher, see Silk, this volume. Women are a much more significant factor in fish processing, making up about 50% of workers in this sector.

3   See J. Tunstall, *The Fishermen* (1962); P. Thompson, *Living the Fishing* (1983); M. Orbach, *Hunters, Seamen and Entrepreneurs* (1977); J. Zulaika, *Terra Nova* (1981). Also, see J. Faris, *Cat Harbour* (1972); M.M. Firestone, *Savage Cove* (1978); R. Andersen and C. Wadel, eds., *North Atlantic Fishermen* (1972).

4   In the early 1980s there were few explicitly feminist academic studies to draw on. They included D. Davis, *Blood and Nerves* (1983); D. Davis, "The Family and Social Change in the Newfoundland Outport," *Culture*, III, 1 (1983); E. Antler, "Women's Work in Newfoundland Fishing Families," (unpublished paper 1976); E. Antler, "Maritime Mode of Production or Labour Process: an Examination of the Newfoundland Inshore Fishery," (unpublished paper 1977); C. Benoit, "The Poverty of Mothering," (M.A. thesis, Memorial University, 1982); A. Matthews, "The Newfoundland Migrant Wife," in A. Himelfarb and J. Richardson, *People, Power and Process* (1980); M. Porter, "Women and Old Boats: the Sexual Division of Labour in a Newfoundland Outport," in E. Garmarnikow, *The Public and the Private* (1983); M. Porter, "The Tangly Bunch: the

Political Culture of Avalon Women," in *Newfoundland Studies* (1985). There is also descriptive evidence in autobiographies and folklore accounts, for example, Greta Hussey, *Our Life on Lear's Room* (1981); H. Murray, *More than 50%* (1979); H. Porter, *Below the Bridge* (1979); E. Goudie, *Women of Labrador* (1973).

5 A son, to Nicholas Guy, related to John Guy; the mother's name is not recorded.

6 In 1766 St. John's, the rate of single Irish men to available women was as high as 17:1, quoted in C. Grant Head, *Eighteenth Century Newfoundland* (Toronto 1976), 87.

7 Quoted in J. Mannion, ed., *The Peopling of Newfoundland* (1977:19).

8 See J. Halton and M. Harvey, *Newfoundland, the Oldest British Colony* (1883:43).

9 For example see M. Chamberlain, Fenwomen (1975); F. Thompson, *Lark Rise to Candleford* (1945); S. van Kirk, *"Many Tender Ties": Women in the Fur Trade, 1670-1870* (1980); B. Light and A. Prentice, *Pioneer and Gentle Women of British North America* 1713-1867 (1980).

10 Quoted in G.T.Cell *Newfoundland Discovered: English Attempts at Colonization 1610-1630,* (1972).

11 In comparing M. Chamberlain's material (*Fenwomen*) with my own, I tentatively put forward two generalizations. Firstly, Newfoundland midwives never developed as many erudite skills, either herbal or surgical. They managed on commonsense and humility. Their hallmark was their accessibility. They would willingly buckle down and sort out the rest of the family or climb into bed with the mother for a warmup and a giggle. See C. Benoit, The Politics of Mothering, for some further comments.

12 There are excellent descriptions of the first stage of processing in G. Hussey, *Our Life,*(1979:38), and W. Wilson, *Newfoundland and its Missionaries,* (1880:211), which show the continuity of the methods used.

13 For a discussion of the role of the kitchen as the boundary between public and private, see L. Dillon, "Black Diamond Bay: A Rural Community in Newfoundland," (M.A. thesis, Memorial University, 1983). Also see J. Faris, Cat Harbour; H. Murray, *More Than 50%*; D. Davis, *Blood and Nerves*; P. Thompson,'Women in Fishing Economies', records community access to the kitchen in Buckie and Shetland. Faris, *Cat Harbour*, stresses that men also met in the shop in the evenings, an arena most other observers, for example, K.K. Szala, "Clean Women and Quiet Men: Courtship and Marriage in a Newfoundland Fishing Village," (M.A. thesis, Memorial University 1978), allocate to the young unmarried of both sexes. Traditionally, the "stores"—sheds on the stages—were men's meeting places, but these were (and are) untenable for the colder months of the year.

Whipping Them into Shape: State Refinement of Patriarchy among Conception Bay Fishing Families, 1787-1825

Sean Cadigan

This paper is based on recent research in 19th century surrogate court records.

RESIDENTS OF HARBOUR GRACE AND PORT DE GRAVE witnessed an unusual spectacle in the summer of 1820. For the first time in almost forty years, public whippings by sentence of the Surrogate Court took place. The surrogate judges ordered that two planters, Philip Butler and James Lundrigan, each receive 36 lashes of the cat-of-nine-tails for their contempt of court. Butler and Lundrigan had supposedly refused to give up property attached by the court to pay their debts to merchants. The punishment was cruel and brutal. Butler, tightly bound by his hands and legs to a picket fence at Harbour Grace, yielded to the court's demands after 12 lashes on his bare back. Lundrigan, tied to a fish flake near the home of his wife and young children, withstood 14 lashes before collapsing in an apparent epileptic seizure. Lundrigan's plight was all the more tragic because the court knew in advance of his predisposition to this illness. When the fit passed, Lundrigan too submitted to the court's wishes (Report, 1821: 2-9).

The writing of Newfoundland history places the Butler and Lundrigan incidents within the context of a rather conventional colonial political history. According to this convention Butler's and Lundrigan's treatment were simply examples of an "outrage" imposed on Newfoundlanders by naval authority in a British possession which had neither colonial status nor representative government. Newfoundland liberal reformers such as William Carson and Patrick Morris, who struggled for colonial representative government, made Butler and Lundrigan a cause célèbre which they used to attack the judicial authority of a Colonial Office-appointed naval governor and his surrogate officer-judges. Few historians say much about the Butler and Lundrigan affairs in their own right, preferring instead to mark them as signposts along the inevitable way to the achievement of Newfoundland self-government. Such historians particularly treat only cursorily the importance of Butler's and Lundrigan's wives in instigating the contempt which led to the whippings (Neary and O'Flaherty, 1974: 66-69; O'Flaherty, 1987: 409-411).

A careful consideration of the meaning of Butler and Lundrigan offers much to those interested in the history of women and of the family about the manner in which the late eighteenth- and early nineteenth-century state could help to shape patriarchal household formation among the Anglo-American labouring classes. Squeezing this understanding out of the scant evidence which remains from the affair is an adventure in speculation. The public record of that era was of a man's world. Men of the gentry and bourgeoisie recorded evidence to suit their own purposes; they assumed that posterity would be concerned with their political issues, and minimized the role and concerns of women in them (Thomis and Grimmet, 1982: 12-13). If we are to learn about the role of women in the Butler and

Lundrigan affair, then we must not be afraid to use some imagination to make much of something otherwise obscured by too little evidence.

Despite its paucity, such evidence suggests that the whippings were a response to a society in upheaval, the product of the severe economic depression which plagued Newfoundland after the Napoleonic wars. In response, the state attempted to stabilize the fishery by encouraging household production based on family labour. A society of families only, government and court officials believed, would enjoy a peace based on people finding their material needs met in the bosom of their households, not by making collective demands for better wages, credit or relief from merchants or the state. Merchants' restriction of credit, and especially their more aggressive use of debt proceedings in the courts, encouraged officials to hope that household production would lessen the need for credit, and consequent legal disputes. The Butler and Lundrigan resistance to court orders resulting from debt suits, however, were family efforts led by the planters' wives. Such assertiveness by women, although characteristic of the labouring classes, was certainly not in keeping with upper-class English views about women's subordination within the family as a foundation of social order. The actions of Butler's and Lundrigan's wives disappointed local officials' hope that a society of fishing families would be an orderly one. Philip Butler and James Lundrigan were most likely whipped as much for their failure to conform to a gentry-bourgeois model of patriarchy as they were for contempt. The demands of living in a society dominated by the fishery meant that the relations between men and women in fishing households, while still patriarchal, were not characterized by the kind of subordination officials hoped would lay the foundation for a more peaceable society.

It is not likely that the surrogate judges ordered the whippings simply because of their naval experience, as reformers at first suggested (*Report*, 1821: 1-17). The surrogate court judges derived their authority from Newfoundland naval governors' civil judicial authority, granted by the British government in 1729. These judges, at first usually naval officers under the governor's orders as commander of the squadron at Newfoundland, were literally the surrogates of the governor. The surrogates' mandate was to dispense summary justice in civil disputes involving small amounts of money, although they sometimes heard criminal disputes (English, 1990: 89-119). There is little doubt that brutal corporal punishment such as whipping was an integral part of naval discipline on Anglo-American vessels in the eighteenth century (Rediker, 1987: 217, 259). The record of sentences passed by the Harbour Grace surrogates, however, does not support any contention that they used naval discipline in their civil jurisdiction. The surrogates ordered whippings only three times, for thefts and fraud in 1787-88, and never ordered any other form of corporal punishment. (PANL, GN5/1/B/1, Box 1, Book 1787-88: 26 Sept. 1787; 10 Oct. 1787, 27, 28 March 1788). By the end of the Napoleonic era, in any event, surrogates were usually civilians rather than naval officers (O'Flaherty, 1987: 409).

The surrogates' harsh reaction to Butler and Lundrigan was much more likely a result of the profound upheaval which affected the Newfoundland fishery and society in the Napoleonic era. The migratory fishery, based largely on labour hired by some form of fixed-wage or share payment, dominated the first half of the eighteenth century. Disruption of the migratory fishery by wars in the second half of the century encouraged the resident fishery. As permanent settlement grew, resident planters resorted less to hired labour, relying instead on that of their families to avoid the additional costs of paying wages. Unique international market conditions established by the Napoleonic wars—the exclusion of French and American competitors from Newfoundland waters, and from Iberian markets—produced unprecedented high fish prices which blunted the trend to family labour in household production. High prices for fish encouraged planters (resident independent fishers) to hire more servants, usually single Irish males, in larger-scale, more capital-intensive operations (Cadigan, 1991: 60-100, 125-56).

The end of the wars abruptly threw most of these single male servants out of work as fish prices collapsed due to the readmission of the French and Americans to the fishery. By the winter of 1816-17 economic disruption had become severe depression. Large roaming crowds of unemployed single men led worried merchants in Conception Bay to demand, without success, that Governor Francis Pickmore round up and ship these men out of the island. His inability to comply left his Lieutenant Governor Captain David Buchan, senior naval officer on the Newfoundland station in Pickmore's absence, to deal with the spectre of famine. Not only had planters responded to the depression by letting their servants go, but merchants tightly restricted credit, giving none to single unemployed servants, and very little to the families of their most dependable planter-clients. Unemployment and credit restriction, coupled with the area's limited agricultural resources, meant that the unemployed single men roaming Conception Bay faced starvation. Many of these men organized crowds to search planter and merchant stores for food. Buchan had not the forces at his disposal to stop the store-breaking which ensued, and resorted to issuing naval stores to calm the situation.

Unwilling to incur the expense of a greater military or police establishment in Newfoundland, colonial officials accepted the advice of merchants that the fishery must be prosecuted in future largely by family labour in household production. Fishing families could supplement their earnings in the fishery by nonmarket agricultural activity. They would thus be able to supply their dietary needs with less credit, and have little time to break open merchants' stores. By 1820, government policy was clear and routinely enforced by the surrogates: all men could have rights to land only for the purpose of raising vegetables for their families. No one could enclose more than their share so that all families might have the opportunity of providing for themselves (Cadigan, 1991: 169-92).

Buchan was one of the surrogates who ordered the whipping of Butler and Lundrigan. Although he never stated why he favoured such penalties, we may guess that Buchan's trips back and forth with his squadron between England and Newfoundland made him aware that a transatlantic social upheaval was in the making in the wake of post-1815 economic collapse. Buchan spent most of 1818 and 1819 in Great Britain (Kirwin, 1988: 114-116). British society at that time was experiencing economic depression and social upheaval based on the collapse on agricultural prices after 1815. As in Newfoundland, high levels of unemployment led to a variety of collective actions by those worst affected, culminating eventually in the Captain Swing uprising of 1830 (Hobsbawm and Rudé, 1968: 29-41, 72-76).

The social dislocation of these years occurred alongside an intensifying idealization of the family as the foundation of a renewed social harmony. This idealization was part of a long trend given voice by English clerics that just as the paternal rule of the King and his magistrates kept social order, so too should male family heads keep order within their families. Wives in particular should be subject to the authority of their husbands in all public dealings, especially the property transactions of the marketplace. Women who would not observe this patriarchal order should expect corporal punishment by their husbands in the interest of the public good (Davies, 1982: 58-80). Capitalist development initially eroded the paternalistic edifice of British society after 1815 by pushing women into the forefront of working-class protests. In the long run, however, bourgeois society ironically entrenched a patriarchal ethos based on the sentimentalization of home and the family which would work against public roles for these women (Thompson, 1976: 115-137). Among Britain's rulers the ideal of the family became a more important comfort as a gentry-dominated hierarchical and deferential social order gave way to the impersonal, increasingly urban, market relations of the bourgeoisie and working class. The new ideology looked to the working-class household head to maintain the order of his family. He represented his family in the public world of court and market, relying on his wife to maintain a passive, ordered domestic domain which would give society no trouble (Davidoff, L'Esperance and Newby, 1976: 142-157).

Buchan's assent to the whipping of Butler and Lundrigan most likely reflected his disappointment that the family plan for social order in Newfoundland had not conformed to this patriarchal ideal. The naval captain should not have been surprised, for the families of the rough British working classes rarely conformed to the domestic ideal of the bourgeoisie. The marriages of people from these classes were both more egalitarian and disorderly than their "betters" would have liked (Perkin, 1989: 6, 158). Northeast-coast fishing families also did not conform to the ideal of peaceable patriarchy which was gaining ground in England.

Fishing households shared with the rest of the Anglo-American world the formal legal structures of patriarchy, particularly in inheritance law. Throughout the late eighteenth and early nineteenth centuries, men inherited property in lieu of their mothers or wives, restricted only by general requirements that they provide for their female relatives. Widows might inherit property in their own right from their husbands, but usually with the stipulation that such property not be alienated from the deceased male's bloodline. Despite such legalities, women often assumed roles as household heads if there was no competent male to assume ownership or control of a household's inheritance. Planter or merchant widows might, for example, continue to direct their sons' work in their families' enterprises. Women without male relatives asserted their inheritance rights to the fishing equipment of their deceased husbands so that they might continue their fishery.

Such women's assumption of very public economic roles reflected the high degree to which Newfoundland households integrated women's work into household commodity production in the fishery. This integration, combined with the precariousness of household survival in such a limited agricultural environment, meant that women were not the docile subordinates that an official like Buchan might hope they would be. Women's indispensable role in the production of cod and domination of the household's subsistence limited formal male authority. Planters' growing reliance on family labour through the early years of the nineteenth century meant that they had to depend on women's labour. While men caught fish, women cured it. Salting and drying fish was a difficult process which required an eye practised at assessing weather conditions. Women's control of the reproductive work of their households allowed them to dominate "shore" work. Women provided most of their families' food, clothing and shelter. The management of the household's subsistence agriculture was their special preserve. Women coaxed root crops from an unyielding soil and tended livestock. Their work was made all the more important by the very limited nature of local soil and climate. Every potato stored away for the winter was a precious achievement on a coast where the prospect of hunger and famine was becoming more and more frequent. Tied to the shore by this reproductive work, women became that part of the family's labour reserve which was available for curing. The limits of agriculture made women's shore work all the more important. Only the best quality fish could fetch the highest prices on a merchant's account book. Only the most careful cultivation could ensure that families would have to take as little food as possible on credit for their winter supply. Both these areas lay in women's hands.

Fishermen depended on their female relatives for their families' survival. The difficulty of such survival pulled people of both genders together as families competed with each other. If one family's pig, for example, ruined the potato garden of another, people could come to blows with each other. The fight might involve two male family heads at first, but both could count on the assistance of their wives or other female relatives if it was needed. While such competition may well have reinforced the patriarchal autonomy of individual households, there is no reason to assume that this entailed extra male subordination of women. The interdependence of men and women within Conception Bay households is suggested by the absence of the newspaper notices by men of runaway wives so common elsewhere in British North America.

No one should make the mistake of seeing fishing communities at the time as not being patriarchal. Not only did public institutions like the courts as well as merchants not recognize women as their male relatives' formal partners, but court records yield many examples of men's brutal discipline of their female relatives. But these records also suggest that women were capable of using violence against each other in disputes over livestock, household goods or topsoil, as well as of defending themselves against male assaults. Women appear to have assumed the role of primary defenders of their households' property from outside threats. The problem was that merchants and courts did not care about women's role as defenders of their households. Merchants generally gave credit to accounts in the name of single males or small partnerships of two or three men regardless of the families which actually used the equipment and supplies purchased on that account for the fishery. Women might see the goods of their households as their domain, but this was of no consequence to merchants. The latter expected debts to be paid, and saw all the property of a fishing household as subject to the obligations of a fisherman's account (Cadigan, 1991: 193-220).

The courts' refusal to recognize women's "personhood" in areas such as household accounts was a longstanding part of Newfoundland legal tradition (Cullum and Baird, 1993: 97-98). The surrogate courts accepted English common law status for a woman as feme-covert, "that is, the very being or legal existence of the woman is suspended, or at least is incorporated and consolidated into that of the husband" (Blackstone, 1765: 430). Women, in common law, largely became subordinate to the commercial transactions of their husbands. Not only did most formal economic power legally reside in males, but common law still allowed men to use corporal punishment to discipline the "misbehaviour" of women. While authorities found such exercise repugnant among the gentry and bourgeoisie, courts allowed, in the interest of order, "the lower rank of the people, who were always fond of the old common law, ...[to] claim and exert their ancient privilege" (Ehrlich, 1959: 85-86).

The conflict between the surrogate court's expectation that fishing families conform to common law patriarchal ideals and fishing women's role as defenders of their households produced the whippings of 1820. Fishing families' need for credit provided the backdrop. Fishing people usually obtained credit from merchants in return for payment from the produce of the fishing season. Merchants pursued delinquent debtors by going to court to obtain a writ of attachment of fishing people's fish and oil or, if there was not enough produce to satisfy the debt, secure the return of what equipment remained in their clients' hands.

The intensive development of the fishery during the Napoleonic wars, however, led many fishing people to look for more credit than usual. Merchants often gave this credit, but in a new way to accommodate the riskier size of the transaction. Although British law for the Newfoundland fishery allowed people only to hold property by continuous usage rather than as real estate, merchants gave mortgages on the fishing rooms, gardens and dwellings of their clients (Cadigan, 1991: 296-97). As a result of these mortgages, merchants now expected that all household property, rather than just the catch and equipment of a fishing voyage, be subject to attachment for debt. The attachment of such household property brought court officials into direct conflict with fishing people.

The surrogate court first encountered the contempt of fishing people for its process in debt cases in 1813. The court's initial reaction was not to mete out harsh discipline. When Thomas Fahey refused to pay £3.7.0 to John Donovan on a note of hand past due, for example, he did so by saying in court that he had no money, "and began to make use of very unbecoming Language." The court jailed him only until he found security for the debt (PANL, GN5/1/B/1, Box 1, Book 1813-15; 15 November 1813).

The surrogate court searched for compromise when the women and men who came before it lived up to patriarchal ideals of appropriate behaviour. The court would only decide in favour of merchant Thomas Danson's suit against P. Ryan for £12.0.8 in 1814, for example, when Danson would accept Ryan's wife's[1] offer "to pay the Plaintiff as soon as she and her Son were able" to sell a part of their fishing room. The son, James, defended himself from a suit for debt by William Danson on the grounds that he had taken supplies on credit "to support his father and mother" (PANL, GN5/1/B/1, Box 1, Book 1813-15; 7 Feb. 1815).

If men alone were the instigators of contempt of court, the judicial response was lenient. William and John Butt's defiance of a court order to leave alone buildings on their neighbour William Whiteway's fishing room in 1814 only earned them an admonishment to cease tearing them down (PANL, GN5/1/B/1, Box 1, Book 1813-15: 18 March 1814). Other actions of contempt in debt cases by Edward Pike and Thomas Fahey (the latter using abusive language against the sheriff) resulted only in reprimands, small fines, and confirmation of earlier judgements (PANL, GN5/1/B/1, Box 1, Book 1813-15; Box 2, Book 1816-18: 25 May 1815, 8 May, 16 Oct. 1817).

At times, the surrogates actually interceded on behalf of defendants in suits involving debt. The court, for example, did not simply decide for Thomas and Peter Ezickle in their suit against the widow Elizabeth Hicks of Harbour Main in 1815. The Ezickles wanted payment in full of the £62 worth of supplies Hicks had taken that year. The surrogate accepted her plea of poverty, and allowed her to pay the debt in yearly instalments of £7 (PANL, GN5/1/B/1, Box 2, Book 1814-15: 21 Sept. 1815). In such instances the court made clear that it felt the interests of the family in its ideal form were paramount when making decisions about the payment of debts. Thus when merchants R.C. Stone, Michael Knox, Nuttall Cawley & Co., and Gosse, Pack and Fryer jointly sued William Smith of Bread and Cheese Cove for supplies he took on credit in 1817 and 1818, the court ruled that Smith had to give up enough property to satisfy their claims. At the same time, however, the surrogate warned the merchants that Smith "being a poor person with a Wife and family he was not to be distressed by selling the property attached without a sufficiency for their maintenance during the Winter ensuing" (PANL, GN5/1/B/1, Box 2, Book 1818-19: 1-2 Oct. 1818).

Philip Butler's was the first of a small wave of contempt cases which began in 1819, peaked in 1820, and lasted until 1825. The incident was one of the first cases in which a merchant attempted to foreclose on a mortgage in Conception Bay as the post-1815 depression deepened. Butler had mortgaged the family fishing room in 1814 to Trimingham & Co. for £236 to obtain credit for his fishery. Defaults on his subsequent accounts and mortgage payments led Trimingham & Co. to seek Butler's insolvency, and the award of his plantation from the court. In 1819, the merchant firm sued Butler for failing to comply with a court order that he yield the property. When asked by the court why he refused to do so, Butler replied "that he had never refused to give up the premises, that it was his Wife [who] had kept forcible possession" (PANL, GN5/1/B/1, Box 2, Book 1818-19: 6 August 1819). The court advised Butler to give Trimingham's the property.

James Lundrigan's debt was much less than Butler's. Graham McNicoll & Co. sued Lundrigan in 1819 for slightly more than £13 credit issued for supplies in that fishing season. The suit was one of many pursued by McNicoll that year (PANL, GN5/1/B/1, Box 2, Book 1818-19: 6 May 1819). Subsequent court minutes simply record that surrogate judges Captain Buchan and Anglican minister John Leigh pressed charges against Lundrigan for his refusal to give up his fishing room after the court sold it to satisfy the debt owed to McNicoll's. The surrogates recorded that they sentenced Lundrigan to the whip because of his "divers contempt of court and resisting constables in the Execution of their duty, and particularly for refusing and neglecting to attend the Surrogate Court" (PANL, GN5/1/B/1, Box 2, Book 1819-20: 5-6 July 1820).

The sentence of whipping was completely out of character with Buchan's and Leigh's sentences for other contempt at the time. They had earlier only fined John Wilcox, a Brigus planter, £1 for insulting a constable who tried to enforce a ruling against him (PANL, GN5/1/B/1, Box 2, Book 1819-20: 2 Dec. 1819). The surrogates excused James Fillier and Thomas Boon Sr. on the same day as Lundrigan's trial for the same contempt as the latter because they were "old and infirm." The surrogates in such cases observed the benefaction implicit in their duty as enforcers of the patriarchal ideal. As a further example, Buchan and Leigh excused Michael Power for a contempt like Lundrigan's because Power "at the time of neglecting to attend was suffering severe family affliction having lost two Sons in boat by a Gale of Wind" (PANL, GN5/1/B/1, Box 2, Book 1819-20: 5 July 1820). Planters John Covyduck and John Dawe had no similar excuse of age or bereavement for their resistance of bailiffs' attempts to seize their property by writs of execution for debt, but Buchan and Leigh did not order them whipped, deciding instead to use more force in seizing the premises (PANL, GN5/1/B/1, Box 2, Book 1819-20: 6 July 1820).

Perhaps the surrogates tired of the increased number of contempt cases, and ordered Butler and Lundrigan whipped in exasperation as a warning to others that the trend would not be tolerated. The unusual nature of whipping as a sentence in English practice by the early nineteenth century, however, makes this suggestion untenable. Whipping, like other forms of corporal punishment, was the direct physical manifestation of the early eighteenth-century English state's view that it was the duty of the magistracy to bring order to society by punishment of the body. People who offended the ideal social order must be treated as a diseased part of a larger organic whole. Corporal punishment was not so much for a particular crime as it was a symbolic ritual whereby the state demonstrated that it was prepared to force individuals to observe the obligations implicit in belonging to a wider network of social relations. The fear of such punishment would act as a medicine to ward off the contagion of unacceptable ideas or practices. By the late eighteenth century, however, the success of liberal reform had supplanted this conception of punishment with a greater emphasis on individual responsibility and rehabilitation rather than on the penitent as symbol (McGowen, 1987: 654-59).

The court's handling of other contempt cases prior to, and at the same time as Butler and Lundrigan, demonstrated that the surrogates did not regard contempt per se as so great an offence of the social order as to deserve corporal punishment. The only difference between Butler and Lundrigan and the other offenders was that their cases involved wives openly defying the ideology of women's passive confinement to the private sphere of the patriarchal family. There is no evidence to suggest that Butler or Lundrigan deliberately chose to allow their wives to act against the court's orders, hoping that the court would not punish them because they were women. Butler's testimony suggests that he would have been quite happy to avoid the whole affair, but that his wife refused to surrender her home. The vigour of Lundrigan's wife in threatening constables intimates that she allowed few people to tell her what to do. The court, in any event, held men accountable for their female relatives' actions. Butler's and Lundrigan's crime was not so much contempt of court as it was failure to be proper patriarchs. The planters' inability to discipline their wives for the good of a wider social order, within the context of post-1815 social and economic crisis, drove Buchan and Leigh to resorting to an earlier, but by their time extraordinarily unusual, style of punishment, the purpose of which was to symbolize and instruct rather than chastise.

Evidence later given at a trial in the Supreme Court for a suit brought by Lundrigan against Buchan and Leigh for damages as a result of the severity of his punishment indicates that the surrogates and their court officers had been deeply disturbed by the behaviour of James' wife, Sarah Morgan. When two constables, Moors and Kelly, initially tried to take possession of the Lundrigan fishing room, it was Sarah who met them with her children. Realizing that the constables had come to take her home and gardens, the means of ensuring her family's subsistence, along with Lundrigan's boats and equipment, Morgan "desired Kelly to be gone, or she would blow his brains out, or words to that effect." Kelly left Sarah to search for James Lundrigan, "not thinking it fit to apply to the Woman for possession." Lundrigan refused to go to the surrogate court, then sitting at Port de Grave, and wished Kelly good luck if the constable felt it necessary to bring back marines to arrest him. Lundrigan was not bothered by the way his wife reacted to the constables, and was not about to interrupt his attempts to catch some caplin so that Sarah and their children might have something to eat (CO 194, Vol. 64, 1812: ff. 6-15). The court's remittance of 22 of Lundrigan's lashes only after he promised to make sure his family left their fishing room suggests that Morgan's forcible possession of the room, rather than Lundrigan's refusal to appear in court to answer for their actions, was what really bothered Buchan and Leigh.

Philip Butler's failure to subordinate his wife to his own, and through him, the court's authority was more clearly the object of Buchan's and Leigh's attention when they ordered Butler whipped. The court took no action against the Butlers when Mrs. Butler barred their door against constables William Mullowny and

Edward Fahey when the latter tried to seize the room in compliance with the outcome of Trimingham's suit. Only when the constables returned and spoke to Philip, heard from him that the room was his wife's property, and "that when his wife came from St. John's he would let them have it if she chose" was Butler taken for his sentencing and whipping. After Butler received 12 lashes, Buchan and Leigh stated that they would forget about the remaining 24 if he yielded the room. Butler agreed, but his wife would not quit the premises with him. The surrogates then "directed the door to be broken open when she opened it & was thereupon turned out & part of her household goods & furniture were carried out" (PANL, GN5/1/B/1, Box 2, Book 1819-20: 7 July 1820).

James and Philip actually appear to have played only a very small part in the actual contempt of court compared to their wives. A number of factors lay behind the wives' vigorous defence of their property. In Sarah's case, the prospect of losing her home and gardens, the pre-eminent domain of women in the reproduction of the fishing household, was probably the main reason for her violent reaction. The surrogate court had departed from previous rulings which allowed fishing families enough property to at least survive a winter. The increased difficulty encountered by merchants in obtaining payment during the depression probably accounted for this departure. For Sarah Morgan, as well as Butler's wife, it must have been a frightful prospect to see the court take the unusual step of seizing their families' fishing rooms (*Report*, 1821: 17).

The issue of the mortgage Trimingham's held on the plantation aggravated the Butler case. Philip Butler may not have even been aware that he had gotten credit by a mortgage rather than as an advance against his season's earnings in 1814. Later suits by merchants against various planters from Conception Bay indicate that those planters did not understand the significance of the agreements they entered into. Fisherman William Gill, for example, testified in a suit for debt by merchant Richard Anderson that he thought he had given Anderson a promissory note "to pay him so much per annum as p. balance of account—he never gave any mortgage of Property to Mr. Anderson. Witness cannot read or write" (PANL, GN5/1/B/1, Box 3, Book 1822-23). Butler, like Gill, may have been unaware that he had pledged his wife's property to pay a debt incurred in his name.

The surrogate court accepted the merchant argument that the credit had been issued for the Butler family's use, and did not care about technical arguments over which particular individual contracted the debt. The judges, without much legal training, appear to have been operating under the assumption that, by common law, all "chattel" property such as clothing, household goods, money, and furniture held by a woman transferred to her husband's ownership by the principle of feme-covert (although the court curiously allowed Mrs. Butler to take some of this property upon her eviction). There is little certainty about how Mrs. Butler acquired the plantation, although it is likely that she had inherited it from her father. It is certain, despite this, that common law did not allow men to assume rights to their wives' real estate. Under English law, Butler had no right to conduct any commercial transactions with his wife's plantation. He could use it in his fishery, but Butler could not mortgage it without Mrs. Butler's consent unless his wife overtly gave it to him, something which had not happened (Macfarlane, 1986: 272-75).

The absence of *de jure* real property rights in Newfoundland may have clouded the issue for Buchan and Leigh, but their judgements demonstrate little concern about property law, and every concern about the appropriate behaviour of the two male planters. The issue, in any event, was supposed to be contempt. Here, the Lundrigan and Butler wives were at least as guilty, or more so, than the husbands. Yet the court singled out the males for punishment. In part, this reflected the English judicial system's preference for believing that women's femininity rendered them incapable of responsibility for serious breaches of public order. English courts, for example, preferred to arrest men as ringleaders during food riots dominated by women, no matter how small their role in the events (Thomis and Grimmet, 1982: 54-6).

More important, however, was the usual practice of the surrogate court not to allow married women to take part in legal actions independent of their husbands. The surrogates, for example, would not hear Catherine Walsh's suit against James Mara in 1820 for damaging her garden unless "it be brought on by a new trial by [plaintiff's] Husband" (PANL, GN5/1/B/1, Box 2, 1820-21: 14 December 1820). Numerous character defamation suits from 1787 to 1825 were brought into the court by men on behalf of their wives. Not only did men feel that insults against their wives constituted a personal damage to them, but the court ruled that men were responsible for damage inflicted by their wives. Thus when Patrick Fitzgerald's wife threatened Maurice Colbert's wife with an axe, calling her a whore, murderer and robber, the court ruled that Mr. Fitzgerald had to compensate Mr. Colbert (PANL, GN5/1/B/1, Box 4, Book 1823-24: 27 November 1823). Whatever the reason, the surrogate court was not prepared to recognize women's public defiance of its authority by prosecuting them alongside their husbands.

The reform movement quickly appropriated the whippings as a convenient outrage they could hold up as an example of the need for constitutional change for Newfoundland. Reformers helped the two planters bring countersuits against Buchan and Leigh for damages in the Supreme Court. The suits became political show trials, embarrassing the surrogates for their use of excessive authority. Reverend Leigh even apologized and promised restitution in the Lundrigan case (O'Flaherty, 1987: 409-11). Neither surrogate ever added to the controversy by openly discussing their reasons for the whippings, although subsequent debates in the British House of Commons puzzled over just how unusually severe was the sentence of whipping (*Mercantile Journal*, 5 July 1821).

We cannot understand the severity of the sentences for Butler and Lundrigan if we accept reform accounts which overlook the importance of tensions surrounding the role of men and women in families in Newfoundland society in the early nineteenth century. Surrogates, to the contrary of reformers' misinformation, did not habitually and arbitrarily perpetuate outrage by ordering corporal punishment. While the jurisprudence of their summary decisions may have often been questionable, the whole legal system of Newfoundland was in flux, without order in a British territory without any colonial status.

The surrogates did know for certain how they were to keep order in a society convulsed by depression. Buchan had firsthand experience with the rioting and storebreaking of the winter of 1816-17, and knew full well that merchants and government hoped that settlement by families would displace the instability of a society dominated by single, unemployed males. Sarah Morgan and Mrs. Butler, by their open defiance, demonstrated that the gentry-bourgeois patriarchal ideal upon which such hope was based, had little to do with the material reality of Conception Bay fishing families. Women were an integral part of their household's production. While families retained a fundamentally patriarchal character, women were not passive subordinates to their male relatives' authority. Women like Morgan and Butler took special responsibility for the governing of their homes and gardens. They, rather than their husbands, made the decisions affecting these areas of their lives, including the decision to publicly resist court officials who tried to seize them.

Philip Butler's and James Lundrigan's failure to exert their own authority over that of their wives is the best explanation for the whippings of 1820. The surrogate judges expected the male planters to hold all of their families' property accountable for the orderly payment of debts. The two planters failed to make sure that their families, particularly their wives, would not disrupt this order. Butler and Lundrigan had not fulfilled their duties as patriarchs. The surrogates' comparatively mild reactions to other contempt involving men alone suggests that there is little other reason for their orders in the Butler and Lundrigan affairs except that they were trying to whip the two delinquent patriarchs into shape.

---

1   Newfoundland court minutes often did not record the name of a woman involved in legal action if a male relative was present. Thus Ryan's wife would only be referred to as his wife. In any case where the record allows, this essay gives the full name of women involved in court actions.

59

Our Life on Lear's Room

Greta Hussey

These excerpts describe the family's summer cabin on the Labrador coast and women's work in the stationer fishery.

Our Cabin

OUR SUMMER CABIN, which was near the bottom on the northwest side of the harbour, measured about thirteen by twenty-four feet with an extension on the west end for a bunk house. The exterior of the cabin was shingled. We used to keep it limed, to give it a more attractive appearance. One end of the cabin was partitioned off and divided to make two bedrooms, one for my parents and the other for us girls. The one door was in front, a little to the right of centre, facing southeast. There was a window on each side of the door. These were very small, each containing four panes of seven by nine glass. One of these windows was in my parents' bedroom. On the back of the house, which was also the back of the kitchen, were two larger windows. One held four panes of twelve inch by fourteen inch glass and the other six panes of ten inch by twelve inch glass. Our bedroom window was very small like the two in front. We had no curtains or window blinds to any of the windows.

A small section in the southeast corner of the twelve foot by thirteen foot kitchen was partitioned off about three by five feet to hold our beef and flour barrels and butter tub. There was just room for two barrels. Over the barrels, there was a shelf where we put our home-made bread and the boxes of sugar that we used. This place was called a cupboard. A wooden bench about six feet long was fastened to the wall and ran between the front door and the cupboard. Over the bench was a mirror and the bench was used for a washstand as well as for a resting place. On the other side of the cupboard, another bench was also fastened to the wall and ran across the kitchen. Two smaller benches, one seating two and the other seating one, were placed on either side of the table, which was home-made and fastened to the floor. Over the inside end of the table were three shelves which held our cups and saucers as well as our plates and sugar and molasses dishes. These shelves were called a dresser. Underneath the dresser was a home-made wooden box about four inches by ten inches and about four inches deep which held our forks and knives and the long-handled fork that was used to take up the duffs. Teaspoons were always kept in a small bottle. Our barrel-oven stove was directly in front of the door and picked up every draught, usually causing trouble. Most of the stoves in the harbour were either Comfort or Waterloo. Ours was named Fisherman. Two fish were crossed on the end doors. We never opened these doors because the stove was quite old and it was lashed up with wire to keep the ends from falling out. The last two or three years that I was in Batteau, we had a Victoria stove which was a vast improvement. The funnelling ran up through a hole in the roof. To the left of the stove were our bedroom door, the woodbox and Pop's Labrador box. Over the wood box was a three-cornered shelf which held small items like a bottle of Sloans Linament, maybe an aspirin or two and a bit of Dragon's Blood which was used as a medicine, although I cannot remember what it was used for. An upturned box, directly behind the entrance door, made a bench for our water buckets.

We had a ceiling in our kitchen although not every fisherman's cabin had one. It was unpainted and two loose boards were sawn off, about eighteen inches long, to make a hatch. It was up through this hatch that Pop kept the hard tobacco which he sold. It kept dry up there. Our floors were board that was unpainted except for a small patch under the stove which was painted with a bit that was left over from the boat. We scrubbed the floor twice a week, Wednesdays and Saturdays. We brought hooked rugs from home which gave the kitchen a more comfortable look although it was hard work trying to keep them clean. For the kitchen, we always had wallpaper which Mother usually picked up before we left home for about eighteen cents a roll. Our bedrooms were always papered with newspapers. The two doors to the bedrooms, as well as the window casings, were painted Emerald Green. The cupboard door was papered.

The latches on the bedroom doors were made of wood. A string of trawl line was attached to a wooden bar which slipped up and down into a cleat in the door casing. By pulling on the string, the latch lifted or fell, to open or close the door. The latch was always on the inside. All that was visible on the outside was a string. The latch on the front door was made the same only it operated with a wooden knob instead of a string.

Water Buckets and Slop Pails

There was no running water in any of the houses. Nobody in Batteau had a well. There was a big spring running out on the inside end of the harbour which was known as "the Bottom." This spring was used by the Labradorians. They would bring the water in galvanized two and a half gallon buckets and fill up two or three barrels that were kept on a platform outside their door. The schooners in the harbour also used this water supply as it was unlimited.

We got our drinking water from a brook which ran down between two hills about three hundred yards from our house. There was no cover, just a place dammed up with sods to hold the water in a hollow into which we could dip our water buckets. As children, we used to pluck a straw of Labrador grass and, using the grass for a drinking straw, we would lie on our bellies and drink the pure water of our brook. All Labrador water is brown in colour. Ours was no exception but we had the best tasting water in the harbour. Water from the Bottom had a sort of groundy taste. People who frequented the harbour year after year got to know the quality of water from our brook and, sometimes, men from these vessels would come in under the bank and remove the sods that we had banked up and they would drain it almost dry. We would then have to go and dam it up again. This didn't happen too often as getting water that way was a slow process compared with the speed of using the spring in the bottom. There were no dogs on our side of the harbour but, if they chanced to stray past our house and sometimes they did, I guess they drank out of the watering-hole too!

61

We had a small pool nearer the house that we could use for slop water and for scrubbing but it was unfit for drinking. A greenish scum was always settling around the edge of the pool. The men used the pool to wash off their boots and rubber clothes.

Bringing water was an arduous task because of the distance and we used to take two or more spells. Sometimes, it was made more difficult by fishermen who had spread their cod traps to dry and mend across our pathway. It was very easy to trip in the twine and fall headlong, buckets and all. We have rolled up many a cod trap so that we could step over it and thereby avoid an accident. I can still remember the stepping stones on the way to the brook. We would put the heel of one foot and the toe of the other on a stone and rock it, causing the black mud to squirt in all directions. This was sport for us and, if we did get messed up, Mother didn't mind too much.

We had no indoor plumbing and no outdoor toilet either. In fact, I don't know of anyone else in the harbour having one except for a family who had sawed an old boat in two across the midships, and the stem half was stuck on end with a door through what was once the deck. The fishing stage was always used. There was a hole through the floor of the stage under the splitting table. This hole, called a trunk hole, was used for throwing away the fish entrails and was often used for a toilet but, if the splitting table was not clean and you were not careful, it could be messy. An ideal place was where two crooked longers met. The gap between made an excellent place but you had to be a sure-shot to direct it straight. At night, if we had to, the girls used a twenty-two pound butter tub which we took down to the water next day. The tub later gave away to the enamel pail.

Saving the Scraps

We made use of everything. Nothing was wasted. We didn't have any food in tins. Everything was bought in bulk form by the barrel, the tierce, the keg, the bread bag or the buttertub. The empty beef barrels and tierce were used to bring home salted salmon and arctic char. The empty flour barrels were made to make hand barrows to lug the fish and also to pack our cooking gear in which we returned home. The burlap bags that held the hard bread were saved to hook mats on, at home, during the winter. The butter tubs had many uses. We used one of the twenty-two pound tubs for a scrubbing bucket, another for a slop pail and, if there was an extra, one to salt cod sounds in. I remember the two popular brands of butter were Sunshine and Primrose, the Sunshine having the edge over the other. It was margarine really but it was all butter to us. It was also sold in ten pound tubs and, sometimes, you could get a five pound tub of Primrose. These five pound tubs were very tidy and were used for our stove polish and brush.

We saved the fat from the salt beef if it was unfit for frying and brought it home to Newfoundland. Mother would boil soap out of this which we would use to scrub the hooked floor mats. The huskies devoured all the rest of the leftovers.

The men's old rubber boots were also salvaged. After using them in the boat and stage for two and a half months, the legs were getting scrubbed and had begun to leak in the upper parts. All the soft part of the leg was trimmed away following the contour of the boot, leaving a tongue on the instep and a high part on the back of the heel. This made it easy for the men to pull these boots on. They were used all the rest of the fall for going from the bunkhouse to the house or to the stage when it was needed for bathroom facilities. These cut-off rubbers were known as pissquicks and were very handy. They were really water-tight slippers.

The Cook's Duties

Almost every skipper took a girl or a woman along as cook for the summer. If at all possible, a family member was preferred for, then, you knew what type of person she was. Nobody wanted to be caught on the Labrador with a poor or dirty cook. Of course, as is always the case, many girls who were not family members had to be engaged. Sometimes, the cook was as young as thirteen years old. In this way, she could help support herself, and her family probably needed all the support that they could get. The skippers promised to take care of these girls and not let them work too hard. I was seventeen years old when I went cook for the first time with my father.

The cook's duties varied. We got up at 5:30 a.m. and washed a table full of dishes that the men had used to have their mug-up before going to their cod traps. We cooked breakfast for the men when they got back around 7:30 a.m. More dirty dishes to wash. Then, we got the dinner pot on and made the duffs. The men had a mug-up again at 10:30. Dinner was ready at 12:00, there was a mug-up again at 3:30 and supper around 5:00 or 5:30. Then, we made the bread for the next day's baking. There was a little break after that. We used this time to sew on a button or darn a sock. There was a mug-up when the men got out of the stage. That could be 11:00 p.m. The last thing we did was lay the table for the morning mug-up. Now, in between all that, we made the beds, kept the place clean, baked the bread, washed and mended clothes. In the fall of the year, when the nights were longer and the men were off the water, we had time to do a bit of crocheting or to go to the square dances. Many cooks were expected to and did work in the fishing stage cutting throats and heading the codfish. We were lucky. We had enough to attend to with the housework and with the few things that we sold so we didn't have to do any stage work unless we wanted to help at night.

Many of the cooks washed and mended clothes for the whole crew although she could refuse if she so wished. We always washed the men's clothes. This had to be done by scrubbing them on a wash-board in a wooden wash-tub that had been made out of a pork barrel. The stained, white articles were then put into a boiler of water into which some Gillets Lye had been added. The clothes were boiled on the kitchen stove, taken out, rinsed and hung to dry. The men's overalls were scrubbed outdoors with a stiff brush and trounced in the salt water and rinsed clean.

We always mended and darned for the men. One thing that the cook was asked to do that she hated was to darn the header's palm or the splitter's mitt. We had knit these for the crew before we left home. The splitter's mitt was just an ordinary mitt for the left hand. The header's palm had no tips on the fingers which had to be free to hook out the livers. Although they were washed as clean as possible, as you can imagine, these smelled to high heaven. You almost had to pinch your nose while doing this job. Another job that we didn't like was patching the oilskins. Most of these oilskins were made out of calico or flour sacks. We had to sew a calico patch over the hole, grease the patch with linseed oil, and hang the oilskins out to dry. When the patch had dried, it was greased again. This was done two or three times until the patch was watertight. This job went out when the men could afford to buy the Black Diamond rubber clothes. This was a happy day for the cook!

The cook also had to act as a nurse should the men come down with a cold, cut themselves or have a case of the water pups. Hers was no part-time job. For all these duties, a good cook got paid thirty-five or forty dollars and assistants got twenty dollars for the whole summer. Some family members never got paid at all.

Food

Our diet on the coast consisted largely of fish, mostly cod and salmon. We also had arctic char which we caught in an old piece of meshed twine tied fast to the rocks near the stagehead. It was fun to see them getting meshed while we watched from the door. As children, my sister and I would take the punt and go the short distance to take them out of the net. The fish were served boiled, baked, fried or stewed. Salmon were also smoked. We used artificial "patent" smoke although there were people who made their own smokehouses and used blackberry bushes for the fire. Once a week, we served fish and brewis. This was made by soaking hard bread and, then, boiling it along with either salt or fresh fish, whichever we had. It was served with pork fat and scruncheons.

Beans were served three times a week: boiled first and then fried in the fry pan; baked with salt pork and molasses or boiled with salt meat.

Tuesdays, Thursdays and Sundays were called "duff days." The regular meals for those days were round peas cooked in a bag and two flour puddings, called duffs, made from dry crusts of bread soaked in water or, if we were stuck, we soaked hard bread. This was mixed with enough molasses and flour to stick it together and, when a cupful of raisins or blackberries was added, it made one duff. There were plenty of crow berries, or blackberries as we called them, growing in Batteau. We always had some on hand. The other duff was always plain. They had to be quite large to feed five hungry men. The duffs were tied up in bags and boiled along with the peas pudding, with plenty of salt meat in a three or three and a half gallon cast iron boiler. That is what made up the meal: salt meat, peas pudding, the two flour duffs and sea birds, if we had them. The men killed plenty of sea birds. In the spring, if we were lucky, we would get a meal of salt water ducks which were a real delicacy. Later on in the summer, we got seagulls and, maybe, a loon or some bawks or hagdowns. The bawks tasted a bit musky so we did not eat many of them. Porpoise, seal and anything within reason was eaten. At least, we knew that it was fresh. Labradorians would never give a bird away without first cutting off the head. Once, when Mother and I were alone, Ben Dyson gave us a meal of seabirds but he removed the heads before doing so. They claimed that to give the head away gave away your luck.

If they were fishing in a harbour where there were no huskies, many stationers would take along their goats and hens to supply milk and eggs. We could never take any animals because nearly every one of the Labrador families in Batteau had a dog team. Where there were huskies, you just weren't able to make a place secure enough to keep the dogs away and, eventually, you lost whatever you had. One year, Uncle Nath Cole took along a pig to fatten but the pig fell over a cliff and met with its doom before the dogs could get their share.

Olsen Sunams, the Norwegian captain of the *Gerd*, was a special friend of ours and kept us supplied with milk all the time he was in Batteau. I've forgotten the brand name but I remember that there was a blue flag on the tins. This was the only milk that we would have after leaving home in June.

Eggs were practically non-existent on the coast. I can remember, one time, though, when my father was visiting Black Tickle and Salmon Bight, Mr. W.H. Greenland, the merchant who supplied Pop, gave him a few eggs for Mother. Pop just put them in the pocket of his overall jacket with the intention of taking care of them. He had to make a trip out to Mr. Greenland's schooner, the *Topaz*, for something or other. Alas for Pop, he forgot all about the eggs until he heard them scrunch against the hull of the ship. Needless to say, my mother never got to enjoy the eggs!

The only vegetables that we had were a meal or two of dandelions and the greens from our small kitchen garden. We grew turnip tops, rape and cabbage plants. Nothing else could be grown out by the coastline because of the short growing season but these greens were very tasty after so long on salt meat and duffs! We soaked fish entrails in a bucket for a few days and, then, poured the liquid on the plants. This was the only fertilizer that we used. If we used the fish as it was, the huskies were sure to get in the garden and ruin everything. Our garden fence was made of posts and twine netting to keep the dogs out, but on one occasion the dogs got in. My father took an end of rope and gave them a lashing. The dogs were afraid, after that, to venture in again.

Soup consisted of rice, salt meat and water. We had no onions but we always made flour dough-boys to give the soup body and to help thicken it. Pea soup was the same only we used peas instead of rice. If we ran out of rice and couldn't get any more, we made our own by dampening a small amount of flour and rolling it into tiny particles between our fingers. It served the purpose and was nicknamed "fresh water rice." Once a week, we also served dough-boys and molasses. That wasn't a very nourishing meal but we had no choice. We also cooked pancakes which we served with fried molasses or molasses candy (molasses, butter, water and thickening).

We baked bread every day except Thursday and Sunday. The kind of yeast that everyone used at that time was dry yeast made into cakes about two inches square. The brand name, I remember, was Royal. These cakes had to be soaked in a small bowl and flour added to make a sort of pudding, called barm. This was set in a warm place to rise. When it had risen, you used it to make your bread. There wasn't any fast-rising yeast then and, usually, the bread was mixed the first thing after supper, the night before baking. After mixing bread and before putting it to rise, we always made the sign of the cross on the dough in the bread pan.

One year, farther up the shore from Batteau, a man from Bay Roberts brought along the family goats to supply milk for the baby. One day, all the family, including the mother, were working outside. One of the older children was sent into the house for something and, after coming out, forgot to shut the door. Well, the goat soon found her way into the kitchen, overturned the barm crock and ate the rising yeast, alas for the poor goat! The next day, her belly began to swell. It just grew and grew and blew up with the yeast. It got so bad that they had to destroy the animal, the best milker they had.

Sometimes, the yeast we had could be bad. Although I was well used to bread baking, one summer I made bread that was sour, one batch after the other. Now, no cook could be excused from making sour bread. I felt quite badly about this but I couldn't seem to find the cause. I thought that it might be the yeast. The next year, I took no chances. I brought some hops and potatoes from home and made my own yeast by grating raw potato, pouring hot hops' water over it and sweetening it with sugar. This was placed in the sun or behind the stove to rise. I used this all summer until my potatoes were gone. I had no more bad bread. Although yeast cakes were only two cents each, I saved quite a few cents by using hops. You could rise bread that way for about a year with a ten-cent package of hops. I didn't even have to buy hops if I didn't want to because it grew wild in Hibbs Cove.

Baking bread was a tedious affair because the oven would hold just two loaves. These were baked in a fairly large worn-out skillet or sometimes, in the small iron pot. Bread baked in the pot always seemed to have a different flavour, much tastier than the rest. Most of our pots, as well as our kettles, were cast iron. Enamel or tinware were sometimes used but they were not as sturdy as the cast-ironware. They were likely to spring a hole at any time. Then, we had to patch the hole by rolling up a small piece of calico and pulling it through until the hole was completely watertight. We could cook for all the rest of the summer in the repaired pot as long as there was enough water in it to keep the calico wet.

For dessert, we made gingerbread and raisin or blackberry buns, without eggs. They were called Labrador buns. On Wednesdays and, usually for Sunday supper, we had prunes which were cheap and sold for nine cents a pound. Everyone could afford prunes. We bought them by the twenty-five pound box. The last few years we were in Labrador, we could afford a pack or two of jelly which was a real treat. In 1939, when I was at Five Islands, we made a batch of ice cream. The men chopped some ice from a berg for us. We crushed it, put it into the wash tub and threw in about a gallon of rock salt. Into a small dinner boiler, we mixed sugar, milk, vanilla, lemon flavouring and a dash of salt. We didn't have any eggs or ice cream powder. We put the boiler into the wash tub and kept spinning the boiler around in the slushy ice until the mixture froze to the right consistency. We had to be careful because the ice cream would burn on the bottom just as if we were boiling it on the stove. This took place on a Sunday afternoon when we had visitors from Salmon Bight. As can be imagined, everyone enjoyed it.

Autobiography as History: The Autobiographies of Three Labrador Women — Lydia Campbell, Margaret Baikie, and Elizabeth Goudie

Roberta Buchanan

This paper was originally published in Newfoundland History 1986: Proceedings of the First Newfoundland History Society Conference, *edited by Shannon Ryan. An excerpt from "Autobiography as Popular Culture: Autobiographies of Labrador Women," a paper presented to the Popular Culture Association, Atlanta, Georgia, 6 April, 1986 is included.*

THE AUTOBIOGRAPHIES of three generations of indigenous Labrador women — Lydia Campbell (1818-1907), Margaret Baikie (1844-1940) and Elizabeth Goudie (1902-1982) — are examples of what Elaine Jahner has called "life history as exemplary pattern," presenting heroic images of strong, self-reliant women (Jahner, 1985: 214). Writing autobiography was a female tradition in this family, and each woman was a preserver of family history as well as a transmitter of Labrador cultural values, folklore and legends.

Lydia Campbell's *Sketches of Labrador Life* was written at the request of an Anglican missionary to Labrador, Rev. Arthur C. Waghorne. It was published in 1894-1895 in 13 instalments in a local Newfoundland newspaper, the St. John's *Evening Herald*. Waghorne, who contributed some articles on Newfoundland folklore to the *Journal of American Folklore*, asked Lydia Campbell to "write me some account of Labrador life and ways," including, apparently, local superstitions. The *Sketches* were republished as a chapbook in 1980, almost a century later, by *Them Days*, a magazine "dedicated to documenting and preserving the old ways and early days of Labrador." An extract of about one-third was also published in *Canadian Women's Studies* in 1981, edited by Newfoundland librarian Anne Hart. She presented it as "a record of a woman, who, like thousands of others, was quietly helping to build a nation" (Hart, 1981: 4). Lydia Campbell's daughter, Margaret Baikie, was "inspired by her mother's account" to write her own *Labrador Memories: Reflections at Mulligan* in 1917; also published in chapbook form by *Them Days* (Baikie, 1983: Introduction). The manuscript was donated by Margaret's niece and daughter-in-law, Flora Baikie, "to help support *Them Days*, which she felt was carrying on the task of preserving the 'story' of Labrador started by her grandmother and aunt" (Baikie: Introduction).

The third autobiography, Elizabeth Goudie's *Woman of Labrador*, by Lydia Campbell's great-niece, was a best-seller, and Goudie herself became a local heroine. She received an honorary doctorate from Memorial University of Newfoundland in 1975 "in acknowledgement of her contribution to the cultural history of Newfoundland," a government building in Happy Valley was named after her in 1980, and a ballad, "Woman of Labrador" praised her as "Sharing everything you had / And living off the land" (Vine, 1982: 16).[1] None of the women had any formal education: Goudie "had about four years in school if it were all put together"

(Goudie, 1983: 7); Campbell's father taught her to read, but she explains that "There was no...school teacher them times hear in this country" (*Evening Herald* 10 December 1894; Hart, 1981: 8).

I have entitled this paper "Autobiography as History." In choosing this title I had in mind implicit assumptions about what "autobiography" and "history" are. I think of autobiography as an individual's subjective account of her own experience; and of history as an objective account of "historical events" — facts and dates which can be verified. Whereas history is about the "public" event — a war, a treaty, a law, the accession of a monarch — autobiography deals with the private sphere of family, emotions and individual experience. However the traditional idea of history as being concerned mainly with politics and the machinations of the ruling classes strikes our democratic age as being too narrow and elitist, and is particularly irritating to women who feel that they have been "written out" of history. To quote from an essay in *Liberating Women's History*,

> Historians' neglect of women has been a function of their ideas about historical significance. Their categories and periodization have been masculine by definition, for they have defined significance primarily by power, influence, and visible activity in the world of political and economic affairs. Traditionally, wars and politics have always been a part of "history" while those institutions which have affected individuals most immediately — social relationships, marriage, the family — have been outside the scope of historical inquiry.
>
> Because most women have lived without access to the means of social definition and have worked outside the spheres of reward and recognition, they have not had a history as historians have defined the term (Gordon et al., 1976: 75).

If the idea of "history" tends to break down when we insist that it should include some acknowledgement of women's lives, so does the idea of "autobiography" if we think of it as, in Stephen Spender's words, that "inside self" which "may have no significance in any objective history of [the autobiographer's] time" (Spender, 1955: 64). But according to Estelle Jelinek in *Women's Autobiography*, "neither women nor men are likely to explore or reveal painful and intimate memories in their autobiographies" (Jelinek, 1980: 10). William Matthews calls this "the human reluctance to stand individually naked" (quoted in Jelinek: 13). Autobiographers in general omit "the detailing of painful psychological experiences" (Jelinek, 1980: 13), thus making them unreliable sources for even their own history. Lydia Campbell, for example, does not write about her forced marriage to "a wild, rough young man," Bill Blake, whom she did not love, after he had succeeded in making her father drunk — presumably because she found it humiliating and also wished to shield her two children from this marriage. We only know about it because she confided "the history of her first marriage" to a Methodist missionary, the Rev. Arminius Young (Young, 1916: 16-18).

Even if we accept the division of human experience into "public" and "private" worlds, and think of history as being concerned with objective verifiable events, can we get some sense of the history of Labrador from reading these three autobiographies of trappers' wives—Lydia Campbell, Margaret Baikie, and Elizabeth Goudie? Their historical chronology ranges from the late eighteenth century and the Napoleonic wars between France and England, to Expo 67. They give some sense of the operations of the Hudson's Bay Company and of the Grenfell Mission with its establishment of schools, hospitals and local industries. They chronicle the introduction of new technology in the twentieth century: airplanes and trucks to replace the dog-team, and the radio, which made such a difference in the isolated lives of trappers.

Through the family history told in the three autobiographies we get some sense of why European settlers came to Labrador. Lydia Campbell records her surprise when her father told her that there was "a better country" than Labrador:

> When I remember first to see things to understand I thought that there was no place as good as this in the world...; but our good father used to take me on his knee and tell me his home was a better country where he came from (6 December 1894).

Why had her father left this "better country" — the "Mother Country" or "Home" as it used to be called by expatriate colonials? As her father explained it, his emigration was due to a combination of a private and public event: the break-up of his family on the death of his father; and the wars between France and England in the early 1800s.

> It was hard to live there after his good old father died, and his mother could not keep him so he stayed with a good old minister...until he died and then he had to come out to this country and to try his fortune in this place, for the wars were raging between England and France and all over the world, and the pressgang was pressing the young men, so he and a lot more English people came out up the shore for wood cutters and sealing fishing and cod fisherys was the highest in those days (Campbell, 6 December 1894).

Thus both private tragedies and public cataclysms impel the individual into a new existence, a new environment.

Lydia Campbell's knowledge of Labrador history was further extended by her father's stories about the first two Englishmen to settle in Hamilton Inlet, William Phippard and John Knocks (Nooks or Newhook):

> They was landed hear by some people looking for a place I think and gave these two people provisions and promised to come after them next year, but they never came back for 3 years; so my Father told us for he saw them when he came from England a prentice boy few years after. Well, they went to a place to live in which there was a river...and that river was called English river to this day (18 December 1894, quoted in Zimmerly, 1975: 55).

There are references to William Phippard in Cartwright's diary of 1778-1779 (Zimmerly, 1975: 53, Gosling, 1910: 240). According to Lydia Campbell, Phippard and Knocks made a double marriage to an Inuit widow and her daughter, but Knocks was later murdered by his wife's Inuit relatives. Campbell had heard the story from the woman herself: "I used to listen to her talking about her young days"

(24 December 1894). At 11 years of age, after her mother died, Lydia was taken by her father to stay with the old woman, now blind and unable to walk, and married to another Englishman, John Whittle.

Lydia's account of this second marriage gives us an insight into the more tragic aspects of women's life in Labrador — the kind of detail which is omitted from most history books, which concentrate on the exploits of the male settlers:

> She told me her husband was hard to her, and he used to leave her be lone [alone]...he used to leave her and her little boy without any provisions, but a little biscuits or little flower when that was gone they had nothing to eat but dog's feed (6 February 1895).

Margaret Baikie, Lydia Campbell's daughter, added some more details in her autobiography: this is derived from oral history, what one woman told another. The details are prefaced by the phrase "Mother told us...":

> Her husband used to beat her with whatever he could get hold of. She told Mother that one day he got a bag of shot and there was a small hole in it, every time he would hit her the shot would fly all over the house (Baikie, 1983: 18-19).

No wonder poor Sarah Whittle solaced herself from time to time with rum, and would "have a boose, [as] they called it" (Campbell, 24 December 1894).

Lydia Campbell has a vivid sense of Labrador history, derived from oral tradition, not printed sources; and from her own experience looking back, from the age of 75, over three-quarters of a century. She notes with regret the decline in the indigenous Inuit and Indian population in a passage which has an elegiac sadness:

> the times to[o] changed now from the times that I have been writing about. The first time that my dear old father came from England...what few whites was hear they was scattered about hear and there. It was lovely he said often about here, no one to see for miles but Esquimaux and mountainnears and they was plentyful, he said that dozzens of canoes of mountainnears would come down out of the big bay as it was called then, what is now called Hamelits Inlet or the Large Lake. They used to come skimming along like a flock of ducks, going out side egg hunting on the island. Well I know it is a pretty sight to see a lot of birch canoes shining red in the sunshine. I have seen them paddling along I have, men steering the women paddling, the children singing or chatting, where are they now, hardly ever see a family now except in winter then we will now and then get a visit from a family or two...Oh our Indians have been killed with drink, and the dirty tobacco and strong tea, how few they are now (Campbell, 6 February 1895).

Zimmerly points out, in his book *Cain's Land Revisited: Culture Change in Central Labrador*, 1775-1972, that this decline was caused by the white settlers and their descendants. Diseases were spread by whites to the indigenous peoples; and white settlers took over the traditional hunting grounds of the Indians, driving them into the interior, as the Indians had driven the Inuit to the coast. The three autobiographies convey the tensions between the three racial groups — European or partly European; Montagnais/Naskapi [Innu] or "Mountainnears"; and Inuit. When the whites first arrived, "The Indians, mountainers, and Esquimaux was at war with each other, but they was kind to the whites" (Campbell, 18 December 1894). Baikie also refers to these wars, in which "the old [Inuit] women heaved rocks sometimes" (Baikie, 1983: 49). Campbell, whose mother was Inuit, echoes the Inuit's fear of the Indians:

> The reason that they [the Inuit] pitched their tents on the ice, was that they was afraid of the mountens [Mountaineers] might come out of the woods and kill them. So we was told when we was young (7 December 1894).

Campbell herself seems to have had friendly relations with the Indians: she and her sister Hannah were invited up Mount "Mookomee, the Drummer's Hill" (so called after the Indian drumming) to stay overnight in a "tent mitchwam" [wigwam] and partake in a feast of deer meat, cooked

> on scivers made of wood — good looking meat dreping with grece. They evokt a nice piece for us..., to let us see how kind they was to us white people as they called us. [Lydia and her sister were mixed white/Inuit] (12 December 1894).

By her daughter Margaret's time, tensions had mounted between the Indians and whites because of the latters' encroachment on traditional hunting grounds. For Margaret Baikie,

> The greatest thing I dreaded was the Naskaupi Indians for they were not to be trusted. They were a wilder set (Baikie, 1983: 45).

Her Inuit maid Peggie cried when she saw the Indians coming, and "asked if they were going to kill us" (Baikie: 45). Margaret Baikie objected to the impertinent way they demanded flour and tobacco: "they begged for everything" (Baikie: 45). In 1926, when Elizabeth Goudie was visited by a family of starving Indians, she was not physically afraid of them — in fact the man was almost too weak to help her carry water — rather she feared they might infect her children with tuberculosis and took the precaution of boiling her dishes (Goudie, 1983: 57-58). The Indians resented the European trappers encroaching on their territory when they expanded their operations to the Grand Falls (now Churchill Falls) district.

> They were so cross about us stealing their trapping... Uncle Bert said the Indians were really nasty then. They didn't like white men coming onto their land. They counted their land from Grand Falls to Seven Islands [in Quebec] and they wanted no white men on it (Goudie, 1983: 154, 155).

Anthropologists David Zimmerly and Gerald Sider see the importance of Elizabeth Goudie's work in its reflection of social changes from a subsistence economy to wage labour; and a change in the class structure, with outsiders — such as the Grenfell doctors and nurses or the Hudson's Bay Company officers — dominating the top of the social hierarchy. Sider, in *Culture and Class in Anthropology and History: a Newfoundland Illustration*, quotes a passage from Goudie in which she tells how she took her sick baby, 17 days old, to the Grenfell Mission hospital, where the doctor arbitrarily named him Esau. Sider comments:

> The precision of the name the doctor gave to her son... — Esau the elder, the

hairy, the hunter, and the disinherited... —expresses with almost overwhelming power the subtle and manifold cruelties of domination (1986: 161).

Goudie quietly renamed the boy Horace, although Esau was the name recorded in the "Hospital Book" at North West River.

Sider, however, does not comment on another detail in the same passage: Goudie's wedding dress, which she bought from Mrs. Paddon, the doctor's wife, cost $5.00 at a time when her wages as a nurse's aide at the mission hospital were only $4.00 a month, working a fourteen-hour day from 5 a.m. to 7 p.m. (Goudie, 1983: 16). If Dr. Paddon's arbitrary naming of Elizabeth Goudie's baby expresses "the subtle and manifold cruelties of domination," was not a charge of $5.00 by Mrs. Paddon for a dress which was, in all probability, second-hand, a cast off of her own, or a charitable donation to the mission, exorbitant? Goudie leaves the reader to draw her own conclusions: "When I got married I did not have much money of my own. I had saved enough to buy myself a washboard" (Goudie, 1983: 20; Sider, 1986: 159).

Perhaps it takes a female sensibility to be aware of the symbolic value of clothes. Margaret Baikie too describes her wedding dress, and compares her own with those of her mother and Inuit grandmother:

> Mother wore a cotton gown and a white lace cap when she was married. When I was married I wore a silk dress and white collar and white cuffs. So you will see the difference in our dresses (Baikie, 1983: 51).

Her Inuit grandmother refused to wear the European dress that her English husband provided for her wedding:

> My grandfather was going to be married so he bought my grandmother a cotton dress. She was ashamed to put it on so she wore a white cloth dickie and white and black pants and sealskin boots. She never wore a dress (Baikie 51).

Perhaps this was an act of rebellion on the part of Lydia Campbell's mother, an effort to resist domination or assimilation into the culture of her white husband. We know from oral tradition in the family that he used to beat her when she ate raw meat in the Inuit fashion. Flora Baikie, daughter of Thomas Blake, Lydia Campbell's son by her first marriage, recalls that:

> Gran used to tell us that before her father would go off anywhere he'd tell them not to let their mother eat any raw meat. One time they killed a caribou and Grandfather Brooks went off somewhere. Grans said she and her mother skinned the deer and cut it up. Every now and again, she said, her mother would eat a piece of the fat. Gran said when her father come home she told him. He took a piece of rope and give his wife a hammering. He hurt her, gran said, cause she cried. I says it wouldn't be only me that got the cracks if t'was me he hammered. Raw caribou fat is real good (Baikie, 1976: 12, cited in Buchanan, 1991: 294).

Women's history is alleged to be "timeless":

> Women's lives ... are characterized by an apparent timelessness: their lives have

focused on bearing and raising children and have been isolated within the confines of the family (Gordon et al., 1976: 76).

However, one does not get a sense of "timelessness" from these autobiographies. Take one small domestic detail: soap. When Elizabeth Goudie started doing housework, making soap took ten days, and was done at home:

> Mother had me stand at the side of the stove for an hour each day pouring the lye into the fat a cup at a time until the fat was cooked. It took about seven days. When the soap was cooked she took about a half cup of coarse salt and about a pint of water to separate the soap from the lye. Then it was put away to cool for three days and then cut out in blocks.
>
> After all this work we would get about three pounds of soap (Goudie, 1983: 10-11).

By the time Elizabeth Goudie got married, "we could buy Gillet's lye so I used to make my soap in fifteen minutes. I had it a lot easier" (Ibid: 11). By 1973, "Dutch Cleanser" was available. Goudie was certainly aware of changes in what one might call domestic technology.

In conclusion, when we look at history from a woman's point of view, what do we see? Elizabeth Goudie seems boldly matrilineal when she traces her family back through the female line. Her first sentence is about her great great grandmother, Lydia Campbell's mother:

> In approximately the year 1806, our great-great grandmother, who was an Eskimo orphan, ran away from down Rigolet Eskimos (Goudie, 1983: 3).

Of the two daughters of this orphan, Goudie comments: "Lydia, was the mother of the Campbells" and "Hannah, was the mother of the Michelins" (Ibid: 3). Yet she also tells of "grandfather Blake," adding on page 5, "This little note was handed down from our forefathers."

I think we see a double tradition, both male and female, in these three autobiographies, for the stories they tell are from both male and female informants. Both foremothers and forefathers are important, as opposed to the patriarchal view of history in which foremothers are regarded as irrelevant and marginal, and often consigned to oblivion. This mingling of male and female traditions is emphasized in the narrative styles of the autobiographies: "I remember Mother telling us about when she was a girl, long ago..." (Baikie, 1983: 8): "Mother told us of her father, when he first went trapping" (Ibid: 9); "Father said we had a very good time..." (Ibid: 14); "now I must tell you of my grandmother..." (Ibid: 49); "First I would like to make a note of my father and mother's life as they told it to me" (Goudie, 1983: 4); "Tom's Uncle John told us..." (Baikie, 1983: 30); "Little cousin Emily said..." (Ibid: 31).

As both male and female traditions and stories are presented, so too are both the public and private worlds: an "historical event" such as the Napoleonic wars which forced young men to seek new lands, to flee from the press-gangs, appears along with the private world of the family with its joys and sorrows — the fear of childbirth, especially alone and far from medical help; sickness, accidents, bereavements, death; the celebration of marriages and New Years; the daily round of work — getting food and cooking it; laundry and housework; baking a special pie for the husband returning from the traplines.

1   Press release, Public Works and Services [Government of Newfoundland and Labrador], 10 April, 1980; Centre for Newfoundland Studies, Memorial University, Name File: Elizabeth Goudie.

Adjusting the Focus

AT THIS POINT, THIS COLLECTION shifts its focus from the fishery before World War II to urban women's history and the interruptions and transformations in women's lives associated with World War II and postwar development strategies. Feminist scholarship on the first half of the 20th century has expanded significantly in the past few years. This section of the book includes some of the newest and best examples of not only academic research, but also creative writing concerned with this period. Feminist historians have recently provided us with the first accounts of the lives of working class, wage-earning women in St. John's. This research focuses on the late 19th and early 20th centuries. Nancy Forestell's paper, in this book, explores the period between the wars. Readers should note, however, that a joint paper written with Jesse Chisolm explores an earlier period (Forestell and Chisolm, 1988). Forestell and Chisolm argue that "[h]istorians familiar with the history of women's employment in Canada will note the emergence of similar themes: the employment of female workers as cheap factory labour; the tensions between poorly paid female help and skilled male workers; the expanding employment opportunities for women during wartime; and the patterns of women's resistance, strike activity, and mobility which belied contemporary images of women as passive and timid" (1988: 142). The authors provide ample evidence that women recruited to work in the manufacturing sector at the turn of the century were not always content with their working conditions.

Like much of Newfoundland and Labrador life, fun "times" as well as the more serious work of sharing and caring during "hard" times depended on women's voluntary labour. Linda Cullum's paper on the Jubilee Guilds in the 1930s concentrates on a particular variant of women's voluntary work: middle-class and upper-class women's reform organizations. She explores the class-based vision of appropriate women's roles found in the Jubilee Guilds and contrasts it with that found in the Co-operative Women's Guilds which challenged the Jubilee Guilds' monopoly on educational work with rural women.

Not all of the "help" provided the poor and the needy in the early twentieth century came from volunteer agencies. Newfoundland's first pension plan was an example of what Mariana Valverde (forthcoming) has recently described as a web of "mixed public-private forms of service provision." This web developed in Canadian society, as in Newfoundland, in the 19th century and has persisted to the present. Although it was funded by the state, access to the old age pension was determined by local leaders. Snell's (1993) detailed account of Newfoundland's Old Age Pension Program from 1911-1949 highlights the gender discrimination at its heart.

Memoir and oral history provide the basis for an exploration of the impacts of World War II on women's lives. The experiences of war brides and of women working on the American bases are highlighted in the accounts by Brown and Benoit.

Times Were Hard: The Pattern of Women's Paid Labour in St. John's Between the Two World Wars

Nancy M. Forestell

This paper, previously published in Labour/Le Travail, *reminds us that a woman's decision to pursue paid work "was most often linked inextricably with the well-being of her family."*

"**I** LEFT WORK WHEN I MARRIED WILLIAM. By that time I was twenty, tired of working at the factory, and glad to be making a home for us."[1] With these words, Mary described the transition in her life from "working girl" to married woman. One stage in her life ended and another began. Born on 31 October 1900, this daughter of a Southside St. John's fisherman and his wife became a wage earner at the age of fifteen. Mary went to work at the city's Newfoundland Knitting Company factory on Alexander Street, sewing knitted garments for $4.00 a week. She gave most of her earnings to her widowed father to help feed and clothe the family. Within two years, she left the knitting mill for the White Clothing Company factory on Duckworth Street where she worked in the pants department, sewing zippers into trousers for a wage of $6.50 a week. After her marriage in 1920 to William, a presser at the White Clothing Company, Mary never set foot in a factory again. She did, however, earn money throughout her early married life by sewing and cleaning, as well as by wallpapering rooms for relatives, friends, and neighbours to supplement her husband's meagre income. She accomplished these tasks while raising her eight children. Mary's eldest daughter, Dorothy, started work at the Browning-Harvey confectionery factory in 1934 at age twelve. Although Mary did not want her daughter labouring long hours in a factory at such a young age, she realized that Dorothy's earnings were essential to the family. On more than one occasion, her daughter's wage of $3.50 a week had to sustain the household because William could find only casual employment, and domestic responsibilities prevented Mary from carrying out some type of paid labour.[2]

Mary's life experience was similar to that of many other women in St. John's during the 1920s and 1930s. Full-time, paid employment outside the home was just a temporary interlude for most between leaving school and getting married. It was part of one stage in their life cycles. While some wage-earning women came from middle-class backgrounds and pursued employment in such occupations as teaching, nursing, or office work, the majority came from working-class backgrounds. For these women, the small wages they earned as domestics, factory operatives, tailoresses or sales clerks, were often an important contribution to the financial support of their families. Once wage-earning women decided to get married, it was fully understood that they would leave their place of employment. Women seldom considered that they would ever have to return to wage labour after marriage, for they expected that their husbands would assume the role of breadwinner and earn a "family wage" while they took on the role of homemaker.[3] Such notions often proved to be the ideal rather than the reality. For many women, their husbands' earnings were insufficient to support their families, and as a result, they had to find some means to earn additional money in order to maintain their households. This paid work usually was performed at home and combined with domestic duties as well as childcare. In certain circumstances such as unemployment, illness, or death of the primary male wage-earner, a small number of women did return to the work force as full-time wage earners. Whether as a daughter or a wife, the decision of an individual woman to seek wage labour was most often linked inextricably with the well-being of her family.

This paper examines the pattern of women's paid labour in St. John's during the 1920s and 1930s. Particular emphasis is placed on changes in women's life cycles as they affected their participation in the city's work force. The argument is made that a woman's age, marital status, and class background were the most important factors in determining whether she worked outside the home or engaged in some form of paid labour within the household. A number of other related factors (including number of children, stage of the family cycle, as well as age and religion) are considered, in terms of their impact on women's labour-force participation and the type of work they performed.

The 1920s and 1930s were years of tremendous political upheaval and unceasing economic depression in the Dominion of Newfoundland (Alexander, 1976; Neary, 1988; Overton, 1988). In St. John's, the unemployment rate was high, and many of those with jobs received low wages and worked only a portion of the year (Forestell, 1987). Despite poor economic conditions, women not only remained in the labour force, but their participation actually increased from 21.4 percent in 1921 to 26 percent in 1935.[4] The number of women in wage employment rose 36.5 percent from 2,822 to 3,866 (see Table 1).[5] An increase in work-force participation by women occurred in most North American urban centres during the 1930s because so many men, especially those of the working class, received small wages, or could not find steady work.[6] This made it imperative that their daughters and wives engage in some type of paid labour. In fact, women sometimes found it easier to secure waged employment than the men in their families because of the greater availability of jobs that were stereotyped as women's work.[7] Men would not even

TABLE 1				
Occupation Groups - Female Labour Force 1921 and 1935				
Occupation Groups	1921		1935	
	N	Percent	N	Percent
Proprietor	78	2.8	139	3.6
Professional	285	10.1	453	11.7
Office Work	433	5.3	592	5.3
Retail Work	445	15.8	498	12.9
Service	1100	39.0	1607	41.6
Semi-skilled	181	6.4	104	2.7
Unskilled	300	10.6	473	12.2
	2822	100.0	3866	100.0

have considered taking such positions. Women were relegated primarily to jobs as saleswomen, typists, garment workers, and domestic servants. This last occupation accounted for more than a third of the female labour force in 1921 and again in 1935.[8] The majority of women continued to be blue-collar workers as opposed to white-collar workers.

Unlike men, women's labour-force participation in the inter-war period was directly related to their age, and more importantly, to their marital status. In general, female workers can be characterized as being young and single. The majority of working women in St. John's at this time were between the ages of 15 and 24 (see Table 2). More than two-thirds of the female wage-earners fell within this age group in 1921, and over 56 percent in 1935. As these figures indicate, however, a noticeable reduction did occur in the proportion of working women under 25, particularly those between 15 and 19; the latter age group accounted for 32.1 percent of working women sampled in 1921, but only 16.9 percent in 1935. This shift towards slightly older workers resulted from single women remaining longer in the labour force because of the bleak economic conditions, and from the rising participation of married women who tended to be older than their single counterparts. Another reason for this shift can be attributed to changes in the city's female population as a whole. Between 1921 and 1935, a reduction occurred in the number of females in the age group 15 to 19, while a sizeable increase happened in the age group 20 to 24.[9] This trend should not be over-emphasized, because women between 15 and 24 continued to represent a substantial proportion of the city's wage-earning women. It should be mentioned that wage-earning women in St. John's tended to be younger than those elsewhere.[10] The youthfulness of the St. John's female labour force was due to the disproportionate number of young women living in the city, as well as the absence of child labour and compulsory education laws in Newfoundland.[11] Women's marital status had an even greater influence on whether they worked or not. Most women worked for a relatively brief period until they married. Single women constituted 93 percent of the female labour force in 1921, and 91.2 percent in 1935 (see Table 2). Perhaps the best evidence of

TABLE 2
Age and Marital Status of Working Women 1921 and 1935

	Single				Married				Separated				Widowed			
	1921		1935		1921		1935		1921		1935		1921		1935	
Age Groups	N	%	N	%	N	%	N	%	N	%	N	%	N	%	N	%
Up to 14	16	1.7	11	.9	—	—	—	—	—	—	—	—	—	—	—	—
15-19	293	32.1	201	16.6	—	—	—	—	—	—	—	—	—	—	—	—
20-24	321	35.2	474	39.3	—	—	2	.2	—	—	1	.1	2	.2	—	—
25-29	131	14.3	207	17.1	—	—	4	.3	1	.1	1	.1	3	.3	3	.2
30-34	34	3.7	89	7.4	1	.1	4	.3	—	—	2	.2	1	.1	3	.2
35-39	21	2.3	58	4.8	2	.2	5	.4	2	.2	1	.1	5	.5	9	.7
40-44	8	.9	23	1.9	2	.2	1	.1	—	—	2	.2	8	.9	12	1.0
45-49	9	1.0	11	.9	3	.3	7	.6	—	—	1	.1	5	.5	11	.9
50-54	9	1.0	11	.9	—	—	4	.3	—	—	1	.1	12	1.3	9	.9
55-59	2	.2	9	.7	2	.2	1	.1	1	.1	2	.2	1	.1	5	.4
60-64	—	—	4	.3	3	.3	3	.2	—	—	—	—	4	.4	4	.3
65 and up	5	.5	5	.4	—	—	—	—	—	—	—	—	6	.7	9	.7
	849	93.0	1103	91.2	13	1.4	31	2.6	4	.4	11	.9	47	5.1	65	5.4

78

TABLE 3
Relationship of Single Working Women to the Heads of Their Households, 1921 and 1935.

Relationship	1921		1935	
	N	Percent	N	Percent
Head	16	1.9	33	3.0
Daughter	457	53.8	577	52.3
Servant	291	34.3	381	34.5
Boarder	42	4.9	41	3.7
Female Relative	43	5.0	71	6.6
	849	100.0	1103	100.0

the connection between age and marital status as factors affecting women's entry into the work force can be found by cross-tabulating them. In 1921, 85.3 percent of wage-earning women were unmarried and between the ages of 15 and 34; in 1935, the comparable figure was 80.3 percent (see Table 2).

The majority of single women who went out to work lived with their parents: 53.8 percent in 1921 and 52.3 percent in 1935 (see Table 3).[12] The available evidence suggests that only a small number of them came from middle-class backgrounds.[13] Only a few were the children of merchants, lawyers, doctors, or even of salesmen. Proprietors, professionals, commercial and state employees were the heads of only 21.2 percent of the households with at least one working daughter in 1921. During the next decade and a half their numbers increased, but in 1935 they still comprised only 24.7 percent (see Table 4). Working daughters were more frequently the children of carpenters, longshoremen, labourers, and of the unemployed. Skilled, semi-skilled, unskilled, and service workers were the heads of 55.2 percent of the households with a wage-earning daughter in 1921, and 40.6 percent in 1935. This sharp decrease was due primarily to the substantial increase in the percentage of unemployed heads of households from 23.4 percent to 34.7 percent in 1935.

TABLE 4
Occupation Groups of Heads of Households With Working Daughters Living at Home, 1921 and 1935

Occupation Groups	1921		1935	
	N	Percent	N	Percent
Proprietor	41	9.0	78	13.5
Professional	9	1.7	15	2.6
Commercial	33	7.2	38	6.5
State Employee	15	3.3	12	2.1
Service	14	3.1	12	2.1
Skilled	104	22.7	125	21.7
Semi-skilled	29	6.3	37	6.4
Unskilled	109	23.1	60	10.4
Unemployed	69	15.1	146	25.3
Unemployed, Age 65 and over	38	8.3	54	9.4
	458	100.0	577	100.0

The small number of middle-class women who worked did not have the same financial responsibilities as did those of the working class. Unlike most working-class women, their earnings rarely had to be handed over to parents as a necessary contribution to the household. They were freer to spend their earnings on clothing and entertainment. When middle-class women were laid off, few of them had to worry that members of their families thus might be denied food and clothing. One woman whose father was a planter[14] on the Southside viewed her job as a waitress in a small restaurant as a temporary position which she could leave at any time. "Problems at work never bothered me much because I knew I could leave whenever I wanted to go home."[15] In sharp contrast, the far greater number of working-class women who worked did so because their wages were essential to the economic well-being of their families. Their wages had to handed over directly to their parents, and were often used to subsidize the earnings of their fathers. The wages of most working-class males did not reach levels high enough to support their families comfortably. Seasonality only made the plight of working-class families more difficult. Having a daughter out working and bringing home an income proved to be a great benefit to many. In 1921, President James Caul of the Longshoremen's Protective Union (LSPU) explained the important contribution made by the children of men who worked on the docks:

> The question of cost cannot be taken into consideration in dealing with the question of wages. Between 95 and 98 percent of the members of the union do not earn enough under the present scale to keep body and soul together. Were it not for the fact that the daughters and sons supplement the earnings of the household a very large majority of the members would be compelled to seek able-bodied relief.[16]

A member of the Newfoundland House of Assembly stated in a 1925 session that, "Families who formerly were in straitened circumstances because they had no breadwinner but a man, are now in comfort through the industry of young women and girls"(*Proceedings*, 1926: 300). One informant, Jenny, was only fourteen years old when she secured her first job in 1926. Her wages were vital to the family because her father did not earn enough as a longshoreman to pay the rent and buy sufficient food for his family. As Jenny explained, "I went to help out our family. I was the oldest girl and my older brother couldn't get work. Times were hard so I went out to work and it seemed as if that was all I did."[17] Her earnings alone had to feed the family when her father went out on strike in autumn 1932.

The wages of daughters were generally used to supplement the earnings of their fathers. Nevertheless, there were numerous instances in which the support of the family was fully a daughter's responsibility, or was shared with another sibling. In most instances their fathers were unemployed, or their mothers were widows. Unemployed fathers became more prevalent between 1921 and 1935. In 1921, only a small proportion of households (3.7 percent) with a working daughter present included a father without waged employment. By 1935, this type of household had increased to 13 percent.[18] A contemporary observer noted that in situations where "the young girl finds employment and her father is at home without a job, she is the first to bring home her earnings" (*Proceedings*, 1930: 235). A much larger proportion of households in 1921 (23.2 percent) were without the primary male breadwinner altogether, and in 1935 this figure had reached 30.8 percent. In these particular cases, widows held the position as head of the household. The overwhelming majority of these widows (84.9 percent in 1921 and 83.3 percent in 1935) did not have any visible source of employment. Under such circumstances, their working daughters and their working sons must have been important sources of family income.[19]

Middle-class women living at home were more likely to be employed as teachers, nurses, stenographers, and saleswomen. [See Table 5.] A retired librarian trained in the early 1930s indicated that there were very few occupations deemed suitable for middle-class women. "You see, by choosing to be a librarian, I was eliminating only teaching, nursing, and office work [as possible job options]. At that time there weren't too many openings, too many avenues. They were the basic options."[20] Working-class women on the other hand, were more likely to be employed as tailoresses, waitresses, and factory operatives, as well as saleswomen.[21] This latter occupation was one of the few which attracted both working class and middle-class women in large numbers. A woman's class background could determine to some degree the work she ended up performing in the labour force. Training for a profession dictated that a young woman had a certain level of education, time, and money. It was difficult for most working-class women to meet all three of these requirements. Only a few were able to surmount these barriers. In order to enter a program in maternity nursing at the city's Grace Hospital in 1924, a young woman had to have passed Intermediate Grade, and pay a fee of $50.00 (*Evening Telegram*, 10 June 1924). Training took twenty months, at the end of which candidates had to write an exam. Women wanting to train at the Grace Hospital or at the General Hospital faced stiff competition because the number of positions were limited. The General admitted only ten to twelve nursing students each year, and the Grace, only fifteen to twenty students annually (*Observer's Weekly*, 4 May, 1937; Nevitt, 1978: 148-50). A substantial number of St. John's women travelled to the United States or Canada to train as nurses. This type of venture most often required the financial assistance of young women's parents to pay for their tuition and their passage to such places as New York or Montreal. One alumna of a private school for girls in St. John's stated in 1928 that, "Many of the pupils leaving Spencer College in recent years have aspired to one of the noblest and highest professions of womanhood — that of a nurse." (*Evening Telegram*, 18 December 1928). She went on to mention some of the places where these women chose to train: Toronto, Halifax, Boston, Englewood, New Jersey, and Providence, Rhode Island.[22]

To work as a stenographer or a bookkeeper, a woman needed specialized skills which she could acquire only by taking commercial courses. Although all of the high schools in the city offered commercial programs that were separate from their regular academic curriculums, they were expensive. At the Academy of Our Lady of Mercy, the tuition fee for one term was $10.00 in 1923 (PANL, Eric Ellis Papers, PN55, Box 1). (The entire commercial program took three terms). This amount only included general courses in "stenography, typewriting, and office routine." There was an extra charge for courses which taught students how to use a dictaphone or a calculating machine. That same year full-time enrolment at the new United Business College cost students $12.00 a term (*Evening Telegram*, 19 September 1923). Commercial courses remained expensive through the 1930s (*Evening Telegram*, 21 April 1929; 9 November 1935).

Why did the majority of single working women reside with their parents? To begin with, their incomes generally were so low that most could not even consider renting a place of their own or boarding somewhere else. For a substantial number of wage-earning women, their parents needed them living at home contributing to the household economy. While there was the possibility that a woman could reside elsewhere and send money to her parents, the sum involved would have been smaller than if she had lived at home. Most parents did not like daughters to live someplace else, where they would be away from their supervision and protection. Concern for the protection of young women, particularly those who worked, remained central. Many people thought that women who worked had a much greater exposure to the evil elements in society, particularly to the dangers of sexual immorality, than women who remained within the confines of their households. Such concerns were rarely articulated in regard to young men working outside the home. Given such prevailing ideas, it is not surprising that parents were reluctant to allow their daughters to move beyond the bounds of their guardianship. Employment did not afford many single women greater independence as it did for single men. In most instances, the parents of wage-earning daughters had a great deal of control over the type of employment they sought, what they were allowed to do with their time away from work, and how much money they had to hand over on pay day. One woman recalled, "Most times I knew when I could have spending money because if my father wasn't working, I always used to get things for my sister."[23] In one extreme case when a widowed mother could not exercise any control over her daughters (both worked at a city clothing factory) to give her some of their earnings, she took them to court. The judge ruled that "the young women had to pay their

TABLE 5
Occupation Groups of Single Working Women, and Occupational Groups of Parents, 1921 and 1935
Occupation Groups
Heads of Household

Occupation Groups Working Women	Proprietor, Professional, Commercial, State				Skilled, Semi-Skilled, Unskilled & Service				Unemployed			
	1921		1935		1921		1935		1921		1935	
Proprietor	N	%	N	%	N	%	N	%	N	%	N	%
Professional	19	4.1	21	3.6	5	1.1	8	1.4	8	1.7	16	2.8
Clerical Work	37	8.1	63	10.9	57	12.4	40	6.9	30	6.6	67	11.6
Retail Work	28	6.1	35	6.1	89	19.4	66	11.4	30	6.6	47	8.1
Service	2	.4	13	2.2	7	1.6	17	2.9	6	1.3	18	3.1
Semi & Unskilled	11	2.4	9	1.6	94	20.5	100	7.2	33	7.2	55	9.5
	97	21.1	141	24.4	252	55.0	233	40.3	109	23.8	203	35.1

mother $1.50 and $2.50 per week respectively" (*Evening Telegram*, 20 February 1925).

Few single working women lived with relatives, as boarders, or on their own: 11.9 percent in 1921 and 13.3 percent in 1935 (see Table 3). Female wage earners who resided with relatives were small in number. They accounted for a mere 5 percent of the unmarried women in the labour force in 1921. Over a decade later their numbers had risen marginally to 6.6 percent. In most instances these women did not have parents living in the city. Either their mothers and fathers were deceased, or their parents remained behind in outports while they sought employment in St. John's. In the vast majority of such cases these women lived with an older married sibling.[24] Female wage-earners living with a relative could contribute some of their earnings toward household expenses, but likely not as much as they would have paid if they were boarding with strangers.

A slightly smaller proportion of women boarded than those who resided with relatives. [See Table 3.] These women tended to be older than other single working women. In 1921, 47.7 percent of female wage-earners who boarded were 25 years of age or older; in 1935, 65.7 percent were (*Census*, 1921, 1935). As the figures suggest, an increase had occurred between the two censuses in the ages of this particular group of working women. These female boarders were employed primarily in white-collar occupations which tended to offer marginally higher incomes than blue-collar occupations. A greater number of women might have boarded if inexpensive places had been available to them. There was a shortage of cheap accommodation where women earning low wages could board. When advertisements seeking boarders were placed in the newspapers, the weekly charge was usually between $4.00 and $6.00 (*Evening Telegram*, 3 May 1921; 15 August 1923; 1 February 1924; 31 September 1926; 1 June 1932; 22 June 1934). Few women held positions which paid more than $6.00 a week. In the early 1920s there were only two homes for "working girls" offering inexpensive room and board, one run by the Roman Catholic Church and the other by the Grenfell Association. The Catholic-sponsored St. Clare's Home, which had been open since 1912, was administered by the Sisters of Mercy (Flynn, 1937: 275). The Home was often filled to capacity with Catholic women as the nuns only required boarders to pay what they could afford. Unfortunately, the home was closed in May 1922 to make way for the opening of the St. Clare's Hospital (Nevitt, 1978: 97). At the Grenfell Association's Seaman's Institute, which had been open since 1914, there was an overwhelming demand for accommodation. The matron of the "Girls Section" noted in her report for 1921 that "Applications have had to be refused for lack of space and there is a long waiting list of girls who would like to become permanent boarders" (The Annual Report, 1921: 32). In 1921 alone, the Seaman's Institute turned down 206 applications simply because it lacked space (Ibid.). In 1926, the Grenfell Association handed over the Seaman's Institute to the YWCA/YMCA. The new administrator stated at the time that "The work of the girls' department so admirably performed under the direction of the Ladies Auxiliary will also be continued and if possible extended" (Seaman's, 1926: 154). Under the guidance of the YWCA, a "House Department" was set up and as many as 55 women at a time boarded there (*Evening Telegram*, 22 January 1927). This one residence could not even begin to fill the persistent demand for cheap places to board in the city. At the annual meeting of the YWCA in 1932, mention was made that the "House Department" could not accommodate all the women wanting and needing a place to board (*Evening Telegram*, 2 February 1932). This issue continued to be raised at subsequent annual meetings during the 1930s (*Evening Telegram*, 11 February 1937; 15 February 1938).

Women who headed their own households totalled just 1.9 percent of all single working women in 1921, and 3 percent in 1935 (see Table 3).[25] These small numbers emphasize the fact that working women during this period found it extremely difficult to live independently. These women were older than their other unmarried, wage-earning counterparts. By this stage in their lives it was likely that at least one or possibly both of their parents were no longer alive. There was little prospect of marriage for these women, so they had to find some means of supporting themselves. The majority of these women were the sole wage-earners in their households (56.3 percent in 1921 and 59.2 percent in 1935). In the case of another substantial proportion (40.2 percent in 1921 and 39.4 percent in 1935) they shared the responsibility with another unmarried sibling.[26] Single working women who headed up households tended to be owners of small confectionery or grocery stores as well as dressmakers, occupations which allowed them to combine their places of residence and places of work, thus cutting costs, and making it easier for them to live on their own.

Religious affiliation was not a major influence on the occupations that single working women chose, but it did have an impact on the location of their work. St. John's was a city where religion created divisions and tensions amongst its inhabitants. City residents accepted the fact that an individual had a much better chance of being hired by a private firm whose owner or manager was of the same religion. In the city's major department stores, Methodists (later members of the United Church) were more likely to be hired by Ayre and Sons, Anglicans by Bowring Brothers, and Catholics by Royal Stores. Such preferments seem to have been an unwritten and often unspoken assumption of the population as a whole. As one woman who worked for Ayre and Sons stated, "You just knew that Protestants looked after Protestants and Catholics after Catholics."[27] Only rarely did one see advertisements like the following in the newspapers: "Stenographer wanted immediately — must be quick at shorthand and typewriting. Protestant preferred" (*Evening Telegram*, 19 April 1921). When this type of preference for an employee of a certain religious denomination was stated publicly, it elicited some criticism. The reaction was quite negative when a sign was placed in the window of one St. John's store in the 1920s asking for female sales clerks with the added notation that "No Catholics Need Apply." The sign was not up very long before it had to be removed because of public pressure.[28] A denominational school system was also firmly entrenched in Newfoundland which meant that a teacher had to be of a particular religious denomination in order to be hired at a certain school. An

Anglican woman, for example, could only teach at an Anglican school in the city. Furthermore, tradition dictated that the denominational composition of the Newfoundland civil service was supposed to match exactly that of the entire country. Therefore, approximately one-third of the government employees in St. John's had to be Catholic, one-third Anglican, and one-third Methodist.[29]

The decision to get married almost always signalled the end of full-time wage labour for women. It was taken for granted by most women that once they married, they would no longer work full-time for pay. One informant noted, "You put your resignation in right away, as soon as you knew you were getting married. There was no such thing as working after you married."[30] Another emphasized:

I gave notice as soon as we got engaged. I was happy to be getting married, that was the lifestyle then. You got married, reared your children and were a helpmate to your husband. That was what was expected of you and you were happy with it.[31]

For many young working women, an impending marriage was eagerly anticipated. It was a time for celebration with friends and co-workers at wedding showers. St. John's newspapers frequently reported these ritualized events throughout the 1920s and 1930s. In September 1924, the female employees of a large book store "waited on Miss Mercedes Wadden and presented her with a handsome silver tea pot and salad bowl to match her contemplated marriage" (*Evening Telegram*, 14 September 1924). A Mrs. Dominy tendered a surprise shower for Miss Alfreda Winslow at her home in October 1928. "Lady employees of the Royal Stores clothing factory numbering about fifty" attended this social event. It was noted that Miss Winslow, along with a Miss Jean Redmond who was also present, would soon be leaving their jobs to get married. All the larger companies in the city had the unwritten rule that women could not remain after marriage even if they wanted to. No written regulations existed in private businesses or in the government prohibiting employment for married women until September 1933, when the Commission of Government instituted the following rule: "On marriage, a woman civil servant shall retire from office unless it is definitely in the interests of the Public Service that she should be retained for a further period."[32] This rule was enforced throughout the 1930s.

Once women married they entered an entirely new stage in their lives. They assumed responsibility for managing their households. Their lives from that point onward became focused upon taking care of their husbands' needs, performing domestic labour, and eventually, bearing as well as raising children. Domestic responsibilities were immense for married women throughout this period, especially those from the working class. Advances in household technology had barely reached middle-class households in St. John's by this time. In addition, unlike middle-class women, few working-class women had the option to hire domestic servants to help them with their housework. Most working-class households still had wood- or coal-burning stoves which required a great deal of attention. A large number of homes also lacked running water, thus forcing women to take empty pails to a nearby tap, line up behind others getting water, and carry a heavy pail back to their houses. This process had to be repeated frequently every day.[33] Hard physical labour was necessary daily to keep working-class households running smoothly. Married women were also in charge of the family budget, which meant that they had to take their husbands' small wages and buy the most they could with them. Living on a low income, always anticipating periods of unemployment, working-class wives often demonstrated great skill in transforming their husbands' scanty wages into decent living standards. In a letter written in 1923, "A Loving Mother" described how difficult it could be to keep a family fed and clothed:

> There is nobody knows more than the women what it costs to keep the home going. It is hard enough when times are fairly good; but it is awful when times are bad and employment is only to be had once in a while. The Women I Say, have the hardest end of it scraping and paring, mending and patching, and trying to make the few dollars that their husbands earn meet all the household expenses (*Evening Telegram*, 12 April 1923).

In a letter one year later, another woman echoed some of the same sentiments. "It is the women indeed who know to their sorrow what it is to live in a city when hard times are upon us. There is the rent to pay, the coal to be got, the food to be bought, the children's school fees, and hardest of all, the boots and clothing to cover us decently" (*Evening Telegram*, 22 January 1924). It took extra time out of an already busy day for women to try to stretch their husbands' earnings as far as possible.[34]

Because most married women experienced such heavy domestic responsibilities, they were reluctant to seek full-time wage labour outside the home even when there was a strong economic impetus for them to do so. They tried to avoid it at all possible costs. The percentage of working women who were married in the inter-war period was extremely small: 1.4 percent in 1921 and 2.6 percent in 1935 (see Table 2).[35] Those few women who did were almost exclusively from the working class. For middle-class married women, waged work continued to be such a social taboo that their presence in the labour force was almost nonexistent. Unlike working-class women, there was little possibility that they would experience the pressure of economic necessity. Most husbands of the married women who worked were skilled, semi-skilled, or unskilled blue-collar workers. A small percentage did not have a job at all.[36] These women's wages were needed to subsidize the earnings of their husbands. In a majority of the households with a married female wage-earner, the husband and wife supported the family (53.8 percent in 1921 and 52.1 percent in 1935), while in a large proportion of other homes one other child aided the family economy.[37]

The married women who did work were substantially older than single wage earners (see Table 6). Relatively few married women worked at an early stage in their family's life cycle while their children were young. The burden of domestic work and childcare at this time made employment all but impossible. Most married

TABLE 6
Age Groups of Married, Separated and Widowed Working Women, 1921 and 1935

Age Groups	N	%	N	%	N	%	N	%	N	%	N	%
Up to 14	—	—	—	—	—	—	—	—	—	—	—	—
15-19	—	—	—	—	—	—	—	—	—	—	—	—
20-24	—	—	2	6.5	1	25.0	1	9.1	2	—	—	—
25-29	—	—	4	12.9	—	—	1	9.1	3	6.4	3	4.6
30-34	1	7.7	4		—	—	2	18.2	1	2.1	3	4.6
35-39	2	15.4	5	16.1	2	50.0	1	9.1	5	10.6	9	13.8
40-44	2	15.4	1	3.2	—	—	2	18.2	8	17.0	12	18.5
45-49	3	23.1	7	22.6	—	—	1	9.1	5	10.6	11	16.9
50-54	—	—	4	12.9	—	—	1	9.1	12	25.5	9	13.8
55-59	2	15.4	1	3.2	1	25.0	2	18.2	1	2.1	5	7.7
60-64	3	23.4	3	9.7	—	—	—	—	4	8.5	4	6.2
65 and up	—	—	—	—	—	—	—	—	6	12.8	9	13.8
	13	100.0	31	100.0	4	100.0	11	100.0	47	100.0	65	100.0

TABLE 7
Life Cycle Stages of Married, Separated and Widowed Working Women, 1921 and 1935

Stages	N	%	N	%	N	%	N	%	N	%	N	%
Up to 45, No Child	2	15.4	4	12.9	2	50.0	3	27.3	7	14.9	7	10.8
Child 11 and under	—	—	4	12.9	—	—	1	9.1	5	10.6	3	4.6
11-15 None over 16	2	15.4	5	16.1	1	25.0	2	18.2	4	8.5	6	9.2
Some or all 16+	7	53.8	15	48.4	—	—	4	36.4	22	46.8	36	55.4
Over 45, No child	2	15.4	3	9.7	1	25.0	1	9.1	9	19.1	13	20.0
	13	100.0	31	100.0	4	100.0	11	100.0	47	100.0	65	100.0

women worked when at least half of their children were aged 15 or older. By this time, their children were already in school (see Table 7). These older, married women tended to be employed primarily as owners of confectionery and grocery stores, and to a lesser extent, as charwomen, boardinghouse keepers, and dressmakers (see Table 8). These occupations allowed women to pursue paid employment while maintaining close supervision of their own residences. In fact, domestic labour could be interspersed with duties related to their paid employment. Such women could tend children while working. None of these jobs would have provided the women with a large income, but it was enough to make a difference to their families' comfort.

TABLE 8
Occupation Groups of Married, Separated and Widowed Working Women, 1921 and 1935

Occupation Groups	N	%	N	%	N	%	N	%	N	%	N	%
Proprietor	9	64.2	11	35.5	—	—	1	9.1	18	38.3	25	38.5
Professional	—	—	1	3.2	—	—	—	—	1	2.1	3	4.6
Office Work	—	—	—	—	—	—	—	—	1	2.1	1	1.5
Retail Work	1	7.7	1	3.2	—	—	3	27.3	5	10.6	5	7.7
Service	1	7.7	11	35.5	3	75.0	5	45.5	16	34.0	23	35.4
Semi-skilled	1	7.7	3	9.7	—	—	1	9.1	4	8.5	5	7.7
Unskilled	1	7.7	4	12.9	1	25.0	1	9.1	2	4.3	3	4.6
	13	100.0	31	100.0	4	100.0	11	100.0	47	100.0	65	100.0

Although working-class married women tried to avoid full-time wage employment outside their homes, there is some evidence to suggest that they were quite willing to pursue part-time paid labour. Resourceful at procuring extra income for their families, women took in boarders, washed laundry, and sewed garments. While only a small number of married women appear in the census as boarding-housekeepers, quite a few had boarders. Keeping a boarder meant additional labour for women who probably were already overburdened, but it was work they could do at home. Washing clothes for others was much more labour-intensive and time-consuming than taking care of boarders.[38] While the work was disadvantageous because the women had to go out to get the clothes, it was a form of paid labour that could be performed at home. The clothing industry in St. John's employed a substantial number of married women as outworkers. Testifying before a royal commission on tariffs, William White of the White Clothing Company stated that until 1920, the industry employed 500 persons in various factories and an additional 200 homeworkers. The economic depression of 1921 impelled clothing manufacturers to cut their staffs drastically, but as many as 65 outworkers remained employed.[39] A large proportion of these workers must have been married women. Constrained by lack of alternatives, the necessity for extra income, and the need to remain at home, married women nevertheless continued to do such poorly paid work.

While most women left the labour force when they married, and were reluctant to pursue full-time wage labour thereafter, the termination of a relationship through separation, divorce, or death caused some to return to work. Divorce was relatively rare at this time. Neither the 1921 nor the 1935 census even included divorced in the section relating to marital status. Only four women in the sample were listed as being separated in 1921; there were eleven in the sample for 1935. Although divorce and even separation were still uncommon, widowhood occurred much more often. Loss of a spouse happened far more frequently for women than men. The death of a husband moved many women to yet another stage in their lives. More than five percent of wage-earning women were widows (see Table 2). A substantial proportion of these women were age 40 or older (see Table 6). Most widowed wage-earners headed up their own households (66 percent in 1921 and 83 percent in 1935). Along with the title came the responsibility for ensuring the economic survival of their families. Like married women, the stage of their family's life cycle had an impact on the employment of widows. Only a small proportion of widows were working at early stages of their families' life cycles. Most worked when at least half of their children were 15 or older (see Table 7). Widows were most likely to be employed as boardinghouse keepers, shopkeepers, and charwomen (see Table 8). As noted above, these occupations provided more flexible hours of work, and gave women who were in charge of their own households the opportunity to carry out domestic duties.

"Times were hard" in Newfoundland in the 1920s and 1930s. Few women in St. John's worked for "pin money"; rather, many engaged in paid employment because their wages were vitally important to the economic survival of their families. The pattern of women's paid work did not change substantially during the inter-war years. Like women elsewhere, wage employment for those in St. John's bridged the gap between school and marriage. The female labour force in this city overwhelmingly was young and single. Working women tended to be under 25, unmarried, and to live at home with their parents. At this stage in their life cycles they were as yet unencumbered by the responsibilities of domestic labour or childcare, and thus free to pursue employment outside the home. Class background proved to be a determining factor along with age and marital status in women's entry into the labour force. Working-class women were far more likely to work than middle-class women, primarily because of the necessity for them to contribute to the household economy. Middle-class women sought wage employment in ever-increasing numbers, but at no time equalled the numbers of working-class wage earners. Class background also influenced the type of employment which women managed to secure. The small number of married and widowed women who engaged in wage labour rarely did so full-time. They worked part-time, at a stage when their children were in school. The occupations that married and widowed women selected allowed them to perform their paid labour, as well as domestic labour.

1 Interview with Mary N., May 1986.

2 Interview with Dorothy F., May 1986.

3 For a discussion of the concept of the family wage see M. Barrett and M. McIntosh, (1980) and H. Land, (1980).

4 Census of Newfoundland and Labrador, 1921, 1935 (Nominal). Their participation rate was significant although slightly less than that of most Canadian cities during those decades. See, Canada, Sixth Census of Canada, 1921, Volume IV (Ottawa 1929), Table 5; Canada, Seventh Census of Canada, 1931, Volume VII (Ottawa 1942), Tables 41 and 57. It seems probable that women in St. John's lagged a little behind their counterparts elsewhere because of the structure of the local economy, with its heavy reliance upon the waterfront where male workers were exclusively employed; moreover, the secondary manufacturing sector which employed a substantial proportion of women was in a constant state of crisis.

5 The figures provided in the text and tables of this article are derived from the Newfoundland manuscript census records of 1921 and 1935. It should be noted that the figures provided in Table 2 and Table 8 do not represent the entire population; rather, they are taken from a sample of every third household containing a working woman. For a discussion of the methodology used, Forestell, "Women's Paid Labour," Appendices A, B. and C.

6 There has been some debate in the American literature on the impact of the Depression on working women. Alice Kessler-Harris (1982: 250-70) and Susan Ware (1982) argue that in spite of public resistance to the employment of women, particularly those who were married, the Depression solidified their position in the work force. Other historians such as Lois Scharf (1980) stress that no substantial gains were made by working women.

89

Instead, they view the Depression as a time of hostility and discriminatory practices, as well as diminished employment options.

7 Kessler-Harris (1976) has suggested that the segregation of women into specific female occupations creates an inflexibility in the labour market which prevents their expulsion during an economic crisis, thus refuting the theory that women form a "reserve army." Kessler-Harris found that during the Great Depression women in the U.S. were actually less affected than men by the contraction of the labour force.

8 The proportion of women in domestic service in St. John's during the inter-war period was much higher than that found in any Canadian city. Lack of other job opportunities in St. John's seems to account for the large number of domestics employed there.

9 In 1921, young women 15 to 19 numbered 2,421, and in 1935, 2,331. Women aged 20 to 24 numbered 2,286 in 1921 and 2,727 in 1935.

10 See, Canada, Sixth Census of Canada, 1921, Volume IV; Canada, Seventh Census of Canada, 1931, Volume VII. For example, in 1921, only 52 percent of the working women in Halifax were under 25, and in 1931, just 46.7 percent.

11 Prior to World War II, there was only one piece of legislation in Newfoundland which dealt with minimum age requirements for employment, and none at all covering age of school leaving. The "Mines Regulation Act" of 1908 stipulated that no boys under thirteen and no girls or women of any age were allowed to work underground in mines (Acts, 1942: 135-44). The passage of the "Welfare of Children Act" in 1944 prohibited the employment of women under the age of seventeen in restaurants and taverns, and waged work for all women between 9 at night and 8 in the morning (Acts, 1944: 303-15).

12 Single wage-earning women living at home accounted for 51.3 percent of the entire female labour force in 1921 and 47.7 percent in 1935.

13 Determining the socio-economic class of working women in this study is fraught with difficulties. There has been a great deal of debate in the feminist literature on the question of ascertaining the class of women (Pat and Hugh Armstrong, 1987; Gardiner, 1977). While realizing the weakness of this method, the class designation of working women in this study is determined by the occupation of the head of the household except in those cases where a woman is living with a relative, as a boarder, or as domestic. It is impossible to determine with any degree of precision the class of women living in those particular circumstances.

14 Planters were middle men in the fishing industry. They did not catch any fish, but instead bought quantities of fish, prepared it for market, and then sold it to fish exporting merchants.

15 Interview with Hazel S., February 1987.

16 PANL, Newfoundland Board of Trade, P8/B/11, Box 11, File 13, Letter from James Caul to the Employers' Protective Association, 16 August 1921.

17 Interview with Jenny F., November 1986.

18 Census of Newfoundland and Labrador, 1921, 1935 (Nominal).

19 Widows did receive a small payment of $5.00 a month from the Newfoundland Government if they could prove they were deserving. In regard to old age pensions which totalled $50.00 a year, only men seventy-five years of age or older qualified. The act governing old age pensions did not include any specific provisions for surviving widows

until 1926. In 1926, an amendment to the old age pension act stipulated that if a widow had reached the age of sixty-five years she was entitled to have one until her death or remarriage.

20 Interview with Agnes O., August 1986.

21 Relatively small numbers of working-class women from St. John's sought employment as live-in domestics. The ranks of domestics were primarily filled by outport fishermen's daughters. For a more detailed discussion of this situation see, Forestell, "Women's Paid Labour in St. John's Between the Two World Wars." ch. 4.

22 Ibid. Some women who could not afford the cost of nurse or teacher training worked for a couple of years to save enough money. Brief notices occasionally showed up in local newspapers indicating that employers of a particular firm were hosting a going away party for a co-worker. Evening Telegram, 23 August 1928; 31 June 1931.

23 Interview with Dorothy, F., May 1986.

24 Census of Newfoundland and Labrador, 1921, 1935 (Nominal). In 1921, 88.2 percent of the working women who lived with relatives were either sisters or sisters-in-law of the head of the household, and in 1935 they represented 87.5 percent.

25 Only sixteen single women were heads of their own households. Such a small sample size poses a problem when attempting to generalize for the entire population.

26 These percentages were derived from data gathered for the quantitative study that relate to the men and women who were wage-earners in the individual households.

27 Interview with Jenny F., November 1986.

28 Interview with Jenny F., November 1986.

29 For a denominational analysis of the Newfoundland civil service see, Newfoundland, The Civil Service in Newfoundland From a Denominational Standpoint, November 1st, 1928 (St. John's, 1928). According to this government report, Catholics constituted 32.9 percent of civil servants, Anglicans, 32.2 percent, Methodists 28.2 percent, and other denominations 6.7 percent.

30 Interview with Stella W., May 1986.

31 Interview with Jenny F., November 1986.

32 PANL, Executive Council, GN9/1, Minute Books, Minutes of Commission of Government, 4 September 1933, #633.

33 Evening Telegram, 21 March 1927. In an article on housing conditions in St. John's mention was made of the fact that there were large areas of St. John's without running water.

34 Relying almost entirely on oral testimony, historian Elizabeth Roberts (1984: 125-68) has constructed a richly textured picture of the lives of working-class women in three towns in northern England between 1890 and 1940. She maintains that most married working-class women devoted their time to domestic labour while also doing everything possible to "make ends meet."

35 For the 1921 census, only thirteen working women in this sample were married and in the 1935 census only thirty-one. Such a small sample size creates problems for generalizing about the entire population. Since the enumerators' instructions for the 1921 and 1935 censuses have not yet been found, it is difficult to determine how they defined whether a person was employed or not. From working with the census closely over a long period of

time, it seems to me that there is a significant undercounting of married women who were wage-earners, especially those who were shopkeepers, laundresses, and charwomen.

36 Census of Newfoundland and Labrador, 1921, 1935 (Nominal). The occupation of heads of households with a working wife in 1921 are as follows: Proprietor (1) 7.7 percent; Commercial (1) 7.7 percent; Skilled (6) 46.2 percent; Semi-skilled (1) 7.7 percent; Unskilled (2) 15.4 percent; Unemployed (2) 15.4 percent. In 1935 the occupation of heads of households are as follows: Proprietor (2) 6.5 percent; Professional (2) 6.5 percent; Commercial (2) 6.5 percent; Skilled (5) 16.1 percent; Semi- skilled (4) 12.9 percent; Unskilled (9)35.5 percent; Unemployed (7) 22.6 percent.

37 Ibid.

38 Advertisements were placed in the city's newspapers regularly by women who stipulated that the washing would be done in their own homes. Evening Telegram, 24 June 1920, 29 February 1927; 9 March 1933.

39 Excerpt of the Report of the Findings of the Royal Commission of 1922 in The Liberal Press, 16 March 1929. It is not know to what extent outwork prevailed in St. John's during the rest of the 1920s and 1930s.

"A Woman's Place": The Work of Two Women's Voluntary Organizations in Newfoundland, 1934-1941[1]

Linda Cullum

This article explores the work of the Jubilee Guilds and the Co-operative Women's Guilds and their roles in state formation.

THE WORK OF WOMEN'S VOLUNTARY ORGANIZATIONS AND NETWORKS in the emotional and material support of women in the nineteenth and early twentieth century has become the subject of historical and sociological study in recent years. These organizations and networks took many different forms emphasizing women's personal interests, the administration of philanthropy and charity endeavors or the generation of social reforms. They were urban and rural based, locally developed or international in scope. Examining these organizations and networks has led to a rethinking of women's lives and work. For example, Carroll Smith-Rosenberg (1975) has revealed that communication links ran between white middle-class women in nineteenth century America, and thus has reformed our notions of the home-centred lives of these women. The importance of literary and study clubs to the development of suffrage goals for middle-class women in central Canada and Newfoundland is well-documented (Duley, 1993). Archival documents from other women's groups reveal their organization around "traditional" women's activities; church organizations or social groups with interests in gardens and flowers abound. As Sheehan (1986) notes, many groups were locally organized and single-purpose, established primarily for the benefit of the women members.

Women's reform organizations were a departure from this personal emphasis. Three international organizations in particular shared the goals of reforming and educating society. The Imperial Order of Daughters of the Empire (IODE), Women's Christian Temperance Union (WCTU) and the Women's Institutes (WI) maintained both local and national structures. They also shared common ethnic, religious and class roots; leaders and members were usually Anglo-Saxon, middle-class and Protestant. Thus, the reform and education advocated by these organizations was defined by a particular stratum of society, one which was shared with the governing elite (Sheehan,1986).

In pre-confederation Newfoundland, a relatively small middle class meant leadership and membership in women's voluntary organizations included the active participation of upper-class women. During the 1920s and 1930s, much of their work focused on the philanthropy and charity central to the alleviation of social problems in Newfoundland. The involvement of upper-class women with both time and energy to provide volunteer labour virtually guaranteed the mobilization of financial and physical resources to accomplish the goals of such organizations. Their fund-raising abilities and their personal and institutional connections were crucial to the sponsorship of many charitable endeavors.

In the provision of these services, the work of women constituted, and was constituted by, a class-based vision of appropriate women's roles. Women were

93

seen as the means to improve the home, family and community, both as providers and receivers of assistance. By their work, women would positively influence those around them. Gendered patterns of involvement emerged. Organizational work was conducted with other women and addressed women's traditional expressive and nurturing concerns in caring for home and family. For example, between the wars, women's voluntary organizations in St. John's provided health and welfare services, especially the provision of clothing and food for children, but women did not undertake the organization of physical outdoor activities or the construction of recreation facilities. Those tasks were left to the men of the Rotary Club of St. John's. This gender-divided provision of assistance reproduced the gender division of labour in middle- and upper-class families.

The work these women performed held consequences for state formation by actively contributing to this formation. To see women's voluntary organizations as playing a key role in state formation requires a particular view of what constitutes 'the state'. For 'the state' is not a monolithic structure, standing apart from, and oppressing, the people. 'It' is not a unitary, cohesive, co-ordinated whole, without contradictions in policy or everyday practices. Rather, state formation is the ongoing production of the active agency of human beings whose activities or practices of ruling are not confined to formal political organizations or government departments.

These everyday activities and practices can be examined as constituents of the "relations of ruling" (Smith,1987). Smith speaks of the relations of ruling as a complex array of practices and activities performed by people in what she calls "multiple sites of power" (Smith,1987:3;1990a:14). These sites include government, business, law and educational institutions. I argue that women's voluntary organizations must also be included as sites of ruling practices, where policies and programs of governance are produced and disseminated. When this concept of ruling is historically grounded in a particular time, and considered as a "process of social activity and organization with historically changing institutions, relations, agents, procedures and knowledges," it becomes concrete and analyzable (Weir,1986:9,14).

Dorothy Smith's work into how ruling is organized has focused on the role of texts (in the broadest sense of the word) in the organization of practices and activities in local settings, and linking those local settings to "the social relations of the larger social and economic processes" external to individual lives, relationships, communities and beyond (1987:152). Thus, it is possible that historically situated ruling practices, located in sites beyond the formal boundaries of state formation, may function to link and articulate local settings and events to the larger social and economic world. This view of the organization of ruling and state formation opens up a space in which to examine women's voluntary organizations as sites of ruling responsive to, and organized in, specific locations and historical circumstances.

In this essay, I examine the work of women through one particular women's voluntary organization, the Jubilee Guilds of Newfoundland and Labrador, 1935 to

1941. Described as a "new form of organization" for women, the Jubilee Guilds was established in 1935 by urban, upper-class women. Their work was focused on reforming the lives of the people of rural Newfoundland by re-establishing "self-help, self-respect, and self-reliance" in the Newfoundland population (Richard,1989:13), principally through the re-education of women. This essay will look at the goals and structure of the Jubilee Guilds and the historical context in which the organization was developed. I will use relations with another, different organization, the Co-operative Women's Guilds, to highlight the disjunctures between the visions held by the Guilds' organizers and the women members who actively participated in both organizations. Further, women's active role in constituting relations of ruling and, more broadly, state formation will be discussed.

My interest in the Jubilee Guilds sprang from the intersection of two personal experiences: membership in a particular women's organization and participation in an undergraduate Women's Studies class at Memorial University of Newfoundland. During the 1980s, I was an active member of the St. John's Guild of Embroiderers, an organization dedicated to the promotion and encouragement of fine needlework. The members, all female, ranged in age and experience. The younger, often less experienced members like myself learned at the feet of the finer embroiderers, absorbing not only the correct techniques but also understandings about, and attitudes toward, their embroidery work and their lives as women.

The effect on my work of absorbing and practising embroidery techniques is more easily described than the subtle shifts in my attitudes and understandings. Yet both carry visible markers: a well-executed stitch; a desire to learn and socialize together; a simple stitchery design and the planning and organizational skill required to execute it; the form and order of a business meeting and the 'correct' way to address issues raised in that meeting; how to dress, speak and participate in a polite, supportive, non-threatening manner. Much of what I learned in the Embroiderers Guild was rooted in certain class-based assumptions about our work and our lives as women. I was only vaguely aware of these lessons at the time.

A Women's Studies class discussion, filtered through my work in the Embroidery Guild, caused me to think more deeply about my own experience and about the work of women's voluntary organizations. A classmate mentioned the Newfoundland and Labrador Women's Institutes as an example of a women's voluntary organization. As we offered what we knew of the organization, I realized our understandings of the Women's Institutes, and their forerunner, the Jubilee Guilds of Newfoundland and Labrador, were very different. The resulting discussion, informed by the feminist inquiry and approaches found in that particular Women's Studies classroom, raised many questions for me about the role, structure and relations found in, and expressed through, women's voluntary organizations. It seemed to me that the Jubilee Guilds of Newfoundland and Labrador, with a history stretching back over 50 years and scores of communities in Newfoundland, would have much to tell about the lives and experiences of Newfoundland women. The work of voluntary groups such as the Jubilee Guilds, or the Embroiderers Guild, is not confined to providing a social space for women. Virtually all women's voluntary organizations have material practices — structures, education programs, reward systems — which serve to organize members' lives and work around the ideology and goals of the group. In Newfoundland and Labrador, there has been little work done to explore the place women's voluntary organizations and their activities hold in the lives of women.

The work of the women of the Jubilee Guilds of Newfoundland and Labrador is examined here in two particular ways. First, their active work in state formation and their relationship to the Commission Government in Newfoundland and Labrador between 1935 and 1941 is explored. I am interested in understanding and illuminating how the Jubilee Guilds may have worked to articulate women's lives to the goals of the Commission Government during this time, thus actively contributing to state formation. By this I mean the way(s) in which the programs and policies of the Guilds worked in concert with those of the Commission Government to organize and regulate the lives of women in rural Newfoundland at a time of political, social and economic upheaval.

Second, the relationship of the Jubilee Guilds to the Co-operative Division and the Co-operative Women's Guilds in the Department of Natural Resources is examined. Through this examination the different discursive practices used by the two women's voluntary organizations are made visible. The phrase, discursive practices, refers to the talk, language, material objects, education programs, official organizational texts and everyday actions of the women and men of these organizations which operated to signify meaning in particular ways. In this case, the meanings of "woman" — the ways of being a woman — are of interest to me in thinking about the work of these organizations. Through different discursive practices, these two organizations attempted to define women as subjects and women's appropriate work in economic production. I suggest that through these practices, disparate forms of social organization were made possible in rural communities. This opens up the possibility of seeing how particular subjects may be constructed and particular forms of social organization established.

Relief and Unrest

Following World War I, Newfoundland faced a new world. War-time inflation, profiteering by local merchants and limited improvements in living conditions, despite a war-time economic boom, had fuelled unrest. Popular political, union and suffrage movements demanded attention for their concerns. With the growth of these organizations and causes, a longstanding concern about popular influence in local politics arose. As Overton (1990) has documented, power relations in Newfoundland were altered by the emergence of organized and vocal opposition to those in power. The upper classes accustomed to exercising control were no longer assured of their position.

By the 1930s, the economic depression and Newfoundland's bankrupt state led to increasing government restrictions on relief. Unrest, protest marches, violence and demands for better relief by the working classes became the order of the day (Overton,1988). However, the upper classes in Newfoundland favoured detailed investigation and rigid control of charity and relief in urban and rural areas. Coupled with this was widespread concern that "indiscriminate" charitable giving would contribute to undermining working class independence and induce "pauperization" of the poor. Pauperization was indicative of a loss of personal initiative and dignity; it was seen as a moral as well as an economic condition to be avoided in the population (Valverde,1991:20). Outport Newfoundlanders were portrayed as lazy and unmotivated workers (*Evening Telegram*, October 18, 1935:19). Disenfranchisement of the poor was proposed by prominent members of society as a solution to problems of unrest (NAC, McGrath Microfilm H1419-20-21:1933).

The Jubilee Guilds

A "new form of organization" was called for, one that promised to promote and encourage the "uplift" of destitute communities. This "new organization" was the Jubilee Guilds of Newfoundland and Labrador. With the Jubilee Guilds, it was argued, the "way to a new Newfoundland" could be found, one which encouraged Newfoundlanders to make "proper uses of the resources and riches around them" (*Evening Telegram*, May 28, 1935:6) Through the Jubilee Guilds, the interests, ideas and knowledge of 'proper' work ethics and civic behaviour flowed from the elite class of St. John's with close ties to the Commission of Government, to the poorer working classes in outport Newfoundland.

The central figure in the emergence of the Jubilee Guilds was Lady Muriel Anderson, wife of the British Governor of Newfoundland. Lady Anderson had a long history of "good works" to her credit, as was appropriate for the leading social figure in the Dominion. In 1933, she formed a charity organization, the British Empire Service League (also known as the Service League of Newfoundland), to collect and distribute clothing to the needy in St. John's and the outports. Through a network of branches, formed and run by the officials and more privileged classes of the communities — ministers, police officers, relief officers, wives of merchants, nurses, teachers — distribution of clothing was made possible. Careful scrutiny of the poor and close control over the definition of who was needy and who was not was exercised by this group (PANL, MG 617, files #1,2,3/3A). Many of these approaches were duplicated in the work of the Jubilee Guilds. Through the actions and practices of this group, work of the Commission Government in controlling and distributing relief was accomplished.

The privileged classes associated with the establishment of the Jubilee Guilds saw "the rehabilitation of Outport life" as their duty (1938 AGM Minutes). The Guilds were to stimulate self-help in rural communities, promote co-operation and social communication (Richard,1989:11) and thereby discourage the acceptance of relief. As founding member Reverend Oliver Jackson stated, the Newfoundland people must work "to build up their morale and bring them back to the industrious ways of their forefathers" (1937 AGM Minutes). He firmly believed the Jubilee Guilds were the path to improved community morale and industry. Others declared the Jubilee Guilds to be "schools in citizenship" that would help the people realize their "duties" as citizens and thus improve "our national life" (*Evening Telegram*, October 18, 1935:19).

With the launching of the Jubilee Guilds, the former Service League emphasis on charity and philanthropy disappeared; in its place was an ardent philosophy of self-help. Individuals and families, through the work of women, were to feed and clothe themselves rather than relying on charity or relief. Program objectives of the Jubilee Guilds were to help "the people of the outports to provide themselves with clothing, make their homes more comfortable, and develop their own local resources to these ends" (*Evening Telegram*, May 31, 1935:5). This was to occur principally through the re-education of outport women, for the upper classes believed that outport people had lost the skills, knowledge and motivation to succeed. Women in rural communities were to "help to change the people from an attitude of despair, to a sense of self-reliance and good citizenship" through the use of local resources such as wool, berries, home-grown food and the production of handicraft goods for home use (1937 AGM Minutes). Importantly, it was argued that the resulting increase in, and quality of, women's domestic reproductive activities would stimulate men's own productive activities in their communities. Thus, the economic betterment of families and communities would 'naturally' follow through increased productivity amongst its members. Women's domestic labour was to restore moral and economic order to what was perceived by the upper class as a chaotic and desperate Newfoundland.

In forming the Jubilee Guilds, Lady Anderson drew on the social elite of St. John's, many of whom had supported her work in the Service League. She designed the hierarchical and gender-divided organizational structure of the Jubilee Guilds. It consisted of a male Board of Trustees, members of the urban business, professional and political elite, and a female Executive Committee, composed of wives, daughters and sisters from the upper classes in St. John's. They were embedded in a complex network of extended social relations through marital, familial, business and social ties which they called upon to support their work in the Guilds. The paid female workers included an Organizing Secretary, usually a single, university-trained home economist, and Field Workers and office staff drawn largely from outport families. Thus, the hierarchical organization of the Guilds located the urban-based, upper-class women in a position of management and control. The rank-and-file rural membership were seen as the subjects and objects of the Guild's educational programming. They were to be reworked, refashioned, reformed in a new image.

The Guilds' program combined the investigation of communities for their "industry" level and the promotion of self-help. The establishment of outport Guild branches was closely monitored and controlled by the Executive Committee and Board of Trustees. Each branch was formally organized, with a President, Vice-President, Secretary and Treasurer. Often women holding these positions in the local Branch were closely tied to the merchant or other privileged groups in the outport. In its first year of operation, seventeen outport branches were formed. Richard (1989) lists the earliest branches as: Argentia, Daniel's Harbour, Flatrock,

Markland North, Markland South, Port Saunders, Upper Gullies, Victoria, Portugal Cove South, Lewisporte, Blackhead and Freshwater, B.V.D., Grate's Cove, Mall Bay, St. Mary's, Gaskiers, Point La Haye and Tors Cove.

Monthly branch meetings included a formal business meeting, brief reports or educational talks and a social hour. From the outset, Lady Anderson planned educational demonstrations and programs divided along gender lines. Women's work was focused indoors. They were to (re)learn the home industries their mothers knew, which Lady Anderson believed needed reviving in rural Newfoundland. In the outports, Lady Anderson believed, women should be creating homespun cloth for clothing, knitting socks and undergarments, learning

> ...cooking, better bread-making and household economy, so as to get the best value out of the materials at their command. There will also be instruction in Weaving and Dyeing; Home Handicrafts; First Aid in Accidents; Infant Welfare; Care of Health; and Home Nursing; Poultry Keeping; Fruit Growing; and Jam Making. (*Evening Telegram*, May 31, 1935:5)

Women were to learn how to 'turn collars and cuffs' on clothing, use technologically advanced preserving, canning and bottling methods and learn about and use ingredients not typically found in rural Newfoundland to 'improve' their cooking. Weaving and knitting lessons taught women patterns imported from other parts of the world. Women were urged to create new colour schemes for their kitchens and plant flowers around their homes. A middle class standard of living was inherent in these education programs — one which did not take into account the difficulties of purchasing flour, let alone flower seeds.

In keeping with government policy and their own concerns about pauperization, the Jubilee Guilds attempted to maintain a "nothing for nothing" policy in their training programs (Trustee Minutes, May 4, 1938). Outport women were required to pay, in cash or in kind, for any raw materials or equipment they were given. The finished handicraft products, woven blankets, handmade clothing, or preserves were designed to "beautify" homes and provide for the "betterment" of families. They were not for commercial sale or to generate personal income. In the words of the second President of the Jubilee Guilds, Lady Eileen Walwyn:

> ...the object of the Guilds is to help the women to interest themselves in every side of home-making for the betterment of their surroundings... I repeat the betterment of the home life of our people must remain our first objective. (1939 AGM Reports)

But outport women were seen to lack these skills of "self-reliance." They required re-education to properly fulfil their domestic role.

Men's work was defined very differently. They were to receive instruction in specific outdoor work: planting and growing crops, keeping livestock such as pigs, sheep and poultry, and canning fish, fruits and vegetables. No instruction in fishing, logging or hunting practices — traditional male occupations — appears in the Guilds' records. An upper-class, urban view of the appropriate gender division of work in rural Newfoundland communities is evident in these education programs.

The idealized results would include a productive, prosperous and civil people. Also evident is the disjuncture between the model contained in the Jubilee Guilds programming and the lives of rural women; it did not address the realities of rural life.

Historical accounts of customary work patterns in outport communities conflict with those constructed by the Guilds. Most outport work was divided by sex, but men's and women's tasks overlapped when required. Women were responsible for work indoors and outdoors as provision of food entailed a chain of tasks from collection of the raw product to final preparation for consumption. The work varied with the season and whether the family was dependent on fishing or logging for their livelihood. Husbands, fathers and brothers engaged in these major economic activities were often absent from the community. Women raised the children, ran the home, planted and tended vegetable gardens and livestock, made butter and cream if the family owned cows or goats and, as Porter (this volume) notes, did the same work as men when required.

Women's skilled labour in the production of salt fish for local and international markets was central to the economic survival of many fishing families. Many hours a day, spring to fall, were consumed by "making fish"; the procedures required great skill and competence. Women worked on shore, often heading, gutting and splitting the fish before washing, pressing and laying the prepared fish out to dry in the sun for several days. Without women's skills, the salt fish would not be a quality, saleable product and the family income would suffer (Antler, 1977). Yet this work was not defined by inclusion in the program of the Jubilee Guilds as work of importance for outport women. The Guild leadership did not acknowledge a situational, family-based division of labour or consider necessary women's acquisition or sharpening of skills required to support this different division of labour.

The Jubilee Guilds attempted to organize the division of labour and gender relations in the outport home through an emphasis on women's domestic labour and family duties. Through their educational programs, the Guilds focused women's attention on perfecting their domestic labour to produce "a happier, healthier and more prosperous population" (*Evening Telegram*, May 31, 1935:5). All this was to be done with local resources to a standard established by the Jubilee Guilds, reflecting an urban class-based ideal of cleanliness, nutrition and attention to domestic detail — an ideal established beyond the boundaries of their own communities. Importantly, women were to be a conduit to the family and community, the ones to improve the lives of others and better the social and economic conditions in rural Newfoundland. They were to work with other women for the "uplift" of their communities and to re-establish moral and economic order and productivity in a "despairing" people. Busy hands and minds would rebuild the country and reinvigorate the outport people.

Notably, women were to be "taught" how to be good citizens in their own country. Through their organized and productive example, order would be restored to rural Newfoundland. Citizenship was a euphemism for quiet, law-abiding people who provided their own family and community support in times of want and demanded little in the way of relief or services from the government. As Overton (1990) has noted, storming the House of Assembly, ill-treatment and disrespect for those in power, and loud, sometimes violent demands for food and work was not the behaviour of "good citizens."

The Jubilee Guilds and State Formation

The potential for the Jubilee Guilds' active role in state formation was evident from the beginning. Government agricultural expert W.W. Baird argued that such a pre-existing "community organization" would result in "more efficient work" by government departments, with a "minimum of cost," in outport communities (*Evening Telegram*, October 18, 1935:6). Immediate, low-cost and legitimated access to a community through the Jubilee Guilds could serve the government well in promoting reconstruction policies and programs. The Commission Government would have access to rural women, a group which government workers had not yet reached with any success. The Jubilee Guilds' connections with the Commission Government were highly visible. Three of the six Commission Government Departments maintained representatives on the Board of Trustees of the Jubilee Guilds, Claude Fraser of Natural Resources, Dr. Lloyd Shaw of Education and Dr. Harris Mosdell of Public Health and Welfare. "[C]lose co-operation with all government departments" was an aim of the Guilds, and their work in the "rehabilitation" of rural Newfoundland was of particular interest to these Departments (*Evening Telegram*, October 18, 1935:6).

The importance given to the Jubilee Guilds as a medium for reaching the women of Newfoundland is explicit in the role played by the Department of Natural Resources in the work of the Guilds. The Department of Natural Resources was one of the major policy-making departments of the Commission, on a par in the Commission of Government hierarchy with the Department of Finance. As Burstyn (1983) notes, this would indicate the Department of Natural Resources occupied a higher, "more centralized" position of power in state formation. This department, headed by a British Commissioner, housed the main resource sectors for economic development: fisheries and fishery research, forestry, agriculture, co-operation (co-operatives), geology and surveys, as well as a secretariat, the Rangers policing force and accounts (Clark, 1951:131). The Rural Reconstruction Program, aimed at rebuilding rural communities and the rural economic base was also housed in the Department of Natural Resources.

In September 1936, Gerald Richardson, then Director of the Co-operative and Extension Department of the Commission Government actively solicited "the co-operation of the Jubilee Guilds, especially in the organization of women" (Executive Minutes, September 21, 1936). Richardson proposed the co-ordination of Jubilee Guild and Co-operative field work activities. The Organizing Secretary of the Guilds, Elizabeth MacMillan, would accompany the Co-operative Division staff when they were forming their co-op educational groups. The Guilds and the Division were to work together to organize men and women in rural Newfoundland.

The Trustee Committee, including members of the government department making the offer, heartily endorsed such a plan.

Further articulation of Co-operative and Jubilee Guild work occurred on many levels. The Co-operative fieldmen began direct communication with the Guilds regarding the formation of branches in areas where the Co-operatives were organizing (Executive Minutes, April 7, 1937). Then, in February, 1938 the Guilds were asked by the Rural Reconstruction Committee to "undertake the direction of women's work in the Rural Reconstruction Programme" under the Department of Natural Resources (Executive Minutes, March 16, 1938). Funds for this work, $9,000.00, were provided by the Rural Reconstruction Committee, and arrived along with a request that "Guild work be started in Placentia Bay" (Richard, 1989:19-25). Once the Guilds accepted financial support from the Commission Government, their work was shaped by government requirements. The Guilds aligned their field work and altered their programming efforts to co-ordinate with government objectives. The teaching of the Guild field staff was organized to include courses in "programme planning and co-operative principles" and the supervision of "the making of upholstery for the demonstration house in the land settlement," a Commission Government program (1939 Annual Reports). The two organizations also worked together on a "social survey" of communities in Placentia Bay conducted in June, 1938. The Co-operative Division co-ordinated and participated in the survey and female workers from the Jubilee Guilds and the Adult Education section of the Commission Government toured communities and homes in Placentia Bay (Executive Minutes, June 23, August 29, 1938 and NLWI Correspondence, August 1, 1938). Subsequently, Elizabeth MacMillan established six branches near Marystown and two Jubilee Guild Field Workers, Eva Parsons and Mary Fitzgibbon, were assigned to conduct courses at the new centres (Executive Minutes, September 9, 1938 and 1938 Annual Report). The Organizing Secretary's Report presented at the 1939 AGM of the Jubilee Guilds, held at Government House, notes that "during the year special attention was paid to this section of the country (Burin District), in order to fall in line with the Government project of rehabilitation" (1939 AGM Minutes). Eventually, the Guilds even adjusted their organizational practices to accommodate government stipulations about workers' salaries, administrative costs and auditing practices (Trustee Minutes, May 4, 1938).

The Co-operative Women's Guilds

However, collaboration soon turned into contestation. By early 1939, members of the Co-operative Division viewed the Jubilee Guilds largely as a means to develop handicraft skills among outport women, rather than skills in community participation, co-operation or community economics. In February, 1939, J.G. Howell, Acting Secretary for Rural Reconstruction observed in a letter to the Commissioner for Rural Reconstruction, "It must be recognized that the Jubilee Guilds have not the machinery or the technique to deal with Co-operative problems" (PANL, GN 31/3A, file #R116). The Jubilee Guilds had come to be viewed as an organization of limited potential in the development of women's participation in the social and economic life of Newfoundland.

In sharp contrast, the male leadership of the Co-operative Division saw women as instrumental to their organizational efforts in rural Newfoundland. Neil Mac-Neil, Assistant Director of Co-operation, expressed strong views about the place of women in the Newfoundland Co-operative movement and community.

> Co-operatives do not hold to the theory that 'a woman's place is in the home' even if her domestic occupation consists entirely of spinning, weaving, making curtains, reading cook books, etc. They must face their share of the responsibility when it comes to the safe-guarding of the village co-operatives. They must have their study club meetings, associated meetings, where all problems affecting the village are on the agenda. They must support and work for any progressive plan to improve the moral, economic, or social condition of the whole village. (PANL, GN 31/3A, C10/11: MacNeil to Gorvin:August 26,1939)

In the same memo MacNeil stresses women's role in the growth of co-operative work.

> "We cannot over emphasize the importance of propagandizing the Co-operative Movement amongst the women. From the standpoint of economic development they are indispensable. No plan or movement dedicated to the re-construction of the village can succeed unless the women are given a place, an important place in its structure" (PANL: GN 31 3A, C/10/11: MacNeil to Gorvin: August 26, 1939).

To achieve these ends, the Co-operative Division began a new initiative in "women's work" in Newfoundland. The January, 1939 issue of *The Co-operative News*, published by the Division, outlined the formation of a new women's voluntary organization, the Co-operative Women's Guilds. Believing that "the women can exercise a more powerful influence than the men" in the Co-operative Credit Societies, (PANL, GN31/3A, file #R116:Howell to Ewbank:February 2,1939), the Division attempted to take control of their work with rural women and to increase women's participation. The Co-operative Women's Guild movement was linked with the Women's Co-operative Movement in Great Britain, America and elsewhere and with the International Women's Co-operative Guild movement (PANL,GN 31/3A, file #R116:Gorvin to Ewbank: February 1,1939).

The Co-operative Women's Guilds aimed to involve outport women in the Co-operative program. Through Study Club programs emphasizing agriculture, health, the development of Credit Unions and the production and marketing of handicrafts, outport women could participate in the economic support of their families and the development of co-operative organizations in their communities. For example, the Co-operative Division believed that the Credit Unions would prosper if women deposited their earnings from the marketing of their handicrafts in Credit Union accounts (Richardson,1940: 20-21). Membership was to be restricted to the wives and daughters of men participating in the Co-operative Store.

Co-operative Fieldworkers Mary McCarthy and Bertha Everson visited communities, talked with women about Co-operative principles and the Women's

103

Guilds and offered training in handicrafts. The resulting groups were less formally organized than the Jubilee Guilds and their approach was quite different. The Co-operative workers supplied raw materials free to their women's groups, and members participated in the production of handicrafts such as woven and knitted goods and leather gloves. The Co-op workers purchased the finished products from the members and arranged for the products to be sold to a third party. Individualized, private production of goods for sale was emphasised as a means of generating domestic income for the outport family. Placing cash in the hands of outport women was key to the work of the Co-operative Women's Guilds. They believed that women were entitled to money for their productive efforts and they paid women for their labour. While women's work remained home-centred and relied on their traditional reproductive skills, women also were constituted as economically productive subjects with a clear and active role to play in their communities.

The introduction of the Co-operative Women's Guilds challenged the government-sanctioned monopoly on educational work with rural women held by the Jubilee Guilds. But they also challenged the particular construction of class, gender and economic relations constituted by the Jubilee Guilds' work. With the Co-operative Women's Guilds, women could gain access to raw materials in order to produce goods for sale. They could use this money to support their community Co-operative Store and lessen their reliance on the local merchant. This was not the vision of the Jubilee Guilds. Indeed, as early as 1935, Lady Muriel Anderson assured the business community that the Jubilee Guilds would not challenge the local merchants.

> ...several people have suggested to me that the Guilds might take away custom from the merchants. My answer to that is that where you raise the purchasing power of a community, which the Guilds hope to do, the merchant is the first to benefit...(*Evening Telegram*, October 18, 1935:19)

The Jubilee Guild's approach did not challenge the status quo of merchant control in the outports and, thus, extra-local capitalist enterprise. Improvements in the social condition of the village were not tackled in the way the Co-operative workers desired; in their view, there was little progressive about the Guilds' branch organizations. In addition, the development of leadership skills among outport women was not addressed by the Jubilee Guilds, according to Neil MacNeil. Rather, the Guilds were run and controlled by the traditional merchant elite in rural communities.

> In many places the merchant's wife 'gives the orders' and the other Guild members just climb back into oblivion. The element of change is not inherent in such a programme....The difficulty in co-ordinating the work of the Co-operative Division and Jubilee Guilds is as follows:
> (1) The Executive Committee of the Jubilee Guilds is composed, for the most part, of women whose husbands are in business. They do not take kindly to Co-operation as a business activity.
> (2) The Jubilee Guild Field Workers very often stay at the homes of local

merchants and usually the merchant's wife takes an active part in Guild work. (PANL, GN 31/3A, C 10/11: MacNeil to Gorvin: August 26, 1939)

In both discursive and material practices, the Jubilee Guilds and the Co-operative Women's Guilds were quite different. MacNeil saw the private, capitalist interests of the Jubilee Guilds' leadership as antithetical to the continual development of rural women's role in economic growth and to the discursive production of women as economic subjects.

The introduction of the Co-operative Women's Guilds did not go unnoticed. Lady Eileen Walwyn, then President of the Jubilee Guilds, wrote to Commissioner of Natural Resources Robert Ewbank complaining of the presence of the new organization. She wrote, in part,

> ...I do not think it was very fair to go in and start some new organization without one word to us. Also it only over laps and makes the women wonder where they are...I hear he [John Gorvin] says the Guilds do not deal enough with the economic side of the Community. Surely it is best, (and indeed the only course to take) to tackle the practical side first, and the other is bound to follow... (NLWI Correspondence, Walwyn to Ewbank: January 30, 1939)

Lady Walwyn was particularly scathing about the work of the Co-operative Women's Guilds conducted at the community of Markland. She defended the limited work of the Jubilee Guilds saying, "the trouble has been that the people have nothing to work with." If the Co-operative workers were successful in Markland, Walwyn charged, "it will only be through 'handing out', which as you know is one of the things the Jubilee Guilds fight against" (NLWI Correspondence, Walwyn to Ewbank: January 30, 1939). Walwyn raised the spectre of pauperization in rural Newfoundland with this argument.

In a February, 1939, meeting between the Jubilee Guilds and Ewbank, the opening statement by the Jubilee Guilds' representatives revealed the antipathy felt by the Executive and Trustees toward "state" involvement and so-called "charity" approaches to the moral and economic development in rural Newfoundland.

> It is noted by the Trustees that the formation of the Co-operative Guild at Markland is the direct result of the need for a medium for the distribution of charity, and to meet this need your Department had appropriated the name 'GUILD', which is the general term used to designate our organization. We submit this action is unfair and unwarranted and tends to defeat one of the chief objectives of the Jubilee Guilds, which is self-help; in direct contradiction to a state assisted and charity dispensing unit such as the Co-operative Guild....We have given study to the objects and scope of this Organization and cannot see where the stated objects are not covered by the constitution of the Jubilee Guilds. It therefore follows that their establishment is definitely competitive. The only difference we can see is the use of the Women's Co-operative Guild by your Department for the distribution of charity, to the destruction of self-help. This being the case the Trustees are unable to reconcile as 'complementary', the two Organizations one state aided where the invitation to join is accompanied by the

lure of 'something for nothing' and the other a voluntary Organization for self-help. (NLWI Correspondence, February 27, 1939)

The old argument of charity versus self-help was raised to support the Jubilee Guilds' central position in the education of rural women. The class location and loyalties of the Guilds' leadership are evident. Neil MacNeil argued that the Guilds confined their efforts to the production of "handicraft apparel for home consumption," rather than production of goods for cash sale, thus limiting the economic possibilities for women. In the words of MacNeil,

the members of the Executive Committee [of the Jubilee Guilds] have no desire to work in closer co-ordination with the Co-operative Division...I am inclined to believe we should be merely 'beating the bushes for witches' if we continue negotiations in an effort to bring effective co-operation into the aims and objects of the Guilds (PANL, GN 31/2, file #318, Volume I: MacNeil to Commissioner: January 12, 1940)

Indeed, by June, 1940, the departure of Gerald Richardson from Newfoundland and silence from the Co-operative Division on the issue of future work together indicated to the Executive of the Jubilee Guilds that negotiations had ceased and "the matter [was] closed for the time being" (Executive Minutes, June 13, 1940).

Resisting Relations of Ruling

While the struggle for control was being played out at the leadership levels of the Jubilee Guilds and the Co-operative Division, outport women were making use of both organizations in many different ways. Despite Lady Walwyn's fears, women appear to have suffered from no confusion about the work of each organization. Neil MacNeil makes this point to Commissioner Gorvin in early 1941 (PANL, GN 31/2, file #318, Volume I: MacNeil to Gorvin: March 4, 1941). Indeed, Co-operative records show overlapping participation in both Jubilee Guilds and Co-operative Women's Guilds, as well as in Co-operative Societies. In some cases, Jubilee Guild outport branches, as well as individual branch members, held memberships in local Co-operative Credit Unions. The Jubilee Guild branch in Change Islands, for example, held membership in the Viking Credit Union during the 1940s. In July 1941, the Registrar of Co-operatives described some of the other connections between the Jubilee Guilds and the Co-operative Movement in a letter to the manager of the Viking Credit Union.

The women were knitting socks, etc, and putting .25 cents on each dollar earned into shares. Members of the Guild were also members of the Credit Society...made 140 pairs of gloves. Junior members were learning about how to make these products... (Carter, 1989)

The Women's Clubs of the Riverhead, Harbour Grace Co-op reported lessons with the women of the local Jubilee Guilds branch given by Bertha Everson, the Co-operative Division Field Worker (Carter, 1989). Thus, handicraft training, production and co-operative saving were conducted together in some communities.

Sometimes women sold their handicraft production through the Co-operative

Division. For example, in 1939, Miss McCarthy, Co-operative Field Worker, received a letter from the Jubilee Guilds branch in Peter's River, asking her if she "would find a market for their articles, as the Jubilee Guilds could not perform this service for them" (PANL, GN 31/2, file #318, Volume 1: December 1, 1939). Apparently this was not an unusual request, for earlier notes on marketing the products of Women's Guilds state that "The number of Jubilee Guilds making things for sale is increasing, as more Guilds come to hear of the marketing Societies through Miss McCarthy" (PANL, GN 31/3A, C 10/11).

The Commission Government Land Settlements at Markland, Haricot and other locations were run on co-operative principles and Co-operative Women's Guilds were established in some of them. In 1941, Commissioner Gorvin described the use made of the Jubilee Guilds by women of the Point a Mal land settlement.

> In a recent report from Point a Mal which, with its 35 families, is, I suppose, the newest settlement in Newfoundland, I found mention of a meeting of all the women in the settlement in support of the Jubilee Guilds Movement, of a Guild social evening which resulted in an addition to the funds of the Guild, and of successful classes in cookery, weaving, sewing and home nursing. (PANL, GN 31/2, file #318, Volume 1)

Clearly, the outport women who were the targets of the programming efforts of both organizations were capable of using these programs to their material and economic benefit. Rural women were not deterred by the animosity between the Co-operative Division and the Jubilee Guilds, nor were they entirely shaped by the social, political or economic visions of either organization.

Conclusion

Neil MacNeil and the other Co-operative workers never succeeded in introducing "effective co-operation" into the Guilds' programming. Nor did the Co-operative Women's Guilds thrive in rural Newfoundland. The original Co-operative workers from Nova Scotia and the United States left Newfoundland in 1940-41, and the Commissioner of Natural Resources, John Gorvin, was recalled to England in a vice-regal move which Neary (1988) argues was calculated to please the business community in Newfoundland. The Jubilee Guilds continued instructing women in domestic arts and good citizenship. By 1947 over three thousand women were involved in one hundred and sixteen branches across Newfoundland.

The work of women in the Jubilee Guilds was a distinct and active part of state formation, contributing social and moral injunctions through their educational programs. This work helped to organize and regulate the lives of women at a time of tremendous upheaval in Newfoundland. A result may have been to eliminate any threat to "the status quo of sexual relations" and to reduce the possibility of women uniting to threaten political stability further by their demands (Crowley, 1986:81).

The Jubilee Guilds also furthered the economic rehabilitation aims of the Commission Government. Without this work, direct intervention in the form of costly social programs would have been required to better conditions for outport people. The Jubilee Guilds stepped into this vacuum, providing access to outport communities and families, an organizational structure, and an emphasis on self-help. The orientation of communities to self-help and the use of local resources to this end fit neatly into some Commission plans for the economic renewal of Newfoundland.

The different material and discursive practices of the Jubilee Guilds and the Co-operative Women's Guild organized their work with women differently. The Jubilee Guilds envisioned rural women as home-centred, nurturing wives and mothers accomplishing an urban, middle-class ideal of domesticity. This was in sharp contrast to the work of the Co-operative Women's Guilds, who saw women as economic subjects, capable of producing cash income for their families and participating actively in support of the Co-operative Movement. The range of options open to outport women, their agency in their lives, differed as a result.

Finally, class and gender relations in communities, and the organization of production and reproduction within families, also may have looked very different under these organizations. Quite specific, historical forms of social, economic and moral regulation were made possible by the work of these organizations. Ultimately, the conflict between the Jubilee Guilds and the Co-operative Women's Guild was over the form of social organization to be established in rural Newfoundland: one that did not challenge the status quo of merchant control and capitalist enterprise in the outports; or one that supported co-operative principles and economic structures outside the control of capitalist interests. Paradoxically, the material practices of these organizations dovetailed in ways that allowed rural women to combine the two organizations to achieve skill development, handicraft production and cash sale to benefit themselves and their families.

The work of these two women's voluntary organizations had consequences for the lives of women and communities. Through quite deliberate and thoughtful activities in the Jubilee Guilds, women struggled against, relied upon and contributed to state formation. The complex and contradictory relations between the Jubilee Guilds and the Commission Government are made visible in the process. It is also clear that outport women were not unresisting recipients of class-based educational programming. Instead, they actively used the organizations, skills, knowledges and opportunities available to them through the two organizations.

An organization is never only one kind of accomplishment; all organizations are contested spaces. My research on the Jubilee Guilds and the Co-operative Women's Guilds in Newfoundland and Labrador demonstrates that even the most unlikely organizations offer us ways of understanding and appreciating what women can do with the realities confronting them.

---

1 For a more detailed discussion see *Under Construction: Women. The Jubilee Guilds and Commission of Government in Newfoundland and Labrador, 1935-1941*, unpublished M.A. Thesis, Department of Sociology in Education, Ontario Institute for Studies in Education, University of Toronto, 1993.

Two Photographs

Isobel Brown

This personal essay, originally published in the anthology Digging into the Hill, *recounts a war bride's experience of her arrival in Newfoundland.*

As I TURNED THE OLD BRITTLE NEWSPAPERS in the A.C. Hunter Reference Library, a photograph caught my attention. A group of young women were crowding a ship's rail. They were a sombre group, grasping babies close, as they stared stonily into the lens of the camera. The white, unsmiling faces and the way they stood near each other suggested an ordeal over and apprehension for what lay beyond the camera and the newspapermen.

I looked at the picture. There I was, at the mid-deck rail, clutching my very travel-sick nine-month-old baby.

The ordeal we had all suffered had had its beginning in many places in Great Britain. Mine had been in Scotland. With other women, I had travelled to Liverpool, England to sail to St. John's, Newfoundland. In common, we shared regrets and unhappiness at leaving home, but also the excitement of at last being on our way to join our husbands, all ex-servicemen. I now recalled leaving the dockside in Liverpool to a band playing Will Ye No Come Back Again and Auld Lang Syne. I'd fled to the cabin to weep into the shoulder of my unconcerned baby.

The rough seas off Ireland, the layover in an Irish sea loch while engine repairs were made, and the March winds that chased us westward and which were a constant presence in our shipboard life are all now a kaleidoscope of memories of the trans-Atlantic crossing. Time, too, was a problem: babies stubbornly ate and slept on British time, while we, the mothers, had to contend with ship-scheduled meals. There was also a problem with the cabins, many of which had three-tier bunks. The S.S. *Scythia* had been a troop carrier and had not been altered for civilian passengers, which included over a hundred children. There was, I remember, a salon made over as a creche with a stewardess in charge. But few used it as babies were too upset by the strangeness of everything.

A major setback arose when the word got around that the ship was not going to St. John's, Newfoundland as expected — indeed promised — but would sail on to Halifax, Canada. Spirits at once hit bottom. Like myself, the other women were worn out from seasickness, lack of sleep, and total care of the children. And though representation was made direct to the captain, we, in fact finally landed, storm-delayed, at Halifax.

There I watched, in envy, the women with older children land and proceed by bus to hotels for an overnight stop before making connections with the Gulf ferry for Port aux Basques and the Transcontinental Train — the posh name given to the Newfie Bullet. I envied those women their night in a non-moving bed so much it hurt. I was to be transferred from the *Scythia* to the Newfoundland coastal steamer, the S.S. *Baccalieu*, and sail immediately for Newfoundland. The powers-that-be had decided that the quicker they got the women who were pregnant or had babies under a year old out of Canada and over to Newfoundland, the better it would be. I

109

remember the rush to claim trunks that had been brought up from the hold and watched in horror as one of the nets swinging the luggage over to the dock gave way. I saw one of my trunks crash onto the dock, burst open and spill the contents into the harbour water.

On board the coastal steamer, I took one look at the below-deck accommodation and declared war on the authorities that were pushing me around. The newspaper I'd just read had a report which stated, "The accommodation was ample; each woman had a bed of her own." A bed of her own? To share with a child in a cabin with three other women and their children! I refused to go below and instead wedged my child's travelling cot between the chairs which were chained to the deck and the long leather-cushioned bench that ran the width of the smoke room. I intended to stay, sleep if I could, above decks 'til I reached Newfoundland.

The sea passage is now a memory of fear, stench and total willingness to die. Off Cape Race, the same storm that delayed our arrival in Halifax lay in wait, as had been forecast by the weather people. The *Baccalieu* fought all night, against driving snow and gale-force winds, for sea room. Winds which seemed bent on driving the boat into the coastal cliffs. I found out later that the same storm pulled down electrical poles, leaving St. John's without light for over five hours. Passengers, and the crew not needed on deck, were battened down below, while in the saloon, I and the other rebels found out why the chairs were chained. My fear of the sea and the storm became terror when some of those chains gave way and the chairs careened back and forth as the *Baccalieu* was broadsided by the North Atlantic Ocean.

I decided that the safest place for my baby was in the travelling cot. I sat on the bench holding onto the cot, and at the height of the storm, we slid back and forth the width of that smoke room. I can remember being so violently seasick that the little container handed out at Halifax overflowed, and there were no replacements available. A woman in the smoke room went hysterical with fear, and her mind went back to some terrible tragedy in her life. In her hysterics, she thought I was somebody who was watching the drowning of someone in her family. She grabbed me and pushed me in: in, for her, was a canal as she screamed, "Save him! Save him!" but for me it was the spilled vomit that sluggishly moved back and forth on the deck. The rancid smell and taste of vomit and the fetor of babies' unchanged diapers filled the air of that tightly sealed room. The sea I saw submerge the portholes could have been on a movie screen for all the fresh salt sea air that penetrated to me. I have memories of the volunteer nurse who was barred in with us, of her always comforting someone or some baby the whole long hours of the storm.

When dawn came, the grey sky and sullen seas did nothing to restore my spirits. Out on deck, away from that terrible stinking room, I met the women who had been battened down below. They, too, were trying to get fresh air into the lungs of their children and themselves. When they related their tales, I was glad I stayed in the smoke room. Later, after breakfast, we again huddled on deck. I think, like myself, the other women felt, if only we could sight St. John's, we'd be safe, but the ice-streaked cliffs now looming on the horizon held no welcome for us nor did the distant cliff-perched lone lighthouse and tower. Then someone cried, "Good God! Look at those wooden shacks and platforms — that can't be St. John's, can it?" For a moment the silence of total disbelief held us all. Where was the city of streetcars, cinemas, shops and parks we had all been talking about, the friendly busy city our husbands had promised us we'd live in. In my mind, I heard again the remarks of various friends and relatives, "He's a stranger." "What do you really know about him?" "Foreign soldiers tell tall tales."

Then the *Baccalieu* steeped inwards and passed the Outer Battery with its storeroom and fish flakes, past Fort Amherst and the Cabot Tower and through the Narrows of St. John's Harbour.

It was as I and the others stared at the approaching dock crowded with people, strangers staring at strangers, that the first newspaper photograph had been taken.

Then, as the *Baccalieu* tossed lines ashore, husbands were seen, and the second newspaper photograph was taken, of smiling, waving women whose tears and fears were forgotten in the excitement of reunions.

I remember my husband yelling, "What's wrong with the baby?" and I replied, "She was very ill — seasick — we need a doctor right away." Other husbands and wives were saying more or less the same thing while the boat's loudspeaker was blaring, "Your wives have to go through Customs. Do not come on board until you are called. You will be called in time to help your families disembark." The voice was still saying this as the men, including my husband, stormed on board and took us off, leaving our luggage to the Customs officers.

So some of the war brides of World War II, as we were dubbed, came ashore to St. John's. I have no distinct memory of the rest of that day. The doctor was called and sedated the baby and me. They told me I slept 24 hours, but then I was ready to explore the city. A city which held many cultural shocks for me. Wooden houses, and in March '46, lots of soot-grimed snow and horse-drawn carts (with runners), delivering coal and goods. The wee single-decked streetcars instead of the double-decked stream-lined, fast-moving tram cars of Glasgow. The policemen on points duty — not just at Prescott Street — with their tall fur caps and long, Prussian-styled great-coats. All this reminded me of pictures of Victorian towns and times. The family-owned shops — I learned to call them stores — lined both sides of Water Street. Bowring's floorwalker in black suit and bow tie welcomed and directed me to the shoe department where I bought my first pair of winter overshoes. They had fur tops. The town itself was small by my Glasgow standards, and while a bustling place, it was very dirty. Winter furnaces had all the buildings soot- and smoke-grimed, but I was promised that after the spring clean-up, I would love the place with its fresh-painted houses and gardens, so I reserved my judgement.

Food was another shock to me. It was March, and most people in St. John's were enjoying their first feed of flippers as the sealers came home. I didn't even know seal flippers were fit to eat. Seal pelts for coats, yes, but eat the flippers? Never! Salt fish was a Waterloo for me. I chopped a piece off the fish and tried to fry it. Fish and brewis assaulted my nose and stomach, but banana splits soothed me and my ruffled taste buds and corned beef and cabbage became an acquired favourite scoff.

Of the promised cinemas, there were six in those days, and the parks blossomed as spring became summer almost overnight. The Peter Pan statue in Bowring Park was worn as smooth by children's hands and feet as the one I'd climbed in Kensington Park in London. I stood or sat by the bandstand in Bannerman Park, listening to the various band concerts, as I would have done back home, and I felt my kinship with St. John's and its people grow.

St. John's people always had a helping hand for a war bride; our accents broadcast loud and clear our identity, and in the stores they went out of their way to help. I went shopping for a teapot, and in the manner of Glasgow, asked for a six-cup teapot. The gentle reply was, "Oh, my dear, a teapot will give you as many cups of tea as you want to pour water in," and I felt the elderly man wanted to pat my head, in sympathy, I think, for my husband saddled with such an ignoramus.

I think it was the birth of my second child in the Grace Hospital that made me a St. John's "townie." I'd scorned the idea of having a baby in what I considered a small cottage hospital and had planned to go home for proper medical attention. I failed to inform the unborn baby of my plans. After the birth, I realized I was the mother of a born Newfoundlander, and thought, surely this makes me a "Newfie."

Over the years, St. John's and I have grown large in lots of ways. The city now has super highways and ring roads. Highrise stone apartment blocks and four large medical complexes. Shopping malls and fancy restaurants now stand in what were fields around St. John's in '46.

Also, over the years, I've grown to love St. John's and call it home and its people my friends. I looked again at the second newspaper photograph of laughing, smiling young women reaching eagerly for the new life waiting ashore, and I realize for me and most of the women, the photograph was prophetic. Even the woman who miscarried after her hysterics stayed on to rear a family of St. John's "townies."

Urbanizing Women Military Fashion: The Case of Stephenville Women

Cecilia Benoit

Introduction

IN 1979, WHEN I FIRST TALKED TO WOMEN IN STEPHENVILLE, some called it a "Welfare Town." Nearly half the families on government assistance were headed by single mothers living in the apartment blocks of lower-class housing built in the early 1970s. Some single mothers were as young as fourteen. Others were grandmothers. In addition, there were widows, divorced women and deserted women. Most of them still saw marriage as their only alternative to social assistance.

There were also women in Stephenville who were both wives and mothers. Many could still remember their rural past, while others recalled their recently deserted military community. Some were young wives and mothers from other industrial towns in Newfoundland, with different memories of their pasts. Whatever their origins, however, these married women typically had one thing in common: economic dependence on husbands. It was the husband who "worked". The wife, meanwhile, was expected to take care of the house and kids, and, moreover, to comfort her male partner when he returned from his day of paid labour. If he was unemployed, a wife performed her usual domestic labour and, in addition, had to console her often depressed husband. Both groups of mothers — married and single — had their domestic labour in common. Their children (and husbands, if they were married) had to be tended upon. The labour force was thus maintained every day, in every generation.

In retrospect, we might say that the joys and burdens of mothering have changed little with urbanization. As late as 1980, women residing in this particular urban environment had limited choices and tended to depend on men or the State for survival needs. What in the 1940s appeared to be the path to freedom from patriarchal control — wage labour "military fashion" — proved to be crowded with barriers similar to those hindering rural women's emancipation.

This paper is part of a larger work on the conjunction of poverty and mothering in a single Newfoundland community (Benoit, 1981). That case study examined the positive and negative aspects of women's lives in both a rural and urban context.

The particular focus here is on the implications of rapid urban development for women in one community. I attempt to point out why, when I last conversed with them in 1980, so many women in this town were ghettoized in the labour market. At the same time, I attempt to explain the specific problems of single mothers dependent on social assistance. Forced to reside in the most economically depressed areas of their urban environment, many of these Stephenville women are aware that they are treated unfairly and, in their own way, are able to explain their fate:

There's a lot of women like myself here in this row of apartments, some like myself deserted and left stranded with the kids to rear up alone, and some more never married and already with youngsters to feed and clothe on welfare handouts. God only knows what their lives are going to be like when their kids are gone and the welfare dries up. The government is not going to look out for them, you can rest assured about that. The Premier don't give a sweet damn about the women herded here in these wooden shacks. We're here just to bring up kids, that's all.

(Single mother, born 1946)

Methods and Data Collection

The focus of this paper is to develop a sociological understanding of mothering — as an institution and as a personal encounter — in one historical instance, as experienced by the women themselves. The time span is 1941-1980, with particular emphasis on the years between 1941 and the late 1960s. The research site is Stephenville, my former hometown, located on the West Coast of Newfoundland.

I chose Stephenville for a number of reasons: 1) I knew many of the older women and believed that their oral accounts of life in Stephenville prior to WWII and during military occupation would be valuable in trying to understand women's position in relation to the historical movement from rural to urban life; 2) I also knew a number of younger women who had grown up with me in the area and had since married and had families; 3) I was aware that the town was one of the main areas in the province where single mothers had been recently ghettoized; and 4) I had decided that in order to understand the problems of other Newfoundland women, I had to also re-examine my own past, in part by renewing relations with my mother and female kin, but also by taking a closer look at my male relatives to see precisely how deeply gender inequality was embedded within my own family.

By use of the "snowball technique," informal tape-recorded interviews were conducted with thirty women and ten men (respondents' ages ranged from 18-65 years) from May to September 1980. Whenever husbands and wives were interviewed together, separate time was allotted for each. This was because my male and female respondents, even those tied by the marital bond, were generally reluctant to comment on "private affairs" (including sexuality, birth control, childbirth) in the presence of the other gender. The interviews ranged from one to two hours, and some respondents were interviewed a second time. Census data and other archival materials, in addition to anthropological studies on the topic, were utilized to complement the transcribed interview data. The analysis presented below focuses on the qualitative aspects of the oral history gathered. This work is descriptive, therefore, rather than conclusive in character.

The Emerging Urban Setting

In 1941, the United States government selected the area locally known in Stephenville as "Back-the-Pond" to construct an airforce base. The Americans needed the town as a stopover and refuelling point for trans-Atlantic flights, since it was ideally

114

located between the United States and Europe, and also because the area was virtually free of fog year-round (Straus, 1967: 555-560).

When this relatively huge project was initiated, many of the adult males from the still-intact village were working as migrant labourers, after years of unemployment throughout the Great Depression of the 1930s. Some local men had signed up as lumberjacks overseas. Others had gone back to the Newfoundland lumberwoods. A few single women from the village had migrated to the nearby city of Corner Brook to work in service, now that the paper town was again providing employment after the slow years of the Depression.

Married women, however, continued, as had always been the case, to stay home on the farm with the older folks and the children. Many of the single girls were left behind as well, keeping things going while the men were away "following the work." Isolation from the outside world remained an essential characteristic of their existence, and most women — young and old alike — took for granted that women did not go "out to work". Their station in life was to labour but not to bring in a wage or have money of their own. Their work day centred around the household and gardens, the children and the men.

The announcement of the Americans' arrival took these women and their families completely by surprise:

> I figured things were going to go back to normal again after the Depression. But they came here and forced us out, just like that. The first time we heard anything about the "change" was one day when this government fellow came to the house. The whole crowd of us had been out picking berries on the bog all day and when we came home he was there, knocking like mad on the door. You should have seen him, my dear. All slicked-up like he was going to a garden party or something. The rest of the men, except for Pop, were away at the wood. He asked to speak to the man of the house, so we knew straight off that something serious had come. He told us that, just like that, we were supposed to pack up and move. Pop was some mad — fit to be tied, he was. It wasn't that we didn't have lots of problems already with the kids and trying to make ends meet. Pop argued till he was blue in the face, but what could we do? The government was always deaf when it came to poor people saying how they felt. Looking back on it now, what I say is that if they had made things any better it would have been fine. But I can't say me or my family got a lot out of it.
>
> (Housewife, born 1910)

Almost overnight the people of this nearly century-old village lost their farms, property, and rural way of life. Most families had lived for three generations off the land and from the sea, with the men occasionally working in the woods and bringing in a meagre wage. Stephenville women had performed the necessary labour involved in reproducing the labour force on a daily and generational basis for over eighty years. Now, with the War and the coming of the Americans, things were about to change in ways that were completely foreign to their usual way of looking at the world. As the women point out themselves, the resulting changes in their lives were a mixed blessing.

They took everything in two lots. It was some sad, my dear. I used to live in the most beautiful spot behind the pond. There was this lake with lovely sea trout and just right for swimming on hot days. There was something about the fresh air and homegrown stuff that was really good for the bones. Anyway, after the Base came and we had to push off, it wasn't the same any more. We still worked like horses in the house and had just as many kids, if not more than our mothers. But there was no time to go at the spinning wheel or get a crowd of women over to card your wool. They bulldozed most of the houses, 'cause we didn't even know where we wanted them moved. God only knows how much got left by the wayside. The last family was the Gabreils. The old man put up some stink, but they uplifted him all the same. He died right away after that, leaving his woman with a whole brood. Ten, I think, there was of them. I can tell you this much, the government didn't do anything to help out that poor widow — just turned the other cheek. The poor soul found a place near the church after that. She lived her days on ten dollars every few months till her oldest girl got big enough to stay home so that she could go housekeeping for the Americans.

(Housewife, born 1904)

Most of the others from Back-the-Pond resettled themselves in much the same way as this widow, packing their belongings, children and memories, finding a piece of land, and starting all over again. The other areas of Stephenville also underwent considerable change, not the least because of the influx of hundreds of labourers, American servicemen, and single women from all over the Colony to serve in the mess halls.

Wage Labour and Domestic Labour

As discussed in detail elsewhere (Benoit, 1981; Benoit, 1990), wage labour had never been a realistic alternative for rural Stephenville women. In general, this was true for most Newfoundland women up to World War II. In all the small outports which dotted the coastline north and south of Stephenville, labouring women had been restricted in much the same way, expected to labour in the gardens, rear the children and tend to the various needs of the men, and often tend to the fish as well. When the call for single women to work in the mess halls was issued throughout the village and surrounding areas, this seemed like a once-in-a-lifetime opportunity to many young women. For one thing, the wages they were offering a "girl" — about eight dollars a week — were previously unheard of. Even domestic work, which rarely paid more than four to six dollars a month, was in no way comparable to this new wage work opportunity. Moreover, working privately in service to some Corner Brook woman carried with it the added disadvantage that the domestic servant was forced to live with her employer and, hence, had little or no control over her work day and no voice in determining the range of her duties.

Now, with the arrival of the Americans, things were different. For example, the work week was defined — Monday to Saturday, with every second weekend free. In addition, work hours were known to the wage earner before she began a job. Finally, living accommodations were better, now that all the mess hall workers (except for the local village women) were together under one roof. Of course, the

116

Matron of the dormitory was strict and hard to take at times, but considering the other option of domestic work, the mess hall job definitely had many advantages.

The job market for single women, and even married women who could somehow arrange private daycare, was relatively good during the war years. Stephenville women remember that the Americans were "crying out" for women to take waitress work and house cleaning jobs. Yet, as I shall show below, the complex status of these female wage earners (from Stephenville itself and from surrounding outports) cannot be analyzed by merely counting how many single and married women found employment. It is important to realize that the labour market was still rigidly segregated along gender lines: women were seldom promoted or granted pay increases. Moreover, they were rarely awarded an opportunity to learn trades or to unionize. Through the Newfoundland Federation of Labour, the average Newfoundland male working as a labourer on the Base during this period was able to avail of many of these options. Furthermore, women's wages were still far below those of their male relatives. For example, while the average Newfoundland male labourer received 40 cents per hour, his Canadian counterpart received, on an average, $1.20 per hour. By contrast, the average Newfoundland woman serving in the Mess Halls received $8 per week, while her Canadian counterpart received 60 cents per hour. (Source: Review of Man-Hours and Hourly Earnings: 1945-1958. *Dominion Bureau of Statistics*, Labour Division, Canada, October, 1959). The dual conditions of low wages and restrictive living conditions under the control of matrons meant that it was virtually impossible for these women to survive financially outside of marriage. This becomes particularly clear when we realize the added problems associated with their gender: sexual harassment, rape, lack of effective birth control and safe abortion, and a loss of many of their former female supports as well. The women remember these contradictions:

> They came from all over this part of the coast. Women from the Northern Peninsula even came down here looking for a chance to earn a buck more than working domestic in the paper town [Corner Brook]. Some worked like myself for a while, in the mess hall serving the GIs and Newfoundland boys. Some other non-married girls went to work as barmaids in the NCO Club or the tavern. Some more ended up minding and keeping house for the bigshot Americans, like the officers and majors. They had their families brought all the way from the States. And the best looking girls got special pay for working in the offices, bookkeeping and typing. As you might guess, we never even knew what a typewriter looked like before the War, so there was no worrying, the best jobs were not for us. The real truth of the matter was that most of the Newfoundland girls from around here, not being able to afford fancy clothes and make-up and that stuff, and with strong Catholic upbringing besides, were never able to get a hell of a lot more than work at domestic chores. When all you ever did in your everyday life was have kids and look out to them and do your garden and housework, then it's not surprising that everybody figured that's all you were made for.
>
> (Mess hall worker, born 1916)

Despite the relatively higher wages and the formal freedom, the new economic opportunities available during the early 1940's were not exactly "revolutionary." One might argue that these women served as a reserve army of labour, drawn on during the war years when many males were overseas, and the American government as well as the "Mother Country" [Britain] needed military bases and women to serve the men who built and maintained these bases.

Single women working on the Base experienced sex segregation on the job market and lacked opportunities to live independently. For married Stephenville women whose children were in school, or who went to work during the night as cleaning ladies or laundresses, the general outcome was the "double shift." The gap between women's work in the home (increasingly seen as women's private sphere) and the wider public world of wage labour in rural Stephenville had become increasingly rigid. But now women, particularly married women, became economically dependent on males to an even greater degree. At the same time, these women were increasingly forced to make ends meet by taking part-time or piece work, typically for very low wages and under extremely poor conditions (*Census of Newfoundland*, 1945). This was particularly true for most widowed and separated women, and both groups of women were becoming larger.[1]

The other side of the relegation of women to the private domain of housework and child care was that these activities became idealized as the primary occupations of married women. In rural Stephenville most women had considered themselves, in addition to mothers and wives, to be weavers and spinners, gardeners and berry pickers, and less frequently, midwives and herbalists. Now, however, they increasingly saw themselves as "just housewives." Mothers, whether married or not, and whether doing paid labour or not, had to bear the brunt of child care and housework within isolated households. It was not mere coincidence, then, that labour in the home no longer was accorded the recognition of "real work." Relatively few women in the village had the necessary land, tools, family networks, and time away from children and work inside the house to perform the important productive activities they had formerly taken for granted. In addition, many of their domestic skills (which had been fundamental to the survival of the extended family in rural Stephenville) diminished in importance as cheaper consumer goods became more readily available:

> Perhaps the worst time for me was when the Base was in full swing during the War. When I was sixteen I left home and went to work for my uncle. I was after getting pregnant and the old man said he couldn't afford to keep me any longer. I stayed on there for five years, never so much as getting a bloody cent for my work. Then I heard tell of the Base in Stephenville and so I packed it all in and went to work in the Mess Hall. I never had seen so many fellows in all my born days. You should have seen some of the other girls. Poor things, so young and still wet behind the ears. They didn't know fellows lied so much, telling them that they was going to marry them and take them back to the States, or some place or other in Newfoundland, if they was native fellows. Being Catholic, and the priest outrightly refusing to marry you to an American or a Protestant, didn't help much

either. How many of them went home to their mothers with a little one on the way! God only knows how many of them got led astray. Me, I met a half decent fellow from Stephenville who was first a lumberjack and then went on construction. Once you started having your family, there was no hear tell of a married woman with young babies going out to work full-time.

(Mess Hall worker, born 1916)

Stephenville women had never expected a lot of help from husbands or other male kin when their society was rural. But at least they had the option to seek support and a helping hand from female relatives in the same situation as themselves. Now, with single women drawn into the labour force and their female kin scattered by resettlement, their daily labour as wives and mothers became more monotonous and far more isolated.

It was a mother's job to look after the babies and keep the food on the table, there's no getting around that. And you had to pretty well do it all on your own, 'cause your relatives were so far away and you couldn't get a serving girl, no matter how hard you tried. Can you believe it, my dear, but I had all my children, the ten of them, home, here in this very house without a woman apart from the midwife, to help me out? Everyone in the family was on some kind of schedule: my husband started at seven in the morning; the youngsters in school had to be sent off by nine; and then the younger ones and the new baby would start in. The Lord must have been guiding me somehow... those Americans, from what I heard tell, were a hard lot. They only were interested in using the people for workers, and the women for a good time, and then they wouldn't look at you after. They were all the time "buttering up" the girls with cheap cigarettes and alcohol. There was lots of chances to be mothers but not a hell of a lot of men around interested in marrying a local girl... Mind you, being a married woman had its trials as well.

(Housewife, born 1916)

For perhaps the first time in their lives, some of the women from Stephenville and the surrounding outport communities had a chance to earn a wage. This paid labour was generally a mere extension of their daily labour within the household, but a little money was better than no money at all. Still, these jobs for women were created because cheap labour was needed for the menial tasks involved in maintaining a transient group of single men. And because women's wages were so low in comparison to those of men, Stephenville women had little opportunity to avoid dependency in marriage.

Sexuality and Marriage

The American presence did little to change the age-old matrix of practices linking marriage, family, sexuality and procreation. Marriage arrangements in rural Stephenville had seldom been what one might call "love partnerships." As I have argued elsewhere (Benoit, 1990), women often married to escape dependence on male kin, and the only option open to them was marriage. The notion of romantic love was all but unheard of for many of them, as was the understanding that sexuality could somehow be disassociated from motherhood.

When the U.S. Airbase was built during WWII, however, the practices of the "good Catholic girls" who found paid work at the mess halls and clubs were gradually seen as "corny" and "old-fashioned." The religious ideology of female virginity and asexual motherhood was now called into question. Instead of the girls going to Church every Sunday and every other evening for prayers, male workers promised them a good time "with no strings attached."

At this historical juncture, both the American and Newfoundland men living in their separate barracks were largely transient workers. The last thing on most of their minds was the establishment of family households. But they were lonely, and probably sick to death of working, eating and sleeping in the same living quarters as other men just like themselves. After their shift was over and the evening meal eaten, there was little else to do but gamble, drink, and try to find female companions. Members of this peripheral workforce competed for the local women, but refused to deal with the consequences of their actions. One female informant put it like this:

> The civilian fellows weren't a hell of a lot better than the GIs [American males] when it came down to it, my dear. What we had was the "Yanks" pulling on one arm and the local fellows pulling on the other, fighting hand and fist over who *owned* the local women. They weren't so keen to fight over the hundreds of little ones that came out of it all.
>
> (Housewife, born 1925)

As this quotation reveals, the seamy side of paid labour was the emergence of new social and sexual problems for women. Although rural Stephenville women had known illegitimacy, desertion and spinsterhood, the women unable to enter into a suitable marriage at least had some protection within their families and community. However, after WWII, single motherhood, it can be argued, became institutionalized. The U.S. government certainly did not want its servicemen marrying local girls and settling down in Newfoundland. Moreover, many of the American male workers already had wives in the United States. But somehow the men had to be entertained. Cheap cigarettes and liquor were partly the answer, and the chance for the average guy to have a woman for a night or for the length of his stay on the Island was another way of satisfying the men. Thus, condoms were handed out and the men were instructed to "watch out for themselves." The civilian workers, as well, were often given this method of birth control so that they could satisfy sexual needs without worrying about consequences.

The Census of 1945 shows that the illegitimacy rate, nevertheless, jumped from a little over 27 percent at the end of the Depression to a high of 53 percent during the War. While the marriage rate increased in many parts of the Island during this period, in the Stephenville area it was not much higher than in previous years and throughout the 1930's (*Census of Newfoundland*, 1945). Many of the local people were quite upset with what was happening to their female relatives and to the other migrant women who had come in search of work. As yet, there were no welfare payments for single women, except for the meagre ten dollars every two months allotted to widows without family income. The situation of single women with illegitimate offspring, often unable to point to the child's father, was an extremely complicated one — for fathers of the single mothers, for the local priest, and for the Newfoundland and American governments as well.

Yet no consideration was given to the idea that some single mothers might want to go back to wage work; might want to remain sexually active, but not have another child; and might not want to be dependents of men or the State. Social services such as daycare, effective birth control and abortion, in addition to equal pay for equal work, were not even side issues at this point. With the war coming to a close, with veterans returning home looking for work, and with the employment-generating construction phase at the Airbase over, reproductive freedom for women would have been disastrous. Instead, the U.S. government between WWII and Confederation in 1949 allotted social welfare benefits to those mothers who "got taken for a ride," as one woman described it. Most girls who ended up pregnant were, in fact, pressured to return home to their outport communities or, as in the case of Stephenville single mothers, to live with their families. Few women were needed in the mess halls after 1945. Even women with someone to care for their children were not able to find full-time work. Some found temporary work as baby sitters and come-by-day servants. Generally, though, both single and married women were no longer needed as cheap labourers. It was much easier for the state to provide these women with some minimum social benefits, for example, a Baby Bonus or a Mother's Allowance, than to provide jobs, daycare, and to satisfy other needs of specific importance to their lives.

Growth and Development

In 1949, Joey Smallwood led Newfoundland into Confederation with Canada, basing his political campaign on two interrelated issues: full employment (for males) and the Baby Bonus (for mothers). It was somehow assumed that if both could be realized, Newfoundland would become an advanced society like others in the Western world.

A year later, the American government decided that, in contrast to the other bases it had established during the war, the Stephenville Airbase would be developed and used as a tanker centre for aerial refuelling. It was therefore assumed that the expansion of the existing facilities meant that the Americans were going to stay for good this time. Hence, there would be a need for two groups of wage labourers: a stratum of temporary construction workers, similar to the group of Newfoundlanders hired during WWII, and a more regularly employed stratum. This two-tier system necessitated once again that women be hired to service the construction workers and, furthermore, that permanent workers be able to marry, settle down in Stephenville, build houses, and feel part of a family and community after their day's work. There would be a need for housewives and mothers to maintain husbands and sons commuting to the Airbase to earn a wage.

According to the older Stephenville women, within a few years it was impossible to recognize the place. All signs of rural life were completely erased, replaced on the Base by rows of duplex family units to house the Americans, and, in the town, by cheaper apartment buildings constructed by local merchants. Stephenville became the fastest growing area on the Island. By 1960, it had a population of nearly 12,000. The local Catholic hierarchy had done well, with a large school, recreational facilities, and a new church. Other denominations also became established. An Anglican Church was constructed and a public school built to educate Protestant children. On the Airbase, a well-equipped private hospital for the American families was constructed during the 1950s, while a cottage hospital was built in the vicinity of the town to serve the civilian population. Private clubs, banquet halls and other middle-class amenities were set up on the Harmon Complex. In the town, public taverns, beer halls, pool rooms and dancing clubs sprang up. Shops and banks were opened. Finally, in more and more houses, electricity and modern water and drainage systems were installed. Of course, various taxes were levied in order to maintain these advantages of town living.

The Working Class Housewife

Other expectations of the local people remained unrealized. Most importantly, perhaps, there were few permanent jobs, since most had gone to male workers from elsewhere who had settled in Stephenville with their families during the 1950s. Local males who had worked briefly and sporadically on the Airbase and at construction work in the town once again had to "follow the movement of capital" — to mainland Canada, to Labrador or wherever else they could find work. Moreover, the mess halls were now closed and the few service jobs in the town were taken up by the better skilled women and men from outside the province:

> My husband tried his hand at it all. He worked in the lumberwoods, tried fishing lobsters, and learned a trade on the Base. But he never had much of a chance to stay around. He worked with the Americans for a few years but permanent jobs were as scarce as hen's teeth for local fellows. Our bungalow was a good three miles away from any relatives. I was alone with the kids three parts of the time. The only time I really saw other people was when I went to Church or grocery shopping. Some days I recall not going outside the door except to hang the clothes or put out the garbage. I'd be up by six or so in the morning to warm the baby's bottle. Then I'd get the youngsters up for school. I had seven in there all at once. If I had a dollar for every bun of bread I made in my time, I'd be well off today. I went through a hundred pound bag of flour every week, and that's not one word of a lie. Sometimes I had to use the whole Baby Bonus to buy the week's groceries and let the kids go to school with hand-me-downs. We had it rough enough.
> (Housewife, born 1911)

Women's domestic duties had indeed changed by 1960. Consumer goods, neatly packed on grocery store shelves and in shopping centres, had replaced the homegrown vegetables and fresh milk "straight from the cow." Expensive restaurants, take-outs and catering services were now available to deliver prepared food, fresh laundry, and housekeeping services on request. At the modern hospital on the Airbase, middle-class women could take prenatal classes, have a physician deliver their baby, and seek out safe and effective birth control. To the "respectable" businessmen, shop owners, and service personnel, many of the options mentioned here were also available. Fraternity with the Americans gave them a status nearly equal to that of the local clergyman, priest and law officers. Unfortunately, for the economically disadvantaged Catholic housewife, the comforts of modern living made her feel like an outsider in her own community. While she no longer had a garden out back and a chance to get away from the house long enough to gather berries and driftwood for her stove, she still had her share of domestic labour. Yet now she was alone, or had at most an elder daughter helping out after school. There were no communal kitchens serving food to her youngsters, or daycare centres to give her a break from the kids, and restaurants, public laundries, and similar services were beyond her pocket book in any case. Instead, she bore a large family, went without monthly prenatal checkups, and served three meals a day. In between, she performed the various other reproductive labours necessary to educate her children and gain the status of a "good" working class housewife.

Women as Wards of the State

For single women — widows and women deserted, separated or divorced — it was nearly impossible to survive on the government's allotted social assistance. Some found work as part-time waitresses, housekeepers, and barmaids. Others supplemented their welfare payments with prostitution. For all of them, it was a daily struggle to keep their homes operating, their children clothed and fed and, finally, to deal with the psychological consequences accompanying their battle for survival:

> My marriage was a complete and utter disaster. I had three little ones before he took off to Toronto. I shouldn't have married him, but I hadn't a sweet clue at the time. My husband was a born alcoholic, I'm convinced of it. His head was a little strange. When he lived here with me and the kids, you couldn't get him to change a diaper. He said it was "women's work." When he'd take to the bottle, he'd hit on the kids or myself — whoever crossed his path. I guess he was half the time unemployed and bored out of his mind. After he left, we had to go on welfare for a while. I got about one hundred dollars for everything then: kids, apartment, food, heat. I never bought a stitch of clothes during those times. I later got a job as housekeeper when the kids were in school. God, I hated the woman who hired me. She was so brazen. She used to run her fingers, all painted up with polish on them, over the end table to see if I got all the dust. She treated me like an "old bag" because I had a family with no husband and I had no education. If it wasn't for lazy people like her, then women would not have to sell themselves. What I had to do wasn't much better, the way I look at it.
> (Separated mother, born 1925)

Most Stephenville widows faced similar financial problems as other women without men. If they received a widow's pension from the State, their family was expected to live on about half of what they had when their husbands were alive and working. Most of them had been married to men from Stephenville and surrounding areas who had been periodically unemployed and, when working for a wage, never stayed with one employer long enough to have a pension. The widows themselves, whose role as housewives had always been seen as their station in life, rarely worked long enough on the Base to earn a pension from employment. Their education level was low and their job options few and sporadic:

> I was a "war bride." I was left with seven to feed and clothe. I couldn't go out to work until the Base was swinging, for the simple fact that women in my situation were not needed outside their homes. Besides, it would have cost me more than I could have made to pay a serving girl. In 1960 I became a "working woman." Before that I got a welfare cheque that allowed me to put a can or two of soup on the supper table. Not much more. I was all alone with a bunch of half-starving kids. As soon as my oldest turned sixteen, the government cut away half of my allowance. So I had to find something. I first started as a sort of cleaning woman on the Base. I had to make 34 beds every day, shine and polish the floors, clean the blinds, and what have you. I used to get $68 every two weeks for my work with the Americans. It was like gold when you used to be living off nothing. Then I'd come home and do my own work.
>
> (Widow, born 1916)

By the mid-1960s, Stephenville's role as a "cash centre" had declined in importance. The Americans and the middle-class professionals who had resettled there throughout the 1950s and early 1960s, moved away. The United States military requirements had changed. The manned bomber was about to be phased out; hence, the Base was no longer necessary to the U.S. military. Consequently, in late December of 1966, the Airbase was closed and officially turned over to the provincial and federal governments. The population dropped to less than half of what it had been during the boom years. Those who rode the crest of the wave moved on to other places where there was still money to be made. Forty percent of the population which remained was of school age. The basic resources of the town — the sea, land and surrounding forests — had long been exploited by outside companies. Only five percent of the men still fished and only two percent were engaged in lumbering. Those who had been involved in maintenance and service at the Airbase now were grouped with the others (including women) who were unemployed. The unemployment rate for males was 43 percent in 1966 (Newfoundland Department, 1964). For females, the rate was almost 100 percent. As a result, nearly half the families were forced to go on government relief. Perhaps ironically, the main occupation of those still employed was that of social worker, the evasive State representative delegated to assist the people living near the poverty line.

The Americans had come and gone. They had left their vacated buildings on the Airbase. Shops and schools were now empty, and there were many single mothers trying to bring up children without help from either fathers or the U.S. military. Other women who had left returned a year or so later, after realizing that the "GI" they had married in Stephenville had another family south of the Canadian border. Some returned for other reasons — poverty, abuse, loneliness, isolation. Stephenville was now both a haven and a trap for poor women who were stranded with children, with inadequate schooling, living alone in small apartments where the Welfare Department kept a close eye on them. Stephenville was more than ever a "man's town." The rule against cohabitation was strictly enforced. Hence, nobody was allowed to live co-operatively with a friend, relative, or person in the same situation as themselves, no matter what their gender or job status. If a woman lived with her parents or if she boarded, she received a hundred dollars at most for herself and a child to pay rent, food, clothing and school books. If a single mother managed to convince the social worker that she "deserved" an apartment, she received a little more to cover heating expenses. But the money came with strings attached: once a son turned seventeen, his mother lost most of her benefits; if she accepted part-time or piece work, she had to subtract all her earnings from her cheque; if she had sick children or was unwell herself, the family just had to bear with it; and, finally, if any male — relative, friend, lover — stayed with her *any* length of time, government support for her and her children was discontinued:

> My first apartment the Welfare gave me and my three little ones cost me almost every cent they handed out. We were cramped into a one-bedroom place where you could almost see through the walls, no word of a lie. I worked at the Red Wood Lounge for a year after that. I had to punch ten to twelve days, all straight time. If I didn't, or complained to the Manpower Office, the buddy who employed me said he'd just fire me and hire some other girl in the same boat as I was. After this thing got real bad around Stephenville, I didn't even have a chance to work part-time. It was a ghost town, if I've ever seen one. So we had to go back on the welfare. The most we suffered from was the bad food, and not enough of it. I couldn't think about fresh vegetables and anything but canned milk for the youngsters. And the poor little things, they had to play right out in the main road. The whole bunch of us were in the same boat: half the time pregnant, Welfare people spying on you, and kids everywhere you looked.
>
> (Welfare mother, born 1946)

All these women — housewives, separated, widowed, divorced, and women never married — still did not enter the category of wage-earner. They became, instead, social problems — women "left over" after the Americans spilled out of Stephenville — and some eventually joined the social worker's caseload. Others were hidden away in private households while fathers and husbands left to earn their keep. Poverty was their story; domestic labour their domain. Motherhood was still compulsory and remained women's major avenue to social status.

Stephenville Women in 1980: Continuity or Change?

As described in detail elsewhere (Benoit, 1981), the people of Stephenville watched a variety of government-initiated projects open and close in the ensuing decade and a half. Despite industrial development and educational opportunities, the situation of local males reported in the preceding pages — low paying wage work followed by economic crisis and unemployment — remained their story. Similarly, the experiences of Stephenville women during this time paralleled those of their female forerunners: service work typically at, or just above, the minimum wage and usually without basic benefits such as maternity leave, child care facilities, and job security. Although these women had by 1980 gained some control over their fertility, typically by taking the "Pill" or undergoing tubal ligations, the local Catholic hierarchy continued to bar access to free and safe abortions.

Yet my female respondents had a positive side to their story that is worthy of note. By 1980, Stephenville women were beginning to articulate their opinions regarding gender issues previously hidden from public view: first, on the very notion of the male breadwinner as family provider; second, on the relationship between sexuality and procreation; third, on the notion that the working class family is based on harmony and consensus; fourth, on the Welfare State as *morally* concerned about the poor; fifth, on the common belief that certain institutions — the Catholic Church, the medical profession, the educational system, the political system and the law — work to help the majority of people; and, finally, on the assumption that women and politics do not go together.

In their own lives, many of my female respondents were slowly taking steps to break away from the common expectations assumed "natural" by their community. Some refused to be battered any longer and others filed for separation or divorce. Many were attempting to teach their own daughters the "ropes," discussing with them the hidden side of female sexuality which seldom gets exposure in the "Family Life Program" in the local Catholic high school. Some married women, and women living in other family arrangements, were even successful in getting their men to take an equal part in child rearing and to realize both the monotony and the pleasures of domestic labour.

Of course, many Stephenville women in 1980 were still isolated and lonely, not least because they were forced to mother in order to survive economically and psychologically. However, in my conversations with even these women, I found them expressing criticism of the State and its patriarchal structures. Stephenville women were increasingly aware of the fact that they were not the only community of women left out in the cold. Through various channels — television, newspapers, their children, women's groups around the Island, and perhaps most importantly, in each other's kitchens — they were discovering their allies and ways to change their situation. Indeed, most of them felt that urbanization, on balance, was in their best interests.

Don't forget, my dear, that it wasn't so very long ago that a woman in Stephenville wouldn't be caught dead with a pair of long pants on in public. And, what's else, she wouldn't be allowed to step inside the Church door if she didn't have her head covered up. Before this, if you were married, no matter if your fellow beat you black and blue, you had to stay with him. It was your religious duty as a wife. Now you can at least get out of a family mess. More and more women are saying what's on their mind, letting it come to the surface more. And some men are listening. Just the other day, I saw a young father with his baby in a carriage. It warmed me up inside. And my own fellow, who never lifted a finger around the house before this, has even taken to getting his own cup of tea. It's almost as good as a miracle. If *he* could change, I say that there's hope yet.

(Housewife, born 1916)

Conclusion

Despite signs of optimism, the prospects looked rather bleak when I said farewell to my female respondents in September, 1980. For these labouring women, though their lives had been drastically changed by urbanization, their particular reproductive problems had not been solved in any significant way. The majority of Stephenville women at this time were still defined as child bearers and child rearers and not as autonomous human beings. It is difficult to focus attention on change in other areas of women's subordination until the struggle for reproductive self-determination — for contraceptive rights, for child care, for natural childbirth, and against forced sterilization — has been won for all women.

1   In comparison to the situation of labouring women during the Depression years, by 1945 a number of things had changed. The death rate had decreased, and the birth rate showed a significant increase by 1945, from a low of 23 per 1,000 in 1934, to a high of 36.3 in 1945. The marriage rate, at least in the area under study, had not risen significantly since the Depression years. In fact, the illegitimacy rate had nearly doubled in the ten-year period. Thus, we can assume that the number of single mothers increased during the war.

Moving Forward

W E HAD HOPED to complement Forestell's analysis of women in manufacturing with an account of the development of nursing and other professional activities in Newfoundland in the early twentieth century. Unfortunately, in this, as in some other cases, the author was unable to produce an article within our time-frame. Readers interested in research on midwifery and early nursing should consult (among other sources) Cecilia Benoit's *Midwives in Passage*, Joyce Nevitt's *White Caps and Black Bands* and Linda White's *The General Hospital School of Nursing, St. John's, Newfoundland, 1903-1930*.

For Catholic women, a version of "professional" status could be achieved by becoming nuns. The history of the Presentation and Mercy sisters in Newfoundland is explored in Whitaker (this volume). Women's work as domestics in St. John's between the wars is explored in Forestell (1987), and their work as domestics in the "Boston States" is discussed in Smith (1984).

Cecilia Benoit's paper on Stephenville extends into the post World War II era, inviting us to look critically at the "modernization" schemes associated with this era and their impact on women. Her discussion of post World War II Stephenville highlights the vulnerability of women caught in development processes shaped by the requirements of the military. This theme returns in a somewhat different form in the paper by Evie Plaice, "Honourable Men." Critical perspectives on government and corporate policies and their impact on women's lives permeate the papers on the Newfoundland fishery since World War II. Miriam Wright examines federal fisheries policy and Bonnie McCay looks at women plant workers in Fogo. Jane Robinson looks critically at the industrial and training policies that accompanied the closure of the Trepassey fish plant in the early 1990s. And views of the fishery over time are encapsulated in Anne Hart's poem.

Women, Men and the Modern Fishery: Images of Gender in Government Plans for the Canadian Atlantic Fisheries

Miriam Wright

W OMEN'S ROLE IN THE HISTORY OF THE NEWFOUNDLAND FISHERY has been a long-neglected area of scholarly research. While the fishing people of Newfoundland have long been aware of the contribution that wives, sisters and daughters made to the economic and social life of the island, only in the past fifteen years have academics and other writers begun to examine the gender dynamics in Newfoundland's economy (Antler, 1977; Porter, this volume). Historically, women were not insignificant participants in the fishery; census data for 1891, 1910, 1911 and 1921 (when Dominion census takers stopped recording women involved in the fishery) indicated that women consisted of over 40% of the fisheries labour force (McCay, this volume). In the inshore, salt fishery that dominated the Newfoundland economy before Confederation with Canada in 1949, women customarily performed the shore work—curing, drying and salting the fish, while the men, either singly or in small fishing crews, caught the fish. In the years following Confederation, however, as Newfoundland's fishing economy underwent substantial changes, womens' relationship to the fishery also changed, although the reasons for these changes, and the way they occurred is not yet fully understood.

Newfoundland's fishery underwent two major shifts after 1949. One was a transition from an emphasis on saltfish production to frozen fish, as many of the older St. John's merchant houses withdrew from the fishing industry, while several frozen fish processing companies began expanding operations. The second change was in the area of government management of the fishery. Confederation brought with it a transfer of jurisdiction from Newfoundland to Ottawa, with the federal government taking control of all sea fisheries, inspections, research and development, shore facilities and exports, and the provincial government retaining control of processing, labour relations and education (Over the years, however, there has been considerable overlap in the two jurisdictions). Yet, the biggest change was not the mere transfer of jurisdiction, but a change in the scale and scope of government intervention in the fishery. Indeed, intervention in the fishery was part of a general trend in the post-war Canadian state which saw an unprecedented level of government involvement in the economy and society as the foundations of the "welfare" state were being laid. The federal Department of Fisheries underwent a major expansion following the second world war, and announced, in 1949, that it was embarking on a fisheries "modernization" program for the Atlantic coast. Implicit in this modernization program was a movement away from the inshore salt fishery towards a modern, offshore, frozen fish industry structured along corporate lines. In the two decades after confederation, much federal (and provincial) money went into building the trawler fleet and assisting large corporations such as Fishery

Products Limited. Other "modernization" policies included educational programs, various household resettlement schemes, and technological development programs. Aside from the extension of unemployment insurance to fishers in 1958, the federal government directed little money to the inshore fishery.

As we begin to reassess the events of the twentieth century Newfoundland fishery, we need to be mindful of the ways that men and women have been affected differently by them. As the production of saltfish gave way to fresh/frozen fish, fewer women participated in "shore work." Instead, growing numbers of women found employment in the burgeoning fish processing plants. Fish harvesting work was still predominantly male, yet Canadian census records for 1951, 1961, 1971, and 1981 indicate that a small but growing number of women were classified as "fishermen" in those years (Canada Census, 1951, 1961, 1971, 1981). In the years following Confederation, different types of jobs opened up in several areas — the trawlers, fish processing plants, and the various branches of both the federal and provincial departments of fisheries. Despite expanded opportunities for paid employment generally, women's earnings in the Newfoundland fishery have remained substantially lower than men's.

Understanding the reasons for the sexual division of labour has been an ongoing area of concern for feminist writers, and it involves looking at such things as class, family relations, industrial structure, and the make-up of the local labour market. In recent years, however, feminists have begun to recognize that in the era of increased government intervention in the economy, the state, too, is an actor in the lives of men and women. In particular, feminist historians and sociologists have focused on the role of the state in the perpetuation, and even shaping, of gender ideology. Historian Linda Gordon (Gordon, 1992), has recently criticized the "gender blind" historiography of the welfare state, saying it has failed to recognize gender as an organizing principle of the welfare state system. Gordon suggests that it is important not only to see how state policies discriminate against women, but how the state supports a whole social system. Recently, some feminist historians and literary critics have tried to follow the creation and development of this social system described by Gordon and others looking at the origins of social welfare policy. These writers, who include literary critic Mary Poovey and sociologist Denise Riley, among others, have been looking at the social construction of gender ideology — the way of conceptualizing "male" and "female" and their respective roles in society — the rationale, if you will, behind sexual divisions within society (Poovey, 1988; Riley, 1988). Both Poovey and Riley identify the ideology of separate spheres, the assumption that men belong to the public world of work and civil society, and that women belong to the private world of home and family, as being the dominant gender ideology of the mid to late-nineteenth century. A particularly middle class conception of gender (and power) relations, this ideal became institutionalized in law, particularly women's property laws, politics, popular culture and later, social welfare policies. Poovey argues that although the separate spheres ideology was dominant, it was not uncontested as demands from women for property, divorce and political rights illuminated the socio-economic basis of the domestic ideal. Despite women's gradual attainment of political and legal rights, feminists looking at the development of social welfare policies argue that remnants of the separate spheres ideal continued to shape government policies in the twentieth century (Gordon, 1992).

While most feminists writing about gender and the state in the west have focused on social welfare policies, feminists writing about gender and the state in third world countries tend to look at economic development policies. For example, Gita Sen and Lourdes Beneria look at the intersections of gender, race and class discrimination in the attempts by the state (and international capital) to develop third world economies (Beneria and Sen, 1982; Sen, 1985). An aspect of their criticism is the application of modernization theory to developing economies. Modernization theory is a branch of economic development theory that was applied to state practices in the industrialized and third worlds in the 1950s and 1960s. With roots in 19th century evolutionary theory and influenced by the work of early sociologists such as Emile Durkheim and Talcott Parsons, modernization theory contains a set of assumptions about societies and the nature of economic change. According to the modernization framework, the world consists of "traditional" and "modern" societies. Traditional societies, according to this paradigm, must be infused with capital, technology, entrepreneurship, education and progressive attitudes before they can become modern (i.e. industrial capitalist). This dualistic approach to development has been under attack for its simplistic, linear concept of economic change, and the values and norms it attempts to impose on third world cultures (Frank, Cardoso). Nevertheless, elements of the modernization theory of development remain in many western and third world countries' economic policies.

Beneria and Sen's point about the need to combine a critique of discrimination against women with a critique of the economic development project itself is germane to the study of the gender politics of the fishery in Newfoundland. Undoubtedly, modernization theory was a part of the federal government's post-war fisheries development project (Wright, 1990). As we build a critique of the federal government's involvement in the attempt to industrialize (and modernize) the Atlantic fishery, we need to keep in mind the links between gender, the state, and economic development. This paper will take a preliminary look at several areas which could provide a means of examining the relationship between gender ideology and state economic policies. First, we will examine a series of visual representations of the Atlantic fishery used for promotional purposes by the federal Department of Fisheries which reveal ideas about gender roles and fishing. Second, we will look at gender ideology in two reports written concerning the future of the fishery in Atlantic Canada and Newfoundland, federal Deputy Minister of Fisheries (1946-54) Stewart Bates' Report of the Canadian Atlantic Sea-Fishery (Nova Scotia, 1944; hereafter "Bates Report") and the Report of the Newfoundland Fisheries Development Committee (Newfoundland and Canada, 1953; hereafter "Walsh Report"). Finally, we will consider the meeting of gender ideology and state practice in policies regarding the fishery. Indeed, several policies such as educational programs and unemployment insurance benefits have had a rather direct affect on Newfoundland women's participation in the labour force.

Poovey's observations on the tension between the dominant domestic ideal and the social and economic realities of Victorian England have some applicability to the case of fisheries planning in post-Confederation Newfoundland. Running throughout this literature generated by the federal fisheries bureaucracy is the assumption that the fishery was a male preserve, and women did not belong in the fishing economy. Significantly, these representations of gender found in the fisheries bureaucracy did not reflect the gender relations of the inshore fishery of Newfoundland. Although a sexual division of labour existed in the Newfoundland fishing economy, the boundaries between public and private were hazy, as women engaged in preparing fish for market as well as domestic chores. Moreover, Newfoundland women continued to be a significant part of the fisheries labour force in the post-Confederation economy, albeit mainly in low-paying and seasonal occupations in fish processing plants. Clearly, the fisheries planners' views diverged from the social and economic reality of the fishery. We are prevented, however, from dismissing their views when we consider that these bureaucrats were in a position of power, and were able to influence the direction of fisheries development. Thus, their ideas about man's place and woman's place in the modern Newfoundland fishery, no matter how disconnected from social and economic conditions, remain relevant to any study of the gender politics of the Newfoundland fishing economy.

Another element in the gender ideology found in fisheries planning is the mythology of the "seafaring man." Found in popular literature, songs and folklore, this mythology is itself heavily imbued with gender stereotypes. The man who earns his living from the sea is rugged, independent, fearless, a risk-taker, somewhat anti-social and strong. Critical theorist Roland Barthes refers to this "mythology", and its tendency to rob the people represented of specific historical context. Although Barthes does not refer to gender in this case, the following passage illustrates clearly the sea-man/land-woman dichotomy which is a part of this mythology:

> If we are concerned with a fisherman, it is not at all the type of fishing which is shown... but rather as the theme of an eternal condition, in which man is far away and exposed to the perils of the sea and woman weeping and praying at home. (Barthes, 1957, 195)

This seafaring man mythology appears, from time to time, in Department literature. However, it is rarely invoked for its own sake, but to "explain" some aspect of fishermens' behaviour. In his Report on the Canadian Atlantic Sea Fishery, Bates draws upon it to show why fishermen needed help from "experts" (like himself) to learn modern attitudes if they were ever going to prosper economically. "Fishermen," he remarked,

> often value highly the freedom and the romantic attributes of the sea; sometimes,

like older European seafarers, they act as if 'seafaring is necessary, living is not necessary' (Nova Scotia, 1944, 107).

Whatever the motive for using this "seafaring man" mythology, implications for gender are more clear. Portraying the fishery as a masculine domain not only obscures women's role, but precludes their participation in the modernized fishery.

Providing a striking visual illustration of gender ideology surfacing in the Department of Fisheries in the modernization era are a number of "institutional advertisements" on the back covers of the publication *Trade News*. This series began in the early 1950s and ceased a few years before the magazine itself ended publication in 1971. These ads covered a wide range of topics: tributes to fishery workers, fishing regulations, consumer information, descriptions of aquatic life, and the place of the fisheries in Canada, among others. An extension of the self-promotional role that the Department of Fisheries assumed in the post-war period, the advertisements were also used in Department of Fisheries displays at fairs, exhibitions and fisheries shows. At least one of the ads appeared in other Canadian magazines. An article in *Trade News* said of the series:

> The Department, with its series of "institutional" ads is not trying primarily to sell a product but to convey ideas and to tell the story of Canada's fisheries as attractively and clearly as possible (*Trade News* vol. 8 no. 1 (July 1956), 17).

The Department was certainly conveying ideas. However, they were telling *their* story, not *the* story of the fisheries. While doing this they reveal a good deal about ideas concerning men's and women's respective relationships to the fishery.

Judith Williamson's influential work on the ideological underpinnings of advertising is helpful in "reading" the Department of Fisheries' ads (Williamson, 1978). Williamson, following Barthes, claims that looking at "*how* an advertisement means" is as important as looking at "*what* an advertisement means." A key to "decoding" advertisements is to see how symbols and mythologies, themselves imbued with ideology, are used to create a meaning. These mythologies are invoked by a "sign," usually a picture of a person or object which embodies the image or idea the advertiser is trying to convey. The sign refers to a larger system of signs, a mythology, a prior "knowledge" upon which the ad's effectiveness depends. Williamson claims that these "knowledges" are not necessarily "true" knowledges, but have been historically constructed.

The "knowledges" upon which the Department of Fisheries draws in presenting these ads are the "sea-faring man" mythology and commonly held assumptions about the public/private distinction and its relation to gender. In these ads, fishers appear as rugged, independent, hardy men and the fishery itself is portrayed as an overwhelmingly masculine domain. Women, when they are shown in the ads, are invariably depicted as housewives and consumers, dependent on the skill and strength of the manly fisher to get good quality fish for their families. Like the writings of the Department of Fisheries officials, these ads obscured the importance of women's contribution to the fishery, while the men shown in the ads have been eternalized, romanticized (and thereby dehistoricized).

A group of these ads focuses specifically on fishermen and their way of life. In all, the physical depiction of the fishers and the accompanying text are strikingly similar. The ad entitled, "the gamblers"(*Trade News* vol. 10 no. 8 March 1958) evokes connotations of a hardy, independent masculinity. The woodcut print depicting three men leaning over the side of a boat hauling fish accentuates the roughness of the physical features. The text reinforces the sea-faring man mythology by describing the "nature" of the Canadian fishermen. "They number around one hundred thousand," begins the ad,

> Independent, hardy, adventurous men they are. Their way of live demands every reserve of wit, skill and strength. They are the fishermen of Canada.
>
> On sea or island lake, no fisherman can ever know ... what his reward will be. It is sometimes great, sometimes dishearteningly small. That is the gamble. But year after year it is taken ... with patience, endurance, perseverance (*Trade News* vol. 10 no. 9, March 1958).

the gamblers

They number around one hundred thousand.
Independent, hardy, adventurous men they are. Their way of life demands every reserve of wit, skill and strength. They are the fishermen of Canada.

On sea or inland lake, no fisherman can ever know, until his net or line is in, what his reward will be. It is sometimes great, sometimes dishearteningly small. That is the gamble. But year after year it is taken . . . with patience, endurance, perseverance. The nation's wealth profits . . . a vital food is harvested for this and other countries. They are good men, our fishermen, as good as you'll find. Good citizens. Good Canadians.

Although directed at the public at large, the ad seems to be an attempt to flatter the fishermen. It concludes: "They are good men, our fishermen, as good as you'll find. Good citizens. Good Canadians."(*Trade News* vol. 10 no. 9 March 1958). Whether or not the fishermen themselves swallowed this flattery (which bore little resemblance to the way the Department treated the opinions of these "Good citizens") is another matter. Significant here, however, is that this ad portrays the fishery and masculinity as inseparable entities. This ad shows that the Department assumed that "masculine" traits such as hardiness and adventurousness were not just assets to the fishery—such traits *were* the fishery.

What are little boys made of?

They're made of a rather wonderful sense of fun . . . a spark of adventure . . . . a good deal of mischievousness . . . and dreams—dreams of what they'll be when they grow up. Right now, the fondest dream of many of them is to have a fishing boat of their own.

And the happy thing about dreams in this country is that they can so often come true.

The fishing industry of Canada will always need men of vision and courage—men to carry on the tradition that has made the industry grow and prosper.

And these fishermen of the future—as well as the men of today—have the assurance that the Department of Fisheries of Canada will continue to do its part in the encouragement and development of the fishing industry.

Through constant research . . . conservation . . . the wise application of regulations . . . and many other essential services . . . the department is making sure that our youth will always have a prosperous and secure future in the fishing industry of Canada.

An advertisement entitled "What are little boys made of?"(*Trade News* vol. 9 no. 6 (Dec. 1956)) suggests that the Department of Fisheries believed in the "masculine" future of the fishery. It features an older man sitting on a dock, telling a story to two young boys sitting at his feet. The older man is gesturing with his hands, while the boys look up, seemingly wrapped up in the old man's tale. Here, the boys and the old fisherman are signs representing the fishery past and future. The text begins by linking the boy, with his "wonderful sense of fun" and "spark of adventure" to the future of the fishery by claiming that many young men dream of owning their own boats. The text then positions the Department of Fisheries between the fishery past and fishery future:

The fishing industry of Canada will always need men of vision and courage—men to carry on the tradition that has made the industry grow and prosper.

And these fishermen of the future—as well as the men of today—have the assurance that the Department of Fisheries of Canada will continue to do its part in the encouragement and development of the fishing industry (*Trade News* vol. 9 no. 6 (Dec. 1956)).

Whether or not the Department of Fisheries would be able to keep its promise to help the fishery grow and prosper, the ad revealed the Department's view of the past and future fishery as "masculine."

Another group of advertisements focuses on the production of fish for home consumption. In these, the stereotype of the sea-faring man is used in conjunction with another sign—woman as housewife and consumer. While women's roles in the production of fish are either downplayed or ignored, much is made of their benefitting from the advances made in the fishing industry. The sea-faring man is somewhat altered as well, losing some of his independent character. The fishermen are portrayed as being part of a team, of which the Department of Fisheries is also a part, working to provide housewives with fish.

One such ad tried to play upon the reader's prior "knowledge" of the "masculine" nature of the fishing industry (*Trade News*, vol. 8 no. 2 Aug. 1955). The ad features six small pictures arranged in a checkerboard pattern. The first five are drawings of men involved in various stages of preparing fish for market—a fisherman, a truck driver, a fish plant worker, a railway worker, a shopkeeper. The last picture, a photograph of a woman's face, stands out from the rest. In contrast to the rough drawings of the men's faces, her face is smooth and softly curved and her mouth is opened in a wide smile. In bold letters beneath the pictures are the words: "The End Man is a Woman."

The headline with the obvious contradiction, and the juxtaposition of the woman's photo in a group of drawings of "working men" are attempts to create an incongruity. However, it is only an incongruity if the reader assumes that women have no role in the production of fish for market. The text reinforces this premise:

The fishing industry of Canada is important to Canada's prosperity and yours. The men who work in it are skilled and hardy—good citizens. It is sometimes hard to realize that even in such a virile atmosphere as this—women play a most important part. But it's so (*Trade News* vol. 8 no. 2, Aug. 1955).

However, the ad does not describe the role of women in the inshore fishery and the fish processing plants. Instead, it explains that woman's role in the fishery is the consumer, the housewife who buys the fish. Working on the assumption held by many that the fishery has a "virile atmosphere," this ad contributes to the myth that the fishery is a man's world and that women do not participate in it at all. The ad ends with an appeal to the "men" in the line to think about the women for whom they are providing the fish:

That is why every man along the line must remember the woman at the end; why he must make it his personal responsibility to see fish reaches her - always - at its freshest, most delicious best (*Trade News* vol. 8 no. 2, Aug. 1955).

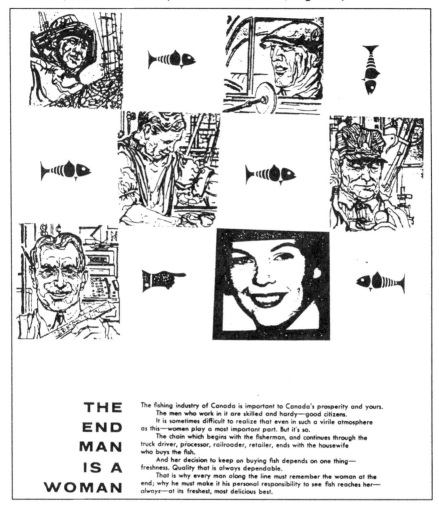

THE END MAN IS A WOMAN

The fishing industry of Canada is important to Canada's prosperity and yours.
The men who work in it are skilled and hardy—good citizens.
It is sometimes difficult to realize that even in such a virile atmosphere as this—women play a most important part. But it's so.
The chain which begins with the fisherman, and continues through the truck driver, processor, railroader, retailer, ends with the housewife who buys the fish.
And her decision to keep on buying fish depends on one thing—freshness. Quality that is always dependable.
That is why every man along the line must remember the woman at the end; why he must make it his personal responsibility to see fish reaches her—always—at its freshest, most delicious best.

However peculiar this ad may seem now, it was apparently considered quite effective in its day. In 1956 it was chosen as one of 50 "Outstanding Canadian Ads" by the Copy Director's Club of Toronto. Said one of the judges: "[the] deliberate incongruity is so intriguing you have to find out how it ends up" (*Trade News* vol. 9 no. 1, July 1956, 17).

Of all the advertisements in this series, only one portrayed women working in the fishing industry. With the heading, "From Dock to Dining Room," the ad shows a group of drawings of all the people involved in the production of fish for market—fishermen, plant workers, scientists, retailers, as well as the ubiquitous housewife (*Trade News* vol. 8 no. 9, March 1956). One of the pictures shows two female workers cutting and packaging some fish. Although the picture is sanitized, in that the women are working in front of a big multi-paned window and there is no assembly line in sight, it does, nevertheless, show women workers. Unlike the other advertisements, however, this ad speaks directly to the fishery workers to make sure they provide the best quality fish possible. In spite of the information they were giving to the general public about the nature of the fishery (i.e. "The End Man is a Woman), the Department of Fisheries officials knew something about the actual make-up of the work force in the fishery.

From dock to dining room

The market for your fish can be maintained and increased only if the fish reaches the dining table in prime condition with unimpaired flavour and goodness. If people get poor fish, there will be a poor market . . . but the reverse is equally true — good fish means good markets.

That is why it is important to safeguard the quality, to make sure that only good fish reaches the customer. The care that is taken in the boats, in the handling and processing, in the packing and shipping, must be such that the people who enjoy fish, and who are your customers, will get a product that is so good, so flavoursome, and so delicious, that they will buy often and buy more.

Guard your markets now and for the future by providing good fish.

Taking the author of the article in *Trade News* on the institutional advertisements at his or her word, we can say that the ads do "convey ideas and tell the story of Canada's fisheries." However, their "story" is one which appropriates only the shell of history and renders the people of the Canadian fisheries into anonymous symbols. In the process, the men are homogenized into essential types and the role of women in both the past and the "modernized" fishery is glossed over and ignored. While the Department of Fisheries paid tribute to the hard work of the male fisher, they had no such accolades for the women in the industry. As we begin to examine fisheries plans and policies in the same period as these advertisements appeared, we will see that a connection exists between this portrayal of the fishery and the ideas of the fisheries planners regarding gender roles.

As the federal Department of Fisheries began mobilizing for the anticipated industrialization of the Atlantic fishery in the years following World War II, several reports were commissioned to provide a blueprint for development. The most influential of these was the *Report on the Canadian Atlantic Sea-Fishery* by Deputy Minister of Fisheries Stewart Bates. Although written for the Nova Scotia Royal Commission in 1944, its prescription of government support for large frozen fish operations was soon to be applied to Newfoundland. A major area of concern in the report was the condition of the labour force and implicit was the assumption that the leaders of the modern economy would be men. Women would only have a marginal role, despite the fact that women had been recruited into frozen fish processing work during the war. Ironically, the strongest "female" presence in the Bates Report is not the women who contributed to the inshore fishery, but the "housewife". The housewife is a key figure in both the iconography of the ideology of separate spheres ("the angel at the hearth") and 20th century consumer culture. Bates made numerous references to "housewives" in an attempt to encourage the fishing industry to develop new food products. He said that housewives expected certain conveniences in food preparation and would not revert to old methods (Nova Scotia, 1944, 11). In fact, it was through the symbol of the housewife that Bates drew the link between the wants and desires of the modern consumer on the one hand, and the need for the Atlantic fishery to modernize to fill those needs on the other. That the issue of providing the housewife with new kinds of fish products gained greater attention than female employment in the industry is indicative of the gender ideology inherent in the Bates Report.

In notes on fish plant production during the war that he made as Assistant Deputy Minister of Fisheries, he indicated that women's role in the fishery would be limited and temporary. In one document, Bates clearly delineated the jobs that women might hold in a description of the job classifications within a processing plant (NAC Department of Fisheries, RG 23, Stewart Bates Papers, vol. 505, box 3. file "Labour in Fisheries—War-Time Problems"). "Class 1" workers were workers who had had two or more years of training, and they included managers, foremen, scientists, accountants, mechanics, carpenters, "line men" and fish salters. He continued his description, ending with "Class 4" workers who had had less than six months training. They included general plant labourers, packers, "line girls", can fillers, labellers and so on. At the bottom of the page Bates added: "Fillers, labellers and line workers may be women, but other general labour in fish plants tends to be heavy work requiring male labour" (NAC Department of Fisheries, RG 23, Stewart Bates Papers, vol. 505, box 3, file "Labour in Fisheries—War-Time Problems").

Almost none of the "Class 1" jobs required substantial physical strength, yet Bates did not suggest that women fill those jobs.

Bates reiterated these assumptions about women's place in the fishery in another note on women workers during the war:

> To women workers the desire to work in a wet plant, among fish guts, is less attractive than many occupations, and it is also less well paid. It is a particularly cold job on hands in winter and anyway, plants require men for carrying heavy fish (NAC Department of Fisheries, RG 23, Stewart Bates Papers, vol. 505, box 3, file "War Conditions and Atlantic Fisheries").

Cold hands and fish guts aside, Bates never considered that women would have to work out of economic necessity and that most women (and most men, for that matter) in fishing communities in Atlantic Canada would not have much choice in where they worked. Although Bates's beliefs about the presence of female labour in fish processing plants after the war were off the mark, his assumption that women would occupy the lowest paid jobs was more accurate (see Neis, 1992).

The Report of the Newfoundland Fisheries Development committee also displays the "ideology of separate spheres" at work in the Bates Report. Written mainly by federal Department of Fisheries representative W.C. MacKenzie in 1953, the Walsh Report was the result of the first joint federal-provincial project regarding the future of the Newfoundland fishing economy. Although the authors were more aware of the role women played in the inshore salt fishery, they insisted that they did not belong in the modern fishery. Moreover, they considered the family fishing crew, and the participation of women and children in the fish curing process an archaic social and economic arrangement. In fact, they saw the break-up of the family operation as a "liberating" (and of course, modern) development. Their thoughts about this "liberation" nicely display his assumptions about woman's true "nature":

> The general social improvement which has been taking place in the Province for some years is resulting in the liberation of women from the hard and unsuitable work of fish-making and allowing them to devote their time to their household duties and to live in an atmosphere of human dignity as wives and mothers. It is also resulting in the liberation of children to pursue their education and receive a formation preparing them properly for a career to which they should have equal opportunity with all other children (Newfoundland and Canada, 1953, 102).

According to this piece, woman's "natural" place was in the home, not working on the fish flakes. She was meant to be a housewife, wife and mother, not a woman contributing directly to the family's earnings. Curing fish was "unsuitable"—incompatible with domesticity and the dominant ideas about femininity. Suggested here is that the inshore fishery was thwarting women from their true calling, thus robbing them of the "atmosphere of human dignity". Modernization, they argued, would "liberate" women.

On the basis of these assumptions, the Walsh Report declared that women would not have any role in the modern fishery:

The committee considers that in a programme of development of the fisheries child and female labour should find no place, except in the case of young women who will be employed at suitable work in plants and senior school children who will undoubtedly continue to help in fish curing during the summer vacation (Newfoundland and Canada, 1944, 102).

Although the report made an exception in the case of young (presumably unmarried) women who might work in the fish plants, women's participation was qualified by the word "suitable." At one level, "suitable" work means jobs consistent with the prevailing gender ideology pertaining to women workers. However, the damaging repercussions for women working in the industry, at that time, and in the present, were that "suitable" work for women was also considered the least skilled and was the poorest paid.

Although fisheries planners assumed the work force of the modern fishery would be male, the descriptions of the future fishery suggest that the model worker was a certain type of man—highly trained, technically skilled, in possession of disciplined work habits and "progressive" attitudes. Bates and the authors of the Walsh Report heaped accolades and high hopes on the young men who would supposedly be leading the modern economy; they were less enthusiastic about the existing work force. To the modernizers, the men who worked in the inshore fishery were almost an impediment to economic progress. Bates frequently berated the inshore fishers for their "backward methods", their "resistance to change" and their ignorance. "The social milieu of the industry was not the kind that encourages the search for modernization," asserted Bates (Nova Scotia, 1944, 61). Although the authors of the Walsh Report were less likely than Bates to proclaim the inshore fishers as "unskilled," they were no less concerned about the sporadic work habits and a lack of industrial discipline in the work force (Newfoundland and Canada, 1953, 72). Modernization, it seemed, required "modern men." Said Bates:

Industrial education may not be sufficient to create the desired habits of mind in the industry, but the attitude to adopt is not to regard such education as having only a remote chance of creating the desired habits of mind; it is rather the only chance (Nova Scotia, 1944, 22).

Because they believed that moulding the workers into the modernization framework was crucial to the success of the program, the Department of Fisheries directed much energy into the educational component. Through education they believed they could obtain not only a work force competent to operate the new equipment required for the large-scale frozen fish industry, but a work force that accepted the values of modernization. In ignoring the role that women had had in the inshore fishery, and directing the fruits of the modernization program toward men, government planners also redefined the possibilities open to women. The first such program was the Fisheries Training Program in Newfoundland, which arose from the recommendations of the Walsh Report in 1953. Other smaller workshop and demonstration programs followed. The most comprehensive was the opening of the College of Fisheries, Navigation, Marine Engineering and Electronics in St.

John's in 1964, a joint federal-provincial effort. Stewart Bates, who introduced the idea of a college of fisheries in his Report of the Canadian Atlantic Sea-Fishery, believed the first challenge was to encourage "young men of ability" to enter the industry (Nova Scotia, 1944, 110). He warned that there were "exceptional men in all branches of the industry", but they could not "lead the industry out of the wilderness." (Nova Scotia, 1944, 110) Apparently, leading the Atlantic fishery "out of the wilderness" required almost heroic attributes, as the literature on the work force portrays these young men as veritable saviours with technological skills. Photographs of College of Fisheries students published in the trade journal *Trade News* shortly after the St. John's school opened in the 1960s show young men in dark sweaters with College of Fisheries insignia concentrating intently on their work. One writer enthused:

> Among the students are tomorrow's skippers and mates of the streamlined and efficient sea-going vessels, the marine engineers who will operate the engine rooms grown highly sophisticated in a world of advancing technology (*Fisheries of Canada* vol. 19 no. 9 (March 1967), 4).

Young men and technology was the magic ticket to rescue a beleaguered fishery. "It is the men," said Newfoundland Premier Joey Smallwood at the opening of the College of Fisheries, "not the money, that will make this great fishery development worth it" (*Trade News* vol. 16 no. 7 (Jan. 1964), 16).

While the young men were channelled into technical courses to prepare them for their roles as "tomorrow's skippers and mates of the streamlined and efficient sea-going vessels," the only educational program related to the fishery in which women were encouraged to enrol was a course in net braiding. Offered at the College of Fisheries in 1966, in conjunction with the Great Grimsby Coal, Salt and Tanning Company of St. John's, the course was designed specifically for women. Employment opportunities for graduates were limited, however. Women who took the course were eligible to work in the company's factory (*Fisheries of Canada* vol. 19 no. 9 (March 1967). Educating women, even in areas where their labour was concentrated, such as fish processing, apparently was not a major priority.

These assumptions about women and men and their relationship to each other and to society pervade the policy concerning the extension of unemployment insurance to fishers. Although this policy was not issued through the Department of Fisheries, federal fisheries officials were involved in drafting the program. Before 1958, self-employed fishers or fishers who worked in a crew on a share system were ineligible for unemployment insurance. According to the November, 1958 regulations, however, fishers working alone or in crews would be eligible. The contribution of each crew member would be calculated by equally dividing 75% of the gross value of the catch made by the crew. There was a stipulation, however:

> If a fisherman's wife shares as a member of the crew, her net earnings are added to her husband's to calculate the value of his contributions, and no contributions are made for her ("Changes in Unemployment Insurance Regulations Applicable to Fishermen," Ottawa, November, 1958).

What is at work here is the assumption that women are not independent wage-earners in their own right, but are economically dependent upon their husbands. Like the nineteenth century British and North American civil laws which rendered married women without legal rights apart from their husbands, the unemployment insurance program essentially alienated women from their own labour. Although fishing crews in Newfoundland often consisted of family members or relatives such as siblings and children, the regulations contained no other restrictions regarding contributions of family members besides husbands and wives.

The regulations concerning crews selling cured fish to a buyer were even more restrictive on women's participation. While male members of the crew based their contribution on an equal share of the cured catch, a fisherman's wife who shared on the crew could not amass any points either for herself or her husband:

> Although a fisherman's wife is counted in the division of the quantity to be shared by the crew, her quantity is not added to her husband's, nor is it assigned to her, and, therefore, she receives no contributions ("Changes in Unemployment Insurance Regulations Applicable to Fishermen," Ottawa, November, 1958).

While the reason for allowing wives' contributions to be added to their husbands' share for fresh fish and not for cured fish are unclear, the implications for women's participation in fish harvesting are. Only in 1980 did the federal government extend unemployment insurance benefits to women who fished with their husbands. Further research on the historical development of such policies as unemployment insurance, education and access to financial programs will provide us with more insights on the gender politics of the Newfoundland fishery.

The directives on labour and education for the modernized fishery written by Bates, MacKenzie, and other fisheries officials give us an indication of how tightly gender ideology is woven into the fabric of modernization. Very early in the program, decisions were made about who would be a part of the modernized fishery and would thereby have access to training and other programs, and who would not. Although an awareness of the relationship between the state and gender inequality in the fishery is but one aspect of the the transition that took place in the structure of the fishing economy in Newfoundland in the post-Confederation years, it is by no means the least significant. Gender inequality and its links to the state and the economy remains a relevant issue as women continue to be an economically marginalized group in the Newfoundland fishery. Not only have the women employed in the private sector of the Newfoundland fishery been the most vulnerable to layoffs and cutbacks, but they have had more difficulty qualifying for government assistance programs such as unemployment insurance and the recent NCARP program. In uncovering the ways in which the state has been involved in perpetuating gender inequality through its institutions, past and present, we will be a step closer to addressing the larger problem of women's social and economic oppression in contemporary capitalist society.

Fish Guts, Hair Nets and Unemployment Stamps: Women and Work in Co-operative Fish Plants

Bonnie J. McCay

Introduction

THIS PAPER offers ethnographic observations on a community undergoing industrialization and trying to keep some control over that process. It describes changing roles of women in the fishery of Fogo Island, Newfoundland, within the context of a remarkable experiment in community-based economic development: the Fogo Island Co-operative Society, Ltd. The entry of women into the work force of the co-operative's fish plants in 1979 completed the transition from "making fish" to "making money" in the economic lives of Fogo Island women. It also raised new concerns and intensified old issues about how and by whom work should be defined and allocated within the framework of an economy sharply moulded by an unemployment insurance system. Field notes[1] on women at work came to read as field notes on the co-operative itself and how it dealt with issues concerning rights to make both money and unemployment insurance benefits. Thus a focus on women necessarily leads to an exploration of the problems of an organization that seeks to maintain financial viability within an industrial capitalist society while also trying to meet the needs and realize the ideals of the large and diverse community that has come to depend on it for its survival.

The Setting

There's no mines, no oil rigs, no f - - - all anything here but the fishery (fish plant worker, Joe Batt's Arm, 1983).

Fogo Island comprises about 120 square miles of rocks, barrens, ponds, and trees set at the edge of the cold Labrador current that brushes the coast of northeastern Newfoundland. About 4,400 people live in the ten small "outports" that hug the shores of the island. Their ancestors came from England, Ireland, and other parts of Newfoundland because Fogo Island is an excellent place from which to fish. It is out on a broad submarine shelf, the Fogo Bank, that supports cod, salmon, lobster, turbot, halibut, flounder, crab, and many other species in season.

Fishing is the major economic activity: in 1980, 874 islanders fished (Fogo Island Co-operative Society, Ltd. 1982), by my estimate this is about 0.9 persons per household. They do not make much money this way. In 1980 the official Canadian poverty line for rural households for four persons (slightly below the Fogo Island average) was $12,035 (Report, 1983). The median income for licensed full-time fishermen in the northeast coast region of Newfoundland—including Fogo Island—was about $7,000. That included transfer payments, unemployment benefits, and wages from other jobs as well as payments for fish (ibid.).

The fishery is inshore and nearshore. Vessel technologies include: inshore "speedboats" (outboard-motored, powered wooden craft 15 to 20 feet long);

inshore "trap skiffs" (inboard-powered, wooden boats up to 40 feet long); and nearshore "longliners" (inboard/diesel-powered wooden vessels up to 65 feet long). Major gears are handlines, longlines, cod traps, lobster and crab pots, and gill nets. Low incomes from fishing reflect not only low prices for fish and irregular productivity on the fishing grounds for the inshore and nearshore fishermen of the region but also the marked seasonality of this fishery. A letter from an islander, dated October 11, 1983, describes the end of a season that began in June: "Fishing is over now. George and the crew got one fleet of nets up. When they next get a good day they are going for the other two fleets. Then they are going in the bay for a load of firewood." They would not start fishing again until sometime in May or June of the following year.

The Fogo Island Co-operative

After Newfoundland's confederation with Canada, Fogo Islanders were caught between the pincers of a declining and erratic resource base and a political economy that limped along toward industrialization aided by tools such as massive resettlement and depopulation of coastal outports (Matthews, 1976; Antler and Faris, 1979). They managed nonetheless to remain islanders, outporters, and fishermen through the 1960s and 1970s, when so many other Newfoundlanders did not. The Fogo Island fishery co-operative has also managed to stay in business through the early 1980s, when so many other fishery firms have not. How Fogo Islanders suffered, fought, coalesced, and were helped by film-makers, extension workers, and others to stay on Fogo Island during the 1960s push for resettlement is depicted elsewhere (Wadel, 1969b; DeWitt, 1969; McCay, 1976). How the co-operative was started; the role of government policies and actors in forming and framing its early development; the growth of its longliner fishery; and the Fogo Island co-operative's halting maturation through the 1970s and into the 1980s into a relatively resilient and viable enterprise are also documented (Sheppard, 1972; McCay, 1976, 1978, 1979; Carter, 1984).

Critical to understanding the issues concerning workers at the fish plants is the fact that the Fogo Island co-operative was created at a time of crisis, with a mission of helping all of the residents of Fogo Island. Accordingly, it is an inclusive rather than exclusive organization: membership is open to anyone, including fishermen, fish plant workers, other employees, and anyone else who wishes to join. Like many "poor peoples' co-operatives" its actions, policies and organization have been informed by social as well as economic goals. This contrasts greatly with fishery co-operatives in parts of the United States which have very selective membership criteria and are run almost entirely for strictly economic benefits to the members (see McCay, 1980; Gersuny and Poggie, 1974). It also sets the stage for conflict and social change as members and leaders of the organization deal with the necessity of helping the co-operative survive in a highly competitive capitalist economy, where profit margins and debt/credit ratios tell all, while at the same time meeting the social needs of the members and the island community.

Creating Jobs: the Fish Plants

One of the most important goals of the founders of the Fogo Island Co-operative in the late 1960s was to find alternatives to fishing for residents of the island's ten communities. Alternatives to fishing were and are critical to the island's economy. Fish were scarce and unlikely to become more abundant in the near future. The major alternatives were labour migration and going on welfare. Shifts in the fishing industry had reduced opportunities to local fish processing and related work. Poverty, unemployment, and welfare dependence had begun to dominate the lives of Fogo Islanders to the extent that government-sponsored resettlement was attractive to many islanders and government agents alike. Leaders of the co-operative felt that the organization could play a major role in creating jobs in fish processing on the island and hence in halting resettlement and the more pervasive process of underdevelopment.

For the first ten years of the co-operative's existence (1967-1977) attempts to create the infrastructure for *in situ* economic development were unsuccessful. The co-operative had trouble obtaining the government assistance it needed to build facilities necessary for processing frozen fish on the island. Government policies were not supportive of co-operatives and overly concerned to "modernize" inshore fishing capacity despite clear evidence of resource depletion (McCay, 1976; 1978). In addition, one of the few very large companies that dominate the Newfoundland fishery and its governance benefited from Fogo Island's role as a supplier of raw material for its fish plant located in Twillingate, some 40 miles away.

However, leaders of the co-operative persevered in their attempts to muster capital for the development of fish processing on the island. At the outset, the co-operative processed saltfish in a plant at the community of Seldom; this function was expanded at Seldom and other communities through the 1970s. Until 1979 the only labour-added value from the fishery that stayed on the island come from the co-operative's saltfish processing operations.

In 1976-78 co-operative leaders made a major push toward obtaining private and government support for improved and new facilities that would enable the co-operative to engage in fresh fish processing, i.e., skinning, filleting, freezing, and packing groundfish and pelagic species. By 1979 the co-operative had obtained the assistance it needed to renovate, build anew, buy machinery, train workers, and start processing several species of fish to the frozen block and frozen fillet products. Plants were in operation in 1979-80 at Joe Batt's Arm and Fogo. A move toward diversification resulted in the construction of a crab processing plant in Fogo that began in 1983.

Right away the new fish plants made a difference to the islanders. In 1980, 460 people worked at the co-operative's fish plants (Fogo Island Co-operative Society Ltd., 1982). Added to the 864 fishermen noted above, this raises the estimate of fishery involvement per household to about 1.3 persons fishing or working at the fish plant. In subsequent years the work force fluctuated, with some expansion, and for the first time women became an integral part of fish plant labour. By 1982 between 50 and 60 of the workers were women (Table 1). Women usually worked on the trimming, grading, and packing lines; men on the cutting or filleting lines and in freezing, boxing, and forklifting stacks of frozen fillets and blocks. In 1983 women's jobs were increased by the addition of 108 shucking-line positions at the new crab plant in Fogo.

TABLE 1: Fish Plant Positions, Fogo Island Co-operative Society, 1981 (Full Shift)

Community Stages	Primary Tasks	Number of Positions	Number of Women's Positions
Deep Bay	Saltfish; salting	5	0
Island Harbour	Saltfish; salting	4	0
Tilting	Saltfish; salting	8	0
Saltfish Plant Seldom	Saltfish; splitting,salting,drying,misc., other (e.g. lumproe processing)	46	0
Fish Plants Joe Batt's Arm	Splitting Cod Fresh Fish Processing (frozen fillet and blocks)	18 / 84	0 / 24-30
Fogo	Splitting Cod Fresh Fish Processing (frozen fillet and blocks)	18 / 65	24-30
TOTAL		248	48-60

From Making Fish to Making Stamps: Women and the Fishery

One of the co-operative's major accomplishments has been to make possible the final phase of a transition (from "making fish" to "making money and stamps") for over 150 women of Fogo Island. The cultural landscape of Fogo Island now includes the sight of women wearing white jackets, rubber boots, and hair nets as they walk or drive down the road to a fish plant. It also includes an awareness that the women, like the men, are earning both money and "stamps." "Making stamps" is a Newfoundland term for earning credits toward unemployment insurance. As we shall see, the issues of fishermen's wives and labour rotation involve the distribution of rights to earn unemployment insurance benefits.

Decline of the Family Fishery

Between 1965 and 1966 the commodity produced by Fogo Island fishing families began to shift from labour-intensive light-salted, sun-dried codfish to heavy-salted codfish that was sent elsewhere (i.e. the Fishermen's Union Trading Company plant at Port Union) for artificial drying. This was a time of great trouble for the saltfish system, and Fogo Island fishermen had difficulty even finding buyers of their fish, a major stimulus for formation of the co-operative. The co-operative's own saltfish plants, once created, hired only men. Fresh fish were sent off the island for processing. There was no fishery work available for women.

The result was that by 1971, when I first came to Fogo Island, only a handful of women were still regularly engaged in making fish. Indeed, only a handful of households were so engaged, most having turned to the production of heavy-salted codfish in community stages or to specialization in fishing only, leaving processing up to the co-operative and companies to whom the fish was sold. The women I talked with seemed happy about their new situation—it was indeed new, having changed for most women only within the previous five or ten years. Housework, child care, church activities and shopping trips were enough to occupy their time.

Getting Paid for Work

The settlement of Fogo Island women into domesticity was bolstered by a home economics curriculum that intensified cultural notions that women belonged in the home and in the shops (Antler, 1977). In addition, the notion of being paid for one's own time, labour and skills was well established by the 1970s, and the idea of working for someone else, even one's husband, without being paid was harder to accept. By 1971 almost all fishermen on Fogo Island were members of the co-operative, and they were clearly being paid for their fish. The bi-weekly cheques they received contrasted greatly with the old truck method of squaring up a household's debts against fish delivered to the fish merchant once a year in the fall. Women had begun to expect that one should get paid for one's work. Accepting for the moment the argument that what their husbands received for the fish came back to them, women chafed that they had not been paid enough for the time and effort they put into making good fish. More to the point, they had never been paid directly: "Remember, we used to kill ourselves making fish, and for nothing." In this spirit, in 1972 women in one of Fogo Island's communities tried unsuccessfully to get a government grant to pay them hourly wages for knitting and crocheting items that would be sold in a tourist centre.

The government unemployment insurance system for fishermen intensified the notion that it was hardly worthwhile for women to work in the fishery. The economy of Newfoundland's coastal fishing communities is heavily dependent on and structured by unemployment insurance because of the seasonality and low incomes of the fisheries and the government's use of unemployment insurance to deal with these problems (Ferris and Plourde, 1982). Fishermen received stamps for how much fish they delivered; although the value of those stamps might be higher for light-salted, sun-dried fish, it did not compensate for the fact that the women who worked in making (or catching) that fish would not qualify for unemployment insurance. Women closely related to the men on fishing crews were not eligible for insurance.[2] In contrast, fish plant work promised to offer women the chance to earn

148

both money and unemployment insurance. Besides, as Fogo Island women often told me, jobs were scarce—even scarcer than fish—and it was "only right" that they should go to men for their households. Underlying this argument was the sentiment, expressed in many other ways,[3] that scarce resources like jobs should be distributed as broadly as possible.[4] As jobs became more abundant after 1979 with the creation of the co-operative's fish plants, it became "only right" for women to work, too, but the egalitarian sentiment remained and was expressed in issues concerning the allocation of jobs and stamps.

Cost and Benefits of Fish Plant Work

As soon as the Joe Batt's Arm and Fogo fish plants opened in 1979-1980, women became an integral part of the co-operative's labour force and have increased in numbers since. I was surprised on my visits to Fogo Island in the 1980s at how completely and smoothly women seemed to have incorporated fish plant work into their lives and expectations, given how thoroughly they appeared, in the early 1970s, to have left the production process and embraced and rationalized narrower and more clearly defined roles as reproducers, consumers, and home beautifiers. Many women I talked with on my visits between 1979 and 1983 were eager to work, some positively glowing when they talked of how lucky they were "to be called to the fish plant." This surprised me because, as they acknowledged, working at the fish plants is cold, damp, hard, messy and emotionally stressful, especially since 1980-81 when the management of the co-operative began efforts to monitor more closely and streamline work at the fish plants.

Fish plant workers receive close to the minimum wage: $4.35 in 1983. Their work weeks are highly variable, depending on how much fish or how many crabs are delivered to the fish plants by local fishermen. There are very poor weeks when some workers are not called in and others may work for fewer than ten hours. There are weeks when workers are called in for over 12 hours a day, including late shifts that extend into the early morning hours, weeks when people may work over 70 or 80 hours. Most weeks are in between and are weighed as "poor" or "good" according to how much money is made and whether the hours worked are enough to qualify for a week of insurable earnings (a stamp).

The variable and often short season of fish plant work on Fogo Island results in low annual incomes from this work. I estimate that the range of annual incomes from the fish plants in the early 1980s was $600 to $4,500. The median, in 1981, was $2,626 (computed from data in Fogo Island Co-operative Society, Ltd. 1982). At the high end were men and women with supervisory functions, particularly foremen, or "floormen" and "floorladies," plus skilled cutters and others who received slightly higher wages and production bonuses. On the average, women had lower-paying positions and worked fewer hours than the men (see also Ilcan 1985 for a Nova Scotia parallel).

The pleasure some women found in such work is related to the fact that their social lives had become severely truncated since the decline of the family fishery. Fish plant work is, at least, done with other adults. A young mother tried to explain this to me: "Well, I don't know, I suppose it's being with the other women, see?" Difficulties of the work must also be balanced against the fact that, in the context of widespread poverty, even small supplementary incomes can make a difference to a household.

Fish plant labour can make a significant difference to a household that has other sources of income. In 1981 the average Newfoundland household had an income of $24,827 (Statistics Canada 1983:61), but rural Newfoundlanders, especially the "baymen" or outporters of the northeast coast and Labrador, were close to and usually below the poverty line for rural households (Report, 1983). This was most evident for households dependent on the income of one fisherman—true for at least half of Fogo Island's households. The Kirby Task Force survey showed total incomes for licensed full-time fishermen in the northeast coast region at $7,000; for part-time fishermen, about $9,000. Medians were considerably lower. It is significant that these sums included transfer payments, unemployment insurance benefits, and wages from non-fishing jobs. The third point is that people were working for stamps to receive unemployment benefits during the long winter season. During much of the year no fishing and little plant work was possible. Low wages could translate into unemployment benefits that could increase wages by as much as two-fold.

The Unemployment Insurance System: Challenges to Women

Women's desire to work in the fish plants was clearly related to their desire to earn unemployment stamps, but fulfilling that desire was not easy. In the mid-1980s, in order to qualify for unemployment benefits once one was laid off, a person had to work a minimum of 15 hours a week for a total of ten weeks (this varied from place to place). If, however, one had not qualified for benefits the previous year, one had to work that amount for a least 20 weeks to qualify. The latter rule came into effect in 1980. Since few women had been in the local labour force prior to 1980, most had the problem of earning 20 insurable stamps at a patently irregular and seasonal job. Their problems were enhanced by the special responsibilities and demands attendant upon being women. The lucky few were those who "made their ten stamps" in 1979 and thus had to make only ten stamps in subsequent years to add unemployment benefits to their incomes.

Making ten stamps was as difficult as the bygone woman's task of making high quality saltfish. Making 20 weeks of insurable earnings was even more so. On the northeast coast of Newfoundland it is unusual to have 20 weeks of good fishing during a year because of vagaries in weather and fish behaviour. In addition, 20 weeks translates to five months of monotonous factory work with the added discomforts and health hazards of standing for many hours on bare concrete or on metal racks above a damp floor. It is five months of emotional tension over being monitored, criticized, and enjoined not to talk with the others with whom one is crammed, shoulder to shoulder, on the lines. In this context, little things come to mean a lot to the women workers:

No, it's not so bad working. You see, they give you the small fish first, and all you're doing is looking ahead to when you get the bigger fish, so you works as fast as you can, maybe two hours, so's you can get to the big fish (unmarried female fish plant worker, Joe Batt's Arm, July 1981).

Most women do not have the opportunity to make their stamps. Twenty or even ten weeks is a long time for women with children (the majority of the female workers) who must jockey unpredictable work schedules, sometimes including all-night shifts, with the demands of their households and the need to find and pay for babysitting. Even grandmothers are now usually paid for child care (women's factory work has an important multiplier effect through babysitting wages). Many women give up working when school begins in the fall, even though they may not have made their stamps, because young babysitters go back to school.

If women do not want to work, they may have economic reasons, some of which reflect the special problems of being women and some the not-so-special problems related to the structure of unemployment insurance:

Yes, maid, a few women here (Seldom) work over to Joe Batt's Arm but it hardly pays. The cost of babysitters, you need to do the housework and cooking just the same, and then there's transportation. Even the unemployment isn't very good. You can't get enough work in one week to get good stamps. This week the women got only two days. You're called to work two or three days, and then you have to take 'low stamps' (wife of an unemployed carpenter, Seldom, July 1981; Seldom is 20 miles from the fish plant in Joe Batt's Arm).

The speaker addressed yet another unemployment issue that affects both women and men and, like others discussed in this paper, molds problems of labour management. A "low stamp" is an insurable week with low earnings. Unemployment benefits are computed on the basis of the average of insurable weekly earnings. Low stamps or weeks with low earnings reduce the average, lowering the incentive to work beyond the 10 or 20 weeks needed to qualify, especially into the fall when fish production is down and hours at the fish plant are irregular and often few. Women tend to have the kinds of jobs that are subject to sharp cutbacks in hours (see also Ilcan, 1985). They are particularly sensitive to the illogic of working for low stamps.

Struggles for Control Over Allocation of Jobs and Stamps

The entry of women into the labour force of the Fogo Island fishery co-operative in 1979 added fuel to a long-simmering fire that, whenever fanned, highlighted the co-operative's central problem: how to combine social goals and economic viability. With the opening of the fish plants at Joe Batt's Arm and Fogo in 1979-80 and the creation of new jobs, including many slated for women, came the issues of whether the wives of fishermen (or their sons and daughters) had any special claim to jobs. The entry of women into the labour force also intensified a more enduring issue, whether a person's need for an opportunity to earn unemployment stamps should be a major criterion in hiring and firing. That these issues were raised suggests the degree to which Fogo Islanders have been unwilling to concede to all of the values of industrial culture including the notion that the conditions of employment are determined solely by the needs of capital.

"Fishermen's Wives"

> If anyone is going to work at the plant, it should be their own (the fishermen's) wives. The fishermen have a good bit to say about what goes on here, because it's their fish that makes it all possible (fish plant labourer, Joe Batt's Arm, July 1981).

The Special Needs of Fishing Households

In 1958 Newfoundland's unemployment insurance system was extended to fishermen. One of the many social effects of unemployment insurance is that peculiarities of fishermen's unemployment insurance, e.g. the fact that benefits do not begin until November 1 and are cut off on May 15, irrespective of fishing conditions, force many households to look for alternative sources of income. "Labour unemployment," or regular unemployment benefits that are not restricted seasonally, are valuable in helping tide a household over the period between fishing and the onset or end of benefits, as well as helping supplement a fishing household's income. Fish plant labour provides these benefits, if one qualifies by earning a minimum number of stamps.

In this setting, the ideal tactic for a fishery household is to have both kinds of unemployment coming in—from a man who fishes and from a woman who works at the fish plant. Thus, if a woman can work enough to qualify for unemployment insurance, her low, erratic income and her costs are more than compensated by what her unemployment cheques mean to the household during the lean months of winter. The fishermen's wives issue arose from widespread recognition of the logic of this tactic.

The Fishermen's Wives Issue

As soon as women began working in Fogo Island's fresh fish plants, first at Joe Batt's Arm and later at Fogo, a question arose over whether the wives (or sons and daughters) of fishermen should be given priority in jobs. It surfaced at the policy level with the board of directors, at the implementation level with plant managers, and within the community in the form of gossip and attempts to use the issue to obtain jobs at the fish plants.

The fishermen's wives issue reflected recognition of the special need of fishermen's households for larger and more secure incomes and unemployment benefits. Despite official and media announcements that Newfoundland's fish stocks were recovering because of reduced foreign fishing and quota allocations among sectors of the domestic fishery, the northeast coast fishery was still in trouble in the early 1980s. Fishermen's catches were irregular, unpredictable, and, more years than not, meagre.

Others on the island were poor and had irregular incomes. The fishermen's wives argument also spoke to the fact that the entire island depended on the fishermen. If there were no fishermen there would be no jobs at the fish plant. With the demise of both, local non-fishing businesses would fail, most people would be on welfare, out-migration would increase, schools, post offices and the hospital would close, and resettlement would occur without government sponsorship. It had happened elsewhere in Newfoundland and everyone knew it.

Longliner Fishermen's Wives?

The fishermen's wives issue revealed potentially divisive differences in structural position within the co-operative, i.e. between fishermen members and fish plant worker members, and between different kinds of fishermen. Most of the impetus toward an explicit policy favouring the wives and children of fishermen at the fish plant came from the longliner fishermen, who not only dominated the board of directors of the co-operative but also provided most of the raw material for the fish freezing plants, where the jobs were.

Longliners are 45 to 65 foot diesel-powered vessels equipped for fishing (with gill nets, longlines, and other techniques) in deeper water than the boats used in the cod trap and other truly inshore fisheries. Longliners tap the fish resources of the midwater reaches of the Fogo Bank and are also taken to the Labrador coast at times when local fish catches are poor. The species they catch are numerous, ranging from cod to turbot, halibut, flounder, catfish, wolffish, and, most recently, snow crab—while catches in the small boat fishery are generally restricted to cod, salmon, and lobster. Longliners have expanded the fishing season and the diversity of species caught and marketed.

Prior to 1979 the co-operative sold longliner fish "in the round" to processing plants elsewhere. The advent of fish processing on Fogo Island created jobs primarily out of the catch of around twenty longliners, the result of the work, investment, and risk-taking of a minority of the fishermen. Inshore, small boat catches are sold through specialized marketing channels (salmon and lobster) or go into the saltfish processing operations of the co-operative (cod). Longliner catches are almost entirely directed toward fresh fish freezing operations.

The perceived inequity recognized by advocates of preferential hiring of fishermen's wives is that most longliner fishermen are as poor as anyone else on the island and poorer than many (excluding a handful of "highliners" or "big fish-killers" who have successfully parlayed skill and luck into investment in superior longliner technology). The costs of this kind of fishing are high; returns are relatively low. Longliner fishermen are heavily in debt, have high operating, maintenance, and replacement expenses, and because of the large crews used (usually four to five men) must share their proceeds widely. In contrast, small boat fishermen, particularly the new breed of speedboat fishermen who use small (15 to 20 foot) open outboards to fish inshore, have few costs, share catches with no one or only one crewman, and make as much money as do longliner fishermen on the average (McCay, 1976). The fish of the speedboat fishermen does not go into the fresh fish plants, where most of the island's jobs and almost all of the women's jobs are.

Fishermen's Wives vs. Labourers' Wives

> Some think that the wife of a labourer should not be hired, just the wife of a fisherman. But I don't see any difference, do you? (Manager of the Fogo Island Co-operative, October 1980).

No one argued publicly that longliner fishermen's wives should be given preference, although the merits of the argument were often discussed in private. Broadening the argument to all fishermen's wives was important. It defused accusations that the board of directors—all of whom were, for a time, longliner fishermen—was self-serving, and it dampened mounting factionalism within the co-operative. It also reflected another concern, expressed in the quotation at the beginning of this section: that it was unfair that a fish plant job be given to the wife or dependent of a man who already had a wage-paying job and hence access to regular unemployment insurance benefits.

There is bitter irony in the situation of a fisherman and his wife who must go to see the welfare officer for short-term social assistance before fishing picks up, while their acquaintances who work at the fish plant are still drawing unemployment benefits from having processed fish caught by the fisherman the past season. That the fisherman may earn more money from fishing and unemployment benefits than a wage labourer at the fish plant earns only makes the irony bittersweet, for he also has more debts and anticipated capital replacement costs for the technology that makes the job and unemployment benefits of the labourer possible.

In sum, fishermen, especially longliner fishermen, came to feel that they were supporting the island and getting few returns. Those who depended on their entrepreneurship, capital, and risk-taking were in some ways better off than they were. Altruism can be its own reward, especially when its generalized returns, such as the maintenance of Fogo Island as a social entity, helped everyone. Still, when new jobs were created or old ones vacated, fishermen had a socially acceptable rationale for their argument that their families, their wives, sons, and daughters, should have first rights to them.

Discussion

The fishermen's wives issue revealed persistent structural problems within the co-operative that challenged the egalitarian sentiments of the community and of the co-operative's "one man, one vote" mode of organization. The co-operative is a worker-owned business, but with two or more classes, as it were, of worker/owners: the fishermen, paid for what they catch, and labourers, paid for their time and skills. The board of directors was comprised entirely of fishermen (and longliner fishermen at that) until 1983 when workers finally gained a slotted position on the elected board. Viewed in one way the labourers in the fish plants were working under the direction of the fishermen through the board of directors, which was made up almost exclusively of fishermen. Viewed in another way, one that complicates the moral economy of the situation, the fishermen were working for the labourers since it was their fish that made jobs possible. Accordingly, they and their wives could claim special privileges.

During an interview in October 1980 on the issue of fishermen's wives, a manager of the co-operative said, "This share and share alike has got to go. That's not business." Regardless of the divisiveness inherent in the issue, it was perceived as (1) a fundamentally egalitarian one; and (2) no good for the co-operative. Soon afterwards, in 1980, the board of directors ruled that fishermen's wives (or any other special group) would have no special status in employment at the fish plants. Nonetheless, until about 1983 the issue of whether the dependents of fishermen should have priority at the fish plant remained alive, expressed mostly in angry phone calls to managers from fishermen's wives who could not get work at the fish plants and who persisted in reminding the managers that another rationality endured.

"Taking Turns"

Managers of the Fogo Island co-operative found it difficult to dispense with "this share and share alike" attitude of Fogo Islanders. Nowhere is this more evident than in the second issue that concerned women, as well as men: allocation of the opportunity to earn unemployment benefits.

Sharing the Chance to Make Stamps

A ten-week hiring policy was in evidence as early as 1970 on Fogo Island (Carter, 1984:164), when most jobs were in the salt fish plant at Seldom and, in much smaller numbers, at collection and feeding facilities in the other communities. In 1980, when the co-operative had begun to run large-scale fish processing lines at two plants, the board of directors decided to phase out this policy to reduce labour costs and help the co-operative survive a developing crisis in the Atlantic Canadian fishing industry (see Carter 1984: 163-164). However, as late as 1983 islanders reported that the policy was still in place:

> They got it all worked out. When the first lot gets their ten weeks, they lay off so the others get their chance to make ten. That's the way it works here (longliner fishermen, Joe Batt's Arm, August 1983).

This policy, also called the "labour rotation" system, was a logical response to the chronic problems of unemployment and dependence of workers on unemployment insurance. Workers were hired long enough to get the minimum number of stamps or weeks of insurable earnings required to qualify for unemployment insurance benefits; then they were replaced by other workers. Inadequate employment and income were thereby distributed. The policy, which was accepted, however reluctantly, by the board and the management until around 1980, clearly fit the co-operative's mandate to maximize employment and income opportunities for its members and the larger community. Reflecting this practice is the fact that there were about 1.8 workers per co-operative fish plant job in 1981 (Fogo Island

Co-Operative Society Ltd., 1982). High turnover within positions contributes to low labour productivity and low average incomes per worker. The policy thus worked against worker productivity and the co-operative's goal of remaining economically viable, and, arguably, helped to replicate the condition of extreme dependency on and adaptation to the unemployment insurance system. On the other hand, it contributed to the goal of distributing income security among the island's households.

Hard Times: An Educational Process

As of August 1983, the fishermen's wives and labour rotation issues seemed to have abated. "It just died down," explained a fisherman I asked, who added: "They had to learn. The co-op has had some rough times." In August 1983 most Newfoundland fish plants were shut down, major fishery firms had withdrawn or gone into receivership, and federal and provincial governments fought over restructuring Newfoundland's ailing fishery. Fogo Islanders felt lucky to have jobs at all, especially since their co-operative had barely survived the summer. The management's message—that the co-operative's goal of providing jobs depends on its viability and hence efficiency as a business—overrode, at least temporarily, members' attempts to coalesce equitable and egalitarian ways to allocate jobs with the business of making money.

Attempts to implement this message began much earlier. Even before the board of directors directly attacked the ten-week hiring policy and fishermen's wives issue in 1980, managers of the co-operative insisted that hiring and firing should be independent of questions concerning stamps or fishermen's wives. Speed, skill, good working relationships, labour productivity and plant efficiency: these should be the criteria used to define, allocate, and reward work. However, the manager had uneven success in implementing a view of the co-operative as a "business." The board of directors, which has the constitutional power to set policy and hire and fire managers, had come to support the notion that jobs and the welfare of the community depend on the profitability and competitiveness of the co-operative. Yet, they too wavered when this notion conflicted with expressions of the earnest and long-standing special needs of the community. They often made implementation of the credo of efficiency very difficult for the managers and plant supervisors despite persuasive arguments and harsh experiences that underlined the co-operative's need to be competitive and thus efficient. In 1980 a manager—a native of the island who had just tendered his registration after seven years on the job because he could not effectively deal with conflicts such as these—complained that the members of the board and other fishermen "…believe in the co-op no matter what. Why should it make money when it is providing work? The co-op started during a crisis and had to make work for the people then. But they refuse to accept that it has to make money to survive."

Local plant managers also wavered in their implementation of the credo of efficiency, enough so that they were often accused by workers and others of being inconsistent, arbitrary and of playing favourites. Like members of the board of directors, they were much closer to the community of workers than was the general manager (an outsider after 1980). The local managers therefore found it harder to put aside the special claims of individuals backed by sentiments of the community.

Finally, in late 1980 the board of directors and a new manager, brought in from the outside to help the co-operative attain greater economic health, decided to phase out all particularist criteria in hiring and firing as part of a package of attempts to rationalize the organization of work and the production process at the co-op fish plants. Hiring and firing would be done on the basis of performance, and those whose performance was good would be hired for as long as possible. While there were indeed equity arguments for giving preference in hiring to the dependents of fishermen, especially fishermen who supplied most of the raw product for the plants, the favouritism implied went against more abstract egalitarian sentiments. More to the point, the board had begun to accept the notion that hard choices had to be made if the co-operative was to survive, and one of these choices was to use the criterion of labour productivity in hiring and firing. By late 1983, others in Fogo Island's communities had begun to accept it too.

Responses to the Rationalization of Fish Plant Work

Despite policy statements to the contrary, labour rotation and fishermen's wives preference continued beyond 1980. This was due to the ability of islanders to force the supervisors and managers to recognize their unemployment insurance needs and because of the very real difficulty facing members, the board of directors, management, and general membership in accepting and implementing a more "rational" labour management policy.

It was difficult for most islanders to accept the change in policy, since it had such evident and immediate effects on the lives of many people. As soon as the ten-week hiring policy was officially on its way out people became hurt and angered, as in this example:

> It's not right, the way they laid people off. There's some who wanted only one more stamp and they was laid off, and there's others who already got their stamps and they are still working. June (pseudonym for the speaker's daughter) got 13, but she's 7 short 'cause she never got enough last year neither. She saved some of her money and she'll get about $200 in her last cheque, but it's no good. She'll be here all winter with nothing to do and no money (mother of an unmarried fish plant worker and wife of a fisherman, Barr'd Islands, October 1980).

The "not-rightedness" of hiring and firing was almost always framed in terms of stamps and often led to individual attempts to persuade the management to do the "right" thing. For example, a young wife of a fisherman had not earned enough stamps during the 1979 season at the fish plant to qualify for benefits. The plant manager promised her enough work in 1980 to qualify, but she was laid off in the early fall of 1980 with only two more stamps to go to meet her minimum. At the time I heard this gossip, she had just gone to the office of the co-operative in Seldom to argue with the plant manager.

"Going to see the manager" was the usual method used to try to redress perceived

157

wrongs and gain personal advantages in hiring and firing. Problems tended to be personalized and worked out in private negotiations like most vertical social relationships in outport and traditional Newfoundland. Nonetheless, they were moulded by and also worked out through the broader community consensus of what was right and what was wrong. That the plant manager allegedly made a promise to the young fisherman's wife mentioned above suggests the pervasiveness of the sentiment that equal distribution of the opportunity to make stamps was very much part of the co-operative's role despite changes in policy. It must be noted that there were few alternatives to going to see the manager since employees at the fish plants had no formal representation on the board of directors (until 1983) and were not unionized.

Another response to the change in hiring policy was to withdraw from membership in the co-operative and to ask for return of share capital. In 1982 large numbers of members filed for return of share capital and withdrew from the co-operative. About half were former fish plant workers who had lost jobs because of the change in policy, since hiring workers for longer periods of time meant that fewer persons could work (Carter, 1984:164). This run on its inadequate capital came at a time of fiscal trouble for the co-operative.

An indirect response was improved participation of fish plant workers in decision-making. The structural difference between fishermen and labourers was manifest in one of the few "job actions" at the co-operative, one that reflected the longliner fishermen's agreement with the management that plant labour efficiency was essential. In 1981 two longliner skippers refused to fish for a week to protest labour inefficiency and sloppy work habits at one of the fish plants. Because they were highliners, their action severely reduced work at the plant and added to other pressures to improve labour productivity and plant efficiency, causing more strains between labour and management at the Joe Batt's Arm fish plant. This in turn contributed to the genesis of the first major "strike" at that plant. On July 28, 1981, the "cutters stuck their knives in" and walked home at noon, in a pre-arranged protest over the efforts at increasing profitability and efficiency (The plant manager broke the "strike" the next day by firing most of the "troublemakers"). Because of this and other labour problems engendered by the decision to phase out ten-week hiring and to implement other rationalizing measures (e.g. an incentive system that included daily monitoring of worker performance, cutbacks in the work force at some facilities, greater standardization and specialization of jobs, resulting in far more monotony and scrutiny), the co-operative added a worker to the board of directors in 1983 and more recently created a system of fish plant committees to which workers send elected delegates.

Discussion

The fundamental issue is whether the co-operative is a special business, tied and responsive to the needs and values of the community, or whether it is a business "like any other," bound by its formal charter and its competitive, capitalist environment to rational criteria in labour management. As a co-operative, the organization

158

is to some degree necessarily both, but it is not, therefore, absolved from conflicts between the two.

The men and women who argued for and against special consideration of fishermen's wives and those who needed stamps for the winter were not only speaking for themselves and their own positions, but also deliberating on what is indeed rational. Industrial culture was not yet so firmly entrenched that people accepted, without question, the idea that the best or most reliable worker should be the one to have a job.

The board of directors of the co-operative wavered on the fishermen's wives and labour rotation questions as well as on the broader question of what the co-operative is and hence whether special criteria, like kinship relationships and household needs, should be used in labour management. Most members of the co-operative and the rest of Fogo Island's population also wavered on these questions.

Islanders who talked about these issues with me presented them as ways that the co-operative was special in being able to serve the social needs of the community. In the fall of 1983, a longliner fisherman, after describing his understanding of the labour rotation system, said, "It's only because it's a co-op they can do it this way." That was not quite true; the labour rotation system has also been observed in privately owned fish plants in Atlantic Canada (Carter, 1984:164; Ilcan, 1985). However, the co-operative is a very special business.

For one thing, as a co-operative it "belongs to everyone." That everyone is very extensive because its membership includes active and inactive fishermen and plant workers: the bulk of the adult working population. Non-members do not feel excluded; membership is essentially open to anyone. For another, the co-operative has become the symbolic representation of Fogo Island. Without it and the political machinations that accompanied its inception, Fogo Island would be nothing but scrubby trees, granite, ponds, and pounding waves. These two interpretations of the co-operative coalesced in the notion that, while the co-operative must be a good business to survive, it must also and a priori meet the special needs of the people of the island, who own it.

For another, the co-operative may have more leeway than privately owned firms do to allow community and household needs to figure in labour practices. Some costs of low labour productivity are balanced by lower costs of labour. Because the fishery and the fish plants are run by a co-operative, in which both fishermen and plant labourers are members, neither the fishermen nor the plant workers are unionized in contrast with those in most other parts of Newfoundland.[5] In order to assure that its members continue to sell fish to the co-operative, in the early 1980s the Fogo Island co-operative's prices for fish were usually similar to those offered to unionized fishermen in the northeast coast region, and sometimes even higher, due to the co-operative's success in developing a program to compensate fishermen for higher quality fish. However, most plant labourers were paid about $2.00 less than unionized fish plant workers, and they did not get overtime and fringe benefits.

The co-operative is also better protected from losses due to job actions since these are infrequent and easily broken because of the lack of a union. The

159

co-operative has share capital from its members, who include not only fishermen but also plant workers. Another point bears upon the fact that both fishermen and plant labourers are members. This has worked against unionization of the labourers because of the structural contradiction posed by a class of workers who are also co-owners in the co-operative sense of the term. On the other hand, it has meant that the co-operative can call upon the loyalty of its members, plus their shared interests in its survival, to justify belt-tightening endeavors. The cooperative has successfully asked members to contribute larger percentages of their earnings as share capital during rough times. Finally, the strong policy role of the board of directors enables islanders to keep alive the notion that this co-operative is indeed special and to modulate how industrialization affects them and their lives.

Conclusion

The dilemma of the Fogo Island co-operative is to stay in business in a competitive and very difficult environment while being responsive to the needs and values of its members. The fishermen's wives and labour rotation issues highlighted this dilemma, and they also showed how an appeal for equity can reveal structural relationships of dependency and inequality. Both policies, when practised, contributed to the economic problems of the co-operative but also realized islanders' attempts to define work as that which benefits the community. Over a longer history than discussed in this paper, the co-operative has lurched back and forth between attempts to enhance economic and labour efficiency and attempts to meet its original mandate to provide a market for fish and to provide jobs in a fair and equitable way for the people of Fogo Island.

Since 1979, when women first came to work at the co-operative's fish plants, issues concerning women workers have been subsumed in the larger issues concerning the co-operative. More truly feminist issues paled in immediate significance,[6] and there has been little sign of the development of a distinctly female worker consciousness. Indeed, women have been essentially silent partners in job actions initiated by men, and most women appear to use the telephone and private meetings with managers rather than public meetings to express their feelings and argue their points of view.

As women gain more experience and knowledge they are becoming more active in the politics of the co-operative. In the summer of 1983 the management asked everyone to contribute to the equivalent of a week's earnings to help reduce accounts payable at a time when debts were high and fish sales low. Loyalty can work only so far in organizations (Hirschmann 1970). Although many people felt this was a reasonable request, a few, including women, objected very loudly that this was illegal and really too much to ask of an underpaid labour force. The suggestion was withdrawn. Happily, production and sales increased soon enough to thwart bankruptcy (this was at a time when other fish plants in Newfoundland were on the verge of shutdown). But it renewed smoldering sentiments about the need for unionization, especially from women who had spent part of the spring of 1983 touring other fish plants in Newfoundland (part of their training for super-

160

visory positions at the new crab shucking plant at Fogo) and had seen big differences in wages, overtime, and benefits.

I visited one of these women one night in August 1983 as she lay exhausted on her "daybed" after 12 hours of work in the crab plant. She said, after explaining the above, "the union, that's the only thing for us." But she paused and then said, "...but if someone came around tomorrow to sign me up (for a union), I don't know if I would sign. The way it is now, at least we're dealing with our own. The co-op belongs to all of us." Her ambivalence is shared by many others, one of whom commented to me while out on the fishing grounds: "The co-op is a union, see. It's just like a union." The co-operative is seen as a union of fishermen and labourers, men and women, well-off and poor, banded together against more distant sources of exploitation. A labour union would make more explicit the divisions of interest, power, and control that exist within this larger "union." It could shatter the egalitarian sentiment that "the co-operative belongs to everyone" as well as the possibilities of realizing that in some small way, Islanders are afraid that a true labour union would upset the fragile system they have created, one in which they feel they are "dealing with our own" and able to maintain some control, sometimes, over conditions of work and the fishery.

1. The observations and field notes on which this paper is based were collected during almost annual visits to Fogo Island between 1975 and 1984 that ranged from one to four weeks, usually in the summer, as well as two years spent on Fogo Island between 1972 and 1974. Thus the date and analysis in this paper refer to the situation prior to 1985. Support for fieldwork came from a U.S. Public Health Traineeship in Ecological Anthropology, a Woodrow Wilson Fellowship, the Institute of Social and Economic Research at Memorial University, and the Rutgers University Faculty Academic Support program. Special acknowledgements go to Marie and Hayward Coffin of "the bottom" of Joe Batt's Arm for their ever warm hospitality.

2. This discriminatory feature of Newfoundland's seasonal unemployment insurance system for fishermen was changed only a couple of years ago.

3. Egalitarian sentiments befitting an "image of limited good" solidity backed by a very limited resource base are expressed on Fogo Island in other ways, e.g. in the design of "winter works" programs, sponsored by the government to alleviate unemployment problems during the winter months while helping, in theory, to develop needed infrastructure. In the early 1970s, when I first did fieldwork in Fogo Island, local committees typically found ways to ensure that opportunities to participate in the "winter works" programs were distributed among all households, and that the households in most distress, usually those of the fishermen, were given priority.

4. It was assumed with good reason that a woman was unlikely to be a head of household (and if she was, e.g. a widow, that she received special government assistance).

5. The gossip is that in the early phase of the drive to unionize Newfoundland's fishery, in the early 1970s, a deal was made between supporters of the Fogo Island co-operative and union organizers to "leave the co-op alone." I heard this gossip from several people including one of the parties in the alleged deal.

6. Other issues affecting women at the fish plants that have not been addressed in this paper, and have received relatively little attention on Fogo Island, include job segregation and income discrimination by sex. It is also noteworthy that individual women have found it difficult, though not impossible, to rise to low-level supervisory positions; one obstacle has been jealous back-biting from other women, which in one case reached the level of anonymous threats to life and property.

Women and Fish Plant Closure: The Case of Trepassey, Newfoundland

Jane Robinson

THIS STUDY BEGAN AS AN INQUIRY into how women were responding to economic restructuring in Newfoundland. It became an exploration of laid-off women's understandings of the fish plant closure in Trepassey, Newfoundland, and of how their knowledge has been overlaid by a dominant discourse of adjustment, supported by the allocation of state resources to specific local institutions. The question I attempt to answer is: How is it that women who are highly productive, industrial wage labourers suddenly become unemployed, unskilled, and in need of being made over? In answering this question, I explore what laid-off women workers are thinking, saying and doing about the closure of their fish plant, and about the government programs rapidly furnished to help them "adjust." I am interested in these women's views on the official adjustment discourse, as it is taken up by politicians, the federal government, and their former employer, Fishery Products International (FPI). I explore how some officials in the adjustment process perceive the work experience and skills of women plant workers. And I examine how the women locate themselves within a new political-economic-ecological conjuncture—the closure of the cod fishery in Newfoundland. I hope that this article will contribute to readers' understandings of gender issues in plant closures and adjustment programs.[1]

The Backdrop: Economic and Ideological Restructuring

Economic restructuring has several dimensions. It involves the realignment of capitalist forces of production, new economic policies, as well as an ideological aspect. Plant closures are a manifestation of the realignment of capitalist forces of production. Economic policies can influence their likelihood and their impact. Neo-conservative economic policies are promoted by powerful western industrial nations and corporations, as well as through international organizations.

It is no secret that Canada is one of the easiest places in the western industrialized world (next to the U.S.) for a company to close up shop (Grayson, 1986). At the same time, Canada's adjustment programs have received international acclaim for bringing together companies, unions and governments to plan the adjustment process. One American policy analyst praised "[t]he successful rapid-response capability of the ... Canadian Industrial Adjustment Service [IAS]" (Hansen, 1988:166). One of the tenets of Canada's IAS approach is to get on with the job of adjustment, not to dwell on the closure itself. This approach tends to divert attention away from the economic and political contexts which underlie the closure. Claire Callender studied a partial plant closure in Wales, and notes a similar tendency in British government policy. "Redundancy," she wrote, "... is understood in an unproblematic way and its occurrence taken for granted and left unquestioned" (Callender, 1987:141).

The ideological dimension of economic restructuring involves not only masking

163

its economic and political contexts but also the promotion of a distinct discourse of development and response to such events as closures. Phrases such as "competitiveness is the key to prosperity", "let's ensure Canada takes on the world and wins", and "training: the wave of the future" are part of the political ideology of restructuring[2] (Cohen, 1992; Burman, 1991). Canadians are being told to adjust or perish.

But the ideology of restructuring does not fit with many peoples' interpretations of their world. This was evident when the federal government placed a moratorium on the northern cod fishery off the northeast coast of Newfoundland and Labrador in July, 1992. Some media reports on the moratorium adopted mainstream economic models for the "contribution" and "importance of the fishery to the Newfoundland economy" by arguing it generated only six percent of industrial revenue in Newfoundland.[3] However, the northern cod fishery employed 20,000 people directly, and many others indirectly. Many of the businesses in the province were kept afloat by the purchasing power of fishery workers. Trepassey fish plant workers told me they were appalled that the high level of employment generated by the fishery was not given value in these media reports.

Economic restructuring also affects men and women differently. Displaced women workers are largely absent from the literature, the media reports and the policies addressing plant closures, adjustment and retraining in Canada. In Newfoundland there is a silence about women in the public discourse on the fishery closure. Rarely are we informed that at least thirteen percent of fishers and about sixty percent of plant workers are women (EIC, 1993; Rowe, 1991). Media reports frequently describe the people affected by the fishery crisis as "fishermen."

Women are particularly vulnerable to unemployment. A gendered division of labour marks them as secondary wage earners to men in the labour market. They tend to be "last hired, first fired," (Connelly, 1978) although their vulnerability varies with class, race, region and sexual orientation. Work in industrial fish plants was one of the few opportunities for women in rural Newfoundland to earn decent wages, and to be involved in a union. In a province where unemployment is notoriously high, the risk that a plant closure will throw women into joblessness is great. Women's gender-defined second shift as domestic labourers, and a strong familial ideology, have operated to keep many of them in wage labour (or unemployed) close to their homes. Men have been consistently more available to meet the needs of labour markets farther from home.

Contrary to familial ideology, many women are single wage-earners in their families, single parents, or otherwise dependent on paid work. How do those responsible for the adjustment policies in the fishery respond to displaced women workers? Do they recognize women's particular needs and their diversity? How do they help, hinder, or otherwise affect women's chances of finding another job?

Research and Theoretical Considerations

This paper juxtaposes grassroots women's thinking about economic restructuring with that found in the federal bureaucracy. In-depth, taped interviews and informal conversations with twenty laid-off women plant workers in the summer of 1992 and notes from three bi-monthly follow-up gatherings provided the data, along with taped interviews with a number of officials responsible for the adjustment process in Trepassey. The plant workers had from three to thirty-four years of work experience at the Trepassey fish plant as trimmers, filleting machine operators, defect removers, sorters, and packers of codfish and flounder. They ranged in age from twenty-three to forty-six years. Several of them held positions in their union local, and in community organizations. Their average education was mid-secondary. They included a widow, single women, and married women. Most of them had lived all their lives in communities within a 30-kilometre radius of Trepassey, or in the town of Trepassey itself.

I entered into this research with some trepidation. As an urbanite, feminist, leftie, and a "come-from-away" (sixteen years before), I went into the community expecting to struggle with the differences between myself and the women I was going to interview. From the start, I tried to be frank about my values and where I was coming from. I was relieved to find similarities among us. Several of the women had had union experience, and some called themselves feminists. Above all, we shared a view that women were left out of the public debate on the fishery, and an interest in talking about the plant closure and the adjustment programs. I resisted a tendency to see the women as victims of economic restructuring. They did not portray themselves this way.

The analysis makes use of a blend of theoretical sources. There is an understanding of capitalism as a system which, at its worst, relentlessly plunders resources for the profit of a few, and produces unemployment through reduction of labour costs and use of advanced technology. The data are, however, interpreted through a feminist lens that is resistant to versions of political economy wherein women's voices tend to disappear.

Post-structuralist interpretations of language, discourse and subjectivity also guide the analysis. Peoples' understandings are shaped by historical forces such as gender, class and ethnicity, and through discursive practices which involve how they talk about, believe (or not), and shape themselves in response to what they hear about issues affecting their lives (Davies and Harre, 1990). Post-structuralist theory views the individual as a site of conflicting discourses, or political interests, through which she must negotiate a passage. In Chris Weedon's words, the subject has become "a site of disunity and conflict, central to the process of political change and to preserving the status quo" (Weedon 1987:21). This approach challenges structuralism, which tends to portray an individual as being almost completely determined by larger events or institutions in her life. Post-structuralism offers women active "agency" in choosing how or whether they will conform to, refuse, or otherwise engage with, subject-positions implicitly prescribed by dominant institutions and ideologies.

Post-structuralism focuses in on the concept of discourse as a conveyor of ideologies. I have used tools of deconstruction in the interpretation of the data collected. Deconstruction refers to "analyzing the operations of difference in texts, the ways in which meanings are made to work" (Scott, 1988:37). For me, this has meant unpacking the gaps, exclusions, differences and concealments, that took place in the talk about retraining and adjustment. This exercise helped me to unveil some of the assumptions and ideologies which guided the adjustment officials, and which silenced and otherwise constituted the women to whom their practices were directed. I also looked for silences in the women's talk, and for what was taken as common sense. I looked for how the women positioned themselves in their talk.

The Context: The Closure of the Trepassey Fish Plant

The Trepassey processing plant first opened in 1953. It was one of the first Newfoundland fish plants to be fitted out for the industrial fishery with its own draggers that could venture far offshore. The original owner, Fishery Products, went into receivership in an industry-wide crisis in 1982. A massive refinancing and restructuring by federal and provincial governments, the industry, and the Bank of Nova Scotia, constituted a new and enlarged corporation in 1984. It was similarly named—Fishery Products International (FPI)—and swallowed up several smaller companies. With a Board of Directors that included major Canadian corporate chiefs, FPI was returned to the private sector in 1986, and reaped tidy profits for several years.

The federal government made severe cuts to the allowable catch of northern cod in 1989. FPI responded by announcing the closure of three of its sixteen New-foundland fish plants in January 1990. Trepassey was among them. Provincial government subsidization delayed the actual closure until September, 1991. Vic Young, Chief Executive Officer and Chairman of FPI, blamed the closures on the federal government's severe reduction of fish quotas (Walsh, Jan. 6, 1990:1). Premier Clyde Wells attributed the quota reductions to "uncontrolled foreign overfishing and resource management shortcomings and mistakes" (*W.I.R.* Jan. 5, 1990:2). A moratorium on the northern cod fishery was imposed in July, 1992, followed by a total ban on commercial cod fishing, moratoria on other groundfisheries, and eventually, a ban on the food fishery.

The Trepassey plant had employed about 621 people. According to FPI, 560 were union members. Most of them belonged to the FFAW, which is affiliated with the Canadian Auto Workers Union (CAW). Of these workers, 46% were women.[4]

The federal government has regarded the Newfoundland fishing industry as "inefficient" and in need of reform for several decades (see Wright, this volume; Matthews, 1993; Report, 1983). The industry was labour-intensive, like the textile industry in central Canada. It was also largely seasonal, with high dependence on unemployment insurance and considered to be "overcapitalized," with more plants and vessels licensed than the stocks could sustain. During the 1982 fishery crisis, the federal government infused hundreds of millions of dollars into consolidating the industry. In the 1990s, with collapsing fish stocks and a context of economic restraint, it has concentrated its efforts on downsizing the industry and retraining its participants for other work.

Soon after the 1990 closures were announced, the federal government unveiled a new Atlantic Fisheries Adjustment Program (AFAP). The AFAP was proclaimed by John Crosbie, Minister of Fisheries and Member of Parliament for the south-western Avalon Peninsula where Trepassey is located. A generous agreement, perhaps designed to appease angry Tory voters, it provided $29 million for retraining and industrial diversification to the area of Trepassey alone. An Industrial Adjustment Service (IAS) committee was established, composed of representatives of the corporation, the union and three levels of government, and it directed the adjustment process. Fishery Products International participated on the IAS committee for a little over a year, but withdrew when the plant gates were closed.

Fishermen, Food and Allied Workers union (FFAW) President Richard Cashin decried the federal government's willingness to let fishery policy be "determined by corporate decisions" (Cashin/FFAW, 1990:6). The union and its members organized several large protest rallies in St. John's. Early in 1990, thousands of women and men drove from the affected communities to a march on the Confederation Building. Supportive local businesses closed for the day, and people were asked to take their children out of school and join the demonstration. In 1992, the FFAW, in conjunction with the companies, held a massive rally to protest foreign overfishing, and sent prominent officials to the Grand Banks on trawlers decked out with protest banners.

In Trepassey, the union has held several public meetings. Some local union officers found employment compiling a data base on laid-off workers for the IAS committee. Some workers also formed a committee called Fishplant Workers Fighting Back (FWFB). It brought together union and management employees, and representatives were elected from Trepassey and the communities where the plant workers lived. The FWFB and the IAS committee initially concentrated almost entirely on searching for a new operator for the plant. These efforts fizzled out when the federal government would not provide a fish quota for the operator.

Women's Analyses of the Closure

Doreen May was thirty. She was married, had several young kids, and had worked at the plant since she was seventeen. She mainly worked as a trimmer, but did the odd stint replacing supervisors. At one point in her interview, she said, "So then when the plant decided to close down, well that left me—jobless." Something about the way Doreen reified the plant as having the power to close itself down made me wonder how women would describe the event of the plant closing. According to post-structuralist theory, people take part in discourses in subtle ways which reflect their locations in a web of power relations. Sarah Hoagland writes that in the construction of the term "battered women," there is a separation between the result of the action, the action itself, and the agent. In fact, as with Doreen May's account of the plant closure, the agent has disappeared (Hoagland, 1988).

To find out the meanings of the Trepassey fish plant closure for laid-off women, I asked them how they would explain the closure to someone who didn't know anything about it.

Rhonda Pike was the youngest woman I interviewed. She came from a large family of plant workers in Trepassey. She commented:

> Well when I first heard about it, I thought well, they want to get rid of the plant, to cut down on their costs. And then all this came out about the fishery... about the stocks being as low as they were, and uh, it's a hard situation, I mean there's so many rely upon the fishery. And here the resource is, it's just depleting, and they can't seem to do anything about it" (A504:16-17).

Rhonda Pike's words suggest that she sees the resource as depleting due to natural causes or at least some unknown agent. This is another example of what Hoagland would call the overt exclusion of the agent. The power relations in the situation are masked. Hoagland suggests that by using such language we may be consenting to the perpetuation of those power relations.

Some women were more willing to attribute responsibility for the closure. Irene Power, who lived in one of the communities outside Trepassey, had this to say:

> Mmm. Well I guess the reason for the closure is just mismanagement. Because, you know, they say that the government keeps a close watch on the stocks of the fishery, but if they have been doing it over the years, they wouldn't give out so many licenses for fish plants—you know, if they knew the stocks were declining. ... And ... they should have cut back their quotas years ago, not just recently. It was mismanagement on the government's part. That's who I blame now.... Because I mean, I can hear Dad and my uncles, and like they've been saying when they were fishing 25, 35 years ago you know, if the government had to listen to them then, there'd have been a closer eye kept on the stocks (A111:11).

Several women referred to mismanagement by federal and provincial governments as the cause of the plant closure. They spoke about there being too many fish plants allowed to operate, stock surveys done incorrectly, international treaties which allowed European trawlers to fish in endangered zones, and, worst of all, the new policy of enterprise allocations, which granted fish quotas to companies rather than the government retaining allocations and companies being given only the right to fish them. FPI was also culpable, according to many of the women. Anne Bulger, who had quit school after grade seven to go to work at the plant, and whose mother had been a union official, told me:

> Well I guess one of the major reasons is that they let the plant almost fall down, they didn't keep doing repairs. Any money that came to Trepassey for repairs they took it and shipped it off to the other fish plants ... If they had to keep her in better condition she wouldn't have closed I don't think, because she would have been a good plant to keep open, and where she's close to the banks, and she's an ice-free port (A107:15).

Scepticism about FPI was most clearly articulated by women who had been involved with the union over the years. Edna Molloy told me: "[T]hey can manage without us. They can still make money right? I think, the bottom line is the shareholders ... [they] are after money" (A116:18). And Carmel Stokes said:

Maybe FPI is just trying to get rid of some of its plants anyways. They're not goin' to come to us, are they? They're goin' to make it look as [if]... the government did it to us. ... Like Vic Young told us "You're in the wrong office. You go to the government. You bring back the fish and we'll open the plant." Would he? We don't know. It's hard to tell, isn't it? There's many unanswered questions. They'll never be answered (A106:21-22).

FPI has done quite well. In 1989, the company acquired Clouston Foods Canada, a profitable sourcing venture which accesses seafood from fish farms in Southeast Asia and South America (FPI, 1989). FPI's reported losses in 1992, even after the first season of the cod moratorium, were small, thanks in part to a tax write-down of its many idle plant facilities (*E.T.* July 28,1992). The company has earned income on the sale of about one third of its trawlers to buyers in Southeast Asia and South America (*E.T.* Oct.20,1992). Since the moratorium, it has also been acquiring cod and other groundfish from foreign sources such, as Russia and Alaska.

Adjustment Programs: Adjusting the Value of Women's Work

In Trepassey, the Atlantic Fisheries Adjustment Program (AFAP) had two elements: an industrial diversification/ small business development package; and a retraining, relocation, and early retirement package. Dick Russell administered the Community Development Fund of AFAP—$7 million over five years, to start up or expand small businesses specifically to assist former plant workers. He was an official at the Business Development Centre (BDC) located in Trepassey, a project of the government-appointed Community Futures Committee. Like Community Futures, much of AFAP came under the umbrella of Employment and Immigration Canada (CEIC). The BDC also offered $1.5 million in small loans for people who wanted to establish and expand businesses in a broad area around Trepassey.

The women I spoke with were under the impression that the diversification funds were set up so as to benefit former plant workers. They told me, however, that the people who had received the loans and grants were either established local business people who had created no new jobs, or others who had never worked at the plant. Anne Bulger and Carmel Stokes had inquired about starting up businesses—one was to meet the need for a senior citizens' home, and the other a clothing store in Trepassey. They were told to phone a woman in St. John's who worked with the IAS. Both ideas were turned down. In a third case, well-known by almost all the women I spoke with, a former plant worker and experienced baker wanted to start a bakery. She complied with the requirements and drew up a complex business plan but was turned down on the basis that she would be competing with other bakeries located a hundred and fifty kilometres away.

When I suggested to Dick Russell that the business development programs could be designed to respond better to women's needs, he responded:

I don't think they've ever thought of themselves as being anything other than fish plant workers.... That's the problem ... they don't have any other skills ...I guess in every community ... there's always the more ambitious in it, male or female, and they're the ones that probably aspire to the foreman type of position, or someone who wants to you know, get some other skills, uh secretarial, or accounting skills and work in an administrative position" (B711:43,38).

To Dick Russell, women plant workers had no skills other than plant work, which he considered unskilled. The extensive organizational and leadership experience many of them had in community organizations and in unions was meaningless. Unless people had worked in an office, or in management, he said, (and he seemed to be referring to the local fish plant office and management), they were not skilled to start up a small business. Virtually all of the women I interviewed had grown up with ideas of training in a field other than the fishery. Several of them had trained and worked in other sectors before returning to their communities and working at the plant. They chose plant work in response to social relations and power relations in their families, communities, and beyond. Their choices were influenced by dominant discourses of femininity and masculinity. These notions showed up in such experiences as Edna Molloy's husband's unwillingness to stay in the city where her work opportunities lay.

Women felt pressured to go to work young, to lessen the burden on their parents. Notions of femininity involved local traditions of marrying quite young, and once married and mothers, there was the necessity to provide for their families. Some women chose fish plant work in response to state modernization strategies, such as resettlement, which created a local labour market in towns where industrial fish plants were located (see Wright, this volume).

Dick Russell's portrayal of plant workers as unskilled, and as never thinking of doing anything other than plant work, revealed a lack of awareness of the experience and expectations of women plant workers. He was acting out of a powerful discourse. Women's so-called 'weaker' attachment to the labour market has been used historically to justify the undervaluing of their work. In most plants where men and women work, men tend to have more seniority. Women's domestic labour of housekeeping, caring for the sick, and, in many cases, child rearing, interrupts their employment continuity and few collective agreements fully compensate for this. Furthermore, work place culture and the way talk gets done (or "discursive practices") at work are typically masculine, and have excluded women from being defined as skilled workers (Cohen, 1991). Indeed both unions and management have historically tended to perpetuate higher valuations for men's work (Callender, 1987; Rosen, 1987). This issue also extends beyond the workplace (Parr, 1990). In many plant closures, rehiring and access to training are based on years of seniority (Callender, 1987).

Without access to other discourses which support them, women themselves may take up the dominant patriarchal idea that their work is not as valuable as men's. This may explain why many women I spoke with did not have a strong sense of what their skills were. Some women equated skill with obedience, with being punctual and co-operative. Other women recognized the value of their work. Here's how one of the women spoke of her years of work as a trimmer:

Well I guess there was a lot of skill towards the fishery. ... how you would cut up a fish, weigh the fish, and make sure that all the bones are out of it, and how the bones are taken out.... [I]f you went to another plant, there would be no trouble that you — just pick up. You would know right away what, what was on there (A116:14-15).

Understandings of women's skill and women's choices can be very limiting if they are simply definitions of one individual at one point in time, or if they are loaded with classed and gendered notions, as in the case of Dick Russell's assessments. Ideological and material constraints condition women's sense of their options, and of the value of their work. Women make choices within multiple parameters which constitute, or form, their sense of what is possible. In Dick Russell's interpretation of adjustment, there was little understanding of women plant workers' skills and experience, or of the obstacles facing women. Their ideas were quashed. This limited women's chances to creatively adapt to the plant closure. It excluded women plant workers from the small business development programs.

Gary Payne worked for CEIC, administering the re-training, relocation and retirement package under the AFAP. One key aspect of the adjustment program, he said, was that it was "client-driven." The words "client-driven" gave me the impression that re-training programmes were responsive to people's needs and interests. Instead I found that this was one of the "newspeak" terms used in the labour market lingo. Gary explained that this term helped the staff of CEIC distinguish between those who wanted to pursue a career interest, and those who wanted to do training out of personal interest:

> [W]hat you will find is when you take that approach to training, you will have a lot of people coming forward merely because of self-interest, of personal interest, doing the course just because it was, it is of interest to them, not because it's in fact a career goal they have (B211:3).

Several of the women I interviewed proposed that a sewing course be delivered in their community, about thirty kilometres from Trepassey. Eleven of these women wanted to make articles for their own households. Four were keen to start a business together. They were confident that they could develop a market, not solely in Newfoundland, for the products they had in mind. The proposal was turned down by the CEIC regional office on the basis that there was no market in the area for fifteen seamstresses, and that eleven of the women had said that they would not move away for work. The women were furious about the rejection. One woman said that they had not understood the implications of the mobility question. CEIC seemed to have used the mobility question to distinguish between a career goal and personal interest (this was hotly denied by a CEIC official).

The personal versus career interest dichotomy is not new, but it goes against progressive notions of women's and workers' educational needs, which contend that career interests often develop out of personal interests (Women's Reference Group, 1992; Jackson, 1989). In this case it was used against women.

Most of the women I interviewed felt that it was much harder for a woman to move away than a man. Some found it very difficult to consider leaving their communities because of domestic responsibilities, because their husbands would not go, or for financial reasons. To take up re-training elsewhere represented a huge shift. It meant, in most cases, leaving their husbands and children and living alone in St. John's, leaving a home of their own, and living in small, often substandard apartments or rooms in boarding houses.

Many women expressed a suspicion that the retraining programs were set up to try to get people out of the fishery and out of their small communities. They compared them to the resettlement policy of the Smallwood government in Newfoundland and Labrador in the 1950s to 1970s. Some of them were determined to stay in the fishery, and/or in their communities. Yet opportunities for re-training within the fishery, developed by the colleges and the union, have focused on fishermen, not plant workers. From the way investments are being made in retraining, it appears that women are being edged out of the fishery.

Yet perhaps because they tended to be women who felt confident to speak out, more than half of my sample either had already done some retraining, or were considering moving to St. John's to do so. Some of them felt there was no future for themselves or for their children in the fishery. Some women saw the retraining package as a chance in a lifetime. A few informal contacts told me that the financial package had enabled women to leave abusive husbands.

Conclusion

This paper has provided a glimpse into the social relations among some women plant workers and male officials in the aftermath of the Trepassey fish plant closure. I have shown how these relations extend beyond the local sites of women's experiences into a web of discourses and practices involving local state officials, their managers, politicians, the media, colleges, unions and other institutions (Smith, 1987).

The messages which form the dominant discourse on adjustment are those which are backed up by institutional resources. These resources empower certain officials to define and delimit the scope of "adjustment" to fish plant closure. In this case study, the officials speak about the need to reduce the number of workers in the fishery. They promote class differentiation within outports, and mobility of people from small communities, through the diversification, retraining and relocation programs. They perpetuate notions of women's work as unskilled, and a sense that women don't belong in the fishery. They promote a competitive market economy model, rather than a democratic approach to community development. They pass on a questionable certainty that retraining will lead to jobs. Furthermore, their approach is focused on the individual, rather than on the social, political and economic aspects of the plant closure. Underlying this is an ideology of adjustment which presumes that economic change is inevitable and all people can do is to accept and fit into it.

In the women's narratives, a more marginal discourse on fish plant closure and adjustment appears—one that doesn't receive institutional resources or media attention. Some women speak about who is responsible for the plant closure and how it could have been avoided. They have a sense of whose interests are and are not being served. They mention a lack of democratic adjustment structures, a withholding of official information, and the mismanagement of funds. They express a determination not to let their communities die, and a sense that retraining is futile because there are no jobs. They speak of increasing alcoholism and social distress in their communities. Some women voice their fears of increasing abuse of women and children.

What happens when so much gender analysis and local analysis gets left out of adjustment policy? Social issues could have been included in the Trepassey IAS committee's mandate—their omission was an oversight, according to the Chairperson.[5] Most of the officials I spoke with complained about the apathy and passivity of laid-off plant workers. They said that this was an obstacle to the implementation of adjustment programs—people just weren't adjusting fast enough. To policymakers in western industrialized countries, adjustment programs are premised on the notion that economic restructuring is a given, and a country will be more advantaged in the global economy if it makes the transition quickly (Hansen, 1988).

The women in this study told me that some of their former co-workers were experiencing a prolonged disbelief, or shock, which kept them from making changes in their lives. I would suggest, however, that some of the so-called apathy represents a form of resistance, in the sense of "the fear, dislike, hesitance most people have about turning their whole lives upside down and watching everything they have ever learned disintegrate into lies" (Lather, 1991).

There is a lot of dissatisfaction and anger about adjustment programs among the women plant workers. Not only have they not been invited to participate in the design of the adjustment process, but their proposals have been turned down and their skills have been ignored. Their basic needs such as child care and after-school programs have not been met at the community level. Assistance for babysitting, as well as counselling services, has been cut back from 1991 levels. Adjustment programs have been loaded with notions of class and gender, with built-in prescriptions for how women should act. Will women, now unemployed in their communities, be expected to mop up after these botched efforts? How will they respond?[6]

1 Pseudonyms are used to protect the anonymity of all persons interviewed for this study. The pseudonyms of the women plant workers are drawn from common family names of the southern Avalon Peninsula. Names given to the officials I interviewed are also false, as are the names of specific communities around Trepassey.

2 *Invest in your own future* Employment and Immigration Canada p.3 n.d.; *An agenda for prosperity* Ministers Valcourt / Wilson p.3 n.d..

3 Interview with Nora Devereaux (pseudonym), July 28, 1992.

4 Personal communication with Donna Crockwell, FPI, October 26, 1993.

5 Personal communication with Dennis Knight, May 25, 1993 (see also Knight, 1993).

6 This article was originally written in November, 1993. It is based on a larger body of research. For a fuller discussion of these issues, see Jane Robinson, 1994. "Women and Fishplant Closure: The Case of Trepassey, Newfoundland," Toronto: OISE M.A. Thesis.

Strange Newes from the New-found Lande

Anne Hart

In 1497 "The northerly course," John Cabot called it,
seven hundred leagues from Bristol.
"I zealously prosecuted the fish," he wrote.

William Vaughan in 1626, playing to the gallery:
"Neptune's sheepe," he called them,
"continually to be shorne."

Poor patient fish
we have done for you, I fear.
We thought you would go on—well, forever—
swimming layer on century layer
so constant, so obedient,
just out there waiting to be called
on that old grey platter
the Grand Banks of Newfoundland.

Dear fish,
come into the parlour.
Perhaps we can negotiate?
We will wear our best suits for you
and handsome women will follow
carrying our briefcases and proposals.

Dear fish,
come back to the table.
Surely, it's never too late to bargain?
Look, we'll save the last of the capelin just for you
and deliver it gleaming, flapping even,
on the softest of old nets.

If She Had The Choice . . .

O RGANIZATION OF THE PREVIOUS SELECTIONS IN THIS VOLUME took a more-or-less chronological approach, and that imposed its own logic on the work included here. The history of Newfoundland and Labrador, as we all know, is tied to the history of the fishery, and this is as true for women as it is for men. Other themes were explored—the impact of the Second World War, for example. The experiences of women who were less closely involved in the fishery were included—first nations women, or women living in St John's. Yet the reader kept coming back to the overarching economic and social reality of the fishery and its fate.

The pieces in this section all look at situations individual women find themselves in and at the choices they do—or do not—have. It takes us away from purely economic considerations, although poverty deprives women of choice in fundamental ways. But there are many other aspects of our lives where whether we have choice or not affects our well being. We live in a world controlled by men and largely organized around their needs. Nowhere is this more apparent than in the area of sexuality. Lorraine Michael testifies to the horrifying impact of uncontrolled male sexuality on young girls and boys. Virginia Ryan's fiction plumbs the depths of one woman's choice in the face of an impossible situation. Some of the pieces in this section draw on the relationship between the church and expressions or experiences of sexuality. Robin Whitaker's paper explores the experiences of Catholic nuns.

Among the most important choices women want to make are reproductive choices. In Newfoundland, as Jaya Chauhan's paper demonstrates, these are not wholly free or individual choices.

Linda Parsons and Evie Plaice examine what it means to be a woman in a community designed specifically for and around men—the mining town of Labrador City and an air base. In both these places, women were introduced to serve certain needs, and these two papers explore some aspects of the problems this creates for women in controlling the choices around their own lives.

Some of the material in this section is raw, alarming and, perhaps, depressing. It certainly doesn't show the romantic idyll of the tourist advertisements. What it does show is a variety of Newfoundland women in a variety of situations either making choices or looking for ways to take control of their own lives.

From this focus on individual experience and struggle, this book moves toward an exploration of women's collective action, protest and organization. A key element in the final selections is the finding of voice—a way to tell stories that have not been told before, to express experience, to draw from experience the impulse for action and change.

"Nobody's Brother": Gender Consciousness in Newfoundland Convents[1]

Robin Whitaker

This paper, exploring the experiences of Catholic nuns, draws from the author's MA thesis at York University.

[Pope John Paul II stated] women's human and civil rights had to be distinguished from their ministries and functions in the Church. Otherwise "false demands" could be presented and "false hopes" raised. The bishops must explain the Church's position to their people. To fail to do so would "amount to a betrayal of them". In not ordaining women as priests, the Church was maintaining a distinction of roles that "in no way favours the superiority of some over others".
– "Pope supports women's rights,
criticises feminist ideology." *Tablet,* 10 July, 1993

Jesus was a feminist.
– Mercy Sister Kathleen (1992 interview)

THE HISTORY OF THE TWO MAIN RELIGIOUS CONGREGATIONS[2] for women in Newfoundland seems in many ways to uphold the optimistic claim that "entering a convent could well mean overcoming the disadvantage of being a woman in a man's world" (Danylewycz, 1987: 160). Becoming a Presentation or Mercy Sister enabled women to obtain a post-secondary education, pursue a professional career, and take an active role in the life of the Roman Catholic Church at a time when such opportunities were very limited. The fact that the Sisters of the Presentation of the Blessed Virgin Mary and the Sisters of Mercy have been contributing in important ways to the education and training of women and girls since their arrival in Newfoundland over 150 years ago also seems to support the description of nuns as "unwitting feminists" (Ebaugh, 1993: 134). Nevertheless, the active articulation of what others might term a feminist consciousness is relatively new. In this paper I speculate about why some sisters have come to identify sexism as a key source of oppression and explore how they have expressed this concern. Before doing so, however, I will provide a brief historical sketch of the two congregations.

In September of 1833, four Presentation Sisters landed in St. John's harbour. They came at the request of the Bishop of Newfoundland, Michael Anthony Fleming, who hoped the nuns would provide both secular and religious instruction for the Island's poor Catholic girls, enabling them to become virtuous citizens and good Catholic mothers (e.g. Dinn, 1975: 16; Howley, 1979 [1888]: 276-277).[3] Fleming felt that this would be accomplished only when young girls could be removed from "the dangerous associations which ordinary school intercourse with the other sex naturally exhibited" (Howley: 276). Despite early setbacks, such as the destruction of their convent in the great fire of 1846, the Presentation Sisters flourished in Newfoundland. Their schools were filled to capacity and beyond. Just twenty years after their arrival they had four houses outside St. John's, and the congregation kept growing in numbers until the 1960s (Howley: 290-293; Dinn,

1975: 19-23; Penney, 1980: 43-46). Moreover, the Sisters' influence extended beyond the education of children, as we can see from their work in Harbour Grace, where they made a foundation in 1851:

> In addition to pupils of regular school age, girls of twenty years of age and over joyfully availed themselves of this opportunity for education, both religious and secular. . . . All the women of the town assembled on Sundays for religious instruction, and girls who could not attend school on week days were taught reading and writing at these Sunday classes (Dinn, 1975: 20).

Bishop Fleming had intended that the Presentation Sisters teach poor children. They proved popular with wealthier families as well. In keeping with contemporary opinion that children of different classes were best served in separate schools (Clear, 1987: 118), however, Fleming felt that Newfoundland needed a school for "respectable Catholic ladies" (in Howley, 1979: 370; cf Clear, 1987: 118-119). He therefore requested the Mercy Sisters in Ireland to send a group of sisters to the Island, for unlike the Presentation sisters, they were permitted by their constitutions to charge school fees.

The early years after the Mercy sisters' arrival in 1842 brought many trials (Hogan, 1986: 30-38), but they persevered, becoming an equally strong presence on the Island. By 1922, the Sisters were running, in St. John's alone: a private girls' school with fees, a day school for poorer children, an orphanage, a teacher training college for women, a commercial school for women, a hospital, and a school of nursing (Hogan, 1986; Penney, 1980: 48-58). Like the Presentation, the Mercy Sisters established numerous foundations outside the capital, providing education and other services to smaller towns (Hogan, 1989; Penney, 1980).

The Presentation and Mercy Congregations were similar in many ways. Both were founded within a sixty-year span in Ireland by wealthy women who had a strong desire to serve God through serving the poor, and who believed that one of the best ways of doing so was to provide them with skills to support themselves (Clear, 1987: 49-50; Dinn, 1975: 3ff; Hogan, 1986: 1-12 *passim*). Prior to the reforms brought by the Second Vatican Council (Vatican II), the congregations' Rules (constitutions governing religious life) had much in common.[4] It is also worth noting that Mercy foundress Catherine McAuley made her novitiate in a Presentation Convent (Hogan, 1986: 11-12). Nevertheless, there were some important differences.

During the nineteenth century, the growing middle classes in Newfoundland and Ireland were dissatisfied with charity schools, yet could not afford the institutions designed for the wealthy. Although McAuley placed priority on ministry to the poor, she also considered that the secular and religious education of the middle classes was a problem in need of address. Hence, Mercy Sisters often had separate schools for poor and middle-class girls, while Presentation Sisters tended to be restricted to charity schools (Clear, 1987: 118; Hogan: 49-57; McCormack, 1955: 2-3). This led to the perception, in St. John's at least, that 'Mercy girls' had a higher status than those who went to Presentation schools.

Secondly, both McAuley and Nano Nagle, the Presentation foundress, wanted to establish non-cloistered institutions, feeling that enclosure would interfere with sisters' ability to minister to the poor. Nagle, though, was frustrated posthumously, partly by her own sisters, who seem to have felt that 'real' religious were synonymous with enclosure (Clear, 1987: 49; Walsh, 1980 [1958]: 168-173). When the Presentation Nuns finally received canonical recognition in 1805, 21 years after Nagle's death, the Pope's Apostolic Brief instructed them "never by any means to pass the limits of the Monastery, unless for the most weighty reasons" (in Dinn, 1975: 11). As a result, Presentation Sisters were largely restricted to their convents and schools prior to Vatican II.

Nagle's scheme was unprecedented in late eighteenth century Ireland (Clear, 1987: 49), which helps to explain her sisters' reluctance to embrace its ambiguous canonical status. By 1830, when McAuley agreed to the Archbishop of Dublin's demand that she transform her charity organization into a religious congregation, she was able to ensure that her sisters would not be prevented from ministering outside the convent (Bolster, 1990: 33-34). Thus, while the Newfoundland Presentation Sisters' work was largely restricted to teaching, the Mercy Sisters were engaged in a range of apostolates (religious works). Indeed, this was one of the reasons for Bishop Fleming's initial request. In addition to teaching, the Newfoundland Mercy Sisters are known for their work in health care and what might broadly be termed 'social work.' For instance, immediately on arrival in St. John's, they began teaching "the basic skills of homemaking" to the poor (Hogan, 1986: 25) and later began running orphanages (Hogan: 87ff).

Strong and innovative women populate the histories of both the Presentation and Mercy sisters in Newfoundland. The differences in rules pertaining to enclosure may have enabled some Mercy Sisters to take a more direct role in public affairs, however. For instance, Sister M. Joseph Fox not only set up a commercial school for women in turn-of-the-century St. John's, but also persuaded the manager of the Bank of Nova Scotia to hire one of her students as a stenographer—the first woman hired by that bank in Newfoundland. Soon thereafter, another Mercy graduate became the first female employee of the Bank of Montreal in St. John's (McCormack, 1955: 35-36).

These differences aside, it must be said that both the Presentation and Mercy congregations were remarkable historically in the extent of their independence from men. Certainly, there are many examples of bishops and priests interfering with the business of Irish convents during the 1800s (Clear, 1987: 53-66), and such events were not unknown in Newfoundland. But here the Newfoundlanders had an organizational advantage. In Ireland the Presentation and Mercy Congregations were diocesan institutions, meaning they were under the authority of the local bishop (Clear). The Newfoundland congregations were pontifical—i.e., directly responsible to Rome—which gave them some protection from excessive meddling on the part of the local hierarchy.[5] This was reinforced in 1916, when Archbishop Roche saw to it that both the Mercy and Presentation convents in Newfoundland were amalgamated. Prior to this, each house had functioned independently; now the congregations were administered centrally by an elected Superior and Council. With amalgamation "jurisdiction in practically all the affairs of the congregation passed from the hands of the Bishops into the hands of the Mother General and Council" (Dinn, 1975: 22). This facilitated the development of institutions and personnel and added to sisters' opportunities for administrative advancement within the congregation (Dinn 1975: 21-22; Hogan 1986: 342-344). Given that sisters generally ran the institutions in which they worked, becoming a nun was "one of the surest ways for a competent woman to rise to the top of large scale educational and health institutions" (Wittberg, 1989: 530). Nuns' life-long professional careers were especially striking considering that the vast majority of female workers in St. John's in 1921 were under 25 years of age (Cullum et al, 1993: 89-90; Forestall, this volume).

While it is important to recognize the ways in which the lives of nuns often contradicted the stereotype "of an obedient, meek, humble servant of the male-dominated Church" (Ebaugh, 1993: 134), readers should be wary of projecting any desires for a feminist utopia onto women of the past. Nano Nagle and Catherine McAuley both believed that women should receive an education, as did many nuns (Clear, 1987: 116-117; Dumont, 1992: 81-82). Yet this was as much due to the conviction that well-educated women would contribute to the betterment of Church and society, especially through their influence in the home and over children, as to a belief in women's rights, as articulated by 'second wave' feminism (e.g. Bolster, 1990: 11; Hogan, 1986: 10, 21; Howley, 1979: 276). Prior to Vatican II, women religious tended not to see gender-based inequality as a social problem (Quinonez and Turner, 1992: 93ff; Wittberg, 1989). How, then, did gender-consciousness emerge?

Naming Sexism as an Issue

Ironically, nuns' earlier lack of concern with systemic sexism may have been partly due to their own opportunities for professional and spiritual growth. Free from the demands of a family and working in congregational institutions, sisters rarely encountered the obstacles that faced other women interested in professional careers. Their insulation from such matters was only increased by the Vatican's 1917 codification of Canon Law, which imposed greater isolation of religious from the secular world (Wittberg, 1989). The Presentation Sisters' work prior to Vatican II was largely restricted to teaching, which may have made them even less likely to encounter such sexism directly than were the Mercy Sisters. But in the last quarter century, nuns' attitudes have been changing along with their styles of religious life.

What has led sisters to question their place in the Church? One factor that seems to have been relevant was nuns' return to university as a result of the Second Vatican Council's call for them to become more effective in modern society (Abbott (ed.), 1962: 467-468). Many Newfoundland sisters spent time in mainland or American institutions during the 1970s and 1980s. Here they had more direct contact with religious from other congregations, and with secular men and women, including the new wave of feminists. The sisters' studies were no longer restricted to education and health care, no longer narrowly defined. Some of their courses offered new, and even oppositional, perspectives on Catholicism (cf Wittberg, 1989: 531). One sister told me she had spent a year doing Scripture Studies in the United States, becoming especially interested in the Bible's female characters. She added, "You don't realize what's there until you look at it from a new perspective."

Sisters were also exposed to a wider variety of viewpoints when postconciliar changes in religious life allowed them greater exposure to print and broadcast media, formerly restricted in keeping with the rules of enclosure. Now convents not only have televisions and subscriptions to a variety of secular and religious periodicals, but some communities regularly watch the news together and discuss it.[6]

As increasing numbers of sisters started working in religious and secular institutions not run by their congregations, sexism began to affect their lives more directly. Lorraine Michael, a former Mercy Sister who served for ten years as director of the Office of Social Action in the Archdiocese of St. John's, wrote about her response to 1989 revelations of sexual abuse by Newfoundland clergy:

> I began to feel so deeply the pain of the victims that I had to ask myself why. And it didn't take long for me to realize it was because I had suffered so much emotional and psychological abuse myself from these same men (Michael, 1991; see also Michael, this volume; Will, 1992).

Another Sister, Kathleen, who is a pastoral minister for a parish, told me that sexism encountered in her work and in religious language provoked a heightened conviction that gender-based inequality is a problem in the Church and society:

> I became very conscious, especially when I started as a reader in the church, that the language we were using—and we're formed by our language—was all male-oriented. How could you stand up and say, "My brothers" when over fifty percent of the people down in front of you are your sisters? . . . And I've so many times said to people, "I'm nobody's brother, don't call me [brother]." So I think the language is perhaps what *really* sensitized me, more than anything else, that we're promoting that gender inequality, just by the way we speak.

Yet experience alone is an insufficient explanation for why some sisters have moved to such a critical position. After all, many women encounter non-inclusive language within the Church (and elsewhere) without being troubled, and women now sensitive to gender-biased language may not have noticed it in the past. Experience is not something that 'just happens' to an individual. Rather it is inextricable from existing discourses, and as such is always "already an interpretation *and* is in need of interpretation" (Scott, 1992: 37). While it is common to identify experience as the cause of emergent political identities (e.g. it may be said that experience of being a woman in a sexist society gives rise to feminism), it is important to recognize the ways in which these politics themselves work to "define and inform experience" (Mohanty, 1992: 86). What happens when women begin to interpret as sexism linguistic forms that equate masculinity with universality? Linda Alcoff suggests:

When women become feminists the crucial thing that has occurred is not that they have learned any new facts about the world but that they have come to view those facts from a different position, from their own position as subjects (1988: 434).

Sister Bridget describes such a shift in her own consciousness:

I always accepted the fact that 'mankind' included me; I'm part of mankind . . . I'm amazed that I always accepted that fact. But now that I have a new awareness, I no longer accept that. . . . I think that we have to acknowledge the fact that women have been just subsumed in the whole human race, and passed over . . . If we're going to address some of what we see as the injustices on a larger scale, we have to start [somewhere]. I don't even see [inclusive language] any more as [a] smaller [issue], because I think it's indicative of a whole lot of other things.

Sisters Kathleen and Bridget thus speak self-consciously as women in the Church, a position from which androcentric language has become unacceptable. While they represent many others, not all women religious share their perspective, as both also told me. There is no neat explanation for why only some sisters come to make "an issue of their femaleness . . . claiming their identity as women as a point of political departure" (Alcoff, 1988: 432). To an extent, women religious have always had an awareness of their gender imposed on them by virtue of how their lives within the Catholic Church have been ordered by it. Perhaps some are now confronted with this 'fact' in situations where contradictions become insupportable, leading to a conceptual shift on the part of the women involved (cf Franco, 1989: xxii; Bartky, 1988: 82-83). For example, Presentation Sister Anne, a chaplain who is restricted from carrying out the full duties of a priest, said her experience has:

given me an awareness of the unfairness in the system and the injustice in the system that says 'men and women are equal, but they're not equal really.' And I think the Catholic Church is doing that. It's saying one thing on one side of its face and something else on another.

Similarly, Sister Kathleen performs marriages in her role as parish minister, but cannot celebrate Mass during the ceremony because women cannot be ordained in the Catholic Church, which has led some of her parishioners to suggest they would prefer to be married by a priest.

Helen Ebaugh (1993: 143-144) suggests that women like Kathleen and Anne experience "great job dissatisfaction" due to their "lack of power and upward mobility . . ." The limits imposed on them stem from their status as women in the Church rather than from the quality of their work. The contradiction of the Church's willingness to let them do parish work and its refusal to allow them access to the priesthood becomes insupportable, so they begin to analyze their experience in what Ebaugh calls "feminist terms."[7] When women undertake such an analysis, they articulate their lives in a new way. This entails an active, discursive reconstitution of self, but it is not a matter of unconstrained 'free will.' Subjectivity (and experience) is constituted in discourse, and identities must be meaningful within the horizons of available discourses. However, conflicts and contradictions between and within discursive systems, and the impossibility of fixing meaning, enable the production of new identities (Alcoff, 1988: 431; Butler, 1990: 147; Scott, 1992: 34). Rather than trying to hammer out a causal explanation for gender-consciousness among women religious then, I want to explore *how* it is produced and played out, looking at the meanings that are created, contested, and deployed during these processes (see, e.g., Stewart, 1991: 399; Scott, 1988: 4ff; Scott, 1992).

Christian Disciples

Lavinia Byrne, a British nun, writes:

'How do women become disciples?' is a specific question and one which is increasingly being asked. In any form of ministry to the spiritual development of women, images of holiness and ministry taken from tradition must be re-examined. Are they a blueprint for women to follow or a minefield we must avoid? How do we grow in the knowledge and love of God? How do we pray? What are the insights we bring from 2000 years of invisibility and cast into the light? What is the certainty we come from and the mystery into which we move? (1988: x).

Sandra M. Schneiders, also a religious sister, suggests that Christian women with a feminist consciousness,

find themselves in excruciating tension with the institutional church and even with Christian faith as it is articulated and practised in the believing community. . . . What is one to do when the male God-image that nourished one's faith from infancy to adulthood becomes at best incredible and at worst oppressive? How is one to relate to a male saviour who represents a male God who is invoked to legitimate the claim that maleness is normative for humanity? . . . What does one do with the endless and exhausting rage that is called forth by sexual apartheid in the church, by ubiquitous linguistic sexism, by clerical monopoly of ministry, by blatantly oppressive liturgy? (1991: 3).

These writers voice the tensions they face as they work to challenge male dominance in the Catholic Church. It is not surprising that their project is framed with questions: women who undertake it move into uncertain territory. What shape might a feminist (or women-affirming) Catholicism take? How will their challenge be construed by the Church hierarchy and by other Catholics? Where do they look for wisdom when much Church tradition, including scripture, has "androcentric, patriarchal, and misogynist content" (Schneiders: 2)? The identities of gender-conscious women religious are made in part through their ongoing responses to such questions. And they must answer as both women and as religious sisters, identities that may, at times, be at odds with one another (de Lauretis, 1986; Riley, 1988).

Given the authoritative centrality of the scriptures to Christianity, sisters concerned for the status of women need a reading of the Bible which affirms gender equality. But Schneiders (1991: 37-38) notes that there is a well-entrenched tradition of using scripture to rationalize the oppression of women. If the Bible teaches that God is male and women inferior to men, then "is patriarchy divinely revealed and therefore divinely sanctioned?" Misogynist (mis)interpretations of scripture abound, but Schneiders argues that the text itself is undeniably sexist:

When the official church invokes scripture to justify its discriminatory treatment of women it does not have to resort to fundamentalist prooftexting or to questionable exegetical methods (Schneiders: 38).

How do Newfoundland sisters respond to this issue? After all, the Scriptures are keystones of their faith. In a joint brief to the Archdiocesan Commission of Enquiry into the Sexual Abuse of Children by Members of the Clergy (the 'Winter Commission'), the Mercy and Presentation Sisters argue that the Church needs to realign itself with Gospel values (Sisters of Mercy and Presentation Sisters, 1990). They connect the occurrence of abuse to "the social sin of patriarchy" (Sisters of Mercy and Presentation Sisters: C91), which they say characterizes institutional Catholicism:

> In such a system, hierarchical ordering and authoritarianism allow one person or group to dominate, exploit or oppress others. This gets played out in situations where men dominate women, whites dominate blacks, the rich dominate the poor. In relationships patterned after traditional gender roles where domination and submission are the models of human interaction, no real mutuality of persons is possible, and the inevitable consequence is the victimization of the powerless. Separation of the masculine and feminine leads to false dichotomies which foster fear, hostility and alienation within and between persons (1990: C90).

They clearly feel that this is *not* divinely revealed, asserting that "the message of Jesus was radically different from patriarchy" (1990: C91). In order for the Church to "become again a beacon of hope for a world crying out for justice, love and peace," the Presentation and Mercy Sisters argue:

> Even as we develop new structures, central to such change is a reinterpretation of scripture, such that we will re-discover the reality of our God as a God of election, liberation and covenant, Who is most fully imaged in the equal discipleship of all of us together (1990: C93).

Such a reinterpretation must involve "rediscovering in the scriptures the feminine image of God and stories about women who have played significant roles in salvation history" (1990: C93-C94).[8] Many sisters go beyond this, to offer reinterpretations of scriptural texts that have sometimes been used to justify maintaining the current sexual division of labour and authority in the Catholic Church (cf Schneiders, 1991: 53-55). For instance, I asked Sister Virginia whether, as a woman in the Church, she sees the Virgin Mary as a role model:

> That has changed [for me]. I feel she was a very brave woman to accept this role which she could have refused, and for an unmarried woman in her day to be pregnant and not married was a tragedy. . . . I respect her as a woman for saying yes to this role and to this commitment, because it was not only a commitment for a short while, but it was a life-long commitment. . . . She was a woman of great courage, and I really respect that—to accept this, not without question, because I feel she did question: the scripture says she pondered it in her heart, and she questioned. . . . But I really respect her final decision, not knowing what the future held for her.

This reading of Mary—as a courageous woman, a decisive agent rather than a passive vessel, and one willing to take risks and challenge social convention—is markedly different from, and potentially subversive of, the one attributed to traditional Catholicism. Here Mary is held up as a model of submission and humility, which Mary Jo Weaver (1985: 201-202) suggests women have been urged to emulate in their relationship to the male hierarchy. Virginia, on the other hand, addresses the biblical text with new questions (cf Schneiders, 1991: 69). Instead of asking how Mary can support existing gender relationships in the Catholic Church (as Weaver suggests the male hierarchy has done), she asks how Mary might become part of a faith that affirms strong, active women.

Similarly, Sister Kathleen told me that during a sabbatical year she had spent much time reflecting on the Gospels:

I became very much aware that Jesus was a feminist. Jesus talked to the woman at the well, and the men who were his followers, or who were with him, spoke against him: "What are you doing talking to a woman, and in public?"... But Jesus broke so many rules as far as their society was concerned. It was the same with the woman taken in adultery—as if she could be taken in adultery without a man being involved [laughs]. But it wasn't the same law for men and women, and he wouldn't let himself be drawn into that. So, while he supported the poor and the downtrodden, among the most downtrodden and the poorest are women, and he stood up for them. That hasn't been blotted out, but it's like we haven't really let ourselves admit that.

By naming Jesus as a feminist, Kathleen asks the Scriptures to speak to address contemporary concerns. She asserts that their "major preoccupations" include a basic concern for justice and the rights of the oppressed, including women (cf Schneiders, 1991: 66, 69). Kathleen went on to say:

... We still have the male-dominated, hierarchical structure. I sometimes call it "the original sin." I think that we will never really be able to realize the Kingdom of God until we see one another as equal, regardless of our physical make-up. I'm surprised sometimes when they say: "Well, Christ chose men, so it has to be men [who are priests]." [Then] I say: "They were mostly Jews, so they should be mostly Jews.".... "Man sees what he wants to see and disregards the rest."

Here Kathleen asserts that the principle of equality is more central to a Christian reading of the Bible than supposed 'facts' about the gender-status of those apostles generally recognized to have been appointed by Christ. With Schneiders, she rejects a literalist approach to reading the Bible—one which assumes meaning is *contained* in the text—in favour of a method which emphasizes the role of situated readers in realizing the text's meaning.[9] It is not that the text can be made to mean anything at all, says Schneiders, but a final interpretation is neither possible nor desirable (Schneiders: 57-64).

Sister Bridget suggested that a commitment to making women more visible in the Church requires an interpretive reading transformative even of Biblical language:

I do prayer services for Congregational things [and] . . . I change the language from the Bible [to make it inclusive] . . . There has been a new translation of the Revised Standard [Version where] the human language is made inclusive, but the God language isn't, and God is still referred to as "He" and "Him". [But] usually if we have prayers now I'll say "God our mother and father" or "God nurturer" or whatever.

The Church hierarchy is responding to some of these issues. The Canadian Conference of Catholic Bishops has published a set of workshops on inclusive language (1990), and a papal letter entitled *Dignity and Vocation of Women* repeatedly asserts "the essential equality of man and woman from the point of view of their humanity" (John Paul II, 1988: 23). On the other hand, this same document reaffirms the Church's conviction that only men can represent Christ as ordained priests:

> *In calling only men as his Apostles*, Christ acted *in a completely free and sovereign manner*. In doing so, he exercised the same freedom with which, in all his behaviour, he emphasized the dignity and the vocation of women, without conforming to the prevailing customs and to the traditions sanctioned by the legislation of the time. Consequently, the assumption that he called men to be apostles in order to conform with the widespread mentality of his times, does not at all correspond to Christ's way of acting. "Teacher we know that you are true, and teach the way of God truthfully, and care for no man; for *you do not regard the position of men*". . . . These words fully characterize *Jesus of Nazareth's behaviour*. Here one also finds an explanation for the calling of the "Twelve". They are with Christ at the Last Supper. They alone receive the sacramental charge, "Do this in remembrance of me". . . , which is joined to the institution of the Eucharist. On Easter Sunday night they receive the Holy Spirit for the forgiveness of sins: "Whose sins you forgive are forgiven them, and whose sins you retain are retained" (1988: 105-106, his emphases; see also 107-108).

Christ's refusal to accept the practices of his era regarding women—a scriptural 'fact' in which sisters such as Kathleen find support—is used here as evidence that women must *not* be ordained. Women may be able to read scriptures in self-affirming ways as Schneiders argues, but the very impossibility of a final reading means that, until women's interpretations have equal authority with those of the male hierarchy, it is unlikely these readings will lead to major institutional changes (cf Asad, 1983: 252; Farrell, 1991: 344).

"With Special Attentiveness to Women"

When sisters express their congregational commitment to work for women, they do so in terms that are meaningful in the context of their faith. At their 1991 General Chapter, the Presentation Sisters adopted a "Directional Statement" for the next four years. While the overall focus committed them to work for social justice, the sisters specifically stated: "Our special concern will be for all victims of abuse, with special attentiveness to women."[10] When the Mercies adopted the goal of "work[ing] towards furthering the place and role of women in our church and

186

society", it was one element of a pastoral plan aimed at enabling the congregation to serve effectively both Church and community.[11] The "Directional Statement" from the Mercy Sisters' 15th General Chapter (July 1993)[12] situates their commitment "to reach out in compassion and service to women and to all in need, especially the poor and the oppressed" within the overarching goal of being "a prophetic presence in our world."

As individuals too, many sisters locate the particular goal of ministry to women within the overall mission of their congregation. For example, Mercy Sister Josephine described to me how her understanding of 'the poor' has changed over time:

> ... In my early years of religious life, the poor to me were those who were actually hungry or cold, ... Now we have more of a world-view of the poor, and we are concerned about the poor in Somalia, for example, and refugees, and women as the poor, children as poor. ... I have a more embracing view of the poor now than I did, say, even twenty years ago.[13]

Likewise, Sister Bernadette indicated that gender-consciousness is part of a spectrum of concerns for her as a Presentation Sister:

> The ministry to the poor: that was always very central to me. The other thing with our foundress was her involvement with people ... It wasn't just her own little community of sisters. She always had other women involved with her, so it was that sense of. . . a community, and working together with people, to minister in service . . . And while I didn't stay with [professional] education, education was part of—most of, I suppose—our foundress's responsibilities . . . That part of education is becoming more challenging for us now because it's not just education in the sense of teaching in school, but even as I was just saying, in looking at the whole role of women in the Church and how that fits into educating ourselves and also helping other women to be educated enough to find their rightful place. And so it's all the ways in which we can educate, that's part of the charism as well.

However, for some sisters, a widened understanding of the congregation's mission means that women should not be singled out *as women*. One Mercy Sister told me: "I don't believe in polarization, and I think we need to look after God's people. If we have a chance to enhance women's self-image and develop those skills and talents, do that." This view merely expresses ambivalence about separating women as a group; 'service to the poor' can also be deployed to *deny* the concerns of some Catholic women, as Mary Jo Leddy, a Canadian Sister and co-founder of *Catholic New Times*, suggests:

> ... one thing I don't appreciate—and many people do this, Church people do it—is hearing women's concerns dismissed as merely middle-class worries about jobs and inclusive language, and being told that what we should be concerned about is the poor (in Leddy et al, 1992: 49-50).

Enclosing their decision to work for women in a faith-based commitment to 'the poor' is part of what constitutes sisters as gender-conscious religious. Situating their views within a discourse which is widely validated in the Church—that is, the 'option for the poor'—may even grant them added credibility in the eyes of Church authorities. This is not to suggest that casting women's rights in a larger discourse of commitment to the poor is merely a tactic to defuse the hierarchy's concern about 'radical nuns' (cf Ebaugh, 1993: 147-148), but it might still have the result of deflecting some opposition. How could anyone in the Church justify an explicit condemnation of sisters' commitment to work against poverty, oppression and injustice? Yet like all discourses, this one may be interpreted, accommodated and redeployed in ways that counter its agents' intent (cf Kondo, 1990: e.g. 299; Scott, 1992: 34; Stewart, 1991).

Women religious draw on, as well as challenge, the authoritative discourses of the Church as they define and reimagine both their situation in the Church and their mission to serve women. Their challenges entail new readings of the Scriptures and other religious texts, but the play of meanings always carries the potential for the subversion of such readings. This risk is compounded by an ecclesial system that reserves certain spheres for men, granting greater authority to pronouncements emanating from these positions. How is this accomplished in a church which claims to stand for the equality of men and women on the basis of their common humanity?

Consecrating Women

The Vatican position on women hinges on the essentialization of gender:

> The Fathers of the recent Assembly of the Synod of Bishops (October, 1987) . . . [recommended] a further study of the anthropological and theological bases that are needed in order to solve the problems connected with the meaning and dignity of being a woman and being a man. *It is a question of understanding the reason for and the consequences of the Creator's decision that the human being should always and only exist as a woman or a man.* It is only by beginning from these bases, which make it possible to understand the greatness of the dignity and vocation of women, that one is able to speak of their active presence in the Church and society (John Paul II, 1988: 9, my emphasis).
>
> . . . even the rightful opposition of women to what is expressed in the biblical words "He shall rule over you". . . must not under any condition lead to the "masculinization" of women. In the name of liberation from male "domination", women must not appropriate to themselves male characteristics contrary to their own feminine "originality". There is a well-founded fear that if they take this path, women will not "reach fulfilment", but instead will *deform and lose what constitutes their essential richness.* . . . (1988: 44, his emphasis).

Of 'women', Riley (1988: 98) writes: "Some characterization or other is eternally in play. The question then . . . is to discover whose, and with what effects." The Pope presents gender as an absolute and all-encompassing attribute. Discursively produced biological categories, masquerading as transparent observations on the 'natural' order of the world, demand that we 'act our gender' or suffer the consequences of our 'deformity' (cf Butler, 1990: 139-140). This works to 'contain' women religious, restricting the ways they can legitimately and 'naturally' express their faith. Such disciplinary mechanisms engender subjects in particular ways. The knowledge of being observed demands a 'competent' performance. For example, one sister told me that when she was away at university she discovered she enjoyed drinking beer from time to time, but added she was very conscious that in Newfoundland "ladies, and nuns especially, don't drink beer." Although she feels there is nothing wrong with drinking beer occasionally, she said that if she did so in public, people would likely disapprove. This may seem a minor example, but its very triviality testifies to the minute and far-reaching ways in which individuals are disciplined to be gendered selves (cf Bartky, 1988; Foucault, 1979).

Nonetheless, I would suggest that the very lives of women religious challenge the assertion that "human beings always and only exist as a woman or a man." Sisters' identity is not limited to the enactment of gender but is also constituted, for example, by their ministries (cf Lather, 1991: 28). Perhaps this is felt most starkly as a challenge to a totalized identity when nuns work in areas once dominated by men, and still largely defined as 'male'. Parish minister Kathleen said:

> I don't hesitate to say [that] what I do here is comparable to what a priest would do in the same position, except that I can't say Mass, and I can't—I can hear confession, but I can't give absolution [laughs]. But that's because I don't have orders.

Neither collective nor individual identities are stable (cf Kondo, 1990: e.g. 44). Kathleen's work as a pastoral minister disrupts ecclesiastical constructions of 'women,' an interference that may sometimes have the effect of heightening her personal awareness of gender. At the same time, assumptions about what it means to be a 'parish minister' are unsettled by the presence of women like Kathleen; their lives challenge the logic that makes maleness a prerequisite for the priesthood.

Yet there are points of convergence between the narratives of sisters and those of the Church hierarchy. The Church's understanding of the equality of men and women, as represented by the Apostolic Letter, is one of 'complementarity': "The personal resources of femininity are certainly no less than the resources of masculinity: they are merely different" (John Paul II, 1988: 44). While some are beginning to ask if equality is really part of the equation or whether this particular 'complementarity' is a thinly veiled excuse for sexism, women religious themselves often speak of men and women as 'equal but different'. However, there are crucial differences in how sisters interpret the implications of 'basic' gender differences, as Mercy Sister Jeanne's thoughts on the place of women in the Catholic Church indicate:

> I have a strong belief that men and women are created equal, and that the roles of men and women in the life of the Church and the world are complementary. I think, historically, because of the Church, the role of women has not been appreciated, or even allowed to operate in the way that I would like to see it. . . . I believe that eventually the whole Church will come to recognize the equality of men and women, and the right of both to participate equally in the life of the Church. And I mean that in every way; I mean from the top to the bottom. . . . I think it's going to be a very slow process, and even though a lot has changed in a short time in my life-time, I think that for us to come to *full* equality, in leadership

and hierarchical positions in the Church and authority and that kind of thing—for women to reach that level is going to take a lot more time than I'll live.

While the Church uses the idea of complementarity to justify excluding women from certain spheres (see also Quinonez and Turner, 1992: 92), some sisters—like Jeanne—make it function in a way that emphasizes how the Church would benefit if it allowed women in all its ministries. Firstly, they suggest that the faithful are ill-served by the shortage of available priests, and that allowing women to be ordained could help to rectify the situation. In keeping with this, some feel it is time to let go of the requirement that priests be celibate. Sister Kathleen reflected: "I think [the Church] would be different if people who feel called to ordination, be they women or men, were ordained." Moreover, they argue, women's differences would enrich the Church if women were allowed to participate at every level. Mercy Sister Josephine:

> In my experience . . . the talents and the gifts of women have not been utilized as they should be. Women are there for service, but it's a very limited service: it's more to do things, but "don't give me your ideas.". . . Women, by their nature, have more feeling and . . . I think maybe some decisions would be made differently if more women were involved in the decision-making. I think women see things differently, look at things with a . . . different perspective, and probably would see aspects of an issue or a problem that all men don't see. So maybe some decisions would be different if there were more of a feminine touch and a feminine input into decision-making . . .

Similarly, I asked Bernadette, a Presentation Sister, whether she thought the hierarchy might change if women were more involved:

> . . . There are other gifts that women bring, in the sense of relat[ing] to people. My experience is that the clergy don't put the same amount of energy and time into developing relationships with people that women do. And I think that that's really key. I think that because of that, when the hierarch[y is] making decisions about people's lives, there's a dimension that's missing.

This focus on the needs of the Church as well as on the rights of women might be interpreted as a strategy designed simply to 'sell' the hierarchy on the idea of allowing women to take a wider variety of positions within the Church. A slightly different view sees women religious as engaging in a creative accommodation of the official Church's position on women, one which emphasizes women's contribution to the Church while also contesting the limits of their placement in the Church. As Dorinne Kondo (1990: 259) suggests, because we "must use the culturally available tools at [our] disposal," complete transformation may be impossible. "But resistance need not be seen as radical rupture or apocalyptic change in order to be effective." Because the sisters I have quoted are committed to a life within the Church, a radical break from its discourses is impossible. Rather, the ecclesial discourses which constitute them in particular ways are also the sites of their agency.

When sisters contend that women can make a unique contribution, they are also expressing their religious commitment to serve the People of God. This explains why several sisters, like Sister Bernadette, told me that while they support the ordination of women in principle, they do not see this as the solution to issues of inequality and privilege which go beyond gender to the very structures of authority in the Church:

> While I had a wonderful experience working in a parish, I would not, at this particular point, want to be an ordained minister if I had to become part of the structure that's in existence . . . I'd rather be clear of that, because I just don't want to put my energies into that at this point in time. I'm much happier with knowing that I have a place in the faith community . . . and that's where I want to work together with people. I don't have the energy to get into that hierarchical stuff—not at this point.

Sister Kathleen suggested the hierarchy could learn from women:

> in the Church it has always been women who have been the most active in really maintaining the Church, but it has always been a role of service, which it should be. Maybe if men could take an example from that and realize that priesthood is a service, not an honour, then we maybe wouldn't have had the kinds of problems [we've had], or at least to the extent that [we have] . . . And if women were to become priests and just go on the same power trips, well, we're no further ahead, you know?

As with their inclusion of women among 'the poor', these convictions characterize gender consciousness among the Mercy and Presentation Sisters. It might be said that, like Latin American feminists, sisters "have found ways of aligning gender politics with other forms of struggle without subordinating gender issues and without sacrificing politics" (Franco, 1989: xxii-xxiii).

Challenging 'Feminism'

As women religious enact their gender-consciousness, they try to do so in ways that affirm their faith, the social site of which, for the most part, has been the very Church they are challenging. Not surprisingly, there is no consensus on these issues. Sister Camille stated:

> I think I have a good relationship with the male hierarchy in the Church. I don't have any difficulty communicating with priests or bishops or cardinals or anyone else . . . I don't have any hang-ups when it comes to talking with them, communicating with them or serving them. I respect them and I think it's mutual.

In contrast, Sister Jeanne said:

> We are still under the male hierarchical Church. Without a doubt. . . . In almost every [parish] ministry that we have, we ultimately have to depend on the goodwill of the bishop in order to be able to continue our ministry there. And that has not been easy . . . They cannot tell us, for example, what we can and cannot do as religious women within our own way of life, and hopefully they would not attempt to in this day and age, in our own institutions . . . But there is still

definitely a strong power that the hierarchical Church has over us within our ministries. If we buck it, we are the losers in some sense.

Some sisters who are otherwise in favour of 'equal opportunity' have difficulty stretching that principle to the ordination of women. For instance, I asked Sister Mary Agnes, a woman in her eighties, for her thoughts on women in the Church. She said that most sisters "are open to and realizing the need for women to have their rightful place, and [that] if a woman is qualified to do any kind of work, she should be allowed to do it." She added, "except a few, a few who will say, 'Oh, that's not for a lady.' But only a few, only a few. And we have on the other end the ones who ... [laughing] want them to be priests even." Likewise, Sister Camille said she thought the church has benefitted from female theologians, but about ordination said:

> Having gone through the whole of my life with a male-oriented Church, I suppose I'm conditioned to that. But I would welcome women ministers. I'm not so sure about the ordination part, but I think that women can do a very good job in instructing people in the ways of God.
>
> I think women have a different approach to things. I think that women who use their gifts and talents to promote the Kingdom can be very supportive of priests and very helpful to priests, and could really unburden the priest and help him to concentrate on the essentials of his priesthood.

Women like Camille and Agnes, who have dedicated their lives to the Church, may find it difficult to challenge some of its most basic elements, practices in which their faith has long been enacted. Such changes can be disconcerting even for more 'radical' sisters as they try to reimagine the Church. One sister who said she is strongly dedicated to working for the equality of women added that she still feels uncomfortable saying, "Our Mother who art in heaven . . ."

Life is messy. Institutions and people can embody affirming and undermining messages at once. Some sisters find in Mother Teresa of Calcutta an inspirational role model, yet not without qualifications, as Sister Anne's comments indicate:

> . . . I don't believe in the way her congregation lives like it was fifty years ago, and they're very highly legislated and all that kind of stuff. I think that's a thing of the past. But the fact that they really *do* welcome the poor is a big plus, and I think we kind of say we do that, but I wonder, do we?

Mother Teresa is many things. On one hand she lives the radical life of service that many gender-conscious religious strive for; on the other she is closer to pre- than to post-Vatican II religious life in many ways. Sister Anne's comment embodies tensions that many religious feel: how are they to go about changing the Church while continuing to affirm what they value in it? Should they align themselves with secular women's groups, and call themselves "feminists"? One Sister who has worked with feminist groups suggested that there is much ambivalence about this as a result of hackneyed stereotypes:

> I'm very involved in social justice activities, and am considered . . . to be

somewhat of a radical [within my congregation]. And some people, even some of the ones that you might talk to, wouldn't approve of working with [feminists], you know, because "half them are lesbians", or "half them are for abortion" and stuff like that.

The Church hierarchy often issues warnings against 'radical feminism' according to Schneiders (1991: 118 n36). She claims, though, that their use of the term lacks precision, and charges: "In general they seem to regard as 'radical' any feminism which calls into question official church teaching, policy, or practice on the basis of gender analysis." But sisters cannot ignore such discourses, and this is part of what gives feminism its particular meaning for them. When Harry Brown interviewed Mercy Sister Elizabeth Davis on CBC Radio, he questioned her involvement with women's groups, pointing out that many of them support abortion rights. She replied:

I find it very difficult when we talk about single issues. I think there are many things that I would support, many values that I hold, that other women would not approve of. That does not mean there are not lots of areas where we do have common ground, areas where we work together to make a better world, a world where women and men can take their full role, and eradicate the kinds of unpleasantness and war and violence and abuse that's present in our society.[14]

Other sisters, such as Bridget, actively confront stereotypes, denying that feminism contradicts their religious convictions:

One of the things that we try to talk about in our sessions around [feminist theology], is that 'feminism' is not a bad word, and when people condemn feminism, many times it is the very radical wing of feminism . . . and that's not what we're all about. We're looking for the equality of the sexes. We're looking to bring focus to the dignity of women and to the place of women in church and society, restoring women to their rightful place. If we go back to the beginnings of our Christian heritage, women certainly have a key role in the church, [but] for some reason, over the centuries, have been relegated to the sacristy. So it's just a matter of restoring that rightful role, and reading the scriptures through a feminist perspective as well, because there is the way Jesus himself dealt with women, and the great women that have been part of our Christian story, through the New Testament and even through the Old Testament.

Such women help to shape the gender-consciousness of other sisters, and are as much or more a part of the context of religious life in their congregations as is the male hierarchy of the Church (cf di Leonardo, 1991: 30).

Women religious in Newfoundland are working to define themselves in ways that affirm both their identities as women and their commitment to ministry in the Roman Catholic Church. In the process, they engage, enact, and push the limits of a variety of discourses, some of which conflict with one another. In so doing, sisters deny that their identities can be reduced to or divorced from either their gender or their religious status. Their aspirations for this multiple project are evoked by these words from Patricia Maher, former Superior General of the Mercy Sisters of Newfoundland:

> As religious communities we can offer still another prophetic sign in the world by the very fact that we are women. The existence of communities where women's gifts have been recognized and developed, where women have exercised leadership and professions, where women have ministered to one another in a variety of ways, takes on a particularly prophetic character in our age. We are in the midst of a new understanding of the dignity and equality of women, one that affects the deepest aspects of our lives—our language, our images of God, our understanding of God's Word, our ways of relating. It should be our challenge to speak out for the inclusion, the full active participation of all women in our Church and society.[15]

1 This paper is a revised version of Chapter 5 of my (1993) M.A. thesis for the Department of Social Anthropology at York University. Archival research and interviews were conducted in 1992 and 1993. All informants' names are pseudonyms, with the exception of archival sources.

2 Technically, the term 'nun' applies only to cloistered contemplative women with *solemn* vows of poverty, chastity and obedience. The Sisters of Mercy and the Sisters of the Presentation of the Blessed Virgin Mary are apostolic (active) Roman Catholic *religious congregations*, which the Church defines as "[i]nstitutes of Christian perfection whose members take *simple vows*, as distinguished from religious orders in which solemn vows are made" (Hardon, 1980: 125, my emphasis). An act against any vow is considered to be a sin, but only an act against a solemn vow is also invalid. Thus marriage by a woman with simple vows would be a transgression, but would be upheld by the Church. Properly speaking, Mercy and Presentation Sisters are called 'religious' or, more popularly, 'sisters' (Hardon: 382, 506, 508, 511, 566; Campbell-Jones 1979: 27). However, sisters sometimes refer to themselves as nuns. The three terms will be used interchangeably in this paper.

3 Elsewhere I discuss in greater detail how the Presentation and Mercy Sisters contributed to the production not only of literate and numerate pupils, but also of individuals with particular gender, class and religious identities (Whittaker, 1993: e.g. 75ff). The situation seems to have been similar in Ireland (Clear, 1987: 116-119).

4 Compare Sisters of Mercy 1954 with Sisters of the Presentation 1958.

5. At least in theory, there were times when bishops overstepped their rights. For instance, one sister told me she had found a letter in which a bishop had requested that a particular nun transfer from one convent to another. She said that it was not his business to have done so. Nonetheless, Wittberg (1989: 530-31) conveys the importance of pontifical status when she notes that American nuns in the 19th and early 20th century "shared techniques and insights on how to transfer their orders from diocesan to pontifical status—a key step in breaking the control and exploitation of the bishops."

6 Cf "A Brief on Community Life", presented at the 1967 General Chapter of the Congrega-

tion of the Sisters of Mercy of Newfoundland (n.a.: available at the Archives of the Sisters of Mercy [hereafter: ASM]), which set out some of the arguments for giving sisters access to current media.

7 Of course women who choose to work in parish and diocesan ministry have already demonstrated their willingness to challenge the status quo simply by entering a sphere traditionally dominated by men. They may thus have been more likely than some others to adopt a 'feminist perspective' even before they encountered sexism in their work.

8 See: Elizabeth M. Davis, R.S.M., August 1992, "Notes from Presentation: Story of Women in Scripture", presentation given at the Mercy Sisters' 150th Anniversary Celebrations (available at ASM) for an example of a contribution to these projects.

9 I contend that a 'positivist' approach is also interpretive but *acts* as if language is transparent and a 'literal' approach to scripture is possible, thus obscuring its hermeneutics (and cf Alonso, 1988: 36-37).

10 Available at the Presentation Congregation Archives (PCA): Box 11.14, Folder 62 ("Fourteenth General Chapter").

11 See: "Goals and Strategies for Pastoral Planning" (Finalized at Pastoral Planning Committee Meeting, September 21, 1991): ASM. 12.Available from the Sisters of Mercy Generalate, Littledale, St. John's.

13 The Mercy Sisters' "Mission Statement" includes a commitment to "ministry with the poor, sick, aged, uneducated and oppressed." Available from the Sisters of Mercy Generalate.

14 The interview took place in September, 1992. My transcription of the interview was deposited at ASM.

15 From: "Opening Reflection." First Meeting of Chapter Delegates, 14th General Chapter, Sisters of Mercy Generalate (October 14, 1988): ASM.

Child Sexual Abuse among the Clergy:
a Churchwoman's View

Lorraine Michael

When this article was written, Lorraine Michael was Director of the Office of Social Action of the Archdiocese of St. John's, and a member of the Congregation of the Sisters of Mercy of Newfoundland and Labrador.

> ... why do men in powerful positions use these situations to sexually abuse women and children? Why do men sexually assault their wives? their daughters? their sons? other women? other children? Why do they try to prove who they are by asserting themselves sexually over those who are less powerful?

RECENTLY, people in St. John's were rocked with the news that three charges of child sexual abuse had been brought against Jim Hickey, a high-profile priest of the Roman Catholic Church. This was a first for the Archdiocese of St. John's, and its effects were beyond belief. But what at the time felt like a massive earthquake now appears as a mild shock wave.

Since January 1988, the people have been hit with one blow after another. First of all, Hickey's charges were multiplied until the final count was twenty. His initial plea of not guilty caused the case to be dragged on for months because of preliminary hearings. The guilty plea and final sentencing did not occur until September, 1988, eight months after the initial charges were laid.

Then in November, 1988, another priest, John Corrigan, had similar charges brought against him. His sentence of five years was brought down in January 1989. People were still reacting to this second conviction when more charges were laid in February, this time against two priests and an ex-priest of the Archdiocese. These charges caused an even greater emotional outburst than previously. Victims' revelations in the media opened a Pandora's box of group sex and planned orgies. They pointed to groups of priests "working" together in orchestrated sexual abuse of minors. This created an awful expectation in the community that there was more to come.

The questions that arise from this unbelievable situation are many. People want to know how a priest could be involved in child sexual abuse for almost twenty years without someone knowing. They are wondering if something about the clerical state—celibacy, for example—has caused this to happen. They are asking if there's something lacking in the training of priests that has led to this. And more than anything, they want to know how and why there could be so many involved.

While these questions, and similar ones, are important, I think there needs to be a broadening of the base of inquiry if we are to fully understand what is happening. As with many forms of sexual abuse, the issue at play here is not sex or sexuality. The issue is one of power.

As a woman in the church, I relate profoundly to the victims of sexual abuse because I have experienced in my work and life the abuse of power by clergy. The sexual abuse of children is just the most extreme expression of the abuse of power that many women have identified for a long time. It is so reprehensible because these men are using positions of trust and power to destroy the lives of adolescents.

There is a danger because of the celibate state of the Roman Catholic clergy to see these cases only in sexual terms. If we do so, we narrow the analysis. Instead we must ask why do men in power positions use these situations to sexually abuse women and children. Why do men sexually assault their wives? their daughters? their sons? other women? other children? Why do they try to prove who they are by asserting themselves sexually over those who are less powerful? These questions are, of course, being asked in the broader society. Their answers are the same as to why Roman Catholic clergy are involved in child sexual abuse.

As well, there has existed in society an unspoken, and very often unconscious, pact that has always protected men who have abused women and children. It is this same societal pact of silence that has protected these clergy. That pact is only recently being broken in this province. It has been only a very few years since rape cases were first reported in the media. It is no wonder, then, that the cloak of silence is only now being lifted in a society where clergy have experienced an incomparable position of power.

I do not talk about the broader societal experiences in order to minimize what is going on with the Roman Catholic clergy. These factors actually become heightened in the church since the Roman Catholic clergy constitute what I have heard referred to as "the most exclusive men's club in the world." Men who are involved in the criminal activity we are talking about use the cloak of a celibate structure to pursue their activities. Also, because there is no structure of accountability outside the "brotherhood" they have felt fairly confident of protection. There is a strong sense of loyalty among clergy, so much so that some priests still find it hard to see why the clergy involved in child sexual abuses should lose their status as priests. And this even in the case of someone who has been convicted of multiple charges perpetrated over a long period of time.

This is incomprehensible to me, but that is because I, too, am victimized. I work as a director of an office in a hierarchical structure where I am never involved in any ultimate decision-making, and never can be as long as all power rests in the hands of the male clergy structure. More than that, individual priests have used this structure to block my work and the work of other laity.

Group reflections that occur as a result of the situation in the St. John's Archdiocese allow people to name this abuse of power. In a group that I was recently part of, participants agreed that the clergy who have exercised power over children through sexual abuse have been able to do so because their abuse of power on other levels had not been named and called. At last the laity, and laywomen more freely than laymen, are doing so. It is most unfortunate that things had to reach such a crisis in order for this to happen.

But one thing is now certain. Our church will never be the same again. Lay people will no longer be willing to leave the church to the clerics. More to the point, women will no longer be willing to leave the church to the men. And there are men who will walk with those women, both laymen who do not want to be co-opted by the clergy, and a handful of clergy who recognize the power inherent in their state.

This is the good that will come from the present evil. It will not come without struggle. But the struggle to create something new will give life rather than drain life as the present situation is doing. Instead of the destruction of an earthquake, we will create the new life of an evolutionary explosion. This is the challenge we face.

Abortion: A Newfoundland Experience

Jaya Chauhan

This article examines social and cultural perspectives on abortion through the lens of personal experience and the conviction that abortion is an individual—and moral—choice.

I AM A SOUTH ASIAN WOMAN, born in Nairobi, Kenya. My family emigrated to England in the late 1960s when Africanisation policies forced my father to flee to Britain. He held a British passport but lived in Kenya where he made a living as a shoemaker. I obtained my Ph.D. in sensory science in July 1982. In 1990, I left my work as a Sensory Scientist at Oxford Polytechnic in England to teach a course called Women and Science in the Women's Studies program at Memorial University. I had been unhappy in my work for a long time, and I welcomed the opportunity to work in a different academic discipline.

Within months of moving to Newfoundland, I discovered that access to abortion services was limited. Abortion is a social issue of serious concern for women all over the world. Prior to 1990, I knew, theoretically, of women's struggles for unconditional access to abortion on humanitarian grounds. For some time I had been bothered by my knowledge that poor black women are often coerced into having abortions in the United States, while Irish women have to travel from Ireland to England to have an abortion. However, it was not until I lived in Newfoundland that I felt in my nerves, in my body, what I knew in my head. In Newfoundland, I became acutely aware of the extent of the barriers women in some areas encounter in accessing abortion. I also discovered how the anti-choice lobby works to silence and divide women, thereby undermining our reproductive freedom. Polarization of women on this issue is just one of many mechanisms for social control in a society structured to reproduce inequities based on race, sex, sexuality, class and ability.

This paper reflects critically on my personal experience with abortion in St. John's, Newfoundland, in 1990. The delays and psychological turmoil and isolation I experienced were not unique. Rather, they were partly a result of the failure of the Canadian government to ensure equal access to free, safe abortion throughout the country. I came to understand, through my experience, that the anti-choice lobby makes the pregnant woman and her reality invisible, while sentimentalizing scientific evidence by ascribing personhood and protection to the fetus.

In Newfoundland, in 1990, there was one gynaecologist in the city of St. John's, performing abortions one morning a week. This was the only abortion service available for the large population of women living in the central and eastern areas of the province. In order for a woman to get approval for an abortion, her family doctor had to recommend termination of the pregnancy on medical/psychological grounds, a gynaecologist had to confirm the recommended decision, and the woman was counselled by two registered nurses. The medical doctors still served as gate-keepers: they either granted or withheld permission to terminate a pregnancy, rather than women having the right to choose. The waiting list at the General

Hospital in St. John's was approximately two months long so that most women were 12 weeks pregnant when the abortion was performed.

It is important to place this situation in historical context. In Canada, prior to January, 1988, in accordance with the 1969 amendments to the Criminal Code, a woman required the permission of a therapeutic abortion committee to obtain an abortion. Not all hospitals were required to establish such committees; the result was that access to abortion services varied by region and province. Essentially, the well-to-do benefitted from a policy that placed the onus for ensuring access to abortions on hospital boards and the therapeutic committees they established, rather than placing it in the hands of the federal government and the courts. Poor, particularly single and young, women suffered from limited access and the often severe biases in the abortion adjudication process that resulted (McDaniel, 1985). On 28 January, 1988, the Supreme Court of Canada held that the provisions of the Criminal Code of Canada that restricted access to abortion, and made obtaining an abortion a criminal offence, except under specified conditions, were unconstitutional (Rogers, 1990). Section 251 of the abortion law was ruled to be a violation of women's rights as embodied in the Canadian Charter of Rights. In 1990, the federal government sought to recriminalize abortion through Bill C-43 which was passed by the House of Commons on May 29. Under this bill, abortion would have been a criminal offence unless "a medical practitioner . . . [was] of the opinion that, if the abortion were not induced, the health or life of the female person would be likely to be threatened" (Bill C-43, House of Commons). "Health" was defined as "physical, mental and psychological health" and "opinion" meant one "formed using generally accepted standards of the medical profession."

With Bill C-43, abortion would have become a crime with a maximum sentence for doctors of two years on conviction. A survey done by the Society of Obstetricians and Gynaecologists of Canada in November, 1990 showed that 343 physicians would have stopped performing abortions if the bill had become law (*Globe and Mail*, Jan. 16, 1991). On January 31, 1991, Bill C-43 was defeated in the Senate. Struggles to decriminalize abortion have been important for women, but they have not entirely ended important limits on women's right to choose.

A recent report by Nancy Bowes provides accounts of 25 individual women's experiences with trying to obtain safe, legal abortion services in Nova Scotia (Canadian Abortion Rights Action League (CARAL), 1991). Each woman's experience is unique and yet each speaks her anger and hurt. Women report difficulties in their search for supportive doctors and delays in getting hospital appointments. The voices of these 25 women provide insight into the largely unwritten and unspoken annals of the abortion reality in the Atlantic Provinces. Their experiences inspired me to speak of my own.

In February 1990, I was a 34-year-old, sexually active adult. I considered myself to be a responsible adult, well-versed in my body and my sexuality, but the journey to that place had been arduous. I did not become sexually active until I was 21 years old. I was raised in a traditional Hindu Indian household. Our culture is steeped in gender ideology: the father and husband act as the sole guardian of wives and daughters; arranged marriage is accepted; and female honour and reputation are to be maintained at all costs. In accordance with East Indian cultural code, going out with boys and attending parties and dances were not part of my life when I was growing up. When I left home for the first time to attend University, I indulged in the activities that I had been barred from previously. I had hungered for intimate relationships and to experience the special bond of heart and skin.

My parents had never broached the subject of sexuality; what I came to know, I learned privately. The Pill was not a contraceptive option for me at the time, because the use of the Pill would have meant admitting to myself my involvement in sexual activity and hence defiance of my gender role. Barrier methods, such as the diaphragm, also required frank admission, and condoms demanded a degree of male cooperation. Hence, initially, my only contraceptive alternatives were the least effective methods of withdrawal and rhythm. Not unlike many Newfoundland women brought up in the Catholic tradition, I had been raised to deny that I was a sexual being in need of expressing desires and feelings of intimacy. This denial limited my ability to freely choose from a range of contraceptives (Davies, 1984). However, with time, my body consciousness grew and this helped me accept increased responsibility for my sexual activity.

By the time I moved to Newfoundland, I was very much in control of my body, acutely aware of my fertility cycle, and using contraception. Each month, I waited with great trepidation for my menstrual periods but, up to that point, they had come regularly and without fail. I considered contraception to be the first line of defense against unintended pregnancy but as long as methods of contraception were less than perfect and women lacked control over their own sexuality, abortion was, I thought, an unfortunate necessity.

In February of 1990, I found myself pregnant and living in my new home in Newfoundland without access to a familiar family doctor. I was married to a supportive partner who lived in Alberta, and with whom I would be reunited once my work contract was completed. My partner felt that "the timing was perfect," and was willing to take on the child care responsibilities so that I could continue with my career. Because risks increase with age, this might have been my last chance for a "safe" pregnancy.

While my partner was delighted, I was far from jubilant. I wanted to echo his joy but felt, instead, burdened by this being growing within me against my will. The prospect of motherhood raised some profound questions that I had not yet worked through. My partner and I had entertained the possibility of remaining child-free; was I to abandon that possibility because of an unplanned pregnancy? I speculated that my mother had had no choice when she had me, and secretly, I think, she was disappointed with me. With four daughters already and living in a culture that places great value on male children, she had hoped for a son. My mother had had her sexuality repressed and was raised in a culture where she had to seek the approval of the authority—Father. I, too, was a product of that culture but was in the process of coming to understand the world from a feminist perspective. In 1988, I had married a non-Asian man against my parents' wishes. It was one of the most difficult decisions of my life, and one I knew would hurt my parents deeply while alienating me from the community in which I was raised. However, I was tired of the role of the virtuous and dutiful daughter and felt I owed myself some responsibility to take control of my own life.

It takes two to conceive but a woman alone gestates a child. This had to be *my* choice, and it was my inner awareness that allowed me to make that choice. My body felt violated and I did not feel as though I could live with myself if I allowed the possibility of another being living against my will within it. I was not ready for motherhood and perhaps I never will be. All I knew was that I wanted my body, this life was being created against my will, and I could not offer a child the care it deserves.

The next two months were the longest of my life. As the days passed, my belly swelled, my breasts tingled with pain, and I felt my body being taken over. As my body lost its physical fitness, I felt disgust toward it, and the emotional turmoil became unbearable. Traditional western images of female beauty had come to inform my body image and I felt bloated, fat and ugly. What had I done to deserve this pain? Thinking back to that time, I am reminded of the Statistics Canada report on therapeutic abortions (1970-1988) which glibly states that the typical Canadian woman who had an abortion in 1988 was less than 13 weeks pregnant: what about the pain during that "less than 13 weeks?"

Communication between myself and my partner began to suffer. I could not say what I felt because whatever I said sounded so different from what I was hearing in me, in my skin, my body. I had one woman friend I was only beginning to know and feel safe with. She allowed me an authentic expression of myself and my being; her empathy was a great solace and I remain indebted to her. A man friend, living in Europe, was another pillar of strength, but I found writing incredibly difficult partly because I was paranoid of the power of the written word and how it could be used against me. I felt alienated from other friends I had thought I was close to; even my feminist colleagues could not be trusted. Everyone seemed so busy with their own lives that I could not risk abandoning the safety of silence. When we examined the abortion issue in my Women's Studies classroom, I found myself in inner turmoil as my students struggled with the interests and well-being of an invisible and unknown pregnant woman. Abortion was distasteful to them and they equated it with killing life, saw it as a selfish act. I felt powerless, voiceless, lifeless next to the fetus growing in me. If only I could have taken the risk and communicated my experience, I think that I would have found some support.

I was pregnant with all the pain from the past, and I yearned for my pain—the wounds that had marked my body and spirit—to be recognized and validated. Being born a female, into a low-caste orthodox Hindu family, into a racist, sexist and classist society had taken its toll on my personal life. As I struggled with the additional load of an unwanted pregnancy, I could not help but think of all the other women in my predicament who perhaps did not have a partner or friends to listen to them. The choice to kill potential life was made by me, a woman with compassion and with commitment to the expression of human dignity. But the word "kill" was not my own. Rather it was borrowed from the media along with 'selfish', 'uncaring' and even 'murderer' (Paczensky, 1990). At the time, I had no idea that the anti-choice lobby was so effective or that it would have such a profound impact on me and my decision to terminate my pregnancy. The anti-choicers' fear of female sexuality and the body worked to keep me silent—a silence that was not freely chosen but forced on me. And my fear, today, in documenting my experience, speaks of this silencing that isolates us and makes us vulnerable.

Why do we tend to see women as having only contingent value next to fetuses? A woman's work, her health, her choices, needs and beliefs are seen as trivial; motherhood is supposed to be based on self-sacrifice. Debates on abortion centre around the sanctity of life: when does an embryo become a human being? From my perspective, neither an embryo nor a neonate is in any existential sense a human being. Prior to the emergence of reflexive consciousness, the embryo and the neonate are nothing other than potentially human; their consciousness, such as it is, cannot be differentiated from the biological consciousness of any other animal. Biological consciousness is not awareness of the world; it represents nothing other than the imperative constellation of survival instincts (Reeve, 1987). It is fetus-directed technology and medical capabilities in neonatal technology that have raised the questions of the independent viability of the fetus and whether the fetus and mother live in "untroubled symbiosis."

When my mother was pregnant, she was simply expecting a baby. She did not separate herself from her pregnancy, her body. Sadrozinski (1989) and Barbara Duden(1991) suggest that changes in reproductive technologies have allowed the fetus to acquire an independent medical identity. Ironically, the fetus has been granted "rights" and status of personhood by many, while such "rights" are denied to many living human beings. As Patricia Williams notes, "if one views 'rights' as emanating from either the body of 'legal' history or from that of modern bourgeois legal structures, then of course rights would mean nothing because blacks have had virtually nothing under either" (1987: 417). In my opinion, every woman has the right and the responsibility to make an informed decision on whether and when to become a mother. Legal, safe and fully insured abortion services should be available across Canada to all women so that they can exercise real control over their reproduction and hence their lives as human beings.

After two months of heart-wrenching struggle, and two days prior to my long-awaited appointment at the hospital, news came from England that my father was seriously ill. I had to break the secret to my family in order to explain why I was not on the next plane home to share my father's last moments with him. He died the day before my abortion, but I did not learn of his death until I got home from the hospital.

For me, abortion, a moral choice, has a deep sacred meaning. I presume it does for countless other women as well. Will someone give their stories a voice, or are they to remain forever marginalized, growing more and more invisible behind the ever sharper images of fetal life conjured by reproductive technologies and flashed across our minds by those who would take away our choice?

Newfoundland Clinic Celebrates 1st Anniversary

Noreen Golfman

This article was first published in Prochoice News *in the summer of 1991.*

IT'S HARD TO BELIEVE that the Morgentaler Clinic in St. John's will be celebrating its first anniversary in November of 1991. The flurry of noise and attention seems a million miles ago now, yet the intensity of the images surrounding the opening will stay with me permanently. I remember myself now both in the thick of things and on the outside looking at myself going through it all. And it gets difficult to distinguish where one's real experience ends and the media's version of it begins. And it certainly was a media circus here in St. John's last November.

If anyone had told me that by the autumn of 1990 I'd be officially directing the media for Dr. "Uncle Henry" Morgentaler in this town, I would have said she was hallucinating. But when faced with Morgentaler's imminent arrival, I had to put all my years of pro-choice lobbying to work.

I'll never forget walking into the Hotel Newfoundland dining room to meet Peggy Misener, the nurse who had moved to St. John's to oversee the preparation and management of the Morgentaler Clinic. The crisp white linen-covered luncheon tables were filled with blue-suited corporate businessmen. Glasses of fine claret were raised to toast the lucrative promises of Hibernia offshore oil development. It's so deliciously ironic to reflect on how subversive our lunch was—there we were, the only women in the room, plotting the invasion of an abortion clinic in the heart of God-fearing St. John's. Anyone else in the room might have guessed that we were well-paid secretaries celebrating our bosses' latest triumphs.

From that moment on, I experienced one of the most frightening and exhilarating periods of my life. And I came out of it stronger and wiser. In the beginning I struggled to keep a secret, not an easy thing to do in this fishbowl, nor an enviable situation for any woman who loves to talk a lot. The next stage involved handling the media and the crowds that we wisely anticipated would gather around the clinic on opening day.

I remember weeks of trying to outsmart the press who were hot on our opening trail, dozens of phone calls with suddenly deferential media bigwigs, artificially polite television producers and well-mannered ravenous journalists from across the country. I learned quickly whom to trust, how to leak just enough information to keep the wolves from the door, and what to avoid.

I remember the generous, unquestioning support from the St. John's Women's Centre—women prepared to go to any lengths to keep the clinic open, and protected from the threatening crowds gathering noisily around us.

When the day in mid-November finally arrived, the sun was shining and the media vultures were circling. I swallowed my orange juice, put my head down, and charged though the day with a combination of fear, necessity and poetic justice. The news conference was dramatic. Pro-Choice and CARAL supporters waved welcoming placards and cheered encouragingly as Henry, Peggy Misener, our lawyer, and I arrived for what was to be over an hour of calmly directed, even intelligent questions. We then headed off toward the clinic across town. GULP. As the car approached we could see yellow school buses, *hundreds* of people, many children, marching with anti-choice placards on the street. Most notably, the then Archbishop of St. John's, the infamous Alphonsus Penny, had dared to show up, significantly undermining the credibility of the anti-choicers bussed in for the occasion. Despite the police being notified, they could not fully anticipate the incredible rage that engulfed the tiny figure of Henry as he faced the crowds and started to walk toward the clinic.

I remember sheer terror. The circle tightened around us. Middle-aged silver-haired men, eyeballs popping, flushed white faces, screaming madly and wildly at Henry: "Murderer! Killer!" and most ironically of all, "Nazi!" The police were nowhere in sight—only an increasingly angry crowd pressed in on us, aiming finally and violently for Henry. Fists started punching towards us. I looked down to find Peggy Misener on the ground below me, face paralysed white, eyes frightened. I stretched my arm towards her, told her to hang on to my wrist, and somehow pulled her up. "Thank God I lift weights," I remember mumbling to her as we inched forward. Meanwhile someone had managed to jab both at me and past me at Henry's shoulder, dislodging his glasses.

Don't ask me how we made it to the clinic door. Maybe sheer will led us towards safety. Once inside, the invited Press immediately went at Henry, who recovered from the ugly ordeal outside in an amazingly short time. I managed to get through the day without surrendering to fear and panic in part because of Henry's extraordinary example.

The rest of the day was neither calm nor predictable, but the worst was over for now. The day's events unfolded in abbreviated form in the electronic media, at once exaggerated and understated, distorted and hysterical. And there I was, caught eternally by the cameras in a moment of terror, with a stubborn look on my face. I had to call my mother to warn her not to get too upset about what she would see on the "National" that night. I had survived the day and, except for the obscene phone calls and ensuing hate mail, I might actually get some sleep in the next few weeks. And the clinic was going to make it.

Since then, hundreds of women across Newfoundland and Labrador have sought help from the clinic, and, except for the intrepid priest who quietly keeps vigil for a few hours on procedure days, the sidewalk outside is quiet. As for me, it took longer to recover from the opening, and the events leading up to it, than I had estimated. For a time in this town I had more media exposure than Madonna!

With decriminalization, the defeat of Bill C-43, and many hard-fought struggles behind us, things are calmer in such troubled anti-choice bastions as this Rock. Yet issues of funding and access for poor and outport women remain, and we know that we can't take the clinic's existence for granted, not for one moment. I learned a lot though this experience—about the media, the community, the dangers that lurk on the sidewalk. But frankly, Madonna can have all the publicity she wants.

Mary Conway

Virginia Ryan

Nᴇᴡs ʜᴀs ᴄʀᴇᴘᴛ ꜰʀᴏᴍ ʜᴏᴜsᴇ ᴛᴏ ʜᴏᴜsᴇʜᴏʟᴅ, out the shore and in to town; news has crept from tongue to tongue how Mary Conway died. How she left the house that evening; how they found her in the landwash; how poor Tom is in the mental, drying out and weeping, raging. Some are saying it's Tom who did it, more are sure he didn't, wouldn't; most believe it hardly matters, because he drove her to it anyway. Some are whispering she was pregnant, and wasn't it a sin, while others say you couldn't blame her, the way they lived, the way he was with her. Some are even blaming Nanny Conway—how she worked the girl, how she always took up for Tom. Some say the whole family was like that, they all knew what Tom was like, but blood's thicker than water. . . . In the city, the sociology department will write a book on the subject. The folklore department will say, at least we've got the family on tape in the archives. The women's groups will say, why didn't she come to us. The Church will say she was a poor, misguided child.

But meanwhile there's a place outside the graveyard for Mary Conway. Outside the graveyard, in the gravelly soil, on the side of the hill, where the shrubby trees lean flattened in the grey sea wind. There lies Mary Conway, saying nothing. And she's the only one who knows. . . .

Mary knows it isn't just Tom, it's more than Tom, poor Tom can't help it, being the way he is. It's just she can't go on with him anymore—and when he finds out, he's probably going to kill her, anyway. She's hanging the cup towel over the stove, to dry; she's listening to the sea outside, pounding on the landwash, and to Nanny Conway prattling on, and to the hall clock ticking the hours away til the children come home and then Tom—so that she must hurry. . . .

Mary must hurry; she must be ready. 'It's a terrible evening,' Nanny Conway is saying, and 'What can you see, honey—is there a big sea on?' and Mary goes to the window, wipes away a little hole to peer out and can see nothing—nothing but the greyness billowing in, part wave, part wind, part nightfall, coming; so she says,

'No, Nan, honey, you can't really see. But it sounds like a big sea, doesn't it, Nan?' and she goes to the stove and pours Nan's tea. 'Have a cup of tea, Nan, honey, and don't mind me while I go upstairs for a little while. I've got to fold the laundry and straighten the boys' room,' and Nan says,

'Yes, honey, you go on. I'll mind the fire and have a cup of tea with you when you come down.'

Mary walks slowly up the stairs, pressing long fingers tight together, thinking, counting, wondering. Wondering, will I do it, can I do it, is everything ready—and yes, everything's ready: the notes have been written, there's enough bread made to last the week, the house is clean, the wood is in, I'm ready. She sits on the boys' bed, pressing her fingers tight together, thinking. I've got to do it. What else can I do? She looks around the room—the old patched quilt, the chair piled high with shirts and trousers, the rosary beads hanging from the mirror, and Vince's things on the walls: posters of rock stars and school compositions, the cowboy hat he won at the garden party, and the photos: photos of both of them, of Vince and Billy—Billy—and Mary's heart goes soft and bleeding, her mind shatters like a dropped glass, and she's thinking, I can't do this, I can't, I can't. And through her rising panic she dimly sees the grim realness of things: Tom's gun on the wall, two little boys cowering on the daybed, an old woman in a rocking chair, wringing her hands and weeping, and no way out, no way out. This is the apparition she has used to bring her to this point: Mary holds it there in her mind, at arm's length, where she can go on seeing it, but says to herself as she sits on the bed, think it through one more time, then, Mary. One last time, just to be sure.

So carefully Mary goes one last time down the dreadful path that has led her here—and every time she comes to a little side road where she could have done differently she pauses and thinks for a while, how things might have been, if she had—but then forces herself on, relentlessly, knowing the side roads are far behind her, irrelevant, and that there's only one choice before her now: to go on, or not to go on. But no, it's more than that, a voice interrupts—because to decide to go on, there must be some way to go on, and that's what can't see, and the tears are brimming. Because that's what she can't see.

Mary thinks of routes she's considered and discarded, one by one. She thinks of Tom's family. Mary has no family—her mother died when she was born, and Nanny Conway took her in as help when she was 10, took her to Lancer's Cove. And there was Tom, so fine, so strong at 15, so sweet to her—and so it went. Tom was sweet when he was 15, sweeter at 20; but at 30 he was not so sweet, and at 40 he was not so sweet at all. Oh, Tom's alright even now, sometimes, when he is sober, but the least little thing sets him off, again, and he goes mad. Mary thinks on the night she left him, she and the boys and poor old Nan—flew in the night to the neighbours' house and from there took a ride to Foley's Harbour, to his sister Annie's. And how good they all were to her, at Annie's, how sweet and condoling, til she spoke of leaving for good, and how their lips clamped tight, then, how their eyes went guarded, and how it was 'poor Tom, sure, he loves you all, honey—what would become of him without you . . .' and just that once she'd tried to tell them, about his rage, and the gun on the wall, and how you hardly knew who it would be: yourself, or maybe even poor old Nan—how you couldn't tell what he might do, after he passed a certain point . . . and they'd said, 'ah, Mary, poor Mary, it's hard, sure, and he's a trial to you, yes, Tom's a trial, and you've the patience of a saint, Mary, honey—but think of the boys, Mary, the boys need their father. . . .' And Mary'd gone back to Lancer's Cove, next morning, to a sober and repentant man, and had set her lips firmly to Annie and the others, and knew she'd never try that route, again. . . .

'Mary, honey, have a cup of tea with me now, before the boys get home'—Nan's thin old voice drifts up the stairs to her, like smoke, like memory. Mary walks slowly out of the room, to the top of the stairs.

'No, thanks, Nan, honey. I've still a bit of work to do—we'll sit down together after supper, Nan . . . The fire's okay?

'Oh, grand, honey, grand' crackles the old voice, warming, 'It's grand to have a good fire in on an evening like this.' And Mary's caught there, on the top step, thinking of Nanny Conway.

They'll blame poor Tom, and they'll blame Nanny Conway. Mary knows that it's too easy to blame—that whoever you blame for a thing, there's a whole set of people and things behind that person that you could blame instead. She doesn't need to look at Nan's hands to see them—to see the hard bumps, the callouses, the exhaustion in those hands. She doesn't need to look in Nan's eyes to see the loss, the weariness of marrying here and being stuck away here, with nothing but work and more work—fish and gardens and dole. When your widowed brother dies, of course you take his youngest son, and as the boy grows, of course you put him to work. And when your own son dies, in the lumberwoods, how hard it is to remember that this boy Tom has feelings, too, and not to compare the two of them, not to make him feel like next to your dead son he's nothing at all, nothing at all. . . . And when you take in a foster daughter, of course you work her—just as you were worked, yourself. And you're delighted when they marry, this boy and this girl—delighted to finally put the whole business by, and be an old woman who rocks by the fire, dreaming of what you might have been. . . .

And Mary doesn't blame Nan—and she doesn't blame poor Tom, either; burn your boats, they'd said, but Tom never had any boat to burn—nothing but a ghost he would never measure up to and a life he would never know how to leave—and the drink, the ugly drink that would start him off so merry, with songs, with stories, with foot-tapping on the floor, the accordion bright and brassy on Sunday afternoons, with a

di-iddle-dee, iddle-dee, iddle-dee
di-iddle-dee, iddle-dee dee . . .

but which would drag him into hell, so that by nightfall, when the visitors and the drink were gone, the smiling man was also gone, with a red-faced, raging demon in his place. . . .

No, Mary didn't blame Tom, but she couldn't love him either—not when she never knew when he'd be like that, next; not when the whole of her life was spent in keeping Nan from egging him on and keeping him from turning and venting on her his years of humiliated rage; and in trying to meet the visitors at the door to swallow her pride and ask them not to bring the bottle in, and in trying to keep little Vince and Billy from seeing the worst of it, and they in such a poor, small house. . . .

So what did she do—she did what so many do, in the back of a car on a summer night—she stole for herself a bit of sweetness, a crumb of desire, a flicker of flame. . . .She and Jim Healey, four or five times, down by the gut, where no one could see. And she didn't love Jim, no—she loved no one but her sons—but what did it matter: other women have chocolates and long-stemmed roses and honeymoons, and romance—she had four or five times in Jim's old Chevy being young again with someone soft and sweet to her in the dark.

Except that in small places, everyone sees. In small places eyes grow in the bark of trees, on bedroom walls and on the road, on outhouse doors and rocks and sticks.

... In small places eyes are everywhere—eyes that see what they want to see, leave the rest, eyes that manage to miss all the good you ever did, to focus on your sins. And women in their thirties who thirst for crumbs of love grow heedless, too, and forget what they've always known, and Mary felt her womb change, and her breasts, and knew what she had done.

Mary knew what she had done, and how it would look, with Tom sleeping on the daybed each night this past year or more and she alone in the quiet room upstairs; and how that was August and this was December, and it was starting to show. . . . Why didn't she go to the priest, they'll say, but Mary knows that you don't go to a priest with a tale like hers—what's he going to tell you? He'll pray for you and give you a penance, and send you back to the man who you know will kill you if he finds out, and not believe you. . . . Why didn't she tell one of the researchers passing through, they'll cry. But Mary can't tell the young strangers passing through—the ones from the mainland with notebooks and tape recorders, who don't mind your honey buckets and eat all your bread and jam and think your life is beautiful, nor the ones from Newfoundland who come with their fiddles and guitars and speak tough and think they know all about you; this surge of young strangers who fill your kitchen and drink your tea and get Nan's stories and Tom's old songs, and whisk back to the city and leave you there, wondering . . . wondering, if you followed them, could it be a road out, wondering could they be a ticket to some kind of answer . . . but when you take the bus into town, twice a year, you can never find them. And when you bump into them by accident on Water Street they're always busy, on their way someplace, and how's Tom and how's Nanny Conway and you must come visit sometime, only they never name a time. . . .

Mary thinks on all the strangers who come to Lancer's Cove looking for something, and leave again thinking they've got it in their tape recorders, in their files. They come into her kitchen with gifts for Nan, and Nan tells them the old names for the hill and pasture and about how her granny came over from Ireland; for Mary there is fruit for the boys and hand-me-down clothing she's glad to get, but Mary has no stories, Mary has no songs; it's Tom they're really after, Tom—with his

di-iddle-dee, iddle-dee, iddle-dee

—all the old songs, the old tunes, and there's beer for Tom, beer and rum and whisky, and oh Tom loves it, loves it, and gives them what they're after time after time, and Mary's heart's rising in her throat and she's praying to Jesus they leave before the liquor gets to him and the smiling man is gone—and somehow by magic they always do, and Mary cleans the tea cups and broken glass later, much later, with the curtains drawn and his rage all spent and him on the daybed, snoring.

But Mary can't blame the strangers, either, with their overfriendliness and their liquor and their greed. It wasn't the strangers who introduced Tom to the bottle, and he doesn't need them to get it, either... and Mary knows her stomach's swelling, and that any day the tongues'll start wagging, as they start to see. . . .

Mary's pacing the boys' room, now, searching, searching in her mind for anything else that she might do—but knows that she has tried it all, that this is just an exercise. She's wondering how Tom will take it, what he'll do...surely he won't harm Vince and Billy or poor old Nan. . . .She lingers on this one, for it's troubled her, before. There's no saying what Tom will do—but the police and the social services will be here in a flash, she knows, and they'll set things straight. Mary thinks how odd it is, that it takes her doing this to get them to come here and do what someone should have done long ago. The boys are swimming before her eyes and she knows she still loves them fiercely, but fiercely her heart's crying why isn't there anyone for *me*, anyone to help *me*, and there isn't, there never has been, so that's why she's got to do this, for herself, and never mind the consequences. When she grows big with this child and Tom sees, she'll be no use to them at all, and life will be hell here, worse hell than it is now, and she'll be waiting for the gun to come down off the wall, and that isn't living. . . . It's mortal sin, her mind is shrieking—Mary, Mary, all the years you've been a good Christian, and now to do this, this, the worst sin of all—but tiredly she reminds her mind that it won't be the first of her mortal sins, and at least it'll be the last. . . .

Mary's fingering her slender throat, gazing out on the December garden, the clothesline, the apple tree, darkening in the dusk. I did try, her heart whispers, I did try. . . . Three weeks ago she got up the nerve, while Nan was napping, to pick up the phone and call St. John's. She'd called Professor Hagerty's wife. Professor and Mrs. Hagerty had come so often to see them, he with his books and his tape recorder, she with her gifts for Mary's boys—and once Mrs. Hagerty'd given her an old fur coat, still new-looking and lovely, and she'd worn it gratefully. . . . When the Hagertys came Nanny Conway would get her to take out the fancy tea set, and make a cake, and drive two coves down to the store for cheese and biscuits and tins of fruit. And Professor Hagerty even had sense about the liquor—he'd only ever give Tom a small amount, and he had more of Tom's songs, now, than anyone did and Mrs. Hagerty so nice and lovely with her two little boys the same age as Mary's, and her nice big house in town that Mary'd been to visit once. . . .

And the Hagerty's were good Catholics, too, so Mary just didn't know... But she'd stewed and stewed it out—maybe Mrs. Hagerty could help her, just maybe she could—so three weeks ago, one afternoon, she'd made the call—but Professor Hagerty had answered. No, Mrs. Hagerty wasn't in, just now, was there a message. Mary? I'm sorry, Mary who—oh, *Mary! Mary Conway*—and he'd been real friendly, then, and promised to have Mrs. Hagerty return her call, and she'd wanted to say to him 'Only in the daytime, please, sir, before four o'clock—and soon, sir, please have her call me soon'—but she'd said none of those things, not wanting him to think of her as desperate, or impudent, or suspect in any way.

And all that night Mary'd waited, tense, for the phone to ring—and how would she be able to say what she needed to say with Tom right there—and how would she explain the call to him at all—and she'd wished she had never picked up the receiver that afternoon, and had thanked Jesus when bed time came with no ring of the telephone.

But next morning came and went with no call, either, and the evening passed, and the next day, too, and Mrs. Hagerty never returned her call...and Mary wondered, did he forget to tell her, or was she too busy—they were so busy, the Hagertys...and she couldn't call a second time, she couldn't—for what if the professor answered, again, and thought she was reproaching him for not conveying her message? And maybe after all it was just as well—how could she have said what she had to say to Mrs. Hagerty, a nice Catholic woman, well-bred, from the mainland—how could she tell them of Tom and the gun when they thought so well of Tom...and how could she speak of Jim Healey's Chevy and her swelling stomach, to such people—what had ever possessed her, to begin with, to imagine she could. . . .

And then last week, the phone bill had come, and as luck would have it, Tom had seen it, and he on the rum, and—'What's this call, Mary?' he'd asked her, and Mary had paled—'Why, I don't know, Tom. A mistake, perhaps—' and he'd said 'I know that number' and taken out their little address book, and sure enough, the devil, he'd found the Hagertys number—he who couldn't usually locate a number or address to save his soul. And, 'Oh, so we're calling the Hagertys, now, are we—and aren't we grand,' he had jeered—'and what would we be calling the Hagertys for, on a weekday afternoon, and we getting so important these days, such high society people,' and Mary had panicked—does he know, does he know—but he'd gone on: 'Here's one for Professor Hagerty,' rolling his r's like an Englishman, 'for the great professor, buying old Tom with his cheap, dirty liquor' and he'd bashed the far wall with a junk of wood. It left a dent, there, a triangle. 'And here's one for the lovely Mrs.'—he bashed the wall again—'and a third for my lovely, lovely wife who is calling them up for tea—' and he'd turned to Mary, who had flown out into the dark night, weeping, her mind made up to act, act soon, sure now that whatever she did she must do it on her own. . . .

Mary can barely make out the clothesline now, which means the boys will be home at any moment. She doesn't want to see them again, their little white faces she's washed and nuzzled, their soft, sweet hair, their eyes, her eyes—but there's no help for it, she has to time this right. If she's gone when they get home they might go out looking for her—and that mustn't happen, they mustn't remember their mother like that. . . . Her eyes are stinging, now, but she's going ahead with this thing. Her heart is breaking but she drags her feet down, over the stairs, and bids it to stop feeling. Soon it won't have to feel anymore.

There's the sound of the school bus; there's Nan's soft wisp of hair showing over the top of the rocking chair; there's her kitchen, her shiny stove, her buns of bread, her table laid for supper, there's Mary's life, there's Mary, in her kitchen, one last time, putting a junk of wood in the fire, feeling its blast of heat crisping her face, her skin—there's Vince, there's Billy, little bundled faces peering in the door at their Nan, their mom, who's longing to hug them. . . . The stormy air gusts into the room, and 'Come in now, quickly, and shut the door,' says Mary, facing the stove so her back's to them, her lips steady, her mind gone cold and hard. 'Get changed and wash up, now—supper's almost ready' she snaps, and to Nan—'I wonder what time Tom'll be home.'

'Any time now, Mary honey, on such an ugly night—don't you think?' and Mary thinks so, too: Tom's been repairing the Hall up in Foley's Harbour, and they let them off promptly, this time of year, and Mary's ready, ready. . . . Mary's bending down over the soup, she's tasting absently, for salt, she's stirring the soup, she's cutting bread for supper, the butter's on the table, the milk, the jam—the little boys are giggling, up in their rooms, and dear God, there's the crunch of gravel, out in the lane, the headlight beam flickers by, goes out: he's home. And Mary must be quick, now—he mustn't see her, he mustn't detain her; she's getting on her coat now, quickly, grabbing the honey bucket she saved, on purpose—

'Nan, honey, I'm just going down to the beach to empty the pail, before supper—tell them to start without me' and she's gone out the front door, hauling the bucket, as Tom's coming in the back.

Down the lane Mary's rushing and stumbling, down the dark lane to the cliff, to the sea. She's set down the bucket, she's buttoned her coat up, the storm wind is whipping her, forcing her back—but she won't go back, she'll never go back. Mary's not herself, now, she's just a machine; you push the 'forward' button and forward you go; Mary's feet feel the edge of the cliff and she breathes 'Sacred heart of Jesus, have mercy on me,' and she is gone.

Half an hour later they find him there; find Tom in the landwash, bent over the body, blubbering, weeping, asking it why. And the news starts creeping from house to household, out the shore and in to town—the news creeps on from tongue to tongue how Mary Conway died.

Labrador City by Design: Corporate Visions of Women

Linda Parsons

This paper, focusing on the lives of women in a "company town," is based on the author's MA thesis.

IN THE FALL OF 1982, Labrador City was experiencing its first economic recession, and I was embarking on my first fieldwork experience. I initially intended to measure the effects of work migration on women in Newfoundland. In the end, however, I focused on the social conditions for women created by the "supercompany" that formed the economic core of the town (Parsons, 1987).

Interviews with 49 women in Labrador City provided the basis for a descriptive ethnographic study of the lives of women who moved to this male-centred company town. Like similar research on women in other northern Canadian company towns, I found the sexual hierarchy in the community was partly a consequence of company policies on hiring, housing, and the provision of facilities (Luxton, 1980). The vision of the "male breadwinner/ female domestic" nuclear family underlay these policies. Luxton (1980), *No Life for a Woman* (NFB, 1979), and my research (Parsons, 1987) all found that the corporate ideal of women's role was to "service" and "reproduce" the workforce. Women did this primarily through cooking, cleaning, emotional repairs, budget and household management, and child-rearing.

This paper outlines Iron Ore Company of Canada (IOCC) policies that affected women (whether covertly or deliberately), including those related to hiring, the recruitment of families to settle the town, and housing. The paper also looks at some of the challenges women experienced in fulfilling the role of dependent housewife in Labrador City in the early 1980s. Women commented most frequently on shopping and the isolation of the town, followed by perceived threats to family integrity from rising divorce rates, and concerns about the frequent use of pornography. In all of these areas, the visions of men dictated the lives of women.

The Setting

Labrador City is a company town built in the 1950s and 1960s by the Iron Ore Company of Canada (IOCC), with assistance from the Newfoundland government. It is controlled by Hanna Mining, an American corporation. The town was constructed expressly to house male company workers and their families, as part of a wider program to modernize Newfoundland. Miriam Wright points out (in this volume) that the Newfoundland government was promoting numerous "modernization" schemes from the late 1950s through to the early 1970s and beyond, in an attempt to "catch up" with the rest of the industrialized world. Its policies included attempts to resettle members of Newfoundland outport communities in centralized "growth" centres like Labrador City to create a labour supply for industrial development. Similarly, other initiatives were intended to stimulate corporate exploitation of provincial resources. The Newfoundland government provided investment incentives including land grants, reduced royalties and taxes, and the building of infrastructure for the town (i.e. roads, schools, hospitals). Just as women at that time were largely ignored in fisheries-related policies, they were also commonly forgotten in modernization schemes throughout North America (Wright, this volume; Hayden, 1981).

In the early years of the town's development, IOCC concentrated on developing a steady and reliable workforce. This proved difficult for a number of reasons, not the least of which was the rigid occupational and social structure of the company and the town. There was a dichotomy between management and unionized workers that was still obvious in 1982 and that had an ethnic dimension. The lower-income, working classes were from Newfoundland, while members of the managerial class were largely from central Canada, or were married to central Canadians. In the 1960s, labour-management relations were far from amiable. IOCC tried many strategies to reduce worker militancy during the "bunkhouse" days. The company unofficially sponsored visits by prostitutes and strippers for workers' entertainment. As housing was built, it initiated policies to entice the wives and extended kin of workers to "settle" in Labrador City. The material and ideological effects of these strategies are discussed below.

The Study

I carried out this research in 1982. Twenty-eight of the first forty-four randomly selected respondents (64%) were at home full-time or were unemployed. All but a few of the rest were working in marginal jobs, largely in the service sector. "Marginal" jobs are usually semi-skilled or unskilled, part-time, with low pay, low status, and few benefits. There are few opportunities for advancement in such positions. Armstrong and Armstrong (1984) and Wilson (1982) have both noted that women tend to be "ghettoized" in these jobs more so than men. One of the reasons for this is the ease with which such jobs can be adapted—or dropped—to suit domestic and corporate demands.

One of my respondents was among the first women to reside in Labrador City on a semi-permanent basis. These women were nurses and female office workers who came to replace the male office workers employed by IOCC until the early 1960s. She treated me to descriptions of the "female staffhouse" days when potentially marriageable women were valued by the primarily male populace. She eventually married and settled in Labrador City.

The role of housewife within a male-breadwinner, nuclear family was generally considered ideal for women. The majority of my respondents moved to Labrador City because of the benefits offered to their families rather than to further their own careers. Lucrative jobs for their men topped the list of these benefits, and IOCC's hiring policies ensured that the family breadwinners in Labrador City would be male. During the development of Labrador City in the 1960s and the early 1970s, there were very few well-paying jobs available to women. This had been the case throughout Newfoundland until well into the 1940s.

Hiring and Kin Networks

IOCC's hiring policies served to ensure that the townsfolk would "fit" the ideals of the male breadwinner family through two different mechanisms. The most direct of the two was the unofficial ban on hiring women to work at traditionally male-defined jobs at IOCC. Women were considered too delicate to do manual or shift work. In the late 1970s, IOCC began paying tribute to the voluntary affirmative action program promoted by the federal government on the recommendation of the 1970 Royal Commission on the Status of Women. Those few women who were subsequently hired as labourers, janitors, or heavy equipment operators in the mine found themselves subject to intense social pressures from both co-workers and neighbours. They were considered to be "bad" examples of womanhood because they were doing such "dirty" work (both literally and figuratively, alluding to sexual promiscuity at the work site). Gossip about women in non-traditional jobs was particularly derogatory during the fieldwork period, probably because of the 1982 economic recession and widespread layoffs at IOCC. A prevalent complaint was that women were taking away the jobs of men. As late as 1990 women were not faring well, numerically, under IOCC's "affirmative action program," comprising only 7% of the total labour force at IOCC and only 4% of the labour force working in the more lucrative "non-traditional" fields.

Since only 36% of my initial random sample were employed, and these at very low-paying jobs, it soon became obvious that the majority of women in Labrador City, as in Flin Flon, relied on marriage for their economic survival.

Women's work both within and outside of the home is often characterized as more flexible than men's by employers and workers alike. Armstrong and Armstrong (1984) note that before the 1980s women were laid off more readily than men: it was assumed that they could return to the home when no longer needed at work. This was certainly the case in this fieldwork in 1982, where many of the respondents had been recently laid off.

IOCC's hiring was also based on nepotism: preference was given to the male relatives of people already working with the company. As a screening process among workers, this ensured less worker militancy. Along with sponsoring new migrants into Labrador City, kin networks frequently provided assistance in getting settled, help in finding a residence and/or a job, and emotional support to the homesick. There were few amenities to ease a family's initial adjustment to the area, and even hotel space was at a premium. In this study, the bulk of this "kin-work" (Stack and Burton, 1993) was done by women as an extension of their domestic duties, regardless of whether the new arrivals were members of their own kin networks or their husbands'.

Nepotism in hiring stimulated the growth of kin and community networks for some residents which helped to banish the loneliness and isolation that women in Labrador City commonly felt when confined to the home. The presence or absence of kin networks (from either the wife's or the husband's side of the family) frequently determined the quality of a woman's experience of Labrador City.

Despite the burdens of the kin-work involved in sponsoring relatives into

Labrador City, some respondents used it to demonstrate their domestic competence. Those of my respondents who felt that they were instrumental in the success of their families' moves seemed to be generally happier with Labrador City. However, eleven of the forty-nine women interviewed moved to Labrador City in hopes of escaping their extended kin. Like many other women and men, their experiences with kin proved to be more intrusive than supportive, as the "ties that bind" can sometimes be.

Women's experiences of Labrador City were very much defined by their roles within the family and the home. Almost all of the respondents in this study agreed that the quality of housing, school, and recreational facilities for children were much better here than in their home communities. Respondents with children testified that they stayed on in Labrador City for the sake of their children. In 1982, schools and recreational facilities for children were much better in Labrador City than on the island of Newfoundland (due to IOCC subsidies), and parents could afford many more material things than they had "back home." This created an important feeling of accomplishment for quite a few respondents, particularly since child rearing was a crucial component of the domestic labour that defined their lives.

Paradoxically, company housing and recreational facilities also restricted women's options.

Housing

Like its hiring practices, IOCC's housing policies were part of its strategy to develop a settled and reliable workforce based on male workers with economically dependent housewives and children. Without consultation with its workers or their wives, IOCC determined the design and lay-out of the houses. In the planning stages of the town, women were expected to take whatever was offered under the guise of "helping the family stay together."

In the early to mid 1960s, IOCC began contracting construction firms to build houses based on plans for two or three standardized bungalows and one row-house that were hypothetically suitable to northern climates (respondents disagreed), and that were cheap and easy to build. There was little room for individuality: houses were arranged in a grid and the style represented a homogenization that is emblematic of suburban life in a company town. Suburban home ownership theoretically corresponded to the male-breadwinner nuclear family ideal. It was promoted as part of a corporate and state strategy to "domesticate" workers throughout the United States from the 1940s through to the 1970s (Hayden, 1981, 1984).

Many of the women interviewed had come from a background of poverty and sub-standard housing in Newfoundland's rural outports. They were promised all of the modern amenities of homemaking in Labrador City, including electrical appliances, running water, indoor plumbing, and television. In considering their neighbourhoods, all but three or four of my 49 respondents appreciated this company-housing style—or at least they didn't mind it—and they liked the "nice tidy look of the place." It was similar to the suburban ideal commonly presented in the mass media during this period (Hayden, 1981). Single-family housing units were a measure of status and progress for these women, as they were for many working-class families. They provided the foundations of privacy and social insulation needed to nurture the nuclear breadwinner family.

This type of housing also had, however, other social consequences for women in Labrador City and elsewhere. Single family home ownership compounded the isolation of women in their role as housewives. It clearly delineated the boundary between "work" and "home" and exacerbated the process of excluding women from jobs outside the home. The long cold winters of Labrador City, its geographical isolation, and inaccessible transportation and other services kept many women and children housebound for much of the year. Housewives were vulnerable to what Luxton (1980) called the "captive wife syndrome" since they did not have external jobs or school to relieve the tedium of the house. Labrador City residents referred to this loneliness and depression as "cabin fever" and described many remedies to deal with it, such as sports participation and leaving town. In addition, most housewives were economically dependent: some had to request money and time from their husbands in order to leave the home even for a few hours, if they could find a place to go. As both "home" and "work," housing was crucial to the well-being of these women. Their lack of control over their domestic environment was striking.

When IOCC began building houses, the demand was overwhelming. The waiting period was extended by construction backlogs that lasted well into the mid 1970s, and which allowed the company a fair degree of control in choosing its town populace and getting rid of the "undesirables" before they had a chance to settle in. As soon as each house was completed, it would be allotted by the company to whomever was judged most in need of it. The definition of this need depended on the supervisor's evaluation of a worker's job-performance, his family ties (i.e. whether he was a "steady family man" or not) and his seniority at work. The first two of these prerequisites could have been interpreted quite subjectively and, according to many of my respondents, getting a house really depended on "who you knew." This was an excellent way to control and discipline the workforce.

The company would never admit to such favouritism, or to the very human fact that its management personnel may have been biased in their evaluations. One company official assured me that housing was allotted equally according to the number of requests that supervisors of the various departments had made. The supervisors would then ". . .try to stick with the seniority system to figure out who finally got the houses, so as not to hurt anybody's feelings."

Yet, only married men were permitted to apply in the first place. Single men had to wait until all of the married couples had been allotted houses, and women had to wait even longer. For the first fifteen years of Labrador City's development, a woman could only live in her "own" home if she was married to an IOCC employee who legally "owned" the house. As in the United States, mortgage policies restricted women's access to home ownership, except through their husbands

(Hayden, 1981). The effects of this policy were augmented by the unofficial corporate practice of restricting women's access to paid employment, particularly after they married.

Another concurrent measure that IOCC used to screen the newly forming populace of Labrador City was its housing subsidization plan. In the beginning, the company sold houses to its workers virtually at cost. Mortgage financing was arranged through a commercial bank, and IOCC would sometimes subsidize the interest payable (which could amount to more than half of the principal owing). Qualifications for a mortgage subsidy were the same as those for an IOCC house: applicants had to be married, male, and of course, IOCC employees in good standing. Married women with families did not qualify until the early 1980s, and IOCC's housing assistance policy was still not available to unmarried women with children in 1982.

In this study, none of the respondents personally qualified for housing assistance and one young single mother, employed at IOCC for more than five years, was quite indignant when still refused assistance during the winter of 1981-82:

> There I was, working at IOCC and trying to get a subsidy from them ever since my daughter was born in 1978, but they always had some reason why I couldn't. Finally I just said the hell with it, got a personal loan from the bank, and bought this trailer. I wouldn't have qualified for a company subsidy anyway, because I'm single. They'll subsidize you if you're married or even living common-law these days, but not if you're single, no matter how many dependents you have. I really got the run-around too. (IOCC clerk)

IOCC's housing policies reflected the company's insistence on marriage (the "stabilizing" factor in workers' lives). Single women obviously did not meet its requirements. Like all non-company personnel, women were finally welcome to buy the home of their dreams (without subsidization) in the late 1970s when the real estate market "opened up." At the same time, however, the market prices of houses skyrocketed. Most women who worked outside the home in Labrador City had relatively low incomes and found it hard to get a bank mortgage.

Some women, like the respondent above, opted to buy a trailer instead of renting. Trailers represented a much smaller personal investment than houses over the long run, but the company considered the trailer park a potentially troublesome area: because they were cheap, trailers attracted what IOCC considered to be an "un-desirable, transient" population. To counteract this, IOCC practised a covert but effective form of discrimination by defining who was allowed to move into the trailer park and by withholding subsidies on trailers. Only IOCC employees were permitted to buy trailers, even after IOCC-built houses were put on the open real estate market. This made trailers particularly difficult to sell since the resale market was small.

Ultimately, potential trailer buyers had to provide adequate proof that they could pay even more (on a monthly basis) for a trailer than for a subsidized house. They had to find their own financing, had to meet higher interest payments, and they had to be that much more "reliable" and "settled." One housewife described some of

218

these company policies, noting that many were used to penalize workers who displayed any measure of disloyalty to the company.

> Really we've been here for years—this is our second house. We had a subsidy on the first one so it was a lot easier to live then. But last year, I got really depressed—just had to get out of here. So we sold our house and went out to look around during my husband's vacation. There's just no jobs anywhere, so we had to come back but we couldn't get another subsidy. Poor Joe—he only left to please me, but you can't tell the company that. They just won't have anything more to do with you if it looks like you might not stay forever.
>
> We tried to get a trailer since we had the cash to pay for it outright, but we weren't allowed to because we had already sold a company house. Now if you had a trailer and sold it to buy a house, that's fine. You're really settling in, then. But they got all these rules and they own everything: the whole town.
>
> The only thing we could get was this row-house. We're paying $408 a month on a mortgage with no subsidy. But it'd be even more expensive if we had to rent it. And it's all because I wanted to get out.

Finally, IOCC stipulated that no one could make a "profit" on an IOCC house, either by renting it out directly or by using it to establish a small business. Self-advancement was encouraged in corporate rhetoric, but not if it involved "company property," for example, the land the houses were built on. IOCC retained ownership of this land as part of the corporate investment incentive package offered to the company by the Newfoundland government in the mine's exploratory days.

This policy extended to all household members. Several women I talked to had to abandon their entrepreneurial ideas and hopes for self-employment through a home-based business.

> That's the whole thing down here: you're not allowed to make a profit in any way off IOCC property. If we decided to build a basement apartment, we'd lose the subsidy automatically. It'd be extra income on a subsidized house and they won't help any more. The mortgage would be $671 per month instead of $372. To make up the difference we'd have to charge the people downstairs $300 a month for a crummy basement, with not much privacy since there's only one entrance. This is why rents are so high and it's better to be settled here, in a house.

Housewives who could not or did not want to accept paid employment outside the home were especially restricted. They could not earn an income at home by providing daycare services, room and board, or crafts production within the community. In this sense, then, the interests of women were regulated and undermined by company policy. By indirectly keeping some wives dependent on their worker-husbands, the company was ensuring that its "stable family man" kept showing up for work. A few respondents pointed out that the company could use this rule to discharge those workers deemed inefficient or bothersome.

Despite these constraints, most of the women with subsidized mortgages were grateful that they were not living and working in Labrador City merely to pay mortgage interest to the bank. They also enjoyed the fairly high standard of living that was maintained through controlled town growth and admission.

219

After the initial 1982 layoffs at IOCC, however, people began to worry about job security and the security of their investment in their homes. The housing benefits offered by the company felt burdensome to those respondents who had recently arrived. They had begun to question the legitimacy of IOCC's claim that its authority over housing was justified by its investment in the town.

There's people here who have been here three, four, five years—and they figured they were pretty safe. The company said "okay, you come on down, we're subsidizing the houses here and we got everything in this town that any young couple would need to start a family," right? So a lot of guys quit their jobs or gave up any other chances if they were just out of trade school or university or whatever, and came on. They bought houses at 55-60 thousand dollars in the late 1970s, worked for awhile and then got laid off. So what do you do with that house, now? Like us. We bought this house about a month before they started announcing the shutdowns. And now, the market is just terrible! There's no resale value on our house because nobody's going to buy it for what we paid for it. So we're stuck with it, or we lose all the money we put into it.

As McQuaig (1991) notes, in 1982 the families of IOCC workers in Scheffer-ville, Quebec were paying a much higher price to maintain IOCC profitability than they had initially expected to. Labrador City families echoed these concerns, fearing the loss of both their jobs and their personal investments in local housing as IOCC began downsizing its operations.

Shopping in a Company Town

Apart from housing, most of the other facilities and services in Labrador City were developed for use by either male workers or children. Shopping, however, was considered a "woman's domain," and while most of the women interviewed in Labrador City agreed that it was quite stressful in a northern company town, it was cited as one of the few entertainments available to women. Juggling the household budget in Labrador City was certainly a domestic challenge, and those who were successful felt not a little satisfaction with their performance.

Shopping was problematic because of the geographic isolation and the relatively small population of Labrador City. In 1982 there were no roads connecting Labrador City to the "outside world" and price inflation was exorbitantly high, far exceeding the 1982 Canadian average of 10.8% (Statistics Canada, 1982). Shipping charges for food and goods were an undeniable part of this expense but in-store mark-ups were always 17% and higher, and the quality of the food, particularly the perishables, left much to be desired. Respondents generally agreed that "we're in the scrap heap here, getting all the leftovers and paying outrageous prices for them."

As in Luxton's (1980) Flin Flon, women in Labrador City were primarily responsible for household money management and many found themselves trying to justify spending so much for so little. Two of the women in this study described their husbands' exasperation at what they perceived to be their wives' "inability to budget." These husbands both eventually assumed responsibility for shopping, but found they could do little better, even with careful plans to economize.

Nowadays, he'll go to the bank—and I'm only too glad to get out of that—and he decides what comes out for payments, what he's going to spend on groceries and what's left over to drink. I keep my mouth shut about it all, like if I think more should be paid here or there; he doesn't trust me much with the money, so I never have any of my own. But at least I don't have to worry over it either, and he always pays the bills—that's one good thing about him.

Cutting household expenses was a major task among the housewives I talked to. For single, separated or divorced women with children, the stress of making ends meet could be overwhelming and many found that they could not afford to stay in Labrador City. The following respondent and her two teenage sons had been deserted by her husband for four months at the time of this interview.

I haven't received not two cents from him all this time. I got a mortgage of $538.00 a month and if you really scrimp you get by on $75.00 a week for groceries for the three of us. This year I'm cutting out oil altogether. I bought five heaters and put them in different places, so the heat will be cheaper but it still cost $200.00 to buy those things in the first place. I had to clothe the kids for the winter and that's not easy! The eldest is a man's size now. Then I had to get them in school with books and supplies and all; the car has to be fixed and gas kept in it, and it all adds up. It's really getting hard on just a waitressing salary (minimum wage plus tips), so I don't know how long I'll be able to last up here.

The high cost of living and price inflation were often cited as justification for women working outside the home: "It's not two people you need working, for Christ's sake, but three! One for the oil bill alone." The frequency of such statements emphasized the changes in family structure that were occurring in 1982, along with the persistent ideals of motherhood and domesticity that made such changes difficult for women. This is the focus of the next two sections.

Challenges to the Domestic Ideal

Few women had any job or other alternatives to the role of mother and housewife in the early years of Flin Flon (Luxton, 1980), Labrador City (Parsons, 1987), and the northern company towns in *No Life for a Woman* (NFB, 1979). This situation changed somewhat in Labrador City during the 1980s as women increasingly entered the labour force and enjoyed greater protection at work under Canada's Employment Equity Act of 1986. Feminist women's groups also ensured that more facilities were opening up to women throughout this period, such as a women's centre and a transition house for battered women in Labrador City. However, Labrador City still did not have a daycare centre in operation at the beginning of the 1990s (Stevenson, 1990), and in 1982, those women who worked outside the home were frequently admonished for ignoring their children. In fact, many of the problems that families and women had in Labrador City were blamed on "working mothers." One example of this was the link that people made between divorce and women's employment.

Throughout North America during the 1970s, divorce, single parenting and female employment all rose, transforming both family structures and the attitudes of women. The one-career, male-dominated family was no longer within the means of most people outside of Labrador City. Moreover, the social value that women enjoyed as housewives in the early years of Labrador City seemed to have diminished by 1982, when they were no longer a "novelty in short supply." As elsewhere, many respondents now defined themselves as "just housewives." They understood that this role depended on the preservation of their marriages and that, consequently, divorce constituted a threat.

Marriage and motherhood were deemed essential by most of my respondents: out of forty-nine women, thirty-eight were married, eight were single (all young women in their teens or early twenties), and three were divorced. These women always referred to themselves in terms of their relationships to the men and children in their families—and rarely as autonomous individuals. The few younger women in my sample who were delaying marriage or motherhood were usually discouraged from doing so by members in their families.

> Me? No way! I don't really like children all that much. Okay for a half an hour type of thing. And maybe I'm spoiled too, because right now I can have whatever I want. If I had to give up this or that for the baby, I think I'd hate it. It costs, these days.
> Of course, my husband wants a couple so we probably will, someday. Not here, though. Can you imagine staying home with small youngsters in Lab City? No way!

In addition, autonomous women in Labrador City were clearly negatively sanctioned through gossip. For example, a local unmarried business woman was rumoured to be quite eccentric. Tales of her successes were always qualified by references to her "domineering," "aggressive," and "reclusive" nature.

Marriage was important to women in Labrador City for other than economic reasons. The importance of the nuclear family structure was elevated by the geographic mobility of Labrador City residents, who lived so far away from extended kin. Although kin networks were encouraged, Labrador City did not always attract the "whole clan" and many respondents felt lonely. Demmler-Kane (1980:11) attributes ". . . increased expectations associated with the marriage bond . . ." to geographic mobility and to the nuclear family. She notes that whenever there is less involvement with the extended family and friends, people also lose an emotional support system. This can place a great deal of extra strain on the marriage, as it did for some of the respondents in this study.

Many cited marital infidelity and family breakdown as common problems in a single-industry northern town, as did Krahn et al.'s (1981) respondents in Fort McMurray, Alberta. Labrador City women often blamed the "surging divorce rates" on loneliness and isolation, depression, and acute boredom: "It's the big thing here now! You're either separated or divorced, or about to be." The threat of divorce exerted pressure on married women to uphold the male-breadwinner nuclear family model where divorce was unthinkable. Economically dependent women in this study often tried to ignore problems which, if taken to heart, could dissolve their marriages. A few of my respondents mentioned "putting up with" husbands who rarely came home, and never for companionship; who left their wives without any cash; and who blamed any emotional problems their wives were having on "nerves," since the husbands were providing adequate food, shelter, and a TV.

Several respondents complained that it was currently "too easy" to dissolve a marriage when any minor problem came up. Their fears were reflected in their hopes for their daughters.

I don't want her out making the same mistakes I did. She's got to get her education and be independent, take care of herself. I know she'll probably get married someday and hopefully it'll be okay, but you never know. She might get stuck with some creep and want to get out but not be able to. She'll need something to fall back on.

Divorce was most threatening to housewives who couldn't get work or adequate training for a job. All recognized and pitied those housewives who had faithfully lived up to the domestic ideal only to find themselves abandoned by their husbands. However, there was a common belief among both men and women that divorce was more likely to occur when women did not fulfil their duties. Indeed, the following respondent's marital breakdown began when she "got a good, steady job at a wage rate higher than his, and he was only doing seasonal work." Her husband's expectation was that she would continue to assume all domestic responsibility:

He never said anything, but he started using all his money to fix up these old wrecks—I was paying all the household expenses out of my money alone.

And then he'd never do a thing around the house, even when he was unemployed. I'd come home from work and he'd be sitting at the table, waiting for me to get his supper on! The dishes he used all day would be there in the sink. His attitude was that "it's okay for you to work as long as your work at home is done." And what could I do? We couldn't afford not having me at work. So over about a year things got more and more strained when once, when I was sleeping in the days and doing midnight shifts, he called me to wake up and get him a glass of water—sitting at the table, three feet from the sink. I did, and then I went back to the bedroom, packed my things and left.

Like the autonomous business woman mentioned above, divorced women were the subjects of intense local gossip. Much of this gossip was sympathetic. For example, "... they have to cut the mouldy bits off hot dog buns"; "... living down in the welfare apartments on Cavendish—that's where they herd all the divorced women and kids"; "... she got fired because she was pregnant and he took off, so she had to go on welfare." Undoubtedly, such gossip heightened women's fears of divorce and its attendant poverty, and reinforced their conformity to the roles of "good" wives and mothers.

Another form of gossip that all three of the divorced or separated women in this study complained of was far less sympathetic. They were accused of being overly promiscuous and they felt subjected to quite a bit of scrutiny from friends and neighbours. Divorced women did not "fit" into either of the two original categories for women in Labrador City: the promiscuous or the monogamous. They were in a new category of women altogether and their sexuality was "suspect".

Sexuality is an important aspect of the social concept of femininity. In Labrador City, as elsewhere, women's sexuality was defined primarily by their relationships (or lack of relationships) to men, but it was also influenced by the prevalence of pornography. Many respondents who felt that divorce threatened family solidarity also considered the widespread use of pornography in Labrador City a further threat. Both divorce and pornography diminished the value of monogamous and married women, and both seemed to present an "other" morality for women that was nonmonogamous and promiscuous. Social expectations of women's sexuality were quite contradictory at times, and this angered a number of respondents.

Ideals of Sexuality: the Domestic and the Pornographic

In the early years of Labrador City's development, pornography was imported as entertainment for the sake of "worker morale." According to the older men I had occasion to talk to, "blue" movies, strippers, and prostitutes who temporarily set up shop were often the only leisure activities available.

When IOCC introduced its plan to encourage a more "stabilizing" element of workers with economically dependent housewives and children, there was an obvious dichotomy of standards for women. Promiscuous women were desired for the sexual needs of single men, but monogamous women were demanded for domestic reasons. Many respondents assumed that different "types" of women would fulfil these varied needs. This may have been one factor leading to the suspicions of promiscuity that separated and divorced respondents had to deal with.

In the early 1980s, women were worried that their sexuality was being measured against a standard set by men and illustrated in the abundant pornographic materials available in Labrador City. To the extent that pornography was used by married as well as transient men, it posed a dilemma to those married women who were expected to fulfil a monogamous and domestic ideal but whose husbands often valued promiscuity in (at least other) women, as well.

In addition, pornography was—and is—often derogatory and demeaning to women. This was unacceptable to quite a few of the respondents in this study. They complained that there were few family entertainments available in 1982, and it was still hard to find the "general audience" magazines in the corner store racks. Almost all movies available were x-rated, whether they were on video or at the local theatre, and striptease acts were the most common form of "live" entertainment in the bars. Many respondents maintained that the demand for pornography was rising, especially among adolescents, as money became more available. They worried that this was influencing relations between the sexes, local attitudes towards women, and violence against women.

Undoubtedly, many of these complaints were informed by the educational efforts of a group from the local women's centre who were actively pressing to have pornography restricted to adults and to speciality areas of shops. They linked the sexual violence against women in pornographic materials to a larger campaign against all violence against women. They were also trying to establish a transition house for battered women and their children who had few resources in Labrador City to fall back on.

Respondents in this study were primarily concerned with the threats that pornographic entertainments posed for family integrity. Even in "pre-AIDS" 1982, these included the danger of sexually transmitted diseases; the example of sexuality that pornography gave children; and the lack of consideration that men had for their wives and children when using pornography.

Of course there's some that see no harm in it, but it can cause a lot of problems for others, all these strippers and that. So many men here spend all their time and money down at the "pit" (a male-only bar) with the strippers.

You take a married man who goes there for a few beers with the boys, gets drunk and puts his money on the table with the rest. Whoever rolls the dice or wins the game of cards gets the stripper for the evening, so he can easily bring home something to his wife a little later on. Or the men would line up at the back door of the pit and pay their money so the woman could do an oral job, just like an assembly line!

Happens all the time around here and it's always the wife who gets stuck, especially if she's got kids and can't leave. There's so many of these sex-diseases up here!

Pornography offended women's ideals of domestic morality including modesty, generosity, emotional centrality, and marital fidelity. Prostitutes and strippers were ". . . just blatantly making a living on their sex." They were referred to as "scum," "sleazebags," "filth." But prostitutes were not always held solely to blame. At least one respondent recognized that they were meeting a market demand: "You could be the ugliest, fattest, meanest old bitch alive; it don't matter, as long as you give them what they want!"

Ideally, married and monogamous women were not allo d to be attracted by pornography, although married men could "indulge." Some tease agents were beginning to cater to female audiences in 1982, and several of the respondents felt that this was a sure indication of moral depravity among women. As the depository of the family's morality, women were not supposed to allow their own tastes and proclivities to descend to the same level as those of men.

It's madness, and it's not just the men anymore! They brought male strippers in here once and they say the bar was so packed, it was unreal! Women were taking their clothes off and trying to kiss the mens' bodies and all that. And if you paid them $5 they'd dance on your table or stir your drink with their 'you-know-what,' ice and all! Now it's all funny enough, but this stuff is getting a little out of hand—it's so public and acceptable now, like no one has any shame anymore.

Almost all of my respondents voiced a sense of outrage that pornography was establishing a standard of sexuality for all women, whether monogamous or not, that they did not find desirable.

Conclusion

This paper has explored some aspects of the lives of women in Labrador City in 1982: the dearth of jobs and recreational facilities for women, company policies on housing, the problems associated with shopping in a northern company town, and the perceived threats to family integrity in the prevalence of divorce and the use of pornography.

Corporate and media visions of women throughout the 1950s designated the homemaker as the ideal: she was a smart consumer, married, monogamous, a devoted mother, and willing to sacrifice for her family. My research found that this notion of sacrifice was important in making the unbearable bearable and in keeping housewives in Labrador City, despite the town's obvious disadvantages. The homemaker ideal was still prevalent in Labrador City in 1982, despite the low value that is usually placed on domestic labour in our culture, since it is neither productive in a material sense, nor paid. In Labrador City, housework was expected to supersede all other activities in the lives of women, whether they worked for pay outside the home or not. As Luxton found in her (1990) follow-up study on the domestic division of labour in Flin Flon, while over half of her "third generation" female respondents voiced ideals of equality and sharing within their marriages, most still assumed the bulk of the domestic labour within their homes. Their husbands' contributions did little to reduce their own working time, since the men would often assume one of a number of tasks that women usually did simultaneously.

Hiring, housing, community services, and sexuality were shaped by the centrality of the male breadwinner, with his homemaker wife and dependent children, to corporate labour relations.

The women in this study had other concerns that I did not go into here, but that were of immediate consequence for them. For example, many felt that their family incomes were jeopardized by IOCC's decision to downsize. They also felt cheated that they had stayed and "put up with all the inconveniences" only to find that they and/or their husbands were facing the same kind of job insecurity and unemployment that they had left on the island of Newfoundland.

These concerns highlight the social constraints—many of which were specific to company towns—that women in Labrador City were living with in 1982. These social constraints were largely a result of the domestic ideal that corporate men envisioned for the wives of their employees throughout the first half of this century. It was an ideal that was difficult to realize with the changing circumstances of women and families in the early 1980s: increasing economic pressures, rising rates of female employment and divorce, and a duality of moral codes for women that were hard to reconcile. Many women found their personal resources strained to meet the tensions of these circumstances.

Partly in response to this, Labrador City boasted an active women's group that recognized the isolation and lack of resources experienced by many women in the town. A transition house for battered women, as well as a family crisis line, were established in the early 1980s. The respondents in this study generally supported the aims of this group, but few were willing to wholeheartedly identify with "feminists." Instead, many felt that solutions could only be found through their individual efforts to "self-improve." They were seizing whatever new opportunities they could get—especially those in jobs and education—to make Labrador City their own home. Whether others acknowledged it or not, they understood that both their domestic and paid work was crucial to their families' maintenance and survival and to the development of the north.

Honourable Men

Evie Plaice

This story focuses on the experiences of civilian women living on a military base. As a piece of writing, it sits somewhere between anthropology and fiction. It is a descriptive account of several weeks spent living on a northern Canadian airbase. These few weeks marked the initial phase of ethnographic fieldwork; as such, they were full of strong images and impulsive partial analyses. Early days in the field are rich in experiences, some of which are hard to incorporate into later, more reasoned analyses. However, although later work benefits from long-term appreciation and deeper understandings of the complex situations in which we find ourselves, it seldom retains the piquancy, poignancy or immediacy of early impressions. I offer this "story" as a means of salvaging some of these potent first impressions.

It has become a "story" for several pertinent reasons. The glimpses of people's lives which derive from my early fieldwork are, firstly, largely residual to my later findings. They have not been subject to any consistent and diligent examination. Secondly, since this was not my area of interest, the insights derived from these experiences are based upon too few examples to support further analysis. Thirdly, the experiences described here involve a certain amount of intimacy, and I do not wish to betray the trust of the people with whom I spoke by exposing these encounters to more critical scrutiny. Despite these shortfalls, the experiences still seem sufficiently evocative—and therefore valuable enough—to write about.

I have tried to salvage the potency of the experiences without giving the misleading impression of analysis. My companions and the circumstances of the events are fictionalized, and I have chosen to write in an evocative and descriptive style. Nevertheless, my created companions provide me with the means by which to relate the thoughts and perceptions I encountered while I was in Sunder Sound. It is easier, then, to describe my attempts at narrative presented below as a "story."

Although the focus is on civilian women living on base, some appreciation of what the women are reacting and responding to aids the description. For this reason, the story incorporates some aspects of the military and other male points of view. This juxtaposition of military perspectives with the perceptions and experiences of civilian women also serves to highlight the enormous gulf between these different people and their divergent aims.

The narrative swings between military descriptions of the purpose of the base, impressions of military personnel using the base, and the experiences of civilian women involved in the service sector of the base and adjacent town. The task I set myself is that the story succeed in evoking a sense of 'being there' among the base girls and the fly boys, the jets and the bars and the open spaces of this region of northern Canada. Anthropologically speaking, it will be enough if I succeed in presenting, or representing, perceptions which help a complex situation in which both military and civilian goals are pitted against each other, often with uncomfortable outcomes.

CELESTE'S HOUSE STOOD, LIKE A WHITE TOOTH IN A ROW OF WHITE TEETH, on a sandy ridge where the wind blew almost incessantly. In winter it was the snow, and in summer, the sand, moving from one bank to the next. Endlessly shifting, sifting, drifting and dropping, drifting and dropping. In winter the ground froze solid and was quickly covered by ice and snow. In summer it baked. The sand and grit got everywhere. Sifting through the fly screens, it covered everything with a fine coat of beige dust. "You may as well," she said, "plan a mushroom-coloured house, since that is what you get."

Sunder Sound Air Base is situated on a wide flat sandy terrace. The terrace is part of a system of glacial features which extends outwards from the Laurentian Shield to the Atlantic Ocean. When the ice had ground its way through the narrow channels in the eastern edge of the Laurentian Shield, it emptied out into Sunder Sound and left behind, in the form of a wide flat outwash plain, the dust and grit of its momentous journey. For the most part, the ground is level and covered with spruce trees and a low scrub of alder, birch and willow. The many treeless sandy glades are filled with that typically aromatic arctic mixture of juniper and crowberry, red, blue and blackberries, sphagnum and caribou moss.

The Proud River curls the south side of the terrace and empties out into Jeannette Lake via Sunder Sound. The Sound gives the terrace a frontage of water. Sunder Sound lies at the head of the deepest fiord along this stretch of the northeastern Canadian seaboard. From the road bounding the Base on the east side, there is an expanse of water which goes via a series of lakes and inlets all the way out to meet the Atlantic Ocean some 130 miles away to the east. It is therefore accessible by water for several months of the year.

The head of the fiord, with its flat expense of sand, is sheltered from the sea so that it is not barren and storm-swept like the coast. But it gains from its maritime position a milder climate than that of the interior. As the ground rises in the west to meet the Laurentian shield, the land becomes barren again, and windswept. Winter wraps a cloak of snow around the woodland of Sunder Sound which is stripped away on the higher ground.

Sunder Sound was built with incredible speed; it took less than half a year to materialize out of that empty windswept plain. Its birth was caused by the urgent need of the Americans to join Europe in the Second World War. An air base capable of handling many thousands of troops being flown to and from Europe had to be as close as possible to the point of delivery in order to be effective. Many sites along the Eastern seaboard of North America were considered, but Sunder Sound was able to provide the proximity along with flat, well-drained land and a reliable climate. Sunder Sound temperatures drop to as much as -40 degrees celsius in the winter months, and rise to extraordinary heights in the summer (37 celsius in 1989). But average temperatures for the summer range between 11.3 and 15.8 degrees celsius, and there is a prevailing westerly wind.

Surveys for an air base began in 1939. Elliot Roosevelt (son of the American President) visited the area in July, 1941 at exactly the same time as the Canadians had set in motion their own survey of the region. Each team carried out their survey under the auspices of their own country's airforce, but, between them, both teams decided upon the terrace above Sunder Sound as ideal for their needs. Their reports wax lyrical over the excellence of the site:

> The area around [North Rapids] enjoys exceptionally good flying conditions, and from there North on a line to Fort Chimo the weather conditions are much improved over those along the coast . . . on clear days visibility is exceptionally high . . . the area around [Jeannette Lake] undoubtedly is the best all-round perspective (sic) district for the location of an airport." (Elliott Roosevelt, Capt. US Air Corps, 21st Recon. sq., Report Number 1 to the Adjunct General of the War Department, July 6, 1941. *Them Days* vol. 12:4, 1987).

Eighteen months later, men and equipment arrived on the scene and the Base was built. It had an integral role to play as part of the airforces' North Atlantic Wing, and was to provide at least two runways, each with a minimum length of 5000 feet, storage facilities for 450,000 gallons of aviation fuel, housing for personnel, and several substantial facilities including a radio station capable of contacting the United States, Canada, Newfoundland and Greenland. Within ninety days of the arrival of the advance construction party, a team of 3,000 construction workers had cleared two 6,000-foot snow-rolled runways: the first aircraft landed on December 3, 1941. By the end of 1942, there were 5000 servicemen and 3000 construction workers living and working in the area. In 1943, 1,789 tactical aircraft were handled by the Base, and by September, 1945 the annual number had risen to 25,000.

The sudden decline in activities at the close of the War was hardly less profound. However, the global-political shift in world affairs that was the result of the Second Word War brought about the cold war. Sunder Sound became a way-station for the Distant Early Warning (DEW Line) systems that sprang up across the Arctic. The level of activity was slight compared to the War years, and facilities and operations on the Base were gradually taken over by the Canadian Government's Department of Public Works. Particularly, the period from the mid-seventies until the early eighties represents a low point in the career of the Base.

There are 745 houses on Base, approximately 500 of which are inhabited (some need rehabilitation, and I saw that underway before I left the area). The houses— quarters for married personnel—were built between 1941 and the mid-1960s, when there were approximately 12,000 military personnel and their families living at Sunder Sound. They are arranged in groups of rows and crescents, both semi-detached and blocks of four units, which vary in size depending upon the size of the family and the rank of the military personnel to be accommodated. There are also barrack buildings and what was once a "hotel" for visiting rather than stationed personnel. The Base was designed to accommodate all military personnel, both transient and permanent, who passed through Sunder Sound, and most military personnel would have stayed on Base where all necessary facilities were provided. There are mechanical and engineering works, a steam plant for the provision of power, a grocery and general purpose store, a cinema, a bowling alley, chapels, schools and a hospital, as well as airport facilities and housing. In effect, the Base forms a separate and completely self-sufficient community in the middle of the northern Canadian wilderness.

Increasingly, civilians have had access to certain of these facilities, especially when the military surrendered management of the Base to the Department of Public Works in 1976. At that moment, all facilities basically became civilian and were opened up for public use. Sunder Sound is one of the few bases, and probably the first of its kind, where there is an emphasis on sharing facilities with civilians.

Celeste's house was part of a row, third in a block of four units. It had two bedrooms, a bathroom, a sitting room and a kitchen. There was also a small porch which acted as a trap for some of the dust, and as a storage area for winter outdoor gear (cumbersome in order to be effective in persistent below-zero weather and strong winds). In the sitting room, a large open-plan area to the front of the house with the kitchen at the back, stood two sofas, a couple of armchairs and a table.

When I first arrived, Celeste was not home to greet me. After riding in the taxi past so many rows of so many houses, all gleaming in the sun, all surrounded by yellowing grass struggling and losing the fight against the encroachment of the sand, I was not at all sure that this was her place, though I had been there before during one of my earlier fieldwork forays. I entered the door, pushed through the porch, and heard the faint sound of a radio upstairs. No one stirred in the house. I put my luggage down and, stepping over debris on the floor by the couch, I started for the kitchen when an overwhelming sense of being in the wrong place, of trespassing, overcame me. I stopped. I had the address in my notebook, and I looked it up. I went outside to find some form of identification on the house. I looked at the neighbouring houses attached to this one, anything for clues of where I was. It seemed the right address, but it still felt wrong. All the houses suddenly seemed the same and I felt I could be anywhere. Conversely, I wondered if I should in fact be in Sunder Sound in the first place. Back inside the house, my sense of being in the wrong place was eased considerably by finding pictures of Celeste and her family on the wall. There was also a pile of mail on the table, addressed to her. I anchored my spirit to the pictures on the wall in the sitting room, and her name on the mail on the table, and began again to expand into the room, the place and my task.

Nowadays, the Base is home to forces from five different countries. It is used as a low-level flight training centre for NATO forces. Low-level flight training requires rather different facilities than either the wartime shipment of troops or the cold war early warning systems operations needed. Besides extensive reshaping of Base facilities, the present flight training takes up a considerable amount of airspace. Airspace in use during the late eighties amounted to 25,000 square miles in two sectors of the Haven Peninsula. In this airspace, between 5,000 and 6,000 sorties were flown each year by a combination of German, British, and Netherlands Airforces.

Sunder Sound Air Base has also been considered as a prime site for further NATO training facilities. The Canadian Department of National Defence has offered the North Atlantic Treaty Organization extensive use of facilities at Sunder Sound in part fulfilment of Canada's obligations as a member in the organization.

NATO needed to develop a tactical fighter weapons training centre where highly skilled personnel could practise specialized manoeuvres in association with low level flying.

Low-level flight training itself has become burdensome on the densely populated areas of Europe. Northern Canada, with its clear skies and low glacial terrain like that of Eastern Europe, seemed ideal. Now, with Perestroika and the dissolution of the Soviet Bloc, the need to develop Sunder Sound is far less urgent; the training terrain of an arid desert would seem far more appropriate at the moment than the heavily glaciated North. And the military is the first to agree that its requirements are anything but predictable. The project to make Sunder Sound into a NATO Base has now been shelved indefinitely. Nevertheless, despite the fast-changing postmodern world, or perhaps because of it, low-level flight training still carries on in this part of the North, albeit without some of the more sophisticated facilities that were in the process of being planned for the Base. Certainly, military activities were in full swing during the summer of 1989.

The requirements, and therefore the effects, of this new development are very different from those of the war years. Military activities during the forties had to do with transporting troops between Europe and North America, and this focused on the Base facilities in Sunder Sound. Although increased numbers of military personnel will be stationed at the Base, some permanently and many more in transit, the present emphasis will be on access to airspace over the rest of the region.

Celeste arrived in the north without forethought, blown on the wind of a fateful adventure. Born of southern European parents and raised in a central Canadian suburb, she had left home early to escape the claustrophobia of her family's yearning for a lost past in the old world. She had worked at different clerical jobs in Ontario and Quebec until, in her mid-twenties, she had tired of city life sufficiently to answer an advertisement for a 'girl-Friday' to join a northern branch of a Canadian business. She had never consciously made the decision to stay, but it had become the place to which she always returned. Now she wrote for a living, furnishing various southern-based weeklies with tales of the far north. To make ends meet, she also worked in the coffee bar at the junction of the road from the Base into town, where she was able to glean tidbits of useful information. She described herself as always on the alert for a "story," and she became very good at packaging her environment into a series of cliched images to which her southern readership could predictably respond. This processing of her experiences and perceptions made Celeste both informed about, but also not part of, the world upon which she commented. She was tall, dark and well-groomed, a striking, stately woman. And yet, Celeste seemed to remain acutely vulnerable.

Celeste had a friend who lived two rows over on the Base. Therese's parents had come from the area, but they had moved to Alberta when she was very young. Therese had grown up in a prairie city quite divorced from her northern origins and had returned out of curiosity. She had found much that she liked, including an extensive family network, but her urban background set her apart from many of her younger cousins. Therese worked in curriculum development for the regional school board. She was in her late twenties, a short, blonde, curly-haired extrovert with a vibrant personality. Of our group Therese was the impetuous one, setting the pace for all of us.

That summer, Therese had a friend living with her. Jolene was a young woman with an ample frame and straight, mousy hair. She was born and raised in Sunder Sound. Her parents had come from Newfoundland during the early days of the Base, had established a small business and had stayed throughout the changing economic fortunes of the town. Jolene worked in the business with her family, but dreamed of travel and work abroad. She felt she could do with more space than her family was prepared to give her. Moving on Base with Therese was a prelude to moving further away; it also meant that the fundamental decision to leave home altogether could be deferred. She was more reticent than either Celeste or Therese, and less sophisticated, but she had an inner strength and independence of spirit which hid behind a self-effacing manner. During my brief stay on Base, the four of us, sometimes accompanied by Jolene's coquettish younger sister Suzanne, formed a group of friends and we often spent time together.

I arrived in Sunder Sound during the summer. The summer is a time that burgeons with more than just a fecund fora in this part of the North. The summer is when the jets arrive in droves. The air sings and vibrates with the high-tech flight equipment of many nationalities. Low-level flight training begins in April and goes on until October. Each participating country has a quota of permissable squadrons able to be based at Sunder Sound at any given moment, and able to use a certain amount of airspace.

I found my way round the Base by bicycle, and, during the summer months, this proved to be an excellent means of transport. Travelling on the straight flat dusty roads of the Base, I often passed the cages, the high wire fences, where the jets sat glistening on the tarmac. I used to stand by the fences with my bicycle, fascinated. These odious yet intriguing machines were usually coloured in a shady khaki which was so much darker than mere black. They looked like giant blackflies, with their antennae jutting sharply from their honed snouts. Indeed, they drank the world's fuel supplies like they were bleeding the sap of life from their host planet. I would stand mystified by these implements of war while the fly boys sunned themselves on the wings, waiting for the call to their next mission. They looked incongruously vulnerable in their human forms against the metallic edge of the technology they flew, despite the fact that their togs matched the colour of the jets perfectly.

For the women of the region, the year could be divided into times of glut and times of leanness. In the summer, the bars swarmed with military personnel from all over Europe—pilots, navigators, mechanics and weapons engineers. Winter meant a death of amorous adventure. One hot, hazy day, Celeste, Therese, some friends and I were sipping our way through a jug-full of "Fuzzy Navels"—the drink of preference that summer. "Let's go get ourselves some Germans!" said Therese. Soon we were out cruising the roads in Therese's truck. The sky was like a shining canopy of blue, the trees at the side of the road looked tortured by the heat and dust. Except for a few main roads, the area was serviced by unsurfaced tracks. The constant churning of dust from passing traffic left a pall hanging over the road. We stopped for some cans of Coke and decided on a plan; maybe we should head down to the river and go for a swim. There were groups of forces lads strolling down the road, visiting the store, driving past in military vehicles. "Let's pick up some boys on the way," said Therese. "If we don't like them, there's plenty more! If we don't like them, they'll be gone by next week, and then there'll be a fresh lot. They're like nothings!"

We took a turn down a track towards the river, and at the corner were some boys in uniform, the black, red and yellow of the German flag showing on their epaulets. There were several but, to us, it didn't matter; they could all sit in the back. They would be ours for the afternoon, enjoyed like a box of chocolates.

Wayne whacked his mug down in agitation. I was sitting in the coffee bar with two unemployed local lads, Wayne and Danny, and we were watching the world go by outside. A group of young women had just left the bar. "We know them. Oh, yes! We know who they are, the Base girls. And come winter, they start hangin' round looking for a date, a party, a good time or something. But we won't go near them. If they can spend the summer fucking military guys, they can stay the fuck away from us!" Both Wayne and Danny were pretty aggrieved. Danny had spent the morning in the last stage of a gruelling interview for one of the rare jobs to come up on the Base. He had been tested for fitness, coordination, agility and academic ability to fill a post as fireman. But he knew that among the hundred or so applicants for the five positions, there had been several ex-servicemen. With their military training and contacts, there was little chance of a local lad getting in, despite fitness or anything else.

Later that week I was taking a shower in the Base gym after an aerobics class. There were some young girls in the next cubicle. "When did you say they were going?" "Tonight. Brian has to fly ahead of them to set up stuff at the next place they're going, so he leaves for Cephlavik tonight." "Will you write?" "Yeah! No. Dunno. Two weeks! Two weeks. Its enough time to get involved, but . . . I dunno. This whole thing is getting on my nerves."

Squadrons can expect to be stationed at Sunder Sound for two to three weeks. Time is of the essence for them; here, they can perfect skills which cannot be put into practice elsewhere, skills which, thus far, have been rehearsed only in simulation laboratories. A squadron is made up of teams of men focusing on an aircraft. Each jet has a pilot, a navigator (except F16s) and a ground crew of mechanics and weapons engineers. This team of highly skilled men stay together as a group within the squadron, a squadron having maybe eighteen such groups. Depending upon the weather, each team can expect to fly two sorties a day, five days a week.

The day begins with a briefing session in which the plans and aims of the day's missions are set out and discussed. Maps of the flying zones are used to plot the course of events, and to identify the targets to be used in the exercises.

The jets take off from the Base runway between 8:30 and 9:00 am. They take off in groups of two or three, one after the other or sometimes in parallel. At the point of take-off, it is quite usual for the pilots to use their after-burners. This adds to the roaring crescendo of the engines building up power for high-speed flight, and flames can be seen darting from the back of the jets. (After-burners use an inordinate among of fuel, and are used sparingly). As the jets lift off the end of the runway they twist back on themselves, their path of flight almost forming a mobius loop, before they shoot off in the direction of their rendezvous. They are back by lunch time. They scream in, circling the Base before dropping onto the runway in close formation. They come in to land with their wings almost touching. Or so it seems from the ground. It is not unknown for jets to land with the tips of trees stuck in their wings. One gets the sense that the lads are having fun.

Suzanne had joined us for the evening to tell us about her new boyfriend. Heinz was a weapons mechanic who was on tour in Sunder Sound with his Royal Netherlands Airforce squadron. His special area was working with the computer gadgetry that controls the weapons on board the jets. Suzanne was apparently quite taken with Heinz; she described him as the cutest man she'd seen all summer, and very sweet.

They had all agreed that I needed a change of image in order to make the most of the bar scene. Suzanne, Jolene and Therese had come armed with cosmetics, a mini skirt and high-heeled shoes. "You are gonna look like you came off the front page of Vogue when we're through with you!" they chortled, and told me to sit on the edge of the bed with my eyes closed. In a surprisingly short space of time, the girls had me made up and dressed to their specifications. We set out for a circuit of the bars on Base.

At the first bar, I was approached by a tall, blonde young man. Suzanne whispered eagerly in my ear; she found him very attractive and wished me luck. The man sat next to me and offered to buy me a drink. As I already had one, I declined his invitation. He provided me with a drink, anyway, and began describing how he photographed women as a hobby when he was home in Germany. He asked me if I would like to be photographed and have my pictures touted round modelling agencies. I tried to show a lack of interest in this endeavour. Somehow, from behind my subterfuge of make-up and heels, I felt utterly unable to communicate with this man. Confused by my inability to express myself as I the person I thought I was, and by the apparent imperative of the outer shell my companions had created for me to be interpreted without reference to me, I retreated into myself and sat there like a dumb animal unable to comment or participate.

Rescue came when our group decided to move on to a bar in town. Here, I was able to slink into a corner and evade scrutiny. Danny was at the pool table with Wayne. They found my outfit amusing, and we began discussing the military men who frequented the town bars. "We call them 'oiks'—the military guys! You know, they come into the bars and do almost anything to get the girls away from us. You know, one night I was sitting at a table and watching. This 'oik' came up to a table where Buddy had gone off to play pool next door. This guy, he comes up and sits down and starts chatting up Buddy's girl. You know, ingratiating himself. Just as

235

well Buddy comes back looking for more change for the pool table, because he sees this guy and knocks the shit out of him!

"There's more fights between the RAF and the local boys, and I reckon its because they can understand what we're saying. You can say what you like at a table next to a bunch of Germans because they don't know what you're saying! But, Jeese! There's some heck of a lot of fighting between the Brits and the boys some nights!"

Once Danny and Wayne had left me to return to their game the barman, who had been listening to our conversation, offered a very different interpretation of things. Gesticulating descriptively with his hands, he said "I mean, wouldn't you rather go with a military guy? Your average northern man expects his girl to stand him the beers, drive him home when he's plastered and beats the shit out of her for her efforts. At least the oiks are gentlemen! They buy the beers; they even treat their women with some respect!"

Facilities on Base for military personnel include kitchens where three hot meals are served each day. The Germans and Americans share one canteen; the Canadians and Dutch share another, and the British maintain their own. The canteens usually provide a segregated area for the use of officers, where there is waitress service, although the food served is the same. Likewise, each participating country has made arrangements for barracks accommodation. Most commonly, facilities rented from the Canadian Department of National Defence have been renovated to meet the specifications of each visiting airforce.

Each participating airforce has an array of rank-affiliated clubs and messes for evening and weekend recreation. Among the most famous of these are Uncle Sam's and the Rover Club. Others include clubs and messes for each rank in the Canadian and British airforces, and a newly opened club for the Royal Netherlands Airforce. Uncle Sam's is one of the oldest clubs; it is American. It is renowned because it is the only mixed rank club on Base, and it is also open to selected civilian membership. Sam's had to open its doors to the civilian public when the American presence in Sunder Sound was reduced after the 1960s. The Americans had only fifteen permanent staff and the club needed a greater membership in order to survive. Civilians who had service contacts with the American military were invited to join. As it turned out, this invitation worked well as a diplomatic manoeuvre during the difficult time of the American withdrawal from Sunder Sound. Because of these unique features, the club has come to be known as a place for military to meet with civilians, and for ranks of all nations to meet and socialize. The RNAF's Flying Dutchman is the newest of the clubs, and it also is non-ranked. But it is as yet only used by the Dutch. The Rover is also a long-standing member of the Base bar circuit. It is renowned as a place where almost anything could happen. For some, it is a little too wild.

It was in the bars at night, during the long evenings and weekends, that I met the pilots, relaxing—as much as they ever can. One evening as I was sitting in one of the more popular bars, a young man came up to me, and, with little more of an introduction than the fact that we were both at the same bar that evening, he squatted beside me. "We're killers, murderers, you know," was his opening phrase. I spent almost the whole night in his company, thus entering another compelling and alien world. Through his talk, I began to imagine his life. He talked about—or he talked around—the problems of socializing as a fighter pilot; the way bar clientele in civilian bars will not share tables with you because of what you do; the way girls are fascinated by what you do, not who you are; the way that flying a jet becomes your living, breathing life with no breaks, no reality outside of the barracks. He described the challenge of becoming a fighter pilot—the initial attraction, with such a high failure rate, is to see if you can make the grade. "I had no intention of letting it be my life" he said. But it soon became his life. He described the pressures of making the grade. Tests—mind tests, physical tests, literacy tests, leadership tests, loyalty tests, technical and coordination tests every day. It seemed relentless, and drew you into a camaraderie with your very competitors, the lads with whom you trained. It reminded me of all the cliched depictions of boot camps I had seen. But here was something even more elite because these young men had also to think, and think fast and independently.

A medical commander on the Base explained to me the qualities that are looked for in recruiting potential pilots. "By normal standards," he said, "they are almost mad." In sum, he said "The mixture of traits that they look for would require that you were almost crazy to start with: intelligence but with no intellectual skills. They cannot be asked to deal with the moral questions of what they do. Their coordination has to be good—excellent. And their memories good also; with ambition and something akin to a kind of drive that negates emotion."

My pilot qualified his initial outburst with the admission that he loved flying jets. He admitted that it could be construed as something totally abhorrent, to fly such a killing machine: "But it is the fastest thing there is on earth—like a motor bike, but so much faster, freer. The ultimate!" At the bar earlier he had joked, saying: "You're waiting for an F16 pilot! Do you wish you were dancing with an F16 pilot?" Of all the jets, the F16 is—or was in 1988—the most admired because the pilots of the F16s fly solo, without even a navigator which the other jets require. The F16 pilots were Dutch. When I did speak to an F16 pilot (his name was Richard Cruise!) he told me that, despite his income and rank, he cycled across the polderlands to visit his girlfriend who to this day does not know what he does for a living because to tell her would be to spoil it all. He says she loves him for who he is and not what he does, and she would either be scared or jealous or awed if she knew he flew an F16.

My pilot sat contemplating the glass-littered table in front of us. "Do you realize," he asked, "that on average, in peace-time, we lose one person a year from our squadron. A squadron is not that big. There's about eighteen of us. We stay in a squadron for about two years and then we're split up and reform as another squadron. If I could get pregnant tomorrow, I'd leave all of these!" He was silent for a while. " 'Top Gun' was the worst thing that could have happened to us," he said.

I would sit out on the step in the sun some mornings, reading and watching the neighbourhood unfold. This morning the little boys from the house across the yard are playing war games. Who can blame them? Their mother hangs out washing on the line—the inner lives of the machismo? Periodically jets surge and rush above the roofs, searing the sky with a shrieking trail of glinting metal and afterburn. Today I sit spellbound by a terrible feeling of apprehension. To even think you may know the person riding that sky demon is unnerving. The statistical chances of a crash are all too clear. I wonder at the families, the people on the ground who are connected to the pilots in the sky. I wonder what they think and what they feel.

My pilot friend of the evening before had invited me to a "Curry Night" at the RAF Officer's Mess on the following Tuesday. Celeste pondered this and said, "They play with you there. What I mean is that they have games they play in which they will try to humiliate you. Did he say he would meet you there; did he make any definite arrangements? You see, you could turn up there and he will be with someone else. Then you wouldn't have an escort, and you can't go without one. It means, if you don't have an escort, that anyone can taunt you. It's not very pleasant. I was there once, even escorted, and they started passing me round, over their heads. They had this game where they weren't supposed to touch you with their hands, but pass you round over their heads using their shoulders and necks. They also get at each other through their girlfriends or escorts. They try to steal you from your escort in order to humiliate him and you. For them its only a game they win or lose. But for you, it's worse."

A few nights later, I spent some time in the company of a ground crew mechanic. He turned out to be a perfect anthropologist's informant as he settled into his allotted task that evening of explaining the weird and wonderful activities of the squadrons in their off hours. "Squadrons are like tribes," he said. "It is very important which squad you belong to. Some are known about all through the force. They've got names for themselves. Reputations. We have nicknames, and so do the squads. Ours is sixteen plus one. We're seventeen, see, but it doesn't do to use your name. Its bad luck. Sixteen plus one; we're lucky. We're a good bunch. A squadron only stays together for two years. They split us up then, and put us in new squadrons. But once you're in a squad, all the other squads are your rivals. We have fights between the best, better than the Army or the Navy. There's a group who don't fit in. Base security. Because they're ground work, its really like the Army. But they are in the Airforce. The Airforce regiment; they protect the airfield and the jets. But its an Airforce Base, and we work with jets! They don't fit in. We call them the "Rock Apes," and we give them a hard time. They can't defend themselves. They're no good. They're neither Airforce nor Army.

"You should see what happens in the clubs. You watch what they do. Squads usually have their own corner of the club, and they stick to that. Visiting across the place is fine, but no invasions. You watch them dancing. You can tell when a guy from one squad is teasing a guy from another. He'll dance up to the guy and start dancing with his girl. Then he'll start making signs at the other guy with his hands behind his back. You watch. The signs mean things. They're meant to get the other guy going. They also dance a certain way. They'll come up behind a guy and use very suggestive body movements—to suggest he's gay. They'll do it even while he's dancing with a girl, especially then. Sometimes a whole group of guys are on the dance floor together, being disgusting. They pull down their jeans and stick their bums out at each other. Sardinia's the worst place. They seem to really get going there. What they do down the local bars is get on the tables, drop their pants, and piss on each other. It is truly disgusting. While they're relieving themselves, they chant the songs of the squadron. Mostly, its famous tunes that are adapted, like "Singing the Rain," or "Nice one Charlie."

"Then there's 'blagging.' You take something from on the Base, you see. You steal it and hang it up in the bar. You just wait till they see it. Then they have to get it back. There's nothing they can do. No one owns up to taking it, but there it is, where they can see it. It really winds them up." Blagging is a kind of thievery that is practised on Base by the men of junior ranks. It involves a squadron stealing some Base property—a flashing beacon, a commander's jacket—something easily identifiable, which is then displayed very prominently at the bar in their club or mess. The point is to trick their superiors rather than avail themselves of property. It is a game played by one rank against another, and yet, in a sense, the honour of the squadron rests on the successful accomplishment of several blagging raids. So, it is also a game played between squadrons.

Therese had made supper. We were almost in the dark; the kitchen light was on, shining through the doorway and the hatch, but that was all. We each reclined on a sofa, sipping schnapps. Each tired and a little depressed. Our feet almost touched; we faced each other across the coffee table. "He was such a gentleman. He acted the perfect gentleman and saw me home. I was so drunk, even thinking about it now makes me feel sick. Humiliated. I'd never let myself get so drunk again. I was so drunk I couldn't do a thing, but I was aware, awake. I was actually being sick, I vomited on the sofa. It made me feel disgusting, all of it. He brought me home, undressed me, fucked me, and left. Who would do something like that? Only the fucking Brits!"

There was a girl, once, an Indian girl. She was brought onto the Base, into the barrack rooms of the boys. They were all drunk, she particularly. They fed her jet fuel and she died. I could never work out whether this was a Sunder Sound myth or a reality. There was no way to verify it; I could find no records.

Celeste told me about what had happened to Jolene. Jolene had had a steady boyfriend who had killed himself. He had been one of the permanent staff, stationed at the Base for two years. When his time was up, he'd been seeing Jolene for almost two years. In fact, they thought they might get married. But he couldn't change his posting. He had to go. He was gone for almost a year, no way of getting back. Jolene started seeing someone else, just casually at first. She was lonely. She wanted to enjoy herself. But she knew her man was getting desperate. There wasn't anything he could do. He started phoning her at odd times. He wanted to know why she was seeing someone else. "It isn't important," she told him. "I'm just finding things to do." In fact, she quite liked this guy. He was a pilot. He seemed keen. Her man decided to plan a holiday back in Sunder Sound. It turned out to be just when Jolene's pilot friend was in town with his squadron. They quarrelled and her man left Sunder Sound without saying goodbye. Jolene knew when his father rang; she could tell. He had taken an overdose.

Celeste said "We none of us expected that. I was really hurt by what he'd done. I got angry but I couldn't show it. It seemed somehow to make him such a failure. He couldn't deal with life." When the pilot heard, he did not phone or come to see Jolene. She waited, but he never came again. "Do you suppose," I asked, "that the pilot thought it was okay to steal Jolene from her man, but not when he quit the game—killed himself? I think they are playing games of honour, but it isn't honourable to quit the game like that—kill yourself over a woman, is it? Nor is it honourable to steal a dead man's girl. But it is fine to play games of honour between ranks and squadrons." "No" she said. "You are quite wrong there."

In the end, I didn't go to the Curry Night. I had caught sight of my pilot friend at the Air Show dance. Indeed, he'd come to see me and said: "See, I'm not drunk tonight." He'd meant we could actually have a different kind of conversation from the one we'd had a few nights ago. It was meant as an invitation, but I did not take it up. My pride would not let me play games of honour with him. Besides I was talking to another military acquaintance about a jet crash, and I had noticed this man wince as the pilot had approached us.

"They need encouragement" Celeste said. "You have to do the running, you know. They have their pride. They're pilots. They're the cream." I wondered if she was being sarcastic. She might as easily have meant it seriously. At the last minute, I'd phone the Officer's Mess: "Squadron 223? No, madam, they left on Wednesday morning. Its the 17th Squadron here now." Two weeks indeed.

I'd first heard of the crash about a week before, while I was out on a trip with some Dutch airforcemen who had opted to spend their weekend at a local fishing camp. I had ended up sitting next to a mechanic. We sat for a while in contemplative silence—at least I was contemplating the setting sun. The water lapped round our feet, kissing the pebbled shore with slow, rhythmic, lapping waves. Colours flickered through a range and back again; orange, peach, gold, peach, orange, black, reflecting first the dying sun and darkening sky, then the hushed landscape and the oily depths of the lake.

The mechanic had been contemplating too. But on other things: "Did you hear about the crash today? It was my jet" he said, staring at his boots. "No," I said, I hadn't. "Is the pilot alright? What happened?" "The pilot bailed out. What happened? We don't know yet. I was the mechanic for the jet. I feel responsible. If I had lost my pilot, I would not have worked on another jet. I would have packed it in." He looked at his hands hanging listlessly over his knees as he squatted on the lake shore. "Today, I've done nothing. They send us to the medics, to get checked. They help us, you see, when something like this happens. Its unnerving. Its upsetting. It upsets the whole squadron. If the pilot had been killed—you don't know. It may have been something I hadn't checked. It may have been my fault. I don't know until they retrieve the wreckage and do some tests. But the pilot is fine. He ejected before the jet crashed. He felt it lose power sharply. He had to decide, and he bailed out. He fell into a lake in the middle of nowhere, and he was marooned there for twenty minutes. He said that it felt like eternity."

A pilot begins training in the RAF at eighteen, but it is easy to become deselected and re-routed to another branch of the force. One has to have perfect health, skills of coordination, a quick and relatively unreflective mind—an agile but not moral intellect. Pressure to succeed builds up with each test, and there are exams and tests on everything, perpetually. Pilots never leave the Base. From rising to breakfast in the barracks until retiring at night to sleep, these men see each other, and see each other in a military setting, almost entirely without pause. They rise together, eat together, are briefed on the day's activities together. From their mid-teens, when they opted for the career of a fighter pilot, they have trained together, and are at once both comrades and competitors, standards for each other. They have become immersed in an increasingly obsessive, compulsive and total world of the jet. There is seldom a let-up; there is always pressure to compete and succeed.

They do not leave Base because their briefing gives them the template for the days activities, gives structure to the day but also links that day and that space in which the day takes place, to the Base, the barracks, their comrades, competitors and the hierarchy of the military setting. In their jets, they don the togs of their trade, headphones, the aircraft even, encasing themselves in their milieu. Contact with Base and with comrades is never lost. Through their headphones, they hear the pilots of the other jets, they hear the Base control tower. They hear their masters' voices. The young pilot who ejected into the northern wilderness, ejected also from his all-encompassing life. For twenty minutes which seemed like eternity, he lost touch with the Base. He had arrived in the North.

At the end of the summer, Suzanne married her young Dutchman. It had been a whirlwind romance. They had only just met during his two weeks on Base that summer, but Heinz had come back the moment he could get leave and they had married in town. As soon as his contract with the airforce was up, he planned to move back to try and get a job with a local computer sales company. Meanwhile, Suzanne was going to the Netherlands with him to meet his family. There, they would set up a temporary home.

That same summer, a young woman with two small children had returned from Germany. She had planned to visit with her parents while her pilot husband was away on extensive training elsewhere, but she had decided to stay on after the end of the summer. Life in Germany had proved too difficult. She had hated the food and the crowded German towns. With her husband away far more often than he was home, and with her struggling attempts at German and her faltering appreciation of German family etiquette, her marriage had encountered severe difficulties. Now, from within the arms of her own family, her resolve to persevere in such a disastrous situation had weakened. She was tired and depressed. And now she was home.

Mainly Because of the Meat

Helen Porter

This story is from the collection A Long and Lonely Ride *(Breakwater, 1991).*

"What's the matter with you, Debbie? You look like you're somewhere else. Anything wrong?"

"Oh, hi, Phyllis. I didn't even see you there. Am I in your way? Hurry up and punch, now. You've only got half a minute."

Debbie stood back while Phyllis put her punch card through the machine. Then they walked together to adjoining check-out counters.

"You didn't answer me, Deb. Is anything wrong?"

"Nothing more than usual. I was just kind of in a daze, listening to what everyone was saying without really taking it in. It takes me a while Monday mornings to get adjusted to this place."

"Same here. Did you have a nice weekend?"

"All right, I guess. Saturday night we went to the Steamer but my feet were so tired I spent most of the night sitting down. Rob didn't like that too well. What about yourself?"

"I was in the house the whole time. No, that's a lie, we did drop up to Mom's yesterday evening. She's not very well lately. But Saturday night we didn't have a babysitter, and no money to pay for one, really, so myself and Dave just sat home and watched T.V. We ordered a pizza, so it wasn't too bad. He was just as tired as I was."

"Yeah, some life, hey? Do you ever wonder what we're all workin' for? The money goes out faster than it comes in, right? And it must be worse for you, trying to save up for a house and everything."

"You should be doin' the same thing. You and Rob are goin' out a long time now, aren't you?"

"I don't know if I ever want to get married. Seems like it only makes everything harder. I looks at Mom and Dad sometimes and I can't help wondering what in the world they're getting' out of it all. Still four more youngsters to put through school and as soon as that's over it'll be almost time for Dad to be pensioned. Then I s'pose one of 'em'll get sick, like so many more do."

"Well, you don't need to have a big family. Thank God for the pill. But are you sure there's nothing else wrong? I can usually depend on you to get me up out of the dumps."

"I don't know, girl. It's just that things get too much for me sometimes. Down to the Steamer the other night I was lookin' at the university crowd. You can tell 'em just by lookin' at 'em. For one thing, they don't dress up like we do. But they're the ones got an easy life ahead of 'em. They'll be doctors or lawyers or. . ."

"Or Indian chiefs. I know what you mean. Some of them got it hard too, though. They're not all rich."

Debbie went to the safe for her cash-tray and put it into the register. Already there were customers in the supermarket and she didn't even have her counter scrubbed down yet. Where in the world did they all come from so early on a Monday morning? That girl with the baby, she came in almost every day. The baby was laughing out loud as his mother spun him around and around in the cart.

"Want to use my pail of water for your counter, Debbie?" Phyllis called out. "It's still hot."

"Heavens, are you finished already? Okay, thanks. I'm slow this morning."

"Good morning, Debbie." Mr. Marshall was standing beside the check-out.

"Good morning, Mr. Marshall." She kept on scrubbing the conveyor belt. It was a hard thing to get clean.

"Everything all right?"

"Yes, I think so, Mr. Marshall."

"You're a good worker, Debbie, a good, fast worker. That's why it surprises me when I have a complaint about you."

Debbie looked up at him and said nothing.

"Mrs. Allen phoned me Saturday night after I got home. You know Mrs. Allen, don't you?"

Debbie knew Mrs. Allen very well. She had gone to school with Mrs. Allen's daughter, Christina. Christina had the kind of bedroom that Debbie used to think belonged only to girls in the old television shows like *Happy Days* and *Who's the Boss*. They had been good friends.

"Yes, I know her. I served her Saturday, almost closing time it was." She remembered Mrs. Allen's groceries: T-Bone steaks, a Tendersweet ham, table butter, fancy cheese and fresh pineapple. And lots of other things.

"Mrs. Allen told me she was missing two bags of groceries. She said she checked very carefully when she got home and she was short several items. I believe you packed her groceries yourself."

"That's right. I did. Tommy was...he was busy doing something else."

"Mrs. Allen will be in shortly to replace the missing items. She said she didn't want to get you into trouble but she had to be specific. I told her you'd just put it through on a No Charge. Of course this means someone ended up with two extra bags of stuff and for sure they'll never report it. You'll have to be more careful, Debbie. The store can't afford to lose money like that. And Mrs. Allen is one of our best customers."

Debbie held her lips tightly together as Mr. Marshall walked back towards the boys who were stocking the shelves. She was finding it harder and harder, lately, to keep from answering back. But she couldn't afford to lose her job, at least not until she finished her typing course. And if she didn't start getting more time to practise she would never finish it. She scrubbed fiercely at the ground-in dirt on the conveyor belt. When she looked up, Phyllis was waving at her from the next check-out. "The store can't afford to lose money," she mouthed, in perfect imitation of Mr. Marshall's lip formation. "Remember that now, Miss Evans." In spite of herself, Debbie laughed out loud.

"It's good to hear people laughing so early in the morning." The girl with the baby was standing at Debbie's check-out. She pushed two oranges and a can of Pepsi towards Debbie, and then pulled a two-dollar bill from her jacket pocket. The baby was eating a chocolate bar.

"My, Jason, you're getting yourself in some state." The girl bent over, moistened a tissue with her own saliva and began to wipe the baby's face. When he squirmed and started to whimper his mother hastily shoved the candy bar back in his mouth.

"Hi, Jason," said Debbie, smiling at him. He grinned back, his small mouth covered with sticky chocolate. "He's cute," she said, handing the girl her change. "How old is he?"

"Almost ten months. No, it's all gone, Jason." She took the wrapper from him and put it on the counter. "Don't cry now, you're not gettin' another one." She opened her purse and took out a ring with two keys on it, which she passed to the baby, who seemed to be considering whether or not it was worth his while to keep on crying. "They're sweet but they'd drive you foolish sometimes," she said to Debbie. "I been tryin' to get a job. Do they need anyone here?"

Debbie looked at the girl's slight frame, her pale skin and tired-looking eyes. "You could fill out an application form. Get one from the office. What grade have you got?"

"Well, I finished Grade Ten. I started Grade Eleven, but then. . ." She shrugged her shoulders, and nodded towards the baby. "I don't know who I'd get to look after him, though. Mom says she's not going to start all over again with someone else's youngsters." She picked up the baby and her parcel, pushed the cart away and started toward the office.

"Good morning, Debbie." Mrs. Allen must have just come in. No Monday morning disarray for her. Every carefully-coloured hair was in place; her face looked like an advertisement for 2nd Debut.

"Did Mr. Marshall tell you about my problem?" She smiled widely, and Debbie thought of her own mother who rarely opened her mouth when she smiled because of the two teeth missing from her plate. She had broken them off years before and was forever planning to go to the denturist for a new set.

"I hope I didn't get you into trouble, dear, but of course I had to call Mr. Marshall when I realized what had happened. None of us can afford to lose money today, can we? You do understand?"

Debbie's own smile was stiff. "Yes, of course, Mrs. Allen. Just go ahead and pick up what you're missing."

"How is your mother, Debbie?" Mrs. Allen seemed determined to be even friendlier than usual. "I haven't seen her at church for several weeks."

"Oh, Mom's all right." Debbie certainly wasn't going to tell Mrs. Allen that her mother had vowed, swearing vehemently, not to set foot inside the church again until she got a new coat. "She's a bit tired on Sundays, usually."

"Oh, I know she has a lot to do, and I think she's wonderful, bringing up such a large family without. . ." Her voice trailed off but Debbie knew what she'd been going to say. "I know you're a great help to her, dear," Mrs. Allen continued, putting her hand on Debbie's arm. "But I hope you're not going to stay here forever. This is just a stopgap for you, isn't it? You always were such a bright child at school."

Debbie said nothing.

"Christina was asking about you in her last letter. She's having a wonderful time in Toronto. I just couldn't stand the idea of sending her to university here. You know what a dive it is, full of drug pushers and other strange types." She paused and then went on. "Tina said she'd been to some sort of lecture on that woman who wrote the *Anne of Green Gables* books. What was her name?"

"L.M. Montgomery." Debbie's legs felt as if they weren't there.

"Yes, that's the one. I know the two of you used to get all her books out of the library when you were going to school. You were always talking about going to Prince Edward Island. Tina said she was sorry you weren't there to hear the lecture too."

Debbie felt herself relax a little. Yes, Christina really would be sorry about that. Sometimes Debbie forgot what a nice girl Tina was.

"My, Tina must have enjoyed that. We really loved those Anne books when we were in Grade Seven and Eight."

"Well, dear, I guess I'd better go and pick up my things. Tell your mother I was asking about her. We're having a sale of work and afternoon tea at the church next week. I hope she'll be able to come along." She pulled out a shopping cart and walked toward the fruit section.

"Hey, Miss?"

Debbie turned around to find a short, fat woman, a customer she'd often served before, standing at the check-out. She had nothing in her hands except a shiny black plastic purse out of which she was taking a cigarette. She lit the cigarette, inhaled deeply, and then looked sideways at Debbie.

"What can I do for you, ma'am?"

"Well, it's like this, see. When I got home Sat'day night I couldn't find half the stuff I bought. Someone else must of took some of my groceries by mistake. Can I pick up what's missing, like that other woman is doing?"

She wet her finger and began to rub at a spot on her red crimpknit slacks.

Debbie hesitated for a moment.

"Did I serve you?"

The woman shifted from one foot to the other. She kept on rubbing at the spot as she spoke.

"To tell you the truth, girl, I can't remember. You often do serve me, but Sat'day night I had that much on my mind I can hardly remember anything."

Debbie couldn't remember either. It had been a very busy evening and sometimes, when she was extra tired, she didn't even look at the faces of the people she was checking through.

"You better go and ask Mr. Marshall, anyhow. I don't see why he wouldn't let you pick up what you didn't get. You know which one he is, do you?"

"That's the boss, is it? Dark-haired fella with the big nose? Okay, I'll ask him."

"Better watch that one, Deb." Phyllis had left her own check-out and was leaning over Debbie's, watching the woman walk toward where Mr. Marshall was standing, "She's a hard case."

"What do you mean?"

"Always tryin to get something for nothing. She was all ears when you were talking to Mrs. Allen. You've seen her in here with that crowd of youngsters, haven't you?"

Of course. Debbie remembered the children now. About five of them there were, noisy and not very clean.

"Yeah, I've seen her. She looks too old to have youngsters that small though, don't she?"

"I believe they're her grandchildren. Something happened to the daughter. I don't know if she got sick now, or took off, or what."

"Excuse me, miss." Debbie turned to find an irritated looking old man at the check-out. "Do you *work* here or are you paid to chat with the other employees?"

The time passed quickly. It was amazingly busy for a Monday morning. Mrs. Allen came back, checked through her cottage cheese, her bananas, her avocados, her cauliflower, her frozen strawberries, her back bacon and her ground steak.

"Everything all right, Mrs. Allen?" Mr. Marshall was forever appearing from nowhere.

"Oh, just fine, thanks, Mr. Marshall. I've got to hurry home now before my cold things get warm."

Debbie packed the groceries with a solicitude that was mostly forced. Mr. Marshall was, after all, watching her every move. And she had nothing against Mrs. Allen, really.

"Thank you very much, Debbie dear. Remember to tell your mother what I said, now. And don't forget to drop Christina a line. She doesn't want to lose touch with her old friends."

The next few minutes were slack enough for Debbie to watch through the big window until Mrs. Allen, after carefully arranging her packages in the back seat, got into her shining dark-green Chrysler and drove slowly away. She thought of Tina in her third year at the University of Toronto. Just like the girls they used to read about in *Seventeen* and *Flare*. Debbie had never in her whole life read a story about a girl who worked in a supermarket.

She turned her head to find Mr. Marshall staring at her from the little window in the office. "Even if you're not busy, *look* busy," she muttered to herself. She moved the magazines around in their racks, although they had not been disturbed yet this morning. When she straightened the candy display behind her check-out she realised that three of the chocolate bar six-packs had been "tampered with," as Mr. Marshall liked to put it. There was a Cherry Blossom missing from each. She smiled as she recalled a skit she'd once seen about an enormously fat shoplifter who was addicted to Cherry Blossom bars. Then she sighed. Mr. Marshall wouldn't have found that skit at all funny.

"Look at your friend," Phyllis called softly, pointing toward the woman in the red slacks who was wheeling a full cart toward Debbie's counter. "I've never seen her get that many groceries before."

Debbie hadn't either. Mrs. Molloy—that was her name, Molloy—rarely picked up more than eight or ten items at a time.

"Can you check me through now, Miss?" Mrs. Molloy sounded out of breath. Her face was red and shiny and her hands were shaking a little on the cart handle. She looks like she might have high blood pressure, Debbie thought.

"I'm in a bit of a rush," she said, pulling some vegetables out of her cart and putting them on the belt. "I got to take one of the youngsters down to the hospital as soon as my son gets back with the car. She've had an earache since Friday and she haven't stopped screechin'." She piled the counter with as much as it would hold.

Debbie rang in a long skinny bologna, a package of chicken parts, a huge head of cabbage and four loaves of bread.

Mrs. Molloy continued to heap her things on the counter. Her hands seemed a little steadier now. Her last three items were a set of water glasses, two colouring books and a spray can of air freshener. As Debbie was checking them through, Mr. Marshall arrived again. He should get a job at the Arts and Culture, Debbie thought. As a magician. I don't know how good he'd be at making himself vanish but he sure can appear out of nowhere.

He looked at the groceries waiting to be packed, glanced at Debbie and then turned toward Mrs. Molloy. "You must have had quite an order on Saturday," he said. "Didn't you get any of it?"

"I got a few things," she said, not looking at him. "But the majority of it wasn't there. I shoulda noticed it at the time but I was so addled with the youngsters I didn't know if I was comin' or goin'."

"Miss Evans," said Mr. Marshall. He always called the girls Miss when there were customers around. "Miss Evans, did you serve this . . . lady . . . on Saturday?"

Mrs. Molloy looked at Debbie and then looked quickly down into the empty cart.

"I had a busy evening, Mr. Marshall. I can hardly remember."

He turned toward Mrs. Molloy. "Who served you? You should remember that."

"I told you, I had that much on my mind . . ."

"That's a lot of groceries you've got there, madam. And not all groceries, either. I've never noticed you picking up drinking glasses or colouring books before." He leaned over her and said softly, "I asked you to pick up only what you didn't get on Saturday. Are you sure you're being strictly honest about this?"

Debbie realized she was holding her breath as she waited for Mrs. Molloy's answer.

"You never asked that other woman what she picked up on Saturday. I had to buy tumblers Saturday because every one we had in the house was broke. My daughter was after sendin' me some money and I wanted to get a nice few things in." Her face was still red and shiny but she wasn't shaking at all now.

"Miss Evans. Try to remember, will you, if you served this woman on Saturday. Just take a few minutes to think about it."

Debbie didn't need a few minutes.

"Yes, Mr. Marshall, I did serve her. I remember now."

"Isn't this kind of an unusual order for her?"

"I don't know, sir. It's impossible for me to remember the kind of order everyone in the store gets." She looked him straight in the eye. "She did have more than usual. And I remember those glasses very plain. I thought of buying some for my mother."

"Are you sure, Miss Evans?"

"Of course I'm sure, Mr. Marshall. And if you're not going to believe me, why did you bother to ask?"

Mrs. Molloy, no longer the central figure in the affair, stared at Debbie.

"All right, then. We'll let it go for this time. But we've just got to be more careful about people's groceries going astray." He walked away from the check-out, his back very stiff.

Debbie began to bag the groceries. Mrs. Molloy was still standing beside the conveyor-belt. She glanced at Debbie and said, "Thanks a lot, miss." Then she looked away again.

"That's all right." Debbie felt uncomfortable, no, not uncomfortable, embarrassed. Then, as she wrapped the glasses individually, she caught Mrs. Molloy's eye and they smiled at each other.

"You let her get away with it," said Phyllis that afternoon when they were both waiting in line to punch out.

"What do you mean, I let her get away with it? She only picked up what she didn't get Saturday."

"Is that right, now? You don't say." Although Phyllis' voice was mocking there was another note in it too. Understanding? Appreciation? Or just plain amusement?

Debbie said nothing more. She listened, without really paying attention, to the bits of conversation going on around her.

When she got outside, Phyllis was waiting for her on the sidewalk.

"Want a run home, Deb? Dave'll be here in a minute."

"No thanks, I feel like a walk. I can use the fresh air. Besides, Mom never starts to get supper until *Another World* is over."

"You going anywhere tonight?"

"Well, I got typing seven-thirty. And I was thinkin' about askin' Rob if he wants to do down to the Strand later on. It's no cover tonight and the band is really good."

"Thought you'd be too tired for dancin' tonight. There's Dave now. Hold on to your wool, boy, and stop blowin' that almighty horn."

"Better hurry up, girl. No, I don't feel too bad now. Some days are worse than others."

"Well, I better go, I s'pose, or Dave'll have a fit and a half. See you tomorrow."

"So long, Phyl. Take it easy, now."

Phyllis got into the car and Debbie, her purse swinging, began to walk briskly down the road.

Researching Women's Organizations in the Labrador Straits: Retrospective Reflections [1]

Linda Christiansen-Ruffman

Introduction

In this paper I will present key findings and enduring impressions from research with women's organizations in the Labrador Straits between one and two decades ago. This paper describes what I learnt about women's organizations and about patriarchal decision-making during times of change. Labrador societies challenged the taken-for-granted assumptions of my culture and the sociological scholarly traditions in which I had been trained.

The research used several sources: newspapers, written material from organizations, interviews with key women and men and participant observation at meetings and in the community. Systematic data were gathered by interviewing women leaders and a key woman in each women's organization during 1978, with the same questionnaire used for research in Halifax in 1975. The analysis is informed by other research projects conducted in Atlantic Canada on citizen participation and the role of women and women's organizations in community life.

Introduction to the Region and Its Gendered Structure

THE STRAITS REGION is a rugged rural area of fishing villages at the extreme south of the Labrador Coast on the Strait of Belle Isle, next to the Quebec border and across from the island of Newfoundland. Lanse au Loup, the largest community, had 531 people in 1976 while the Lanse Amour area (including Lanse Amour, Fox Cove and Point Amour) had 54 people. The population of the entire region in 1976 was 2,141.

Historically, the region depended on the fishery. Some people also moved temporarily in search of work. For example, I was told about men who left to cut wood in winter and Straits families who were attracted by well-paying jobs on work crews and in food canteens during construction of the Churchill Falls hydroelectric facility in the 1950s. During the 1960s and 1970s, Straits society underwent tremendous changes in its employment and class structures as well as in its integration with the outside world. Some full- time jobs in government services were introduced to the Straits as well as unemployment insurance (UIC), government subsidies and short-term job creation programs such as LIP and Canada Works. Along with these changes came the idea of employment as distinct from work, an increasing use of cash and need for cash income, an increase in time free from subsistence requirements and the institutionalization on the Labrador coast of new, permanent, waged, male sex-stereotyped jobs. (*Decks Awash*, 1986). Within living memory, dog sleds and foot travel were the only local transportation in winter; telegrams and radio provided the only communication links. By the 1970s these were supplanted by snowmobiles, pick-up trucks, telephones and aircraft service.

In this paper, some comparisons will be made between the Labrador Straits and Halifax. Both are coastal communities in Atlantic Canada, oriented in part to fishing, but the similarities end there. Halifax is a major port and provincial capital, with a 1976 population of approximately 250,000. Since its founding in 1749, it has been a site of civilian and military governance linked with the rest of the world by transportation and communication networks. Labrador's development has been different. By 1972, only one community had a municipal council. In 1977 when the Straits did not even have a doctor, and was opening its first bank, Halifax had numerous hospitals, universities, government offices, stores and businesses. The contrasts between the two regions were great in terms of geographic, political and social isolation.

In 1976, the gender structure of the two regions also differed considerably. There was greater social differentiation and segregation between men and women in Labrador than in Halifax. At a meeting or dance, for example, it was not unusual to see married women sitting on one side of the room or at one table and men in another place. This social segregation meant that women had a clear sense of themselves as women, and unlike Halifax, women did not need consciousness-raising groups.

As elsewhere in rural Atlantic Canada, both men and women had their "work," and work was not associated with employment but with chores. As Muir (1977:5) found:

> "Work" as a category of labour had NOT been distinguished from "housework."
> Island women will speak of "my work;" meaning housework, in the same way
> that men mention their "work." I found that the question "Would you like to
> work?" (commonly asked between acquaintances and in questionnaires in in-
> dustrial society) was greeted with indignation and with the tart response that
> women DO work, harder than most people with jobs.

In spite of an ideology of male dominance, patrilocal residence patterns and female roles oriented to support and serve the male, women played an indispensable and central role in the Straits society. Compared with women in Halifax, Straits women were, were seen to be, were supposed to be, and were recognized as being, hard-working.

In the 1970s the Women's Liberation Movement tended to associate equality with the practice of women playing the same socially valued roles as men. I arrived with this stereotype, and with an interest in how women could become more involved in decision-making. I saw stark differences between men and women in Labrador that were supposedly associated with "traditional women," but the stereotype was quickly shattered and I began to realize the inappropriateness of many of my assumptions—about equality, about sameness, about linear "progress," about community participation, and about decision-making abilities. As I pointed out elsewhere (see Christiansen-Ruffman, 1979), women in Labrador had more "personhood" than women in Halifax.[2] Their contribution to the community was recognized by that community as important. As one woman explained:

Here in Labrador Straits is different from other areas in the province. Women were always equal when it comes to decisions and policy-making.

In Labrador, in contrast to Halifax, women were much more articulate about their importance in community life. Clear community interest and commitment were conscious features of life experiences in Labrador Straits. Compared to men, according to one Labrador woman:

Women are more interested in the community. They help and raise so much for the community. Things would never get off the ground except for women. If there is a project everybody gets involved.

An admittedly shy woman compared female and male teachers. The men were on one committee at most and had interest in other things. The women were fully involved with children's recreation and with community activities. And this was a gendered pattern, with moral overtones:

There's no problem with the women. What will go, will go. For example, the cemeteries. The UCW [United Church Women] cares for two. They are all painted and nice. The men on council are supposed to be looking after the third, but it is run down; the fence is half down and not painted. . . .
The men don't want to take time to get involved. They are self-centred. It's always been that way. Women are more involved.

Women's Organizations in the Labrador Straits

In the Straits in 1978 there were eight women's organizations, five of which had branches in more than one community. Three others were associated mainly with women: the Red Cross, Agricultural Committees in several communities, and the Labrador Craft Producers Association.

Of the eleven organizations or committees, two were church groups, the third was a charitable organization (the Red Cross), and a fourth, the Orange Lodge, had religious as well as charitable and social functions. Three other groups were oriented toward education and recreation for young people (Nursery School, Brownies/Girl Guides, and the Community Club which ran an annual Christmas Party in one community). Three of the remaining committees or organizations had ties outside the area and were associated with education and community development: agricultural committees, the Labrador Craft Producers Association, and the Women's Institute. The remaining organization for women—the Dart League—was mainly recreational.

The oldest women's organizations on the coast were organizations connected with the Anglican and United Churches.[3] The "Guild" or the "Ladies' Aid" met weekly. Women talked about and created community while they sewed and made goods which were then sold to raise money for the church; informally they were known as the "sewing class." The income raised for needed materials such as furnaces, paint, kitchen facilities, or material to build a new church was, in local terms, substantial. As one woman said, "If there were no Church Women, there'd be no church at all." The women not only raised money necessary for the church's survival, they supported it with their time and labour: they decorated, cleaned, cared for its physical needs and fulfilled its community functions such as visiting the sick. Women's significant and multifaceted role in the Straits compared with other areas was especially clear to clergymen who moved to Labrador from parishes elsewhere in Canada. One Minister expressed great surprise at having women on the Church's Board of Stewards. He exclaimed, "Women have their roles—to support the church, but here there are both men and women involved." In fact, in a few communities, the women's group was effectively the Board of Stewards. They raised and controlled the money, decided what was needed and paid the bills. Several incidents were reported to me where new clergy attempted to take authority away from the women in their congregations and to re-establish patriarchal relations.

The women's church group served not only as a sacred but also as a community institution. In one community, it was reportedly the only one. As one woman explained:

> In this community, that's all there is. There's no council; the men have no organizations. . . . The women have to keep this place going.

Women did not have to be members of a church or denomination to join the church's women's group (although most were). In the past the women's church group absorbed and shared other groups' functions—and even their names. In one community, the women's church group—or Guild—was also the community's agricultural committee and its Women's Institute:

> There's the women's Institute and the Guild. They're exactly the same. It's all one crowd. We meet once a week; sometimes the minutes are taken for the Guild, the last week of the month for the Women's Institute. When we raise money, half of it goes to the church and half to the Women's Institute. The Women's Institute bought the community hall for $1000. It was renovated by an LIP[4] project but now we have to keep it going; there's insurance, an awful heat bill and lights.

In other communities, greater organizational differentiation had taken place by 1978, but extensively overlapping group memberships were still common.

The role of women's organizations in most Straits communities in the mid-seventies was especially prominent because of the absence of other community institutions. Before municipal offices, women's organizations provided the locally legitimate means through which community needs were identified and met.

The relative flourishing of women's organizations in the Straits reminded me of the growth in women's organizations during the late 19th century when middle-class women were freed from work by changed circumstances and devoted their energies toward organizing charities. Although in Labrador, there were no idle middle-class women, one might hypothesize that the flourishing of women's organizations during the 1970s was one response by women to their new conditions, to social forces undermining community and to the erosion of the basis for the relatively equal communal relations they had experienced in the past.

The Women's Institute: A Case Study

The Women's Institute (WI) was a particularly important organization in Labrador Straits in the mid 1970s, with seven branches and a district council. Most of the branches were formed in 1972-3, after area women heard about the provincial organization from officials of the Royal Commission on Labrador. The organization was greeted enthusiastically by women of all ages. Its appeal was multifaceted, and it addressed squarely and directly problems of isolation, employment, and community needs. It was community-based and altruistic and, at the same time, economic, educational, political, recreational, inspiring, quasi-religious and entertaining.

Women's Institute branches were easily incorporated into existing community structures. Each branch felt free to pursue any aspect of community involvement and development or group education it wished under the name of the Women's Institute.[5] The sense of continuity between the Women's Institute and existing organizations was especially strong in communities with only one church, but even in these, the new organization was breaking isolation and forging new structural relationships. One of the most important features of the organization was its explicit tolerance of different religious denominations. It was one of the few organizational forums where Anglicans, United Church Women and Catholics worked together. Women expressed regret that women in the other major denomination, the Christian Brethren, were not allowed to join any organization; this religious prohibition prevented complete community membership.

The meetings and interactions between branches both reinforced traditional community patterns and forged links with new segments of local, regional, provincial and global communities of women. The District Council was the first regional association in the Straits. The Women's Institute also reduced the actual and perceived isolation of the region, in relation to Newfoundland and Labrador and the larger world. Regular contacts and communication with the Provincial Office in St. John's and with other branches of the international Associated Country Women of the World expanded women's sense of geographic space and provided "a great sense of involvement." Trips to meetings and organized exchanges expanded Labrador women's horizons not only geographically but socially. Members sent news of their activities elsewhere and made new contacts.

The organization's multi-faceted nature accommodated and strengthened continuity while generating new ideas and challenges. Initially at least, this resulted in some striking differences among branches and in the way in which the organization was viewed by different members. Issues such as female property rights that were raised by the Provincial Organization and discussed in local meetings were especially important. Land was in the process of being converted from common land to private ownership, and concepts of private property were being instituted by the state and mortgage companies. The President of one branch was particularly interested in the diverse issues that the branch was regularly called upon to address by way of resolution. The Women's Institute she described lived its motto: a University for Rural Women. Not only did the President see an educational role, but she looked to the organization for women's liberation. Presidents of other branches stressed community-based sociability, fund-raising, community development and crafts.

Meetings of the Women's Institute combined education, development, food and fun. I attended one annual meeting where branches entertained each other with skits and songs reminiscent of popular theatre. The spirit and warmth in the room at meetings, the hectic community activity, the vibrant political culture and the enthusiasm of Institute members is reminiscent of Porter's description of "The Tangly Bunch" of members in eastern Newfoundland (Porter, 1985).

In Labrador, the Women's Institute also played a major role in initiating development efforts and in increasing the scope of community interests. The complexity of its role in the development process is illustrated with the example of crafts. All branches were involved in crafts, but there were differences among branches in terms of what was produced and for what purposes. The interest in crafts built on a tradition in each community of women sitting together in the evening and sewing and/or knitting for community needs. Several branches saw themselves as quite explicitly involved in community work and in raising money through crafts, card games, community concerts, suppers, fairs and bingos for community purposes and for charity. A Branch President explained a process that created funds for both individuals and the community.

> We do all crafts for the institute and [once a week] we hold a card game for fund-raising. We give out materials to the women in our community. They make it up in crafts, then we pay them for doing it. When the finished product comes to us, we put it into the Women's Institute until someone asks for donations. Then we give these products for their sales or money. . . . We give donations yearly to school, church committee, community council and girl guides.
>
> The purpose is not only to do crafts but to get women out working and involved in community life. I think women are more involved in community development than men. Women are always involved in something. They have a number of organizations.

In a few communities, the Women's Institute was appreciated for teaching women how to make new crafts and learn new techniques. Another community saw it as playing an important function in upgrading the quality of crafts. Still another advocated research into different crafts. The Women's Institute also operated a regional craft shop.

The regional craft shop and other development projects had begun to transform sewing from a community effort to an individual source of income, and this became a source of considerable debate. In 1975 the Women's Institute applied for and received an $1100 grant to buy materials and to pay women a fee for their goods. The crafts were then sold at a craft shop during the summer months and the money used to buy more materials. The popularity of the revolving money led to a debate about whether men and other nonmembers should be allowed to join the Women's Institute or to sell their goods at the craft shop. A brochure produced by one branch appealed for new members in the following way:

We would like to see more members joining the Women's Institute who are interested in getting more crafts done so that our Craft Shop can be open longer than 2½ months in the summer. . . . The Women's Institute can provide extra money, the more you knit or sew, the more money you earn, you get paid for everything you do. Why not come and see what's going on; you don't expect to know unless you attend. We would like to see as many as possible attending our meeting and joining our institute.

Some of the leadership in the community did not like the idea of pay for crafts, and felt that doing community work as a business was counterproductive. They felt that the Institute was getting too involved in crafts, in quality control, and in individual rather than group work, and said that it should be "spread out in the community more." But many Labrador women also felt that they should be paid for their labour as men were paid for theirs.

The development efforts of the Women's Institute did not focus solely on crafts. In fact, the President of the Lance Au Clair branch felt that one of the benefits of the Women's Institute was that it allowed women to apply for government grants. The WI had some of the first regionally based government-sponsored grants (from both the provincial and federal governments), and it was represented as an organization on two new government-sponsored regional associations: the Southern Labrador Development Association (SLDA) and the Community Employment Strategy Committee (CES).

The Women's Institute as an organization developed a variety of projects for community betterment. It supported a Nursery School and initiated a proposal for a tourist information centre and museum. Its official organizational form was seen as beneficial because it allowed women access to government grants. Despite some discouraging proposal rejections, women with whom I talked remained relatively confident that they could participate in development efforts as well as men.

Most government projects supported mainly male employment by favouring material rather than social infrastructure development. A typical project provided males with construction jobs. Despite the sex segregation in the community, a number of women expressed strong views about the rights of women to construction jobs, if those were the jobs available. One Women's Institute member complained about being refused employment on a renovation job:

No women were on it. I tried and couldn't get it. They said if they could get men, they wouldn't take the women. I figured I could do the work as well as men. . . . They took boys with no experience, even outside of the community. Women is turned down every time—when there's a dollar in it to be made. . . . I thinks I's as good as any man there. The crowd here, there's no problem men to women. Men seemed more dominant there than here.

As part of job creation and development efforts, the Canadian government supported several job creation programs in the 1970s. Both women's groups and men's groups in communities applied for Canada Works projects which would provide income for work previously done by community members without pay. In

1977, the women's projects (knitting, handicrafts) tended to be rejected because of a fear of paying for work which had previously been done as a matter of course. The opposite judgement was made for men's projects which had previously been volunteer (e.g. constructing a church or community hall). The double standard and the implicitly patriarchal ideology on which these decisions were made was not a subject of public discussion, but it did not go completely unchallenged. In 1978, despite previous rejections of proposals, half of the applications for Canada Works were "women's projects" from women's organizations.

In 1978, one Women's Institute branch submitted—and received—their own building repair project as a result of the Canada Works competition. It made an application to renovate a building for community use and planned to hire all women. The group selected the project in part because previous building projects had been supported. This example raises an interesting parallel between the experiences of the Straits women and well-paid urban women. In order for work to be valued, to be considered "of worth," women have to prove themselves equal in a world controlled by male standards.

Centrality of Women's Organizations in the Labrador Straits Compared to those in Halifax

During the 1970s, Halifax had a wide variety of women's groups with specific causes, interests and concerns that ranged from flying clubs to churches; from poetry to being a mother of twins. In 1975 there were 130 women's organizations with an additional twenty-six considered mainly women's organizations (156 in total). Twenty-eight organizations had several branches, including a church group with over 40 branches in the metropolitan area. At the time, only 21 or 13% defined themselves as actively working to improve the status of women, and most of these had been formed since the Report of the Royal Commission on the Status of Women (1970)(Christiansen-Ruffman et al, 1975).

An obvious difference in the character of women's organizations in the two areas was their relative numbers. In absolute terms, the urban area had a larger number of women's organizations. On the other hand, an examination of the women's organizations per population indicated that organizations were more prevalent in the Straits than in Halifax, at least at that particular time. Perhaps more importantly, in the Straits a considerably larger proportion of women belonged to a women's organization than was the case in Halifax. Their role and the importance attributed to women's organizations by women in the community was hence more central.

In the Straits almost every woman leader had been or was important in women's organizations. This centrality of women's organizations contrasted sharply with the situation in Halifax, where a large number of women community leaders neither were participants in women's groups in the past nor had any current interest in women's group membership. Women's organizations in 1976 were defined by Halifax women leaders as uninteresting and marginal, and most women community leaders interviewed appeared to be pleased that they were not members of women's organizations.

The relatively peripheral community status of women's organizations in Halifax is further confirmed by comparing what women community and organization leaders in Halifax considered to be important problem areas with what women's organizations actually were doing in 1975. The most important problem area was considered to be housing (54% of women cited it). This was followed by transportation, daycare, employment and education. But when we looked at the issues that women's organizations were actually working on, we found that most—twenty-five—were working on education, nineteen were working on health issues, fifteen on culture and fourteen on social services. Women's organizations were not addressing areas that the women themselves defined as the most important problems in Halifax. There was, if anything, an inverse relationship. The issues being addressed by women's organizations in the Straits were more central to community needs, more important to the community and recognized as more significant than those being addressed by women's organizations in the Halifax area. Hence, women's organizations in the Straits made a relatively greater contribution to the community than did organizations of women in Halifax in the 1970s.

A comparison of women's organizations in Halifax and Labrador challenged a number of then "common sense" assumptions about "traditional women" that I had gained from the general community, feminist community, and academic scholarship. My experience forced a re-examination of taken-for-granted assumptions such as the dichotomy between "traditional" and "modern, liberated" women.

Conceptual Lessons: Multi-Faceted Women's Groups Are Not Misbehaving

In Halifax, the focus of women's groups tended to be specialized. Organizations were built around specific services such as aid to hospitals, firefighting, female offenders, family planning and abortion referral rather than general community well-being. It was possible to categorize a particular organization as having a focus on one of the problems mentioned in the previous section. A few groups in the Straits were also at least superficially easy to classify—one group was established to deliver daycare services and the dart league was clearly recreational. But the Women's Institute, with its multi-faceted and interlocking objectives, resisted classification. Upon further examination, a number of Labrador women's organizations—and also those in Halifax—had multiple goals which they often carried out together. Moreover, a number of groups in both places (e.g., Junior League in Halifax and the Women's Institute and Church groups in Labrador) identified gaps in community services and initiated new projects each year to meet these needs and thus the group's institutional focus.

I have treated women's realities and perspectives as central and as a starting point for discovery of the community-based work of women. I do not see their broad, well-rounded character as a problem of misbehaviour. From my perspective, women's groups often create a variety of forms of wealth—material, political, moral, social, cultural, human and economic resources. Rather than misbehaving, women's groups point to problematic assumptions embedded in existing patriarchal concepts of wealth and development (see Christiansen-Ruffman, 1987:12).

Conceptual Lessons: Women's Community Work

Women and women's organizations in the Straits and in Halifax demonstrated an active concern for their communities and for the well-being of people in them. Approximately two-thirds of the organizations in both places fulfilled important community service and support functions. Some organizations such as church groups were oriented broadly to community service, whereas others had one particular focus, such as meeting the educational and recreational needs of children. All these women's organizations did unpaid public work for the community by volunteering to do necessary service tasks and by financially supporting charities and projects. They also identified and filled gaps in services to individuals, families and groups. Namely, they did women's community work.

Especially in the 1970s, patricentric society and scholarship had rendered women's community culture invisible. It was not of interest to scholars and remained largely untheorized. In an early attempt to understand women's community work, Davis (1979) applied the work-leisure dichotomy to women's volunteer association activity in a Newfoundland outport. I remember my negative reaction to the resulting characterization of women's community activities as "play." It seemed to bear no relationship to the reality of the Labrador Straits or to the other Newfoundland communities I had known. The characterization of "play" seemed to trivialize women's activities. I understood it as a classic case of a false dichotomy, developed from male experience. The fact that women in organizations have a good time is an expression of a vibrant women's culture and the multifaceted nature of women's community work, not proof that women's activities are unimportant, non-work. Indeed, all women's organizations to some degree provided important social and recreational opportunities for women and, in fact, one of the few legitimate social activities for women outside the home. In the Straits, at least, they were also actively engaged in creating and maintaining community.

In an unpublished paper (1985), Leslie Brown and I described women's community work as "a third part of the puzzle" and as distinct from household labour and paid labour. Our detailed review of the literature on work found that the sociology of work literature tended to exclude or at least obscure women's community work. Even when included and rendered visible, women's community work was typically characterized as less important than what we called "paid work," as supportive, complementary and low in status.

It is striking now, although I did not recognize it at the time, that in Labrador, some of women's community work was, in fact, not unpaid but paid work. The typical community-based fund-raising efforts of the Straits' communities point to a practice of monetary reimbursement for labour that was funnelled for the public good. Under those circumstances, women's community work clearly had a monetary value, but for the collectivity rather than for the individual. For example, women made baked goods or catered dinners with the proceeds of their labour going to the community or to the church.

Research in Newfoundland in 1993 found women and women's organizations to be engaged in sophisticated forms of community-based fund-raising but, paradoxically, of an increasingly individualized nature. For example, church groups and clubs had organized elaborate ways of producing dinners which were delivered for a fee to individual households rather than served in halls. It is one of the contradictions of this development that as women organized increasingly focused and efficient fund-raising efforts, these efforts were transforming and potentially losing their communal and community-based character.

Conceptual Lessons: Women's Political Culture

Although women in the very different communities of Halifax and the Labrador Straits tended not to see themselves as engaged in politics, their common orientation to "getting things done for the community" was striking and led to my theorizing about a closeted women's political culture. I defined women's political culture as a set of orientations, morals, values and beliefs about the nature of a just and caring society, one that meets human needs. Women's political culture helps identify socially valuable goods and services and strategies about how to maximize women's goals. It has a material base, not a biological or essentialist one. This material base is rooted in the social organization of women's experience which involves the nurturing of children, caring for people and ensuring distributive justice. Because of their responsibilities for the daily care, maintenance and support of children, women are concerned with the arena within which children live and the social forces which damage this environment. Their societal position extends the sphere of women from the home into the surrounding community. Thus it is not surprising that women in both Labrador and Halifax created community facilities and activities. Two major features of women's political culture that are reflected in the actions and recollections of women's groups in both communities are its rootedness in multiplicity and its confidence in women's morality.

The conception of women's culture being closeted is useful because it allows one to think of the continual, structurally generated orientation of a women's political culture while also recognizing its uneven appearance and articulation. It helps to explain the consistent themes such as peace and community well-being that have been articulated by women in these different communities as well as in other community-based groups over the centuries. It is no accident that it is women who initiate and organize urban reform movements involving housing, welfare and the environment. Even when closeted, the latent power of women's political culture can be mobilized to act politically with remarkable force, as in Japan between 1882-1884 (see Sievers, 1981), in Barcelona between 1910-18 (see Kaplan, 1982), in women's constitutional gains in Canada (see Kome, 1983), and in the significant but unrecognized contributions of Black women in Nova Scotia (see Hamilton, 1993).

Relative to their own communities, women in rural Labrador had more resources, more control and received more recognition than did women in urban ones. The rural women were also more likely than upper-middle class urban women to take for granted the exercise of day to day control over the home. Both the control of women and the importance of women's work in rural areas was symbolized by the big centrally located kitchen which was the family gathering place. In the Labrador Straits the kitchen of each household served as a common space, not only for the family but for the larger community as well. Community members were welcome to enter at any time; there was no custom of "knocking" to ask permission to enter. It is only recently that the significance of this space for the promotion of women's political culture has become clear.

Conceptual Lessons: Women's Political Culture and Feminist Political Culture

Feminist political culture draws on women's political culture but also brings additional political resources through its conscious challenges to patriarchy and other forms of power, including racism, classism and colonialism. Feminist political culture attempts to articulate women's diverse material realities and strengths, women's oppression and women's commitment to social betterment. This knowledge has been developed from the wisdom of women working in groups who draw on their own realities, perspectives and experiences, from feminist activists within the women's movement, and from feminist scholars who are grounded in these movements. Women in Labrador did not have access to such feminist resources whereas some women in Halifax, as part of the women's liberation movement, were beginning to establish a feminist political culture. Thus although women's organizations in Labrador were generally more prominent and addressed more important issues than those in Halifax, the feminist organizations in Halifax were even stronger in some respects. The importance of feminist political culture and of women's conceptions of the political are explored in Christiansen-Ruffman (forthcoming).

Conceptual Lessons: Patriarchal Changes

Empirically and theoretically, I have documented the strong presence of women's community work in the Labrador Straits. Although women's strength was locally recognized, it was the men and not the women who were approached by visiting development workers and government officials. When government officials wanted to set up committees focused on agriculture or the fisheries in the Straits communities, they typically summoned men to a meeting. These bureaucrats had totally ignored the fact that women traditionally cared for the gardens and processed the fish. Women in one community described how they learned about a meeting and got information; the agriculture committee continued under their sponsorship. These women said that agriculture committees never worked or ceased functioning in communities where women were not involved.

Government officials from outside not only helped to create new male committees. In the early 1970s the men's community improvement organizations were encouraged by the Newfoundland government to form community councils. Women's organizations, despite their prominence, were not asked. There was a suggestion among some women that recent organization of male-dominated community councils happened in part because the Women's Institutes were seen as a threat to men when they started organizing regional and community activities.

Women were not only ignored or passed over when it came to newly developing facilities, but their resources were also systematically undermined. One example of the pressure away from women's control of community resources imposed by the outside, is in the control of community halls. Women Institutes in a number of communities had equipped and run the community halls which were built by men under short-term employment projects. When community councils were established consisting almost totally of men (although a woman is head of the council in one community), the women were "relieved" of the hassle and expense of running the halls because they were taken over by the councils. The councils, as quasi-official bodies, were able to cost-share the upkeep of community halls with the provincial government on a 50% basis. The expensive heating and upkeep thus cost the community less if controlled by the male-dominated community council instead of female-dominated groups under whose guidance they came into existence. The offer of 50% was worth the loss of control for some women's groups but others were strongly resisting the "logical takeover."[6] The result was a loss in women's power and control over community facilities.

In 1978 I ended my paper with the prediction:

What women in the Straits are likely to be facing are the forces for discrimination which undermine community values and women's position, forces which have historically accompanied the so called "development" of the economy and the modernization or colonialization of the community.

In subsequent trips to Labrador I heard anecdotal evidence about the pressure women felt to leave their jobs so as to distribute jobs more evenly among families and to preserve community values. Some succumbed and some resisted the strong community pressures.

Conclusion

The call for further research in the Straits is especially poignant with the profound crisis of the early 1990s which closed the northern cod fishery. I wish I could be in the Straits doing this necessary research, and knowing how each individual, in each family, in each community of the region is doing—and how each is reacting, individually and collectively, over time, to the government imposed ban and to the suggested "solutions." I also wonder whether contemporary Labrador women recognize "instinctively" the patriarchal nature of the bureaucratic and government-appointed decision-making bodies as clearly as women there once did. Richard Cashin, the head of the all-male task force appointed to make recommendations on the future of the fisheries, recognized at a public meeting in Halifax in December, 1993, that forty-year old women would be most harmed by the crisis.

Patriarchy's acceptance of women as victim prevented him and his colleagues from paying attention to the problems of these women and adopting policies focused on their needs. Instead he and his task force developed solutions clearly against the interests of women, children and communities such as those in the Labrador Straits.

Feminists internationally have called for people-centred development. As DAWN explains:

> This means not only that people's subsistence, survival and well-being be the goal of development, rather than economic growth per se, but equally that people participate in economic and social decisions through decentralization of resources and power. . . . The values which sustain this vision are those that are widely held and shared in the international women's movement, namely, cooperation, sharing and responsibility for others, accountability, resistance to hierarchies and commitment to peace.

Women's contribution may well be this people-centred development, if patriarchy has not blocked all the means for them to be heard and to influence the future.

1 This paper is based in part on an unpublished paper presented at the 9th World Congress of Sociology, Uppsala, Sweden, August 14-19, 1978, entitled "Women in Community Development: A Comparison of Two Regional Communities in Atlantic Canada" and in part on a paper presented at the 3rd annual conference of the Canadian Research Institute for the Advancement of Women, Edmonton, Alberta, Canada and published in *Resources for Feminist Research: Special Publication No. 8, 1980*. The research was assisted by many individuals, and I thank in particular my research assistant, Ellen McDonald, her family, and the many other individuals in the Straits area and elsewhere who assisted my research over the years. Directly or indirectly, Saint Mary's University, the International Development Research Centre (IDRC), the former Minister of State for Urban Affairs, DPA Consultants, and the Canada Employment and Immigration Commission partially financed this research.

2 For the purposes of this paper, personhood is defined as the extent to which an individual's contribution to the community is recognized by that community as important. More specifically, the personhood of women is analyzed along three dimensions: (a) the extent to which women's activities contribute necessary resources to the community and to the family unit; (b) the extent to which women exercise control over resources in the household and in the community and (c) the extent to which women are respected in the household and in the community.

My analysis began with three then current but misleading propositions concerning the personhood of women in rural areas:

(1) Women in rural areas, often called "traditional women" and characterized by relatively rigid sex role segregation, are relatively deprived of personhood compared to their more sophisticated urban counterparts.

(2) Progress toward personhood is gradually being made as communities become more urban and industrialized.

(3) Women in rural communities and generally in Atlantic Canada are conservative and are not innovative or politically active in community life.

3   For different reasons, the other two churches in the Straits— the Catholic Church and the Christian Brethren—did not have organizations exclusively for women at that time.

4   LIP was a Local Initiative Project, one of the first of a succession of short-term employment creating projects sponsored by Employment and Immigration Canada, at the time called the Department of Manpower and Immigration.

5   This was the finding of Ellen McDonald, my research assistant, after extensive interviews in 1978 in the Straits. Although there were prescribed provincial programs for each month, the Straits branches saw themselves as relatively autonomous and different branches within the Straits pursued a variety of projects under the Women's Institute aegis.

6   The takeover, incidently, would mean a considerable loss in community social activities as well, since it is through bingos, card games and other community "do's" that the funds to pay for heat and utilities are raised.

Women and the Fishery

Victoria Silk

This is an account of one woman's experience as a fisher in Petty Harbour, Newfoundland.

Introduction

Recent years have seen social scientists taking a closer look at the roles women have played in fisheries throughout the world, discovering that women and fish are inextricably linked in many cultures. In *Women of the Praia*, Sally Cole documents the involvement of Portuguese women in their fishery as licensed boat owners and skippers dating back into the 1800s; as early as 1876, a crew of eight women were shipwrecked while returning home with a load of fish. *Winds of Change*, a book about women of the Northwest fishing industry, follows their roles as processors and producers over the past 50 years. Siri Gerrard, a Norwegian anthropologist, has been researching women's contributions in the fishery of her homeland, bestowing upon them the name "ground crew" in recognition of the roles they play. Her research points out that women's contribution to the fishing industry is so vital that it provides "a premise for preserving the settlement structure and the coastal fishery for the future and for turning the ideal of equal opportunity into something more than empty rhetoric for women in the fishing districts" (Gerrard, 1987). Women have also played intricate roles over the past two centuries in Newfoundland's fishery, although it is not so much through the eyes of historians that we see this as through the more recent work of feminist social scientists such as Neis (1994), Porter (1988), Davis (1983), McCay (1988) and Antler (1977). With all due respect to those who have made fine contributions to our knowledge in this area, the record of Newfoundland women's lengthy and rich contribution to the fishery remains sorely neglected.

My paper will look at women and the fishery from one woman's perspective as a harvester in the inshore sector.

My Story

I LEFT TORONTO IN 1978 shortly after a young boy was brutally murdered eight blocks from my home at Queen and Spadina. One evening, not long after the murder, my four-year-old daughter disappeared from our yard for an hour. The police were called in and all ended well; however, the combination of incidents convinced me that I needed to 'single-parent' in a healthier, safer environment. Several months later, following an unsuccessful search for an out-of-town home, I accepted an invitation to baby-sit the goats and chickens of an acquaintance for the summer months in Petty Harbour/Maddox Cove. The pace of outport life appealed to me, and by the end of the summer, I had resolved to stay in Newfoundland, convinced that it would be a safer and healthier environment in which to raise kids. The following winter I traded a beautiful, solid body electric guitar for a leaky eighteen-foot boat with as many half-inch gaps in it as there were planks. Ten pounds of oakum later she was primmed up and I was ready to go fishing.

It was the summer of 1979 when I joined Newfoundland's inshore fishery, the sector where fishers leave home on a daily basis in the wee hours of the morning, generally returning home by dusk. This was two years after the 200-mile limit had been declared, and federal and provincial governments alike were exceptionally optimistic that this new declaration would be the "panacea of" Newfoundland's economic woes. This confidence inspired the infusion of large numbers of subsidies into both the harvesting and processing sectors. According to the International Commission for the North Atlantic Fishery (ICNAF), the commission responsible for managing the fish stocks of the northwest Atlantic, our stocks were healthy enough to support not only our own activities, but those of the European community as well. I knew little of all this, only that the summer I commenced fishing you could catch fish the size of dogs on any of the traditional fishing grounds and that is what counted.

Although my first summer on the water went reasonably well, my first few days fishing are certainly worth mentioning. I started fishing on a Thursday and during the first three days I caught three sculpins. Having never been on the open ocean, that great expanse of cold, grey Atlantic looked formidable. As soon as I cleared the harbour's mouth I hove anchor, hoping for the best. On the second day I lost the grapnel. I knew nothing about ropes, by-ropes and tripping anchors; it just got caught down on the bottom and I couldn't get it up. So, doing what any sensible person would, I attached my life jacket to the anchor rope, marking the grapnel so I could get back to it another time. I'll never know how much mileage the fishermen of Petty Harbour got out of that incident, but a good few of them came up to me asking if the berth had been so good that I marked it to find my way back the next day!

On my third day of fishing, a prominent fisher approached me and, in the most tactful way, explained that he was "born and reared a life time in Petty Harbour and had never seen or heard tell of anyone ever fishing that ground." He informed me that if I wanted to catch fish, I'd have to head out to the "ledge," that "sou'dard" piece of ground three miles from port where the handline boats, no bigger than specks on the horizon, were catching cod. Monday morning, bright and early, I set out for the ledge as though I was headed overseas. I finally arrived, hove anchor and caught 436 pounds of Northern Cod. Arriving back in the harbour around noon, hardly able to contain my excitement, I was greeted wharfside by a family of Americans who were making home movies and were so delighted to see a female fishing that they filmed me, the boat, the fish, then bought some fish—what a star!

My summers went smoothly in most respects but all of my learning was basically by trial and error. One of the major obstacles for women who want to become harvesters is that they have been excluded from access to traditional knowledge. While young boys follow their fathers or other male relatives down to the stages, onto the wharfs and into the boats, gaining the wide range of knowledge needed to pursue the fishery, young girls are excluded from these male-dominated territories.

The confidence and knowledge required to tackle the fishery is a reserve for young men. I can see this in retrospect, but at the time, I figured my big disadvantage was being a "Come-From-Away" (someone born and raised outside of Newfoundland).

The gear I was using at the time was simple: an outboard. Within a year, I graduated from my 18-foot wooden boat to a 22- foot fibreglass boat. Depth sounders (fish finders to some of us) and radios came into the community a couple of years after I started fishing. People had had very successful seasons with no fancy electronic equipment; it was the decline of the stocks that forced them to move towards more sophisticated fish-finding technology.

When I started fishing, I was the only woman fisher in Petty Harbour, and according to most of the community, the only woman to ever fish out of the Harbour. At that time, there were approximately 11,000 licensed fishers in New-foundland and Labrador of which approximately 350 were women. Needless to say, there was much talk and discussion about it and I was the brunt of many, many jokes. One fellow asked if I'd like to crew with him, be his cook and in my idle hours be his masthead. One young fellow was quoted on the CBC evening news as saying "no women ever fished in Petty Harbour and its nothing but a disgrace— they belong home cooking and tending the youngsters." Some of the older generation believed quite firmly (or so they professed) that it was bad luck to have a woman in the boat.

For all this, I had my moments of glory. A neighbour of mine who had started fishing one year before I did sold his fish to the same plant. For some reason, day after day, I consistently caught more fish than he did. This mortified him—he was tortured mercilessly each day by other fishermen and plant staff who suggested that he crew with me awhile to learn the ropes. As you can imagine, that was one relationship that never really blossomed into much.

CBC got wind of the fact that a woman was going out fishing on her own and approached me about doing a documentary on my fishing activities. I agreed and after several days of partial interviews on land, it was time to film me at sea. The plan was that I would spend a regular day fishing and the crew would join me on the water filming from another boat. The morning started out well, with moderate winds, sun and a nice run of fish. As noon approached and there was still no sign of the film crew on the horizon, I realized that a north easterly wind was brewing. A close friend had been kind enough to explain that when black clouds appeared over the north head of Motion Bay, accompanied by a good breeze, it was time for me to head in. This warning was accompanied by the advice to never cross over a shoal called the Ledge, which often breaks in a North Easterly, but to steam north until I cleared it. At the time, I was anchored about five miles from port, well outside the bay. I hauled in my anchor with great difficulty and headed for home. I came into the bay, turned broadside into the wind and realized that I had grossly misjudged where I was—I was on the north end of the Ledge. Two things happened simul-taneously: the stern of my boat went under the waves three times, causing it to fill three-quarters full of water, and the CBC crowd appeared out of nowhere in a great big super sloop just in time to film what I thought might be my final few minutes on earth! One of the crew was singing out "throw everything forward" and fortunately the weight of my fish and gas reserve were enough to keep the stern out of the water long enough for me to clear the shoal and limp home to port. I was safe and sound with another lesson tucked under my belt, and the CBC had an action-packed story that they advertised about three times a day for six months before airing the show.

I fished late into the fall that year, attempting to get as many insurable weeks of earnings as were necessary to open my first UI claim. Early in November I filed my claim, contented with my first season's labour, only to be thrown into a tail spin three weeks later by a disentitlement letter from Canada Employment and Immigration Commission (CEIC). The details of this battle are too lengthy to go into here, but the upshot of the case was that I fought the disentitlement, winning at both the Federal and Supreme Court levels. After the lengthy three-and a-half year battle, a regulation was dropped from the Act, to the benefit of many. My court case resulted in the fishers' qualifying period of twenty-six weeks being changed to fifty-two weeks, and this meant that fishers could combine insurable weeks of earnings from November to March with summer stamps.

During my first three or four years I geared up, buying more licences and eventually fishing for capelin, herring, squid and cod. The latter provided the main source of income. In my third year of fishing, I teamed up with a partner: I brought my licences and boat into the partnership, and my partner contributed a lobster licence and many years of traditional knowledge. We continued to fish together until I quit fishing in 1986.

Overall, I was successful at fishing. However, I encountered some problems that were never totally resolved, ones that ultimately contributed to my decision to leave the fishery. My skills as a fisher were never really acknowledged by my peers. I think that everyone strives to find acceptance and approval within their work community and over the years, it was at times discouraging to feel this missing. Something that always stands out in my mind is that, although people knew that my partner had sold his gear to join my enterprise, when someone wanted a loan of the boat or my gear, they would always approach him, not me. If he wasn't home, they'd call back later.

I'm not sure if I was ever looked upon as part of the fishery work force. People tended to view me as an oddity, and it was not uncommon to find people treating me with kid gloves rather than as an equal.

The pressures of parenting got a little lighter as time went by, but the problems that come with mixing kids and fishing don't go away. The long, arduous hours leave little time for interaction with children and there is a tendency for women to lose valuable time on the water due to family issues that arise. Unless one has good live-in help, it's difficult to fish the long hours while kids are still in school. Men who fish generally have women in their lives, either mothers or wives, who produce meals, clean clothes, make beds, shop, bank and baby-sit, often while holding down full-time paid employment. Women rarely enjoy these same advantages.

Another problem for women is that the Department of Fisheries and Oceans' definition of full-time fishers relates to a specific length of consistent fishing activity during a defined season. Although it varies from one area to the next, generally speaking late May, June, July, August and September must be fished to qualify as full-time. As already mentioned, women's child care commitments can make this difficult. Being classified as part-time, or being downgraded to part-time, can restrict one's access to limited entry licences which are only available to full-time fishers of 3-5 years.

Towards the end of my eight years of fishing the economic pressures created by declining stocks, combined with health problems and other concerns inclined me towards a change in direction. I had survived one near-drowning, a Supreme Court case, a severe bout of pleurisy, two years as a member of the Atlantic Fisheries Licensing Appeals Board and I had a chronically bad knee—yes...I was DEFINITELY ready for a change!

Conclusions

The theme of women's invisibility runs through the whole history of the fishery. It can still be seen in today's moratorium that finds government and industry officials refusing to look at gender issues, insisting that people be treated as individuals, ignoring the well-known reality that due to "occupational segregation, the wage gap and women's responsibility for work in the home" women will always be affected differently than men (Rowe, 1991).

Women are often viewed as lending a helping hand to a family business as opposed to being acknowledged as workers of equal status. I can recall being on the wharf listening to one fisher tell another that "Martin had a grand load today—2700 pounds." Not Martin and Silk, or Silk's crowd (that day I caught my biggest load ever, approximately 1200 pounds, hook and line, one at a time). From the day Martin joined my enterprise there seemed to be a tendency to downplay my role both as owner of gear and as a contributor of labour. When I fished alone, I was a novelty; the media picked up on this and made a special show about me. Yet there were many women fishing with male partners who were not viewed in the same light.

As late as 1981, there was a CEIC regulation that prevented women who fished with their husbands from qualifying for UI. This was successfully challenged in the Supreme Court of Canada by Rosanne Doyle of Witless Bay, Newfoundland, and since then women have been able to fish with their husbands and open winter claims.

The change in the law, combined with economic pressures, may have encouraged several women in a nearby shore community to go fishing during the summer of 1991. These women took to the boats with their husbands. However, the local plant was reluctant to purchase fish from these women, questioning whether or not they were only out to get insurable earnings to draw UI in the winter, otherwise referred to as "getting one's stamps." Meetings were held, and an effort was made by the all-male management to try and determine under what conditions a female could/would be considered eligible to have fish receipts in her name. All of this was accompanied by a good deal of public debate! The consensus was that a woman should be in a boat a minimum of three to four days a week to qualify as a deserving fisher. There was sympathy with the idea that women had to have a couple of days off to shop, bank and tend to household responsibilities. This intense scrutiny had to be unnerving for women who were on shaky ground already by virtue of their "trespassing" on traditionally male territory, and this serves to highlight the hidden barriers that help prevent women from accessing the fishery.

It seems appropriate to close with the recent comments of one middle-aged man about some women who went fishing. After hearing that one of them had lost the compensation package he commented: "There's not one of them fished more than the other; if one fished they all fished, but, if the truth be known, neither one of them could ever be called a fisherman because there was never a woman fished Petty Harbour."

What Is Women's Work? Gender and Work in Grand Falls

Elke Dettmer

THE STUDY Women's Economic Lives in Newfoundland, carried out between 1988 and 1990[1], focused on trying to develop an overall picture of the way in which women in Newfoundland related to economic structures, and how these affected women differently from men. It took the broadest definition of 'economic activity,' and looked in particular at how women's domestic responsibilities and roles in the family both constituted economic activity of many different (and usually unrecognized) kinds, and conditioned the ways in which they could relate to more formal 'economic activity'. As part of this study, we selected three contrasting communities as 'case studies'—a fishing town in Trinity Bay, a remote fishing community in Placentia Bay, and Grand Falls as a larger community with a non-fishing economic base.[2] What follows is based on the work I did as the researcher in Grand Falls.

In 1905, the publishers of the *London Daily Mail*, the Harmsworth brothers (Lord Northcliffe and Lord Rothermore), anticipated that they would run short of pulpwood, and went in search of new sources. They found the timber stands along the Exploits River and Red Indian Lake in central Newfoundland suitable, and chose a site near the grand falls of the Exploits River on which to found the Anglo-Newfoundland Development Company, and to build a mill and a town, to be known as Grand Falls.

When it opened in 1909, the mill was the largest industrial building on the island. The Anglo-Newfoundland Company tried to plan the town as a "garden city," following the models being tried in England at the time. The streets were to be spacious and planted with trees; the houses generously proportioned and carefully organized to accord with the status of the occupants as workers or managers at the mill. For the next fifty-six years—until 1961—the mill owned, managed and controlled the town. Only people connected with the mill were allowed to live in Grand Falls. Even widows of mill workers were expelled from the town after the deaths of their husbands. The company built houses for its employees, and later sold them to the occupants at low prices. Every need was taken care of, including a company-owned and -operated dairy farm to supply the town with milk. The company provided schools and augmented teachers' salaries; it took care of recreation by building a bowling alley, a skating rink and a stadium, and Lady Northcliffe donated money to establish a small hospital.

Meanwhile, across the railway tracks, the town of Windsor grew up around the railway station without any of these advantages. It was haphazard and unplanned. It was populated by people who did not qualify for residence in Grand Falls by virtue of their jobs at the Mill, or who were unacceptable on ethnic or other discriminatory grounds. Most of Windsor's population were less well off, and certainly less economically secure, than their Grand Falls' neighbours. Windsor began as a huddled settlement around the railway station and continued to focus on the vicinity of the railway, where two Jewish families—the Cohens and the Riffs—established retail stores, two of the success stories of Windsor.

Even today it is easy to see signs of these different origins. The Mill's contribution continues to augment Grand Falls' tax base, and the municipal authority is thus able to afford amenities denied to many poorer Newfoundland communities. Visually, the contrast is evident between Grand Fall's spacious, wooded streets and numerous, well appointed public buildings, and Windsor's less elegant sprawl. While officially two communities until recent amalgamation, it is clear that Grand Falls-Windsor constitutes one community, divided along class lines. Citizens of Grand Falls continue to ignore and disparage Windsor, which to them is simply the 'wrong side of the tracks'. This disdain was nowhere more obvious than in the outraged reaction of Grand Falls Mayor Henessey when amalgamation between the two towns was suggested by the Liberal government. Threatening to resign with all his councillors, his views were certainly shared by the prosperous burgesses of Grand Falls who couldn't be expected to foot the $12 million to bring Windsor facilities up to their own standards.

Grand Falls is a good place to live if you are affluent, married and a member of an old established family, which gives you right of entry into the various groups and cliques which dominate the social and economic life of the town. But this closed status- and class-conscious town is a hard place for outsiders—the less well-to-do, newcomers or single women. After a year in Grand Falls, the wife of an outgoing mill engineer complained that she had not once been invited for a cup of coffee. Social problems tend to be hidden in Grand Falls, and most women would rather take their psychological problems to a psychologist in Gander, who has confronted the pattern so often that he refers to it as the Grand Falls syndrome. Meanwhile the husbands join a buddy system that involves playing cards, hunting, golfing, curling and making careers together, a process that either excludes their wives or involves them in an unending stream of activities designed to enhance the family status.

Grand Falls is not only dominated by men in political and economic terms, it also lacks support systems for women. A women's centre was short-lived and has not been replaced. During the last decade there have been several efforts to establish a transition house for battered women. Each attempt was thwarted by the neighbours of the proposed shelter claiming that their property values would go down, that irate men might come looking for 'their women' and enter the wrong house or, most revealingly, that there was no need for such a shelter in Grand Falls because there were no battered women in the town. At one Town Council meeting, a (male) councillor persisted in his view that he had never seen a battered woman—until a woman at the meeting announced that she had been battered.

In other words, we found that Grand Falls (in association with Windsor) forced us to face issues of class in ways that were not so apparent in other Newfoundland communities. This also meant that we had to consider the connections between class and gender in trying to understand women's economic lives. Class was mediated by gender, but so was gender by class. At the most simple level this means that poorer women in Grand Falls, especially women on their own, have fewer

271

supports and economic possibilities than elsewhere. Middle-class women, on the other hand, find themselves with two responsibilities. 'Status', which is overwhelmingly important, has to be maintained both by the purchase of the appropriate commodities—house, car, cabin et cetera, which is difficult on a single male income. Middle-class wives, therefore, have to find jobs to provide the essential 'second income.' At the same time, it is also their responsibility to ensure that the family participates in a punishing round of social and service activities that entail considerable amounts of work to organise, cater for, fund raise for and dress for. Most of this work falls to the women.

Class consciousness begins in kindergarten, where the right address and the right clothes are important factors in obtaining invitations to the right birthday parties. While teenagers of the affluent families enjoy all the privileges that money can provide, including trips and university educations, there are no resources in Grand Falls for less affluent youngsters, who can be seen hanging out on the streets or crowding into the cinema on Friday and Saturday nights. For teenage girls, desirable job opportunities are few, and many still consider pregnancy and/or early marriage as a 'way out.' Here again, class operates in conjunction with gender to limit the available opportunities.

Most Grand Falls men work at the Mill (as do many men from Windsor) or in well paid professional or managerial jobs, but where do the women work? Both middle- and working-class women in Grand Falls face difficulties finding appropriate work in a tight labour market. For working-class women, or women on their own, the main problem is to find a job that will pay enough to support them. This is made harder by the strict sexual division of labour that characterizes the Grand Falls labour market. Most women's jobs simply do not pay a living wage. Middle-class women are even more restricted in the jobs they can find, as they are more bound by the notion of what is appropriate work for women. They also share with other Canadian women the same poverty of choice and low pay and uninspiring working conditions in the traditional female jobs that are available to them. In this piece, we will examine what happens to Grand Falls women when they enter the labour force under these conditions.

Grand Falls operates on the assumption that men are the breadwinners and women the homemakers, even though most families are desperate for the wives' second income. A major source of traditionally female work is in the clerical sphere, in businesses, government offices or with the schools or hospital. Among the most sought after traditional female jobs are the nursing and ancillary jobs in the Regional Hospital. Even the lowest-level positions at the hospital are relatively well paid and secure. They are coveted jobs but indications are that it helps 'to know somebody' to get a job. The laundry, for example, was staffed with so many members of the same family that the place was all but deserted during the funeral of one of their relatives.

Health work is considered women's work. More than 85% of health service and hospital workers are women. The nursing profession is still overwhelmingly female. Health care jobs reflect the institutionalization of traditional women's work—nurturing, caring, cooking, educating and cleaning. In the context of Grand Falls, where the men often oppose their wives working outside the home (even though they need their wage) nursing is seen as an acceptable job for women, especially if it constitutes a 'second income' and thus does not threaten the primacy of the 'male bread-winner.' Many of the nurses in Grand Falls are tied to the area because they are married to men working at the mill; in fact, a good many of them have been at the hospital since its inception.

Nurses in Grand Falls, as elsewhere, report the heavy workload as a major cause of occupational stress. A recent study in Ontario found that 87% of nurses experienced stress related to work overload. Nurses are also vulnerable. They are accountable to the hospital, to doctors, to fellow staff, to patients and their families. They can be readily blamed, and are increasingly liable to be sued for errors. They find themselves under constant stress because of the pressure not to make mistakes coupled with an ever increasing patient load (Walters and Haines, 1989).

In the hierarchy that prevails in hospitals, nursing assistants rank lower than nurses, and do not belong to the Nurses' Union. They work as hard, physically, as nurses, but do not have the same burden of paperwork or responsibility. Take, for example, Andrea, who has worked as a nursing assistant at the hospital for twenty-three years. She works in Emergency and Day Surgery, registering patients, taking temperature and blood pressure—the same work as a nurse would do, with the exception of administering drugs and starting IV treatment. But even though she escapes the high stress load of a nurse, Andrea's life is typical of many of the women 'in the middle,' around 40 years old, especially those in health care. She gets up at 6.00 am every morning, works until 10:00 pm and "then I can sit for an hour, before I go to bed." On work days, she does her laundry and pins it on the line before she leaves. She takes care of her household, her husband and three children as well as sharing the care of her physically handicapped mother with her sister. She is also a Girl Guide leader and active participant in the women's group of the Salvation Army. When she and her husband retire, they want to travel, but meanwhile both of them work as many hours as they can to enable two of their children to go to university.

Bernadette trained to be a nurse in the 1950s at St Clare's, then a small private hospital in St. John's. Her life demonstrates many aspects of the lives of health care workers. Her training was tough, and the students got their keep, but no more. After working in a number of cottage hospitals, Bernadette returned to Grand Falls in the early 1960s. Soon after, her father suffered a heart attack. Realizing that her parents would not be able to keep their standard of living without her help, she decided to stay in Grand Falls, where she already had a job at the new hospital. Even then, she found conditions much more stressful than in the cottage hospitals. Each nurse was responsible for ten patients, regardless of how much care they might need. This would often force her to deal only with the most urgent matters. She was already noticing the imbalance in the power relations within the hospital, the (male) doctors who liked to be "buttered up" by "cute nurses" who "kept running with the coffee cup," instead of spending time with patients. She also had difficulty getting the doctors to listen when she indicated that something was wrong with a patient. "Some doctors have terrific egos." They may feel professional jealousy or even fear when confronted by a nurse, but it is the nurse who is in closer touch with the patient and who often has better opportunity to observe. "You got to go and tell him," Bernadette says.

The same problem cropped up when Bernadette was chosen to represent some of the nurses' grievances about excessive shift work and long working hours. "I was as polite as I knew how to be, but what I was told was that the door swung both ways and I could go or I could come."

The fact that Bernadette was a nurse simply made it more obvious that she should take care of her father. She did it gladly, never regretting her decision to stay in Grand Falls for her parents' sake. When her father suffered a second heart attack, her parents had no health or drug plan, no sick leave and her father's pension was not enough to live on. By paying board in her parents' home, Bernadette could take care of them and contribute financially. With her professional care, her father survived several more heart attacks, but with each one her parents became more dependent on her. In the mid-1970s, her mother developed a severe kidney infection which required prompt treatment and then further care. Because she was a nurse, Bernadette got even less help from the hospital and home care services than other people did. She was, after all, a professional; it was assumed that she could cope.

Bernadette's father died in 1982, and around that time her mother developed Alzheimer's disease. She died in 1987. Thus for more than twenty years, Bernadette's life was dominated by the needs of her sick and aging parents. Her brother, who lives nearby with his family, took no part in the care of his parents. Bernadette excuses him. "After all, he has his own family to take care of," and "He is not the kind to see much sickness around. He could never give up his weekend." But it was impossible not to resent the double standard: "men are spoilt. They never have to cope with that kind of stuff." In the end, "women are tougher than men."

Eventually, caring for her parents took its toll on Bernadette. "It starts to tell after a long time because you get more irritable," and as much as she loved her mother, the caring was also very hard work. "You can't say you do all things selflessly. You resent. You do resent. . . ." For years, when her mother could not be left alone, Bernadette forwent the things she loved, such as plays at the Arts and Culture Centre. After her mother died, Bernadette was exhausted and burnt out, and it was only then that she found herself incapable of coping with her job. She went on medical disability for a year and finally took early retirement in December, 1988.

Many studies (eg Kaden and McDaniel, 1988) show that women predominate on both sides of the care-giving equation. While older men often receive assistance from their wives, older women are more likely to be cared for by their daughters, as women outlive men. Caring for frail, elderly relatives, usually women, is a growing aspect of 'informal' health-care. Recent research suggests that in the USA, the average woman will spend seventeen years caring for her children and eighteen years caring for aged or infirm relatives (Weinstien, 1989). Aging itself appears to be a women's issue— associated with widowhood, low income and poor health on the one hand. On the other hand, we find the 'women in the middle,' of three or four generations, who take on the major responsibility for informal health-care (Kaden and McDaniel, 1988:6).

Women encounter the health-care system as workers, as patients and as care-givers. But, more importantly, they provide primary and secondary care, inside and outside the formal health-care system. We see nurses like Bernadette being paid to care for patients, caring for their own parents, and having to pay someone else to care for their parents, while they work in the hospital. It is easy to find examples of the variety of ways women take on increasing burdens of caring, unobserved and unhelped by formal agencies.

In many ways, the health-care workers, especially the nurses, are relatively privileged in the Grand Falls female labour market. Women in Grand Falls, as in the rest of Canada, are concentrated in certain job categories and at the bottom levels of each occupation or industry. Among such jobs typically reserved for women, banking provides some of the most notorious examples.

Shirley worked in banking for twenty years, and loved her work. She even made a career of it as she moved around the province with her husband (a teacher), until they settled with their children in Grand Falls. Her experience and manifest capability meant that for many years she was chosen to train men to take positions higher than her own in the bank. Finally a sympathetic manager promoted her to the rank of Administrative Officer. At that point she thought, "Well, that's as far as you can go being a woman." However, working conditions at her bank, which had always been friendly, if demanding, deteriorated when a new, relatively young manager was brought in from St. John's. His approach was "tough." He wanted her to "keep everybody on their toes," to meet targets, and he wanted to prevent tellers from "associating with the public." He also seemed bent on getting rid of the existing, relatively well paid regular staff and replacing them with part-time workers to make the operation more efficient. After only eight months, Shirley left. She felt it had become a choice "between my salary or my sanity." She felt bitter and went as far as complaining to the board of the bank, but she was too exhausted and demoralized to go further. She also feared that if she complained to the Human Rights Commission, she would become known as an 'instigator,' and consequently would never get another job, at least not in Grand Falls. Shirley was replaced by a younger, less experienced man, but one prepared to go along with the new manager's ways and to treat the women employees with the "toughness" he demanded.

Shirley subsequently regretted that she didn't fight harder, so it is instructive to learn from the experience of a group of bank workers at the Bank of Commerce branch in Antigonish, Nova Scotia. There, eleven women workers walked out in order to get a pay increase due to them. Despite the difficulties they faced, Baker (1991) found that the experience had not only empowered women and had a positive impact on their perception of themselves and their jobs, but that several of them emerged as leaders and their action won the support of the community.

In Grand Falls there was no such communal action. The situation worsened after

Shirley left. Within eighteen months, fifteen of the original nineteen women on staff had left their jobs because of a deteriorating working environment and stress, and out of solidarity with employees who had quit. It also seemed as if they were being systematically pushed out and replaced with younger, inexperienced women willing to work part-time, although the bank never admitted that this was a policy. The bank was now staffed by employees who were cheaper and more expendable than the experienced, mature women who had once worked as a friendly team. One unfortunate aspect of this affair was the way it pitted women of different ages and status against each other. Several of the older women gave examples of inexperienced but young and obviously pretty women being taken on to do jobs for which they were manifestly unqualified—unless they were actually being hired as sex objects as the older women argued.

In April of 1989, Jane, a competent woman in her early forties, became the sixteenth woman to quit the bank. She had worked in banks for the previous seventeen years. When Jane first left the bank, she was shocked but also angry enough to fight back, if only for the sake of her own sanity. This was the point at which we met. Together we explored ways to lodge a complaint or to start an investigation. The situation was awkward. She had left 'voluntarily' so she had no case for civil damages—nor did she want her job back while the conditions remained as they were. We decided to try to prove sexual discrimination. Jane wrote a long letter to the Head Office of the bank. This was signed by six other ex-employees, including Shirley, the former Administrative Officer. It became a form of collective protest against the harassment these women had experienced. The letter eloquently portrays the situation of these women and their predicament.

"Central Bank"[3], Toronto, Ontario

Dear Sir/Madam,

I have been employed as a bank teller for twenty one years, the last seven with the "Central Bank" in Grand Falls, but on April 6th, I was forced to quit. . . .

Changes at this branch started when Mr "Brown" arrived and staff turnover began almost immediately. For us tellers, however, things really got bad when "Joe Smith" was transferred to this branch as the Chief Administrator. My first encounter with him occurred one afternoon, shortly after his arrival when, after the bank had closed at 3 o'clock, I balanced and went downstairs to the bathroom. When I exited, Mr Smith was waiting for me outside the door and told me that in the future, I was not to leave my post for any reason without first getting his permission. . . .

Since Mr Brown and Mr Smith joined our branch there have been, to my best recollection, sixteen employees who have resigned or just walked out. Doesn't this tell you something? Don't you think that something is wrong? I don't blame Mr Smith completely, although he is a major part of the problem. He is young, inexperienced and struggling to climb to the top by whatever means he thinks is necessary. I believe his approach is terribly wrong, degrading and harmful to all who come under his supervision. I hope, for the sake of Central Bank, that he does not learn his philosophy at management training seminars. I do, however, blame our manager, Mr Brown. He is the one who should realize that something is wrong and take the steps to correct it. A manager should not be there just for the company. He should also be there for his staff, to ensure their rights are met, that they are content and to motivate them to take pride in their work. At this branch, the only motivation is to work like a slave or get out.

In December, I was temporally assigned as head teller. One Monday morning there were in excess of thirty night deposit bags to be deposited when I started work at 9 a.m. Despite this, I was expected to have this completed and my booth open by 10:00 a.m. This was impossible, but despite some sympathy from the manager, I was still reprimanded. In February, after returning from lunch at 1 p.m., the day was very busy, and I had customers steadily up to 4:30 p.m. At that time I needed desperately to go to the bathroom. I put up my 'Next Teller' sign to go. However before I could leave, Mr Smith was over and said I could not go while there were customers in the bank. I remained for another five minutes. However, the call of mother nature was too great and I just had to put up my sign and go. Despite the fact that I was only gone a few minutes, I was called aside by Mr Smith, reprimanded, and told that if I couldn't stand on my feet for a seven and a half hour day without a break or going to the bathroom, I couldn't do my job. Although I did not know it at the time, I was a month and a half pregnant, pregnant for the first time after fifteen years of marriage. Unfortunately, a few weeks later, I had a miscarriage. I'm not saying this incident had any effect on my pregnancy, but possibly it was the reason I had to go to the bathroom so badly.

On April 5th, I had just returned to work and was downstairs in the break room talking to one of the new part-time tellers. We were talking about how hard it was to have an eleven o'clock dinner hour and having such a long afternoon to put in when one of the loan managers walked into the room. We immediately stopped our conversation and went upstairs. The next day I was called into Mr Brown's office as soon as I arrived at work in the morning. He told me that what he was about to say was very unpleasant. It had come to his attention that I was telling the new girl how bad it was to work in this bank. I asked if I was fired and he said "No," but that he would investigate further and if the allegations were true, then I would definitely be fired. I started to defend myself and he abruptly cut me off. I am not sure of his exact words because I was almost in shock but, it was something to the effect that "another word out of you and I won't be responsible for the action I take."

I certainly could not stay with a threat hanging over me like this. I decided it would be in my best interest and probably, safety, to put my keys on my desk and leave, which needless to say, I promptly did. I am writing this letter for several reasons. I want to let you know of conditions at the bank, although you should suspect something because of the high turn-over. All the others, both those who have quit and some still working at the bank, keep saying that something should be done to stop this man, and most importantly to clear my name; to stop this man from ruining my future plans of employment by his lies and deceit.

I trust this letter will not fall on deaf ears.

Yours sincerely,

signed by Jane, Susan, Elizabeth, Glenys and Cindy

Jane eventually received a polite, half-page response from the bank. Young Mr. Smith quit his job during the next summer. Manager Brown was eventually transferred to a different line of work at the bank.

This paper has looked at two groups of Grand Falls women workers. They exemplify some of the problems that women face when they enter the labour market. For women do not enter the same labour market as men do; nor do they do so on the same basis; nor do they encounter the same conditions when they get there. In Grand Falls, as elsewhere, married women define themselves primarily in terms of their location in the family. First and foremost, they are wives and mothers, and their chief responsibility is to the family unit This is significantly different from the male responsibility to do well for himself in his career, which will, in turn, benefit his family.

Women arrive in the labour market already disadvantaged by their own and their employer's definition of them. They enter the traditional, low paid, dead end jobs, reserved for women—a mischief compounded by everyone's definition of their job as 'secondary.'

There are many ways in which the women of Grand Falls are the envy of many outport women, many of whom have expressed a longing for the urban delights of consumer goods and the clean, dry jobs of bank tellers, nursing aids and so on. But, in many ways, the experience of Grand Falls women workers exemplifies the traps that might await such women if or when their own communities are transformed into the same kind of economic and social entity as Grand Falls.

1   The study was funded by SSHRC, in the Strategic Grants Programme on Women and Work, and directed by Dr. Marilyn Porter, Department of Sociology, Memorial University.

2   Various elements of the study were carried out in all three communities. A researcher lived in each community for a period of time. The material in this paper is taken from the Grand Falls study. Most of it is based on ethnographic observations and interviews, but some is drawn from survey material.

3   The name of the bank, and all personal names in this letter and in the rest of this article are pseudonyms.

Women in an Uncertain Age: Crisis and Change In A Newfoundland Community

Dona Davis

This article was written after the author returned to a South Coast community following a twelve-year absence.[1]

Today, to an extent unprecedented in the past, rural women who live in communities which have traditionally been fishery-based are facing new and multiple challenges. These include challenges to livelihood, family and community organization, as well as threats to the very continued physical existence of progressively marginalized communities. The purpose of this paper is to describe how these challenges can affect different women in different communities in different life situations and at different stages of the life cycle in different ways.

The challenges individually and collectively faced today are the result of the current North Atlantic fisheries crisis. Provincial and National attempts to streamline the fishery have resulted in the ascendancy of capital intensive multi-national corporations. High tech fisheries have undermined the potential for competitiveness among the smaller scale fishers. Overfishing, pollution, faulty estimates of fish stocks, a national recession and an emphasis on the development of offshore oil as the key to the economic future, have all combined to jeopardize fishers and their communities. Plant closures, the support of one fishery at the expense of another, and governmental unwillingness to support peoples in non-productive communities have secured the economic viability of some communities and left others fighting for survival.

It is against this background that I present the following account of women in a community which inhabitants fear has become expendable in the overall design for the future development of Newfoundland's rural, coastal communities. As an ethnographer, I offer some perspectives on the recent past, the present and the future for women in this community. Hopefully the insights I offer can, in part, justify my intrusion in their lives.

Women of a Certain Age

My first experience doing fieldwork in Newfoundland was as a doctoral student in anthropology investigating the possible effects of women's status on their experience of menopause (Davis, 1983). At that time (the late 1970s) the concerns of middle-aged women focused on a single issue—coming to terms with the social changes that had accompanied "The Road," which had recently connected the community to others and replaced the sea as a safer and more dependable conduit of people and materials to and from the village. In everyday use, "The Road" referred to the reality of the end of isolation and the pervasive modernization and dramatic changes which it brought to the community in the 1970s. But "The Road" had also become a metaphor for passing judgments on the comparative merits of traditional versus modern ways of life. As I came to understand it, "The Road" marked a far more important change in the lives of middle-aged women at that time, than had any change of life or individual life cycle transitions.

Throughout my fieldwork, the discourse of blood and nerves, rather than menopause, came to constitute a complex and confusing puzzle worthy of, and begging for, ethnological interpretation. My conversational, interview and observational data on nerves and blood seemed to reveal more about women's status and the life history and life cycle changes they had experienced than did more conventional anthropological or sociometric indices of female status. In my analysis or interpretation I saw these terms—that described the body, bodily processes and characters of women—as complex metaphors for a pride in shared heritage and a strongly felt sense of occupational community as well as powerful mechanisms for social control.

I came to see their "community" as clearly defined, tightly bounded, basically egalitarian, cautiously cooperative and dominated in both its domestic and public (landbound) spheres by women both as individuals and as groups. The soul or expressive essence of the community was derived from the shared heritage of the Newfoundland fishery. As the men adapted to a series of fluctuations in fishing technologies, the women, especially the middle-aged ones, had become the moral adjudicators or key actors in blending the best of the old with the best of the new.

Women in an Uncertain Age

In 1989, I returned for another period of fieldwork in the same village. This time I found myself in the vortex of a storm of change with far more ramifications than the changes wrought by "The Road." "The Fisheries Crisis," more commonly referred to as "The Crisis," now pervaded local discourse. Unlike the case for "The Road," there was no score of years of tradition-laden hindsight against which to work metaphors for the dramatic demise of the inshore fishery. Stoic endurance and passive resistance, once touted as the way to survive bad times, were in the preliminary stages of being superseded by a language of hopelessness and despair. Residents were facing the realities of becoming either a permanent welfare, make-work/UIC community or "reservation" ("like for the Indians"), or a "ghost town." Simply put, there were no fish to be caught by local fishermen. The fishing seasons of 1988-1991 had been a disaster. My abstracted "glue" of high self-esteem and egalitarian moral order, which had once pervaded the community and held it together had dissolved.

By 1989, the community had become delocalized and decentralized and its very geographical survival was in great jeopardy. No longer did community, or family, lie at the base of moral consensus or social order. Today, metaphors of collective and individual identity no longer permeate the discourse of local life. Instead each individual speaks for their own predicaments and strategies for survival in this uncertain age.

During my absence, profound changes had occurred. My reference to the community as delocalized describes the process by which the community has been progressively integrated into the wider popular culture and structural contexts of

280

North America. Cable TV from across Canada and the United States has brought the rest of the world into the households. Soaps (and VCRs to record them) remain a popular pastime, and Wrestlemania has become a new one. The evening news is followed by more households than ever before. People have a more informed recognition of how events which take place in political and economic arenas far from home may have a profound effect on local life.

Community integrity has also been undermined by changes on the local level. The family is no longer a cohesive unit of production and reproduction. A consumer, cash, culture dominates family life, and government payments free individuals from collective family responsibilities. The community no longer binds people in; instead, it pushes them out. The village secondary school has closed, and teens are bused to a nearby town to continue their education. They are taught by highly admired and extremely dedicated teachers who urge them to get their education in order to secure a future outside of their communities. Men and women, to a far greater extent than ever before, migrate in and out of the community to find work. Every year more young people leave for military service, college and trade and technical schools. Vacationers travel to the mainland and organize Christmas shopping expeditions to Bangor, Maine. Many villagers are building summer cabins or second homes in a fog-free valley about 60 miles away, where their houses are interspersed with those of neighbours from other West and Southwest coast communities. These days, people are more likely to choose spouses from outside the community. Elders, who fifteen years ago displayed morbid ideation concerning travel by automobile, now gamely travel by train or car to Toronto and other popular destinations in the United States and Canada to visit children, relatives and tourist sites.

One of the most dramatic changes concerns the internal structure of the community. In the 1970s, I was repeatedly told "we all come up together or we don't come up at all;" now the capstone phrase is "it's everyone out for himself." Today, factions dominate village life. In the fishery alone, there are many sources of conflict between different interest groups, for example, inshore versus offshore fishermen, fish plant labourers versus fishermen, those who continue to fish versus those who in discouragement have given it up, and day shift versus night shift at the fish plant. Fishery conflicts were exacerbated by a vicious fight over union affiliation, past mismanagement of the local plant, and the future status of the plant for which neither buyer nor leaser can be found. The members of the community development committee, tourism development committee, and town council are censured, by locals, as being out for their own interests, nepotistic and ineffectual. All pretence to an egalitarian social order is gone. Successful family members now try to socially and geographically distance themselves from their less successful kin. An internal village stratification system is emerging where teachers (and professionals like nurses and social workers) are on the top, followed down the hierarchy by other government or salaried workers, merchants, fishermen and fish plant labourers, those on UIC, welfare and a tiny group best characterized as hard-core poor. Very clear material demarcations and differences in life styles have come to characterize these strata. As one woman put it:

Today there's some as make you feel inferior. We got uppity-ups here now. They're the ones that are ignorant [rude] for doing it, but just the same there's some houses here I don't feel welcome into. It used to be you could go anywhere, now I know there's places I am not welcome. It used to be we was all the same, now just look at who has the tarred driveways and peach coloured curtains and you'll know who is who around here. My dear, today it's as plain as the nose on your face.

This internal stratification system is overlaid by emergent, non-local, middle, working and welfare class identities. The village also has lost its traditional prominence in relation to the other settlements on the coast. Once the most successful of the community fisheries, it is now one of the least productive on the coast, the one whose future is in greatest jeopardy.

Changes in gender relations also reflect and contribute to the decentralization of local life. Divorce is common as is living together. The number of female-headed households continues to escalate and peripheralizes men from family concerns. Illegitimacy is common and always was, but now it is planned. Children are still highly desired but there is much less pressure to marry. On the controversial make-work projects, women's self-esteem is protected by working hard while men tend to buffer the humiliation of no gainful employment with passive-aggressive resistance. Single and divorced adult men and women have forged new, largely unregulated, and controversial mazeways of sexual expression. Financially strapped women commonly report that, due to the nature of welfare regulations, the decline of the fishery and drinking and consumption patterns of men, they are economically better off without them. Alcohol abuse among adult men and women as well as among pre-teen boys has become an issue of concern. Fights, especially between men who are fighting over women, are not uncommon. The ensuing acts of escalating violence and revenge have become popular topics of gossip.

In the recreational sphere, the church and the women's associations no longer bring people together. The church, for some years, has lacked effective leadership and the once powerful middle-aged women who ran the church, oversaw major rites of passage and directed the more expressive, recreational spheres of collective life, are now viewed as pathetically behind the times—anachronisms of a bygone era. Weddings and showers are no longer community affairs. Even new attempts to bring the village together, such as a week-long winter carnival, can create as much hard feelings and controversy as good times. Ironically, it is young people, those most committed to leaving, who through their nightly socializing or walking the roads, comprise the current core of collective community social life.

This is a harsh portrayal of contemporary life. But it is a picture of crisis drawn by the local people themselves. As we shall see, it is not all negative and a large part of the blame is believed to come from the outside, not from within. Local people attribute negative changes to forces over which they feel they have little control, such as excessive fisheries regulation, bad plant management, and unfair competition between local and non-local fishermen.

How do we portray the world(s) of these current Newfoundland women? Women in this uncertain age no longer talk of "enduring" and of "being bred for toughness"; instead, they speak of "getting out" and of "being trapped."

It is against this background that I update analysis of the relationship between this sample of Newfoundland women and their community. To do so, I draw on data from a questionnaire which I administered to men and women in three age groups (15-25, 35-45, 55-65). I asked women about what they felt had changed most in their community during my absence. I also asked them about what was best and worst about life in the community, about the fishery and Newfoundland in general. Each woman was also asked about the future and about what I would find if I came back in ten years. In addition, I asked what I should say or write about in the next book I planned to write about them.

Although I used specific age grades to select the women I interviewed, I came to realize that age, social status, and personal predicaments are not always in accordance. For example, a woman in her early twenties, who is married with children, finds herself in a much different situation than a woman who is unmarried or divorced at a similar age. In addition, education and employment make a big difference between the ways in which women see themselves in terms of the community. Women can and do, however, shift from one category to another. As I see it, four key themes govern women's outlooks on their current situation. The themes are age-related but not age-exclusive. They are labelled and summarized as follows: 1. the "up-and-outs" or young women completing high school or pursuing post secondary education who feel pushed or pulled out of the community; 2. the "trapped" or more settled, young to middle-aged women with young children who feel trapped in the community; 3. the "satisfied" or middle-aged women, with grown or nearly grown children, who have come to terms with the life choices they have made or who see their most important wants and needs as still being met by the community; and 4. the "pensioners" or elderly women who feel that the times have already passed them by and who are embedded in worlds of meaning that are no longer seen as relevant to contemporary life. Each of these will be considered in turn.

The more you gets; the more you wants.

This phrase may be seen as a condemnation of the consumerism and materialism of the younger generation by the older generation. To the younger generation, however, the phrase suggests actively seizing opportunities. The sentiments expressed below tend to characterize the discourse of young women, 17 to 25, who are finishing high school, attending college or are college-bound. There is more uniformity and consensus in this group than in any of the others.

> Today we young people are exposed to more communication. The more you know, the more you want. Because we have more choices, the younger generation wants more for itself than the older [generation] did.

"Wanting more" entails a disaffection with local life and a concerted effort to prepare yourself for a "future." The term, "a future," is a gloss for leaving the village and often Newfoundland altogether. The following statements illustrate a variety of emotions but a shared sense of direction, best expressed as "up-and-out."

> I'd love to live here, but there is no future for me here. I don't want to leave but I know you have to leave to get anything.

> I've got this boyfriend. He has his grade seven and is a fisherman. He would marry me in a minute, but I've got to have a career and income of my own. I never want to become dependent on a man, never, never, never, in my life. Either he leaves here or I leave him.

Preparation for success means the best education possible, working hard to maximize income-earning talents, and getting out into the wider world. The following statements show that "getting out" is believed to be the key to success. This category of young women reject the world of their parents and community. What they want to become or aspire to, however, is not as clearly articulated as what they do not want to become—welfare recipients, plant workers or women prematurely saddled with marital or family obligations, as they feel their mothers were. Hindsight, rather than foresight, shapes the decision to leave.

> There's no future for me here. College is my ticket out. I will go anywhere the jobs are.

> Maybe the fishing will pick up. Here, it will be fishing or nothing. No other business will come in. I will get my secretarial degree. I'd like to stay nearby, but I doubt that I can. It really won't be that hard to move either. It's nice here, everyone is friendly but we really aren't any different from people anywhere else.

> Mom's generation settled for less. They married early, worked at the plant and played darts. They had a house and a car and did all they could for their kids. They thought they had it made. Now they are stuck here for good. There's no work here. It's too late for them but I'm going to make my life different.

Young women report that they want careers. They dream of becoming professional salaried women. They aspire to a rather narrow range of careers—nurse, social worker, school teacher and secretary (in contrast with young men who want to be engineers, teachers or soldiers). The role models for many of these young women are the new local elites; the first generation of young women to pursue a college education and a career were in college during my first period of fieldwork. A good number of these women came back into the community and are in the few plum positions available to professional women. Many of them married men who were far less educated than themselves, but it is these career women who have set the lifestyle standards that underlie their high social and material standing in the community. Just getting out is not enough; social mobility is what counts. Nor do mobile young women emulate local women who have taken a more traditional route to financial success by becoming local entrepreneurs (general and speciality store owners).

Although the "up-and-outs" feel they must move away for success, the decisions to move are not made without a sense of personal sacrifice. Nor does this category of young women totally reject more traditional values.

There's no future here. Things have got to change. There is nothing here. Young people with their grade 12 who stay here will be getting ten weeks work and living off of UIC back and forth for the rest of their lives. People could leave and lots do, but they give up a lot. Fishing plus people make this community. Take away one and you don't have the other.

When you write your next book tell about the drastic changes that are not for the better. Tell what's happening. The fact is there is nothing here. Tell the cold dark truth. It hurts my heart to know that Mom will never really get to know her own grandchildren. She's looked forward all her life to grandchildren. To her its the best part of having a grown daughter. She'll get her grandchildren but she won't have them [around or near by]. You know what I mean?

These young women, on the verge of adult life, view their own life histories in the village as marked by some positive changes that have facilitated their mobility. The following statements show the more positive aspects of the "more you wants" theme.

Women today, have a lot more work (outside household, paid labour). Some have fishery licenses, some work at the plant, some go to trade school. A lot more opportunities have opened up for women, even here.

Some women find it easier to leave than others. A number of young women, married or in committed relationships, often with small children at home, report a feeling, more overwhelming in some than others, of being trapped. They are in a period of their lives when their dreams and reality are being painfully reassessed. In their mid-twenties to late thirties, these are women for whom the discourse of being trapped can take a number of forms.

There's no help for it; I keep getting this closed in feeling.

This poignant statement encapsulates a sentiment of frustration that characterizes the responses of my second grouping of women—the "trapped." They feel that their life decisions have already (perhaps prematurely) been made, that opportunities have passed them by, and that life circumstances have trapped them, for the time being at least, in the village—a post-fishing, welfare economy which can no longer offer them and their families a viable, meaningful living. This thematic type is derived from the accounts of the young population of married women in their twenties and thirties. They live in houses that they own outright and have young children at home. Many have husbands whom they married during a teenage romance, and whose lack of education severely restricts their opportunities for employment outside the community. Others have husbands who are committed to what they call the "outport" or "country" way of life and have no wish to leave the community. These women see their standard of living declining. They see little opportunity for the future. They commute in groups to take self-improvement courses at a community college, in case they ever have the opportunity to get out. They are envious of their peers who, less tied to family obligations, have sought success by moving away. Also in this group are the young women who have completed their education and have not gotten married or started families. Unable to support themselves, they continue to live with their natal families and find themselves trapped in a form of perpetual childhood, roaming the streets by day and populating the clubs at night.

Being trapped or held back from pursuing more gratifying lifestyles by a lack of education, their own or their husband's, is a commonly expressed theme among this group. It is interesting that a good percentage of these women were casualties of the relocation of the high school. In the mid-1980s, a regional high school was built and local youth were bused to and from it. Mixing with children from other communities, being taught by strangers, being taken so far from home on a daily basis or just the trauma of the bus ride (e.g., peer hazing) itself, were cited as reasons for dropping out of school at grade seven or eight.

> I dropped out at grade 8. You tell me where I'm going to go? There is nothing out there for the likes of me.

> My children will get their education and get out. If my husband could get a job tomorrow you'd find a for sale sign up in our window.

Being trapped by a lack of education is also expressed in a commitment to make sure children are able to capitalize on the education offered to them. Whereas the previous generation left education up to the aptitude and inclination of the individual child, the present generation of young parents take their children's education very seriously. They spend hours helping children tackle homework assignments. If the child's level of learning has passed them by, parents turn to neighbours or relatives or phone all evening to get the correct answers to the homework assignments.

Women also report being trapped in a dependency on unreliable and unsatisfactory employment.

> The worst thing about being stuck living here is that there is no work. I work at the fish plant. I hate the work. I like working with my hands. I'm a cutter and that pays the highest. But I hate the fish plant.

> What do I do for a living? I could tell you I'm a fish plant labourer, but then I'd have told a lie. I haven't even got enough work for stamps the last three years. If I was free you wouldn't even see me leave this place. I'd be going so fast all you could see would be a flash.

Still others report being trapped by marriage and/or family obligations.

> I have my grade 11. I'm good at school. I would like to go to trade school so I could move and have more satisfying work. But, you see, my husband only has

his grade 7. He can hardly read. As a husband and father he is the best kind. He's a hard worker, but what does he have outside of here (fish plant work)? I'm trapped, I can't figure how to get out. All I can do is tell my kids to do well in school so they can get out.

I'm stopped in time and place. I don't like working at the fish plant. But my husband would be at a disadvantage outside of here. Here he has his family and his work skills. He has lots of time for me and the children. He redid the house all by himself. He would be misplaced outside of here. I can't demand that of him.

Unlike the more mobile women, who see positive changes as having occurred in the village (such as the increased flexibility of sex roles) women who fall into this thematic type are more likely to portray changes in the collective essence of the community in negative ways. Less tangible or more esoteric expressions of feeling trapped come from a sense that the community is changing in character and not for the better. Some of the comments in this group are quite bitter.

I'll tell you this and I'm not afraid to have you put it in a book, just like I'm saying it. The people around here have changed. People were friendly, now they are pigs. They are so jealous they would cut your throat for a dollar. They're ignorant [rude]. You keep hearing how people from Newfoundland are so kind. Well, many are not. People here are real jealous of what you have.

I just don't have any best friends. I feel so isolated and alone. Even real close kin won't have nothing to do with their poor relatives. It didn't used to be like that.

This group is also the most likely to report that their sense of esteem has been undermined by their increasing knowledge of the wider world. The incursions of the outside world intimidate and anger them.

I've been away and I know a lot more now. If your not a townie you're low class. If you aren't from a town you're nothing. They consider themselves to be way up there. They dress in different fashions and are ahead of us. They think they are higher class with their noses up in the air. This even if they are on welfare or UIC too.

As seen by their mobile counterparts those who get away have it made and those who stay behind are failures. This is the group that stayed or has been left behind—the group that the "up-and-outs" dismiss as losers.

Others, who have repeatedly tried to get away, report that they are called back by attachments to home and family and traditional values. Their frustration is compounded by their sense that they "had their chance and blew it."

We lived in Halifax, when my husband was in the service. We lived in a 20-story building. We were on the 20th floor. I could look out the window and see everything. It was unnatural. There wasn't anything to do in Halifax. We could walk in a park and shop in a mall. The bar my husband went to wasn't fit for me. There was nothing for us or me to do in Halifax. I should have stuck it out, but I insisted we come home.

The preceding quotes represent the conflicting sense of values and hopelessness of some of the young women I interviewed. It is not necessarily a child, husband or lack of education that keeps one rooted in the community. Products, themselves, of the first generation of small families characterized by intense and emotional parent/child relationships, some young women find themselves trapped in an emotional as well a financial dependency. This 22-year-old woman demonstrates how difficult it can be for some young women to break away, especially from very close ties to one or both parents. This woman not only wants to continue living with her mother, she wants to live her mother's life.

> I know I have to leave home. Mom won't let me stay here forever. She doesn't want to do it but she will have to kick me out. To be honest, I'd rather live in the past than now. If they had toilets everything else would be okay. I wished I was born forty years ago. There were less problems in those days, things were cheaper, there was no town council and people didn't have to have an education. Hard work was all that counted. I often dream of living in the past. It would be so much easier.

It would be easy to overemphasize the maudlin. Not all of the young women with small children feel trapped. There are young women who are forging ahead with new or experimental lifestyles, yet such women comprise a tiny minority. Some, like the educated elite, are experimenting with less permissive styles of childrearing and feel that a rural setting is an ideal place to raise children. They also feel less cut off from the wider world and are secure in the sense that their achievements are recognized. A few village women are married to or about to be married to men who make their living on the transport boats of the Great Lakes. Called "Lakers," these men earn incomes that are large by almost anyone's standards. These young couples are contentedly involved in building large, expensive, well appointed homes, which conspicuously demonstrate their newfound wealth. Other women have sought to increase their enjoyment of country life by adopting elements of what was once the male lifestyle.

> I have a fisherman's license. I like the outdoors life just like a man does. I like hunting and fishing and going down the bay. I like working with my hands. I do carpentry and I'm good with a hammer and saw. I would really like to be in forestry or wildlife preservation. I'd love an outside job like that. I'm not a woman who likes to cook and clean and stay in the house. I'm a tomboy and like the man's life.

> Fishing is hard. It's a hard job, but I've done it and some of the hardship stuff is bullshit. It isn't so hard as they say. [Of] course it don't make no difference if its men or women fishing if there's no fish.

Some women at this life stage are very active in the community, running its Sunday school, dart and recreational clubs, participating on development and other committees, and running local stores. Yet, they feel defeat more keenly than accomplishment. They take on these responsibilities amid a great deal of controversy over their motives for community leadership, and their extensive persuasive and organizational talents, entrepreneurship and emotional fortitude go largely un-recognized. A good portion of their discouragement comes from a sense of being beaten down or defeated and finally burning out.

> You can't get people out like you used to. Everyone just sits at home and bitches. They cut one another's throats. I have tried and tried and tried to make things better here, but they beat you down till you just have to give up. We're going to lose everything we have if we don't pull together and fight, but don't look to me. This soldier has been wounded in too many battles to ever fight again.

Those who feel trapped are uncertain women. They are uncertain about what they want in life and are fearful that life has already passed them by. These are the women of an uncertain age. They are those whose careers and the careers of their families are most drastically affected by the decline of the fishery. They are caught in a world that no longer values them and that they no longer value; yet they have little real opportunity to get out, and little confidence that they have any skills to make life in the community better or more amenable to the futures they want for their own children.

> I've lived here all my life; I couldn't live anywhere else now.

This statement refers to a grouping of middle-aged women with grown children who have lived their lives, made their adjustments and are unwilling to move or uproot. They have come to terms with what they've got. What they perceive as the safety and security of the community holds them there. They are the "satisfieds."

When we talk of women who straddle the modern and more traditional eras we are not necessarily talking about "old" women. Although teenagers feel that "before The Road" was ancient history, their parents, not grandparents, spent their early childhood in this era. Women who are today in their mid-thirties remember what it was like before the modern conveniences and improved communication that came with "The Road". This group, more than any other, reflects a mindset rather than an age. Local people recognize this category and will describe a particular woman as a "traditional woman." These are women who still make bread, keep their houses immaculately clean, are actively involved in extensive kin networks, and are still trying to live the fishing life because they know no other.

This group of "satisfieds," like their younger counterparts, derive financial security from the fact that they own their homes and property. They are married to fishermen rather than plant workers, although they may be or have been plant workers themselves. I wouldn't call them trapped. I'd call them rooted. To them the future is not all that great an issue because the future has, by and large, passed them by.

> I was born here and never wanted to live anywhere else. My roots are here.

> We got no learning, my husband and I, We can't even read signs, how are we going to get about in the city? Even if all our children moved away, we would probably stay here. We have a nice house and it suits our ways.

Yet not all women share these sentiments. This age/life-stage group has its malcontents. Some women fear that once their children are gone, their husbands will drag them even farther into the country. Others fear that there is no future for old people in the village either.

> My husband has ten years of work left. If we stay here what do we have to look forward to? There will be no fishing, no post office, nothing for young people. We can stay in our homes and watch TV like old folks do today, but that's no kind of life.

Others, like their younger counterparts, simply do not like local life.

> The place could burn down for all I care. I have never liked the place. I don't like living here, I don't see why people would like living here.
>
> Getting out has been a lifelong dream, but it's a dream that keeps getting put off until tomorrow and probably always will be.

Interviews with this grouping show that the fishery still plays an important role in their lives and the expression of their identity. I found themes in today's women of 30 or 40 that I found in the 1970s in women 50 and over. Yet, unlike their mothers who adapted to the vagaries of the fisher life, this group is faced with the inevitable demise of the fishery. Many of these women, whose lives have been shaped by the fishery, are still reeling from its decline. Their husbands, some of them the more successful fishermen in the village, seem willing to ride it out until its absolute end. Unlike women of the past, whose discourse of fishing featured timeless, well-worn notions such as worry, suffering and stoic endurance, many of today's fishers' wives talk about fishing in terms of the immediate and wider environmental/economic/political ramifications of the current crisis. They are militantly vocal and cynical.

> The fishing is no longer reliable. It's a hard way of life. Right now they are phasing out. The inshore fishermen can only catch certain species. It used to be that you could catch anything. Fishing and even fishing just for the stamps makes it hard to survive . . . They went and issued so many inshore dragger licenses and then they let any foreigners fish off our waters. Why do they do it? It's only killing us. Something has got to be crooked if you ask me. Why did they sell our plant to the wrong people? The minister of fisheries couldn't tell a cod from a hake. Selling the plant was a political decision made in Ottawa.

Yet the more traditional notions of worry and self-sacrifice are not altogether absent in this group. Whether the fishery succeeds or fails, women have invested their lives in it and it in turn has shaped their lives.

Like the "trapped" grouping, this more "satisfied" grouping want their children to be educated. The achievements of their children are an important aspect of their own measures of success. Yet, their attitudes towards the younger generations are also ambiguous. A recurrent theme of this age group is a condemnation of the next generation.

When I was young, we didn't have half enough. Today children get too much. They want more than we ever had. We are no worse off for it though.

When we were young we took no for an answer. They don't.

Today they want $200.00 stereos not just fruit for Christmas. Today I buy a bag of fruit and it rots in the fridge. The apple or orange we got for Christmas meant the world to us.

Like those who feel trapped, this more satisfied grouping actively and energetically contributes to the community. Yet like their younger counterparts, their contributions go largely unrecognized. The following quote from a man in his mid-thirties who compares his mother and wife illustrates this point.

My old woman was man and woman together. My father was always away fishing. We don't have the same work today. Women worked real hard then and so did children. My wife and kids wouldn't do that today.

This wife was an extremely industrious woman. She was raising three kids, regularly took in up to six boarders, and was active on one of the local development committees. She was a skilled seamstress, who made elaborate garments and altered store-bought clothes for others. Moreover, she took self-improvement courses, bartered for a new family car and bottled her husband's meals in advance so that he would have a month's supply of home-cooked meals when he was away at trade school. But unlike the mother, her contributions go unrecognized. Her hard work and accomplishments are taken for granted by her husband and children. Women in this age group, although satisfied with local life, do not receive the recognition of their contributions that the more proficient, self-heroizing women of the same age and life stage received only 15 years ago.

The discourse of today's satisfieds reflects the practical economic and political contingencies of the real world they live in and the challenges for survival of the fisheries around which they have built most of their lives. The life choices that provided a degree of certainty for the satisfied grouping were early marriage, a family, home, "dependable" jobs at the fish plant and commitment to place. Yet these choices are rejected by their own daughters, who search for security and certainty elsewhere. Today, the satisfieds offer themselves as negative lessons in life to their children, for example, "I chose to stay here and look what has happened to me." "If you don't get an education this can happen to you too."

Here we turn to the current status of the cohort of women who, during my first period of fieldwork, had so successfully drawn upon local lore and fishery traditions to maintain a positive impression of themselves and the worth of their contribution to the community. Today, the blood and nerves crowd of the 1970s are in the eldest age grouping—the "pensioners." As is the case for the other groupings, the dilemmas faced by this group are complex and tied to the contemporary fisheries crisis.

Oh! Me nerves!

One of the first things that my friends did when I returned to the field was to show me mugs and T-shirts (designed for the tourist trade) emblazoned with bold letters stating "Oh! Me nerves!" At first I shared in the humour and even felt a little vindicated that others could recognize the importance of nerves as a local idiom. I did wonder at the phrasing. My English/Anglican informants had always said "My nerves..., never "me" and never "oh." I figured the particular phrase, "Oh me nerves", probably originated on Newfoundland's more Irish east coast. Yet, in 1989, "Oh! Me nerves!" had become a common expression in all but the oldest age groups.

Unlike the serious intents that could underlie nerve talk among my middle age informants in the 1970s, the new phrase was regarded as a joke—a statement made with a wink or a smile. Today's teens show a contempt for the older generations that I did not notice 15 years ago, as the following statement from a woman in her late teens illustrates.

> The generation gap around here is unreal. They just don't understand us. I get sick to death of hearing all the talk about the old times and what tough old birds they were. If they were all that special, what do they have to show for it?

It could be said that the trivialization of nerves reflects the trivialization of the life experiences of today's pensioner women. In the 1970s, the recentness of the "past" had made the experiences of middle- and old-aged women more relevant to the largely shared experiences of other generations. World views were insular and localism predominated. Middle-aged women at that time had bridged two eras and had set the moral tone for others in the community. The shared occupation of fishing continued to unite generations. Now horizons have expanded. Two generations have grown up in a modern world of mass communication. Fishing no longer binds people together.

Today's pensioners are doubly women of a certain age. They are "old" and they are viewed as survivors or as anachronisms of a largely bygone era. They are appreciated for their contributions to a world that no longer exists. As an older woman told me, "our days were better, younger people respected older people." "Our days" refers to a bygone era—not long gone, because it was the topic of my first book. During that time it was their days indeed. They were the arbiters of the local moral order. They were important enforcers of an egalitarian social order that no longer exists. Their community of judgment no longer solidifies middle- to old-aged women as a group. Among them you will still find the values of traditional family, hard work and stoic endurance.

> When we were growing up we didn't have so much. When I was 16 I worked a full day at the plant and then came home and cleaned old people's houses for them. I didn't expect any money for it either. We had to carry coal too.
>   When they had the scarlet fever epidemic around here years ago, my mother used to go tend and help those who were sick. She knew she risked the danger of

carrying the infection to her own family but she would not leave suffering people unattended.

In hindsight, they have not lost the well articulated discourse of the hardness of their lives. Their life histories seem, ironically, to centre around having had nothing and having had it all. This duality refers to a comparative sense of relief that they lived their productive years during the time of a viable fishery. They feel they have earned the financial security of their pensions through a lifetime of hard work. They are content with the times as well as the timing of their lives. This is a nice time to be old. No pensioner wished to go back to the former age.

> My dear, I grew up in a little place so I appreciate all the services we have here today. I can walk to the stores, the post office and the clinic. We had next to nothing in the old days. Now we've got everything. I wouldn't want to be young these days but it is a good time to be old.

But unlike in the 1970s, these women may feel that their values will no longer serve the best interest of the younger generations. They are regarded as having little relevance or little to contribute to contemporary life. Yet, it would be misleading to say that these older women have been pushed aside. If they have been peripheralized by changing structures of the community, they have also actively withdrawn from or peripheralized themselves from its current concerns. Like the younger groups, the pensioners no longer see the fishery as viable. In their own way they have become somewhat smug about their own financial security and about the fishery always having been an option during their productive lifetimes, despite its up and downs. I had anticipated that the older villagers would blame the decline of the fishery on laziness, rampant materialism and/or the softness of the younger generations; however (with very few exceptions), they did not.

> My son is a good boy and a hard worker. He's got 8 stamps from fishing. He's got to get two more in the next week. He won't get them and he won't get on no project either. That is really sad. We had hard times but we always had our pride and our work. Where's his self-respect supposed to come from these days?

They do not judge the unemployed young men so much as pity them. The old today are as hopeless about current conditions as the young, and feel that nothing in their past has prepared them for the extent of today's crisis.

> They weren't born drunks you know. There's no fish and it's all because of the government now. My dear, I've watched them leave the harbour [go out to sea] for over 70 years. But it's gone now. It's been kilt dead and won't ever come back. It's really frightening. We might have had the merchants to contend with, but this is entirely different.

The valuation of the old has changed. Those left in the village do not like to be thought of as "old." They fail to support senior citizen's organizations or attend activities traditionally organized around the old. For example, the church used to be a major focus of elderly women, but due to a lack of ministers, these women are now less involved. Also the voluntary organizations of today require literacy skills that this generation often lacks.

The very diversification described in this paper has undercut the control of the aged. Everyone is searching for different agendas, even the old. The "nerves" generation held the stage in the local drama of collective life in the 1970s. They, like others in the community, have different interests today.

Conclusion: Community and Commitment

In summary, the different groupings of women, [2] I have just described, represent different levels of commitment to the local community. The "up-and-outs" are committed to making a new life for themselves, to pursuing professional careers, or to finding jobs with more lifetime security than is currently offered by the local fishery. Many of the "pensioners" are also moving out in order to be closer to medical service centres and to live in the new houses they have built over the years in fog-free valley. These pensioners have a sense of being entitled to a retirement from community responsibilities. Those pensioners who decide to stay cite what they perceive as the relative safety of the community as their primary reason for staying. It is the "trapped" and the "satisfieds" who, more than the other groups, show a continued commitment to the community. The commitment of the trapped is a reluctant one, while that of the satisfieds is more positive. Both of these groups are active in the day-to-day maintenance of community life. But both groups fear that they are riding the tail-end of an era. They both actively encourage and force their children to leave. Their continued commitment to community, at present, seems to take the form of refusing to move in the face of government policies which make it more and more difficult to live in an increasingly marginalized social and economic setting. This refusal to move should not be confused with the endurance of adversity or stoicism of the traditional past. Instead, it is a passive-aggressive strategy of community survival, as one pensioner told me, "they [government] resettled us once and we lost everything, we won't let it happen again."

As I mentioned at the beginning of the paper, I had found writing about the Newfoundland women I had met during my first period of fieldwork to be a very pleasant experience. On the local scene, my book, *Blood and Nerves*, got mixed reviews. Some people thought it was a fair portrayal. Others did not. Writing about this community in the 1990's is not a very positive experience for me, but my dilemmas are minuscule compared to the challenges which confront my respected friends and informants, who find themselves in a community ridden with conflict and on the verge of economic collapse. I realize that what I have written and my characterizations of the various coping styles of the "up-and-outs," "trapped," "satisfieds" and "pensioners" will be controversial. In so doing I have taken the lead from my own informants who are less and less inclined to shirk controversy in their own lives. When asking what I should write in my next book on the community, I was told over and over again to "tell the bad as well as the good," "everyone knows the good stuff about Newfs: what we need is a frank discussion of our problems like drugs, alcoholism and broken families," "let them [outsiders] know what they've done to us and that it isn't pretty" and "be honest." I hope I have met this challenge: time will tell.

1   Acknowledgements: The original period of research was funded by the National Institutes for Maternal and Child Health in a grant administered by the University of North Carolina at Chapel Hill Population Center. The 1989-1990 research period was funded by a Canadian Embassy Faculty Research Grant, a University of South Dakota Research Institute Grant, and a Memorial University of Newfoundland Institute of Social and Economic Research Fellowship.

2   I am currently working on a similar characterization of the responses of men to my interview questions. They are considerably different from those of women.

Doin' Time on the Protest Line: Women's Political Culture, Politics and Collective Action in Outport Newfoundland

Barbara Neis

This paper was originally published in A Question of Survival *ed. P. Sinclair, 1988*

Introduction

Feminist research on women and politics has not only documented the hidden history of women's political action; it has also gone on to explode traditional notions of politics and power, which are inherently male-biased in that they exclude women's activities and struggles from study. Definitions of politics and power are too often limited to formal political mechanisms and institutions such as elections, parties and government policies. However, as feminists have argued, those aspects of our lives that are socially defined as personal are also political.

This revised understanding of politics has been reflected in recent research on women in Newfoundland. It has been argued, for example, that despite continued male dominance of formal positions of political power, women in Newfoundland "have achieved a piece of subversion that should not go uncelebrated; but more than that, the latent power of the organized rural women of Newfoundland is, as yet, unrealized" (Porter, 1985b: 89). Women in rural Newfoundland have created and sustain a network of women's organizations. Within these organizations they pursue goals and engage in activities that are both cultural and political, thereby generating a women's political culture. In contrast, working-class males and male petty commodity producers are often trapped in inappropriate political institutions (Porter, 1985b:87). However, the power of women's political culture is, to some extent, latent in that the organizational strength and ideological understanding evident in these organizations could be directed towards a range of goals and issues that tend not to be the focus of women's collective struggle.

This paper explores what can happen when the untapped potential of this political culture is released in a new context. It begins with a theoretical examination of some of the problems that plant shutdowns in North America today generate for organized labour. It then goes on to examine the strategic role women can play in struggles to prevent plant shutdowns, focusing in particular on single enterprise towns. Following this theoretical introduction, the paper analyses women's participation in one community's fight to prevent the closure of its local fish plant. This analysis documents women's participation at one level of that struggle and attempts to explain the factors that shaped that participation and allowed it to take place. Particular emphasis is placed on the way in which women's political culture and organizational networks within the community influenced their involvement in the fight.

296

Opposition to Plant Shutdowns: Women's Strategic Potential

The rate of plant closures in North America and elsewhere during the late 1970s and early 1980s reached a level unprecedented in the postwar period. Not surprisingly, sociologists and others have demonstrated growing interest in this wave of closures. The rapidly expanding body of literature which has emerged concentrates primarily on the social impact of shutdowns, but, to date, relatively little research has been conducted on efforts to prevent planned shutdowns from occurring (see, for example, Bluestone and Harrison, 1982; Feltham, 1968; Slote, 1969; and Stern, 1971). The apparent lack of interest in resistance among researchers in this area can be attributed to the infrequency with which sustained opposition has emerged. Indeed, one of the most striking features of plant closures in North America has been the fact that, despite the devastating social and economic consequences they can involve for workers and communities, the vast majority go ahead, as planned, with relatively little opposition. The lack of resistance can, in turn, be attributed in part to the legal and political constraints that confront organized labour in North America.

In a very real sense, organized labour's opposition to plant closures is a struggle on new terrain. Furthermore, this is a struggle for which the agreements negotiated between unions and employers, and between unions and the welfare state during the post World War II period provide poor support. In the case of union-management relations, the "managerial prerogative clause," which is typical of most union contracts, explicitly allots control over investment decisions to management and keeps them outside the sphere of negotiations. Legal constraints on strike activity further limit organized labour's ability to fight such decisions at the level of the shop floor. Few companies are foolish enough to announce and/or carry out shutdowns when workers are in a legal position to strike, and although wildcat strikes do occur, they are always difficult to sustain.

Welfare state policies further contribute to the forces inhibiting sustained resistance on the part of the workers affected by a shutdown, because striking workers are not entitled to unemployment insurance or welfare benefits. The disincentive to strike activity which this ruling creates is further augmented, in the context of plant closures, by the possibility of low incomes for the duration of the strike and permanent job loss.

Despite these structural barriers to resistance, there have been several cases where closures have been opposed, sometimes successfully. On some occasions, such as the case of the pulp and paper mill in Temiscaming, Quebec, this opposition has taken the form of an employee takeover. It is significant that, where organized, sustained resistance to plant closures has occurred, it has relied not only on the efforts of affected workers and unions, but to a substantial extent on those of other members of the community (Metzgar, 1980). This resistance has also tended to arise in single enterprise towns where plant closures are a threat to the workers, their families and to the entire community. Even if the community survives, a shutdown will transform its complexion, and frequently workers must find both a new job and a new home. In this context, there is a fairly high potential for cross-class alliances and for the recruitment of local political and religious leaders into efforts to oppose the shutdown.

By themselves, these community leaders can appeal to politicians and other influential people in an attempt to prevent the closure from going ahead. They can also organize demonstrations and various other media events. However, so long as the workers continue to go to work and the dismantling of the plant is allowed to go ahead as planned, these strategies will have limited effectiveness. Direct interference with production and the process of plant closure places pressure both on the company and on the government to respond to the community's demands. It also increases the likelihood of media attention. If such interference is to be sustained, the equivalent of the picket line is required. The so-called "protest-line" which has been used in organized opposition to plant shutdowns in some communities in Newfoundland provides this equivalent.

Protest lines are organized by members of the community who are not employees of the company that is shutting down. As in a strike, they set up a line across the gates to the plant. The purpose of the protest line, however, is not to keep out scab labour, but to provide employees with a legitimate excuse for not returning to work. Because they are not on strike, workers who refuse to cross a protest line can still qualify for unemployment insurance. Thus a protest line serves to disrupt the company, while preventing employees from having to turn to welfare.

Protest lines cannot be openly organized by unions and do not involve the workers themselves. It is thus interesting to explore how they come to be organized and who participates in them. In the context of single enterprise towns, possible participants in protest lines include all who are not directly employed in the plant: senior citizens, those employed elsewhere in the community, local politicians and other leaders, and family members of plant employees. Perhaps, ironically, the largest single group of individuals who are in a position to take over the protest line are the female relatives of plant workers. Precisely because of their historical exclusion from the labour force in most industries associated with single enterprise towns, it is this group whose participation is least constrained by welfare state and industrial regulations despite their direct material interest in the outcome of the planned shutdown.[1] Like the women in coal mining towns in Britain who played a crucial role in the recent miners' strike, these women "have remained caught in a time-warp of male breadwinner and dependent family...They and their children are dependent on the male wage, and if that fails, from separation, death or industrial conflict, their only recourse is the welfare state" (Rose, 1985: 25).

Women played an important and multifaceted role in the British miner's strike. They created an alternative welfare system in the form of soup kitchens and children's parties and participated in attempts to stop the use of scab labour. Women's involvement was a crucial ingredient in that strike as well as in others, including those in Sudbury and Sydney, Nova Scotia. Less visible to the state and less subject to legal constraints than the workers, women are a more difficult target for state intervention and a more likely focus of media attention than the workers themselves, a reality they may consciously exploit.[2]

Working-class actions that make strategic use of intervention by non-strikers are not new. Sympathy walkouts, demonstrations and mass picketing are old strategies based on the same basic premise. Unlike these other strategies, however, the protest line involves prolonged participation by a group that is not formally organized, that is, working-class women in the community. Significantly, while women's interests could, in principle, lead to their intervention in most contexts by forming a protest line, this has been an infrequent occurrence. Collective action of this kind requires more than objective interest because power, based on organizations, consciousness, solidarity and resources, is also necessary. In the case of women who are minimally involved in the labour force, primarily in the non-unionized clerical sector and in part-time work, these elements of power are not generated primarily in the workplace. They must be found elsewhere. An examination of the socio-cultural roots of women's political culture and collective action in Burin suggests that this power originated primarily in those women's organizations commonly defined as "expressive" and hence, by definition, "nonpolitical."

The Context of the Burin Protest

During the winters of 1982 and 1983, a wave of fish plant closures swept round Newfoundland. These closures were precipitated by the same economic crisis that led the federal government to establish the Task Force on Atlantic Fisheries, chaired by Michael Kirby, in 1982. While the government was studying, yet again, the problem of the Atlantic fishery, the threatened bankruptcy of the three major fish companies in Newfoundland resulted in plant closures and months of uncertainty and hardship in deep-sea fishing communities.

Responses to the shutdown of fish plants in such places as Ramea, Fermeuse, Grand Bank, Harbour Breton, Gaultois and Burin varied from community to community. In some cases, members of the community relied heavily on local leaders' appeals to MPs and MHAs to lobby on their behalf in Ottawa and St. John's. In other communities, collective strategies for blocking the closures were tried. The town of Burin on Newfoundland's south coast was one of the communities where local opposition was multi-faceted, collective and sustained. There are many aspects of the Burin protest that make it an interesting case but only one, women's involvement, is dealt with here.[3] The following discussion provides a brief history of the community of Burin and analysis of its structure. It then documents the events associated with the Burin protest and the character and roots of women's participation in that protest.

The Community

Like many other communities on the Burin Peninsula, the history of the town of Burin is dominated by its association with the fishing industry. Despite substantial dependence on the fishery, Burin has become a single enterprise town only in the past 20 to 30 years. In 1943, Fishery Products Ltd. built a small fish plant in the community. The plant co-existed for some time, however, with local merchants involved in the saltfish trade. Today, the decline of the saltfish trade is reflected in the old and empty stores of some members of this merchant class. A relatively complex fishing industry with a range of businesses has been replaced by an industry with only one major employer, Fishery Products Ltd., and a new class of small store owners who are involved in retail sales but not directly in the fishery. In 1983, the fish plant in Burin was serviced by its own fleet of trawlers, both primary and secondary processing were carried out, and there was a trawler refit branch responsible for all of the trawlers in the company's fleet. There were 500 to 600 employees, of whom over 75 percent were male.

The single-enterprise complexion of Burin has increased further over the past several years as a result of the ascendancy of Marystown, which has become the centre for employment, administration and retail trade in the area. Indeed, prior to the announced closure, some Burin residents worked in Marystown. As is often the case in older single-enterprise towns (see Lucas, 1971), the Burin plant had been unable to absorb the new generations of workers and/or the wives of plant workers who, in response to the same pressures confronting working class families elsewhere, desired to enter the labour force. At this time, there was widespread unemployment among women in the area. Most of the women interviewed desired a job, but many had been unable to find one. According to the 1981 census, labour force participation rates among women were low in Burin and in the nearby communities of Port au Bras and Fox Cove-Mortier, ranging between 18 and 34 percent. Among these women, unemployment ranged as high as 60 percent. Those who had jobs either worked in the plant or were employed in local service industries (such as restaurants, lounges, stores and the hospital), or the schools. Some worked in Marystown.

The Closure

Fishery Products' announcement of its intention to close the local plant and consolidate its processing operations in Marystown, roughly eleven miles away, came as a shock to local people. In its August, 1982 Newsletter, the company had maintained that the fish plant in Burin was "its most productive plant" and that this fact alone ensured "the continuity of operations" there. The announced closure came in November, only three months later. February 26, 1983, was the date set to complete the dismantling of the plant and consolidate processing in Marystown.

The Burin Action Committee was set up almost immediately in response to this announcement.[4] The committee began its struggle to reverse the decision to close the plant by appealing to the company and to government. They soon decided, however, that if these appeals were to have any effect, they must be backed up by organized collective action at the community level. Following the example of nearby Grand Bank, which had faced a similar threat the previous year, the committee decided to set up a protest line across the gates to the Burin plant. The protest line was intended to prevent trawlermen, returning to work following the Christmas layoff, from sailing in any of the nine trawlers that were tied to the wharf. It was also intended to stop the dismantling of the fish plant, which the company planned to carry out over the next two months, and to serve as a source of media attention. The trawlers and the contents of the plant, including 700,000 pounds of frozen processed fish, were held by the Burin Action Committee as collateral in the committee's confrontation with the company and the provincial and federal governments.

Trawlermen respected the protest line, went home and applied for unemployment insurance. Plant workers soon followed. Both groups were able to draw unemployment insurance so long as they did not participate in the protest line. This helped them endure months of deliberation by the company and the governments. The economic support provided by unemployment insurance also helped ensure that plant workers would be less likely to undermine the protest by applying for the limited number of jobs Fishery Products was offering in Marystown.

The date scheduled for dismantling the plant came and went. In February, the Task Force on Atlantic Fisheries Report, *Navigating Troubled Waters*, was finally released. Despite vague references to "excess plant capacity," and to the need to consolidate to ensure the "economic viability" of the industry, the report did not address the issue of which plants in Newfoundland would be kept open and which would be closed in order to achieve these goals. Having already endured several months of uncertainty, people, in what came to be called the "endangered" communities, were being asked to wait still longer.

The final agreement on the restructuring of the Newfoundland fishery was not signed until September, 1983. By that time a growing number of Burin plant workers had taken jobs in Marystown, the trawlermen had returned to work, the frozen processed fish stored in the plant and held by the Burin Action Committee had been released, and the protest line, a fixture in front of the plant gates for six months, had disappeared.

Doin' Time on the Protest Line: The Creation of a Female Institution[5]

The first individuals on the protest line were members of the Burin Action Committee. An appeal to the rest of the townspeople to support them brought out many others, both men and women. During the initial few days, protesters came when they could and stayed as long as they felt was possible. Because of their responsibility for work in the home and child care, women found this arrangement difficult. Many complained that they could not get their work done, and others noted that there were problems with an unorganized protest line in that, during the day, the only time the trawlers were permitted to sail, there were few people on the protest line than in the evening and at night. Also, there was a general sense that the protest had the support them would give advance warning if any attempt was made to pressure trawlermen into returning to work.

A shift system gradually began to develop, but for the most part members of different sections of the community found they were coming at the same time every day. This was also problematic. As one woman pointed out, women with young children did not always want to be on a shift from 12:00 pm to 4:00 pm when their children were awake and active. All of these factors contributed to a decision by a few women to approach the Burin Action Committee with an offer to establish a rotating shift system for the protest line. The Committee agreed, but pointed out that they expected the women who had come forward to organize the shifts and take responsibility for them. These women took the list of names of individuals who had agreed to participate in the protest line and organized several teams from different parts of the community. They approached twelve people in different areas and asked them to become team captains. Four of the team captains came from Burin Bay, a section of the community consisting almost entirely of plant workers' families and inshore fishers. Eleven of the twelve were women. Members of each team were required to spend four hours out of every 48 on the protest line, and the shifts rotated. A schedule covering several weeks was drawn up and posted in the Masonic Lodge where protesters could see it during their breaks.

The reorganization of protesters was followed by the introduction of a few basic amenities on the line. Protesters and their supporters brought a baseball dugout, which they walled in and equipped with a barrel stove. Men brought supplies of wood and someone donated a kerosene lamp and an electric light which could be hooked up to a car motor. The Masonic Lodge was left open so that protesters could go there during the lunch break and have access to a phone. It was understood that if anything actually happened at the plant gates, protesters would have quick support. This support would be recruited through a system of chain telephone calls in which, one woman maintained, three initial calls could bring one thousand people onto the line.

This reorganization of the protest line had the effect of producing a structure that could be expected to endure, and it transformed the line into a female institution organized and maintained by women. If we wish to understand this transformation and the substantial success of the protest line, which was maintained twenty-four hours a day, seven days a week, for nearly six months, it is necessary to study the wider context out of which it emerged.

The remainder of the paper examines two basic problems: (1) why the protest line became a female institution; and (2) the social and cultural roots of women's protest in the community of Burin. With regard to the first problem, it is important to note that although the protest line became a fundamentally female institution, some men did participate. For example, a few male members of the Burin Action Committee dropped by periodically and spent time on various shifts. One retired man came regularly with one of the shifts and a couple of men were regulars on the midnight to four in the morning shift. A couple of younger men came on the eight to twelve shift in the evening but were not attached to any particular group, and the night watchman at the plant spent brief periods on the line when he was coming off and on duty. Significantly, those men who participated in the protest line were there only to help out. They provided support services: helping to keep the fire going, cleaning the lamp, getting more kerosene. They were helpers, but it was the women who were in control.

The gendered character of the protest line had its roots in the social organization of the community. The few existing studies of women in rural Newfoundland emphasize the sex-segregated nature of these communities. For example, sex-segregation is evident in the rigid sexual division of labour that exists within the fishery with only men involved in harvesting the catch. It can also be found, to a significant but somewhat lesser extent, in fish plants and in the home. At the community level, women and men tend to participate in their own segregated organizations (Porter, 1985b; Davis, 1983).

Burin is not an exception in this sense. In the context of work, draggermen and inshore fishers are all male, as are those who work on trawler refit onshore. Prior to the shutting down of the fish plant, workers were divided along gender lines with men responsible for cutting and maintenance, and women working as packers and on the cooking line. Outside the fishery, in local service industries such as the hospital, work is also sex-segregated.

At the the community level, there is a similar pattern. Formal politics has long been the preserve of men within Burin itself, although there is now a woman on the town council and there are several women on community councils in the surrounding area. Women participate in a dense network of voluntary associations including the Red Cross, church groups, dart leagues and softball leagues. Similarly, men have their own organizations which include soccer, softball and dart leagues, as well as the Kinsmen, the Society for United Fishermen and the Voluntary Fire Brigade. These last three organizations have women's sections which are separately organized but affiliated with them. There are also a few mixed-gender organizations including mixed darts leagues, the union local at the fish plant, and a very active senior citizens' club.

This cultural context of sexual segregation in work and in the community no doubt played a role in shaping the gendered character of the protest line. For example, women in Burin, as elsewhere in rural Newfoundland, enjoy spending time together and customarily engage in a range of activities. In Burin, this camaraderie and these activities were transplanted onto the protest line where they were essential ingredients in shaping that institution and ensuring its survival. Significantly, on those occasions when men came around, in particular men who did not regularly spend time on the protest line, this atmosphere and the associated activities were disrupted. Lone men were often the butt of sexual and other jokes and when groups of men came by, their visits were brief and conversation confined to questions and answers. On one occasion I observed a group of men enter the shack. After a very brief visit characterized by awkwardness and silence, they set off marching in unison with their arms linked. The women stood on the road watching and doing a parody of their walk.

In a community with a tradition of sex-segregation, such as exists in Burin, it seems unlikely that a mixed-gender institution would have persisted in a context like the protest line where groups were small and people spent hours together inside or outside the shack. It would have been too awkward. The protest line had to be either male or female. The majority of plant workers and trawlermen were male and they could not go on the protest line. Older men and younger men not associated directly with the plant were not organized to the same extent as some of the wives, girlfriends and mothers of plant workers, draggermen and their friends. Each of these factors played a role in shaping the dominant gender and culture of the protest line. However, in themselves, they do not fully explain the ability of the women to organize and maintain the protest line for almost six months. A search for the roots of women's power takes us back to the community and to the connection between the organization of the protest line and the "latent power of women's organizations and political culture" in families and in the community.

Those women involved in the protest line were wives, sisters, mothers, sisters-in-law and girlfriends of plant workers, trawlermen and local store owners. Kinship and marital ties were an important factor in the recruitment of women onto the protest line. Recruitment was not, however, related simply to ties to males, but also, perhaps even more crucially, to kinship and/or friendship ties to other women. Despite the industrial character of Burin, kinship ties are still extensively maintained and the extended family represents for many people the most important institution, followed by community. There is a widespread understanding that individuals have certain responsibilities of their "own." For women, your "own" is defined in a variety of ways depending on the context, but it generally includes members of their own and their husband's family including parents, brothers and sisters, and their children.

The women on the protest line were there partly because of the obligation they felt to "their own" to help protect their jobs and their community. But there were other reasons for standing on the protest line. As is evident from Olive Hiscock's song "Doin' Time on the Protest Line," women had no difficulty recognizing their objective interest in keeping the plant open. At a time when married women were finding it difficult to manage on one salary, the absence of a fish plant meant hard times, poor food and extra work in the home, as well as less likelihood of finding work in the future. Several of the women on the protest line pointed out that they hoped to get a job in the plant one day.[6] One maintained that when the plant reopened she would go and sit on the steps until they gave her a job. She believed that having participated in the protest, she had a right to one. Women also understood that the shutdown meant their teenage children would no longer be able to find summer work and, as the song suggests, women shared the pride of local workers in the quality of fish produced in the community.

The company argued that the protesters in Burin were objecting to no more than "an eleven-mile drive down the road," a claim that angered women on the protest line. They knew the decision would mean an immediate loss of several hundred jobs and a long-term decline in employment opportunities for themselves and their relatives. But there would be other negative consequences as well. For example, they knew from talking to workers who had gone to Marystown that the shift to Marystown would mean a direct cut in pay for most workers. It would also mean loss of seniority. No matter how many years of seniority workers had in Burin, they would have less than anyone in the Marystown plant with the exception of other former Burin workers who had less seniority than they did.

The Burin workers who went to Marystown were all placed on night shift.[7] Some women saw this as a threat to family life as they had known it; in some cases, their husbands had not worked on night shift in years. For these women, the shift to Marystown meant their husbands would no longer be home with the family in the evening for company or to take care of the kids if they wanted to go out. There were also the added costs and difficulties associated with getting a job which was several miles further away when, in some cases, families had neither a car nor a licensed driver.

Those trawlermen's wives who stood on the protest line were there to support others who worked in the plant, but they also had a personal interest in keeping the plant open. If the plant closed, their husbands would be landing fish in Catalina or Trepassey, several hundred miles away. The added travelling time associated with this change would reduce the already short period of 48 hours between six- to ten-day trips which trawlermen spent with their families.

The women on the protest line not only demonstrated a clear understanding of the problem that would be created by the plant closure, but during the protest they also exhibited considerable awareness of how to deal with the RCMP and the Unemployment Insurance Commission, and of the repressive, contradictory aspects of these institutions. For example, individuals drawing unemployment insurance were not allowed on the protest line because, it was argued by the Commission, if you were on the protest line, you were not "ready and willing to go to work." (This argument was used to keep plant workers off the protest line even after they had been laid off because there was no fish to process.) As the women pointed out, if plant workers were on the protest line, they were as ready and willing to go to work as they would be if they were up in the woods or in the union hall, as many later were. Furthermore, it could be argued that the participants in the protest line were in fact "fighting for a job."

Women maintained that management at Fishery Products Ltd. were keeping track of the protest line and making reports to the Unemployment Insurance Commission. Those who participated in the protest while drawing unemployment insurance avoided the risk of being cut off by coming only during the 8 pm to 12 pm shift or later during the night, and by not putting their names on the list posted in the Masonic Lodge. Those who came with a regular shift refused to provide their names to strangers on the line.

A similar strategy was used as a mechanism for dealing with the police. Protesters maintained that at one point, when police were issuing summonses to individuals on the line for interfering with the company's attempts to remove some of the processed frozen fish, only those whose names were known by the police were actually given a summons. In one case, when the police tried to find out the identity of a woman who participated in this incident, they were told that her name was "Dolly Parton" or "Joan of Arc." She was never served with a court summons.

Women's understanding of the contradictory and repressive character of the UIC bureaucracy was no doubt rooted in their own personal experience and that of their friends. The often temporary nature of the local employment available to women in the service sector and in the fish plant had given them ample personal experience with policies that insist they be ready and willing to work at jobs that don't exist.

Women's consciousness of their own objective interest, kinship and friendship ties to each other and to the workers, and experience with government bureaucracy and the police, played a role in the success of the protest line. There were, however, other factors rooted in the organizational and cultural features of local women's organizations that were also important in achieving this success.

In the existing literature, a conceptual distinction is commonly made between "expressive" and "instrumental" institutions. According to this distinction, the majority of the organizations in which women participate in outport Newfoundland are expressive, i.e. "organizations the purpose of which is to satisfy the desires of individual members as opposed to those designed with the goal of enhancing the power of members in the wider society" (Davis, 1983: 27). However, as Marilyn Porter (1985b) argues, this distinction is not very useful. Indeed, there are several difficulties with this approach. First, as Porter documents in her study of women on the Southern Shore in Newfoundland, it ignores the political processes that are an inherent part of so-called "expressive" institutions. For example, on their way to and from meetings and during the meetings themselves, the women do not confine their topics of discussion to the activities that are the immediate goal of the organization. On the contrary, discussions are often wide-ranging and include regular reference to the fishery and other economic and political topics. As Porter (1985b: 84-85) also suggests, these organizations have provided a framework within which women have developed relatively unique democratic forms and leadership patterns which are not inconsistent with the strong egalitarian ethic common to many outports.

At another level, the assumption that the goals of these organizations are nonpolitical (if we understand politics to gear to issues related to power) can also be questioned. For instance, through this rich network of organizations women can exercise a significant degree of control over the ways in which a portion of the economic surplus that exists in their communities is spent. An examination of the extensive fundraising activities in which they engage provides the clearest evidence in support of this claim. Dart leagues and softball teams set up by women, for example, allow them to spend time together and "get a little exercise" without spending a great deal of money. These types of recreation can be contrasted with the privatized and costly forms more typical of urban settings. The money collected from participants in various activities in Burin is used to buy the equipment necessary to ensure the continuation of the league and often to pay for a dinner and dance held at the end of the season. It thus remains in the hands of the collective participants rather than ending up in the pockets of private individuals.

Through their various organizations women not only exercise some control over the local economic surplus and the way it is spent, but they are also able to influence the cultural values and goals that dominate in those organizations and, indirectly, within the community. The goals of women's organizations in Burin reflect the priorities of women. Thus, the various organizations that raise funds for the fire

306

brigades reflect women's concern for the safety of their homes and families. And, the emphasis on "enjoyment" and "fun" rather than "competition" and "excellence" in recreational sports reflects women's preference for organizations in which membership is broad and inclusive, rather than narrow and exclusive. A rigid conceptual distinction between expressive and instrumental institutions ignores a range of fundamentally "instrumental" or political aspects associated with these institutions in the context of outport Newfoundland. But there is a further problem with this distinction. Studies of the nineteenth century working class and of nineteenth century women have argued that there is an important relationship between organizations that facilitate adaptation to the existing system and those that play a role in the development of sustained resistance (Walkowitz, 1978; Ryan, 1979). In the nineteenth century, local clubs and pubs provided the basis for cementing male working class cultural values and goals that were distinct from those in the wider society. Working-class women's organizations can have a similar impact. The relationship between the protest line and women's organizations in Burin allows us to document this criticism at an empirical level.

Like most women's organizations, the protest line combined a formal organizational goal with expressive activities such as eating and card-playing. For many women, the time they spent on the protest line was an enjoyable experience consisting of time free to associate with other women, joke, play games and just "be foolish." Since young children were not allowed on the protest line, those with young ones at home often enjoyed the break from child care and meal preparation. During the protest, conversation included recurrent jokes about the way they looked in their skidoo suits and about their shack, the "table" they had built, the "curtains" on the window and the paper on the walls. On some shifts, parties were held and elaborate meals prepared. In the jokes about their own appearance and the various amenities they incorporated into the shack, as well as in food preparation, knitting, card-playing and other games, the women linked the shack and the fight to keep the plant open to their own political culture. The shack became their domain and the protest line a symbol of their ability to fight the company and both levels of government.

The voluntary character of the protest line was another aspect of its similarity to women's organizations in the community. Should someone refuse to participate, the organizers and participants who had counted on their help had no real sanctions they could impose beyond talking about those who were not present and speculating about why they were not there. Participants were informed about the shift or the team that they were working with, but beyond that, their participation was basically their own responsibility. They were expected to find out when their next shift was and to be there. It was understood that they wanted to participate and that they would be there if possible. Unless problems developed, the team captain and/or organizer did not call the participants to find out whether or not they were going and why. Finally, teams were put together in such a way that they included more than enough members to cover any shift. It was recognized that, because of other commitments such as work, sick children and meetings, not all participants would be able to attend all the time.

The voluntary character of the institution necessitated certain kinds of organizational strategies with which women, because of their involvement in other voluntary institutions dependent on their participation, had extensive experience. The similarity of the shape and character of the protest line to that of other women's organizations in Burin was, no doubt, an important factor in making it a success. Local women's organizations tend to be non-authoritarian and characterized by widely dispersed responsibility and control. Those responsible for organizing a particular event or group basically agree to carry out a set number of tasks and formal organization was minimal.

The woman in Burin who was primarily responsible for organizing the protest line had experience in both labour and community organizations. She had been President of her union local and was also involved in the local branch of the Red Cross. The local Red Cross consists of 11 women who engage in a range of fundraising activities throughout the year. They also organize an annual blood donor clinic and loan out equipment owned by the local branch to members of the community. They do most of the work for the major fundraising activity (a canvass of the entire community) and the blood donor clinic. As with the protest line, they begin with a list of phone numbers of individuals and/or organizations who have expressed interest in the past and attempt to recruit them to help. Members of the Red Cross are basically a steering committee who undertake a range of activities on their own, but who mainly rely on the community to help out with major projects.

The team captain system used on the protest line is more typical of dart leagues, baseball and other sports organizations than the Red Cross. However, the same basic practice of decentralized control, with organizers responsible for setting things up but not exerting direct control over members, is common to both the Red Cross and other organizations (Porter, 1985b).

In the case of the protest line, those who criticized the organizers for setting up the shift system were told that they need not abide by the schedule but could spend as much time on the protest line as they wanted. The organizer pointed out that the goal was to get lots of participation. If someone wanted to come at a different time or had no alternative, then there was nothing wrong with that. As with the Women's Institutes in the Calvert-Ferryland district (Porter, 1985b), women involved in leading women's organizations in Burin are organizers rather than leaders with any substantial power over their members.

Conclusion

The protest line in Burin is now only a memory. It gradually ceased to exist during June of 1983. The federal and provincial governments signed a restructuring agreement in which it was decided that the Burin plant would be reopened, but only for secondary processing. Local women attribute the continued operation of the plant at least in part to the success of the protest line. The plant is now in operation again but with a transformed labour force. The removal of primary processing has meant a sharp reduction in the availability of jobs for men in the plant. In some cases, former plant workers were without jobs long enough to lose whatever seniority they had accumulated and have had to go back as new workers with no initial job security. Most of the women formerly employed in the plant have returned to work and others with little or no experience are now being recruited. There is substantial optimism regarding the future of the plant, although at the moment the number employed is much reduced from the past.

This study of the protest line has allowed us to examine a situation in which the latent power in women's organizations in outport Newfoundland was released and directed towards achieving ends not normally within the realm of women's collective activities. In their struggle to keep the Burin plant open, these women, with the help of others in the community, contested the right of a corporation to make investment decisions regardless of their impact on the community. Within Newfoundland, they were part of the grassroots mobilization that ultimately contributed to a decision on the part of the federal and provincial governments to take control of the largest fish companies rather than simply bail them out of this latest economic crisis.

1 This is not meant to suggest that women in these communities haven't tried to find wage labour just like women elsewhere in the country. They have, and labour force participation rates in these communities, in particular among women with dependent children, have been on the increase. See, for example, Luxton (1983). For a general discussion of women's labour force participation rates in forestry industry towns in British Columbia see Marchak (1983: 213-248). See also, Meg Luxton's (1980) discussion of the gendered division of labour in Flin Flon, a mining community.

2 Barnsley Women Against Pit Closures (1984); The Wives Tale, DEC Films. Initiatives of this kind on the part of women do not seem to be prompted by unions and the extent and character of union involvement in them is often a somewhat contentious issue.

3 One of the other interesting facets of the Burin protest was the extent to which the leadership expressed strong opposition to further bailouts of the company by government. The Burin Action Committee maintained that the big fish companies had mismanaged the fishery. At one point they insisted that Fishery Products turn the plant and the draggers over to the town for the sum of $1.00 because they belonged to the townspeople anyway. They were also a leading group in grassroots pressure against further bailouts and in favour of a government takeover of the industry.

4 Material in this section is drawn primarily from interviews with members of the Burin Action Committee and others in the community.

5 This section of the paper is based on observations recorded during several periods on the protest line and on interviews with the organizers and some participants in the latter.

6 It is important to recognize that jobs in the fish plant both in the past and today, pay substantially better than other nonprofessional jobs available to women in the community.

7 Many of those who went to Marystown ended up on night shift for over a year and a half. It was only after the night shift staged a wildcat strike in the summer of 1986 that rotating day and night shifts were introduced in Marystown.

Women's Economic Lives: Research in South East Bight

Carmelita McGrath

This paper draws on work in "the Bight" during the summer of 1989. It was published in a slightly different form in Waterlily *magazine.*

"There's no life like the life of an outport, no matter what you say."[1]
Clara Whyte, South East Bight

WOMEN'S ECONOMIC LIVES, an extensive study of women's work in Newfoundland and Labrador, was undertaken in 1988 by Marilyn Porter, Elke Dettmer, Bev Brown and myself. The study focuses on the variety of women's work—including paid labour, household work, child care and that vast field of work often loosely defined as "caregiving."

During the summer of 1989, I was in South East Bight to conduct the third community study included in Women's Economic Lives. This project had also focused on women in Grand Falls and Catalina. South East Bight in Placentia Bay, with 120 permanent residents, was by far the smallest community to be included in the study. Having come from an outport myself, I was more than willing to take the ferry out to "the Bight," and slip into the slower pace of life.

The pace, however, was slower only for me. In July, South East Bight was at the peak of the fishing season, with both men and women involved in the inshore fishery. A collector boat from National Sea Products came to collect the fish. With no plant work available, in South East Bight if you want to be involved in the fishery, you fish. While young women in South East Bight may be new to going out fishing, there is nothing new in the involvement of women in the fishery. Older women told me stories of "making" fish on the beaches; however, only in recent years have women gone out in boats, usually with their husbands, to fish. As one woman recounted, getting so directly into the fishery was not always an active, thought-out choice, but a natural consequence of economic circumstances:

He (her husband) was by himself, he had the old punt then. And I started going back and forth with him. I was working too and that was another thing. One of those Canada Works projects, and I had sixteen stamps, because that was all I could get, so I wanted to go for twenty for my unemployment. So I fished in the summer and I got another six.

"And did you like it?" I asked:

Oh yes, I liked it. That's not saying that I didn't get sick when I started. But I got used to it. And I like it.

In South East Bight, faith in the fishery had not been misplaced. Catches in the years just prior to 1989 had been adequate to support families, and sufficient for the people involved to get enough stamps to receive Unemployment Insurance in the winter. As in many Newfoundland communities, Unemployment Insurance (UI) is an integral part of the economic structure, providing security for the long winter between the end of the fishing season in the fall and the beginning of the new one in the spring. Still, there is often a long break between the time of "making a claim" and actual receipt of benefits—a period of as much as a month. Predictably, this dry period happens just when it is most difficult for families: before Christmas.

Given the recent scrutiny of the use of UI in Newfoundland by both politicians and the media, people in South East Bight were predictably sensitive about Unemployment Insurance. "You're not one of the 10-42 crowd, are you?" a woman asked me the first time I met her. I assured her that I was not. Like many people, she felt that an "expose" done by CBC Television's the *Fifth's Estate*[2] on make-work projects in Newfoundland was biased, unfair, and sensational.

> They came looking for the worst. The worst they could find. And they did the damage. I wonder—will we be able to get any projects at all now?

Because a key part of my work involved observing how Unemployment Insurance fit into the economies of families and the community, I had to ask questions that inevitably brought me under suspicion. I might be from the federal government, there under the cover of research, to dig out any economic arrangements that the "feds" might question. I could be from any number of regulatory bodies, there to check up on any number of things. If from the university, I might inadvertently collect and circulate information that could harm people who were simply trying to "make the best of what we have here."

Such fears were understandable, particularly in communities like South East Bight, where UI is an integral unit in balancing the family budget, and winter projects have often provided the means to create basic services and infrastructure vital to the survival and stability of communities. Such services and facilities were hard-won in the Bight which, in the 1960s, was targeted for resettlement. But despite threats of total withdrawal of any kind of support services, the community persisted. In the end, only six families were left. As one elderly woman remembered:

> They were all going, except for a few. Even the priest came to the door one day and he said to me. "Oh, you'll leave too. When the old rooster goes, the old hen will follow.' And I said, 'Well, this is one old hen that's staying.' Now my husband, he was inclined to go along with them and leave, but I talked him out of it.

The determination that caused people to stay began to manifest itself in organization. Women were key players in committees formed, battles with government fought and services obtained. In the midst of all this, women were key players. The landmark achievement was electricity. People fought for and kept their school. They kept the ferry service. And after electricity, they got telephones. While traditional merchants had left, new stores opened up. And people who'd left began to filter back, finding little elsewhere in the government's promise of 'a better life.' This period saw the beginning of projects which provided wharf and breakwater facilities necessary to the fishery. There is concern now that, as actual proposed changes to UI and Canada Employment projects come into play, such gains can be eroded. As one woman angrily pointed out,

> Last year they gave us $1,500.00 to fix up the government wharf. $1,500.00! Now we're building on (to the house) and I could tell them how far $1,500.00 goes.

The determination to hold on to their community, together with a sense of the fragility of the gains that had been made, and an awareness of how easily positive developments could be reversed by "policy changes" produced an atmosphere in which my detailed questionnaires seemed both intrusive and irrelevant. By the middle of the summer, my research efforts had shifted to discussions at kitchen tables—some taped, some not—and the construction of stories by picking up narrative threads in one place and carrying them to another. The stories collected covered a wide range of experience and spanned four generations of women. In accounts ranging from child care arrangements while making fish on the beaches to becoming a fisher in the 1980s to moving away only to return, a larger, more cohesive narrative emerged. This was a narrative of what makes a community a good place to live over time, and also of how a community's benefits and services can be enhanced through local organization and the use of funds and programs from the outside. It was the narrative central to Clara's statement, and also the one which—since it contained a cycle involving threats to survival, gains, stability, threats of losses—served as a constant reminder of how outside intervention is both needed and suspected.

Many of the concerns which emerged, once it was decided I was not "from the feds," were related in one way or another to Unemployment Insurance. One concern was the change to an emphasis on projects which involve training. Several times, people voiced the question of what people could reasonably train for. "Train them to go away," And, as the federal government leaned more towards programs such as "Section 25" projects on which people work for a top-up of their UI benefits, and became less inclined to fund traditional "winter works" projects, the number of people in receipt of benefits might decrease. This put a pressure on those not involved in the fishery, especially the young, to leave.

While there is little likelihood that people so determined to stay would be inclined to leave without a fight, the community in 1989 could look ahead to many challenges in the future. Certainly, changes in government funding policies will play a large role in this.

Again and again during my stay, I asked the women what they would like to see for their community in the future. In the Bight, women indeed are the logical ones to ask, as they have been traditionally active in everything from building a new church to the local development committee. One desire echoed repeatedly was for a community water system. Dry wells in summer and freeze-ups in winter contribute to an already heavy workload for families. Women also agreed that they wished the school would continue up to Grade Twelve; in 1989, young people had to go away to finish the last years of high school, and this meant that many did not finish. As well, most of the women I talked to felt a need for improved health care services. In 1989 a doctor came by helicopter for a clinic every second Tuesday. If the weather was bad, you had to wait until the next scheduled visit. And who can rely on it not to be foggy in Placentia Bay on any given Tuesday? The only other option was by boat. At the time I was there, South East Bight had only five elderly residents. However, the adequacy of such a health care system would certainly be stressed as the population ages.

The one thing I could find no agreement on was the possibility of a road linkage to the Burin Peninsula via Monkstown. While some people seemed to think it a good idea, others felt that it would destroy life as the community knows it, and that it would open up an easy way for the young people to leave and not return. And it would definitely mean the relinquishing of certain securities. One woman I discussed the issue with was looking out her kitchen window. Her children were disappearing over the crest of a hill,

> Look, (she pointed), I can let them go out and I don't have to worry about them. I know where they are. If I don't, I can ask someone, 'Did you see the boys?' I know who's in the community. If a stranger like you comes, I know about it. But a road—how would you know? You wouldn't know who's here, or what they'd be at.

And for the woman looking out the kitchen window, a fisher whose work day often began at 4:00 am and ended after dark, such security means one less thing she has to worry about.

Postscript, 1994

Re-reading what I wrote in 1989-1990, as well as reviewing my journals from the summer, I become aware of how many of the issues raised by women in the Bight have been echoed and expanded, since the failure of the fishery, throughout the province. Concerns over "useless training," pressures to resettle, lack of maintenance of infrastructure, fears about the erosion of UI, and anger over how decisions are made concerning the survival of communities are even more real and more pressing in 1994. One woman's comment especially stands out: "We'll hang on," she said, "as long as the fish don't go." In the end, it was the resource that made everything else tenable; it was the fish which held all the stories together. I wonder what this woman is feeling now.

1 Clara Whyte is quoted with permission. In fact, "I don't mind if you use my name," was a common response to questions during the summer. All names in personal accounts in the larger study, *Women's Economic Lives*, were, however fictionalized.

2 The Fifth Estate program mentioned here was notorious in rural Newfoundland for two reasons: 1. it was seen as being constructed out of an uninformed point of view about what constitutes work in a Newfoundland community, and 2. it was absolutely an "outsider's" perspective, and one that could only harm public opinion about the role of Unemployment Insurance in seasonally structured economies.

Take Off Your Shoes!: The Culture of Feminist Practice in Bay St. George

Glynis George

This article is based on a year's fieldwork done in preparation for a University of Toronto Masters Thesis.

Introduction

IT'S 9:30 AM ON A SUNNY MARCH DAY. Two officials from Corrections Canada arrive at the Bay St. George Women's Centre in Stephenville, and enter through the side door of the large four-bedroom bungalow. "Take off your shoes!" directs one of the women. The men, clad in suit and tie, shuffle uncomfortably, but quickly oblige. After all, it is a "home." Michelle, the President of the Women's Council, turned down their request to assemble in the formal environment of a hotel boardroom and offered the Women's Centre as a more comfortable meeting place.

They are greeted cheerfully by the co-ordinator of the centre, offered coffee or tea, then ushered into the living room. One is directed to the large, comfortable couch, while the other, eager to sit beside his colleague, is gestured instead to a cosy loveseat. Once everyone is seated, the Council President introduces an agenda and the participants, who include an RCMP officer, two sex abuse counsellors who work for Mental Health and the local School Board respectively, two single mothers, and two Women's Council members.

The officials are here to respond to concerns raised by a myriad of community residents over the implementation of an experimental sex offender 'recovery' program which was to take place in town and which would house sex offenders in the local halfway house. Those administering the program were proclaiming, through media reports, an 80% recovery rate for those men who undertook the 10-week treatment program.

Minutes after the introduction, domestic hospitality is quickly eroded by intense and, at times, confrontational discussion over the program. The Corrections Canada officers begin aggressively enough, by defending their program with a lecture of explanation. The 'audience' is informed that they have simply misunderstood the major elements of the program. Soon after, however, these men are faced with assorted, informed arguments from all sides of the room. Marie, the RCMP officer, wants a detailed account of how surveillance and protection will be maintained. Jim, the sex abuse counsellor, begins to cite other reports that question the utility of this therapy model and the possibility of 'cure'. Rhonda, a single mother who lives across from the halfway house, recounts experiences with other halfway house residents and expresses anger that claims of 'recovery' in the media, may provide false comfort for neighbourhood mothers.

Enfolded in the comfort of thick homemade quilts, the officials, separated and flanked on both sides, begin to squirm awkwardly from side to side while fighting to keep their socked feet planted firmly on the floor. After two hours of heated discussion, the Corrections Canada officials become thoroughly disarmed; soon after, they nod in agreement to many of the suggestions and criticisms presented.

The meeting is called to an end and the officials make their way out. Seated around the kitchen table soon after, the other participants chat, recreate their favourite moments over tea and toast, and declare their meeting a success.

This incident manifests complex contemporary issues surrounding community activism, sexual violence, and gender relations. It shows how the Bay St. George Women's Council reshapes women's traditional arena of power to confront the diverse inequalities that shape the life experience of women in this region of western Newfoundland. Moreover, it contains the elements of my argument in this paper: that deeply-rooted cultural notions of family, community and domestic space are combined with emergent forms of social and political power that women have recently acquired to enable the council, informed by the practices of a broader feminist movement, to contest major male-dominated institutional sources of power, and empower women from diverse backgrounds.

I further argue that, while the Bay St. George Women's council does not represent a 'model' organization, whose structure and activities can be applied to any social setting, an examination of this council and its particular cultural context permits an assessment of how the ideas of feminism become part of a local way of life.[1] To do this, I examine the historical constitution of gender, work and domestic space which Bay St. George feminists both contest and embrace.

Gender and Work in Bay St. George

The Bay St. George Women's Centre is situated in a residential neighbourhood in the town of Stephenville and is distinguishable from other homes on the street by the large feminist symbol suspended by the front door. The centre is just two blocks from the town's commercial district which begins at the bridge over Blanche Brook and continues seaward for several blocks where it meets the shoreline road that leads to the Port au Port peninsula. On the other side of this bridge, beyond the narrow river, lie the numerous buildings that once comprised the Ernest Harmon Airforce Base which operated from 1941 until 1966. The base initiated the development of "the town" and provided employment for a few thousand women and men who came from other parts of the island in search of jobs. The houses "on base" are pastel blue and yellow boxes, organized in tidy rows and loops which bear the imprint of American hegemony through names like Montana Drive and Oregon Avenue. Their uniformity forms a sharp contrast to the diverse styles of homes "in town," some of which were built before legal standards were imposed. These architectural distinctions are visual reminders that the town owes much of its infrastructure to American hegemony, and that American military life co-existed alongside Newfoundland civilian life.

In Bay St. George, a cultural tension between rootedness and migrancy is apparent, perhaps to the outsider from away, through the varied recollections of assorted residents. For some, Sandy Point, a deserted community across from St. George's Bay, evokes fond memories and the heyday of the herring and salmon fishery whose 19th century pre-eminence lingered into the early half of this century. Francophone families who reside at the tip of the Port-au-Port Peninsula trace their family line to Acadians and French fishers who began to settle the area to fish lobster and cod, from the 1870s onward (Mannion, 1977). Many residents in Stephenville proper can easily identify the names of the oldest families who farmed and fished here, "before the base" and after which some of the oldest streets "in town" are named. Newcomers to the area, in contrast, recall the community or town, which they or their parents left in search of jobs from the opening of the base to the present.

The political and economic development of this region, one of the earliest settlements on this western coast known as the 'french shore,' created the rural-urban enclave of Bay St. George. On the one hand, each small community and the town of Stephenville itself constitute discrete entities which are bounded geographically and politically through local governments, family land and intimate histories. At the same time, the past is, in part, shared through prolonged economic interdependency, flexible borders and the movement of residents through marriage and work. Within this shared historical context gender relations were structured and female social roles that are now labelled 'traditional' emerged. Male and female roles are not static; nor are gender relations and the relative autonomy and control that women and men exercise. Rather, they have shifted over time, through life cycles and across a changing rural and urban landscape.

As family members, women were responsible for child and elder care, and a variety of subsistence work in gardens and the home.[2] Many husbands worked away for extended periods, in the wood camps, in construction or as fishermen. The prolonged absence of husbands and sons fractured marital and family relations and conferred upon women greater autonomy and authority as well as responsibility for children and household finances (Benoit,1990). Says the 88-year-old widow of a fisherman:

> When I told a male friend that I was deciding what school my son would go to, he said, 'you west coast women, you west coast women'. . . . It's true. Women on this coast rule the roost—they make the decisions, they handle the money.

The construction of the Ernest Harmon Airforce Base precipitated the introduction of a vast and 'modern' infrastructure, a few thousand men in uniform, and a military culture which celebrated masculine bravado, and alcoholic and sexual abandonment; family and community life were dramatically and unevenly altered throughout the area. Specifically, it provided women with new choices, the consequences of which were somewhat determined by their relationships to men. Many worked "on base" as clerical workers; others married American soldiers. Although the base closed in 1966 after 25 years, the urban culture which it created persisted through the cycles of boom, bust, and out-migration that followed. In sum, this historical development generated a variety of social and economic hierarchies throughout the area that cut across communities and households.

Today, cultural tensions of migrancy and rootedness are further manifested through traditional work practices, which have been structured by seasonal demands, and co-exist with more recently introduced nine-to-five and shiftwork occupations (Hill,1981). Large numbers of men, more in the rural communities, but also in town, work 'away' seasonally as construction workers, farm labourers, wood cutters and tradesmen. A large number of households rely on social assistance and unemployment insurance. Although unemployment has stabilized at a rather high rate of 25% for the last decade, it is not spread evenly throughout the region; rather, unemployment rates are much higher in the outlying rural communities (CEIC, Stephenville).

Historically, women's participation in the paid labour force was considerably lower than men's, especially in the rural communities. Although their participation has steadily increased since the 1970s, large numbers of rural and urban women do not engage in sustained paid work, if they desire it, because of inadequate child care, lack of training and most importantly, lack of jobs. Those that do work full or part-time are concentrated either in the low-paying and often temporary or seasonal service and retail sectors, or among the higher-paid, unionized government service sector, as clerks, teachers, nurses, and social workers.[3]

Women's involvement in the paid workforce has generated shifts in the organization of the household economy and marital relations. Moreover, it has created new hierarchies of power among women. These hierarchies are rooted in differential incomes and job securities. Such financial guarantees conjoin in varying ways with forms of social power that accrue to nurses, social workers, teachers, for example, who have access to information about, and decision-making powers over, other residents.

Nonetheless, women's paid and unpaid work continues to be rooted in age-old social roles which entail nurturing and caregiving. Motherhood remains an important and highly valued part of women's social identity. Whatever forms of labour women engage in necessitate extensive social interaction as well as responsibility for others in the most intimate aspects of everyday life.

Today, women's paid and unpaid work constitutes a crucial contribution to the household economy. In many households, women have equal or more control than men over household finances and decision-making. At the same time, women's roles are constructed within relations of power that inform the culture generally. Thus, it is insufficient to look at the economic contributions and roles of men and women exclusive of the social relationships in which such work is embedded .

Cecilia Benoit argues that, in the first half of this century, Stephenville women rarely conceived of notions of individual freedom; rather, their lives were "tightly interwoven with significant others" (Benoit,1990:175). These sentiments are also reflected in the numerous life stories of women from age 20 to 90 that I collected. These stories suggest that the 'tradition' of female social roles continues to have meaning and to shape the choices women envision . Importantly, the women I interviewed rarely conceived of their tasks as merely or exclusively work per se. Rather, their tasks and their social identities were always tied—socially, morally, and economically—to a household, a family, and in some cases, a community.

Family, Place and Social Space

Women's identities as mother, daughter, wife and worker are structured by the various demands of making a living and raising a family in Bay St. George. Moreover, women's identities are informed by ideologies of family, church and gender which provide a cultural framework for evaluating 'womanly' behaviour within a patriarchal culture. The culture of everyday life, however, emerges within social arenas that link women to various households and the community; within these social spheres, women exercise autonomy and control . While there is considerable continuity in women's roles per se, the contexts in which they take place, the social and economic value they are assigned, and the social relations which surround them have shifted. Women absorb this history of shifting gender roles in such a way that numerous contradictions between female power and dependence pervade in everyday life and through ambiguous cultural understandings of 'womanly' behaviour (Weedon,1987; Parr,1990).

Historically, a woman's roles were centred in domestic spaces, primarily her own, and secondarily, those of her friends, neighbours and relations. Even women's activities in community organizations, within the church for example, derived from female domestic roles. Such roles were rooted in social expectations and norms of behaviour that were informed by the ideologies of the church, the Roman Catholic church in particular, whose leaders preached chastity, marriage and procreation, and that women were to be protected by their fathers and husbands (Benoit, 1990:178).

> It wasn't my choice to have 10 children. I kept getting pregnant. I used to burn through them. I didn't want to get pregnant but my husband was a faithful church goer and that was the message in church—go forth and multiply (grandmother, remarried widow, born 1934).

Family and domestic responsibilities circumscribed women's circulation in the public arenas where men regularly gathered for work and leisure.

> I was married at 18, and had 11 children. I didn't work then, well, I didn't work outside the home, but I sure worked . . . it's a sin really, but my life started when my husband died. I wasn't a person when I was married. Everyone knew my husband and my husband was all about town while I went nowhere" (widow, b. 1935).

Within the domestic sphere, women could assert control over children and the organization of daily activities. Moreover, because the gendered division of labour created separate social spheres for women and men, women relied on the company of other women within the neighbourhood and extended family. Within these social networks, the private domains of families conjoined within the community, through female work and leisure. In this social arena, women expressed their opinions, exchanged information, provided support, and could be "a power to be reckoned with" (Benoit,1990:183). Traditional roles within the immediate and extended family structured relations between women that hardly conjure a harmonious past of female equality.

My husband and his brothers, they're all mama's boys—she always has a crowd for Sunday dinner, and she cooks up a big salt beef dinner, and turkey . . . but they are steadfastly loyal to her, and they gossip, judging this person and that...but she's a good enough person; she finally told me to get rid of Al, (her husband) and to come back to my house which is right beside hers (separated mother of three, b. 1952).

Moreover, depending upon the woman herself and the amount of female support she could rely on, such female control was exercised within the domestic space and circumscribed men's behaviour within the home.

Mom was always on the go—baking bread, cooking, cleaning never smiling . . . and when Dad was drunk, she would yell at him and boy, she let it out—'you devil' she'd yell and she'd shout. . . . Dad never drank in the home—he drank outside in the shed. (married mother of two, b.1960).

This history of women's privilege in the domestic realm,where much of her crucial activities were centred, is reflected in current attitudes that women have regarding the home as **their** social space, the place where they strive to create an ideal family, in which they can exercise forms of power that derive from their social roles.

I'm a big one on control . . . I like to have the house just so, . . . its not a fifty-fifty division in our house, but its my own fault. My husband, he just 'babysits' our little girl. . . . I gotta learn to let go of her a bit more (married, mother of one, b.1964).

The ideal family of male breadwinner, motherly wife and children, then, prevails although reproductive technologies have expanded women's control over their bodies, and freed female sexuality from the limits of a purely procreative function. Popular ideas of appropriate female behaviour continue to shape women's understanding of sexuality, masculinity, femininity and the choices they actually make. Such ideals inform women's personal evaluations and criticisms of their social relationships. This is reflected in the importance they place on the nuclear family as an ideal for which they strive.

I knew I was in a bad marriage, but I wanted it to work so badly. . . I wanted kids, and a nice home and I wanted someone to take care of me (a divorced mother of three, b.1964).

Yet, there are limits on female control within the domestic arena which are most dramatically manifested in the stories of women who have experienced physical and sexual abuse as children or adults.[4]

Mike, my first husband, was just no good. He was so possessive and domineering it got so bad he wouldn't even let me use the telephone. He watched every move I made and it got so he would never let me out of the house. . . . Things got so bad, he cut the telephone wires. . . he was always hurling insults at me. . . he beat me to a pulp. It took a long time to leave him, but I did (mother of two, remarried, b.1957).

Cultural ambivalence towards female behaviour is reflected in local perceptions and institutional treatment of 'single mothers' in Bay St. George, some of whom are grouped in subsidized low-income housing in Stephenville; others are dispersed throughout the area and integrated within larger extended families. Some 'single mothers' may be connected by close ties of neighbourhood or friendship; as a group, they are united by common experiences that render them socially disadvantaged through persistent negative stereotyping, and economically disadvantaged by the persistent gender division of labour that gives primacy to their childrearing responsibilities without concomitant support. Within this underemployed region, it is difficult for 'single mothers' to progress in educational institutions and occupations that pay a family wage.

Women experience inequality in different ways and their responses to life circumstances vary according to individual character and available support. In general, they do find ways to exercise autonomy and control, value their social contribution and gain personal satisfaction within patriarchal structures . At the same time, the family is rarely an exclusively private domain; nor do women have the privacy of personal choice. Rather, they are constrained by the social pressures and cultural norms that bridge the domains of family and community.

In 1980 I was pregnant. . . I needed to save face. . . so I got married. I cried. My choice was either to go away or get married. I would have raised it alone away, but not here, there were too many judges (divorced mother on one b.1958).

In Bay St. George today, women adjust traditional social roles to accommodate new economic circumstances, job opportunities, and changing perceptions regarding family and gender. Although the social arenas in which women circulate have shifted and expanded as women enter the work force, the domestic arena remains a social space in which many of women's activities and social roles are still carried out.

In sum, the arenas of 'family' and 'community' are both ideal and relative constructs as well as material contexts which tie women and men together in distinct ways (Parr, 1990). The community is comprised of the ideas, institutions, social roles and citizens which embrace the family and the home. It is through the community that social behaviour in the home is either sanctioned or denounced, made public or kept private.

The Bay St. George Women's Council

It is within this social context that the Bay St. George Women's Centre is situated and the ideas of feminist practice must unfold. The Women's Centre is operated by the Bay St. George Women's Council, which seeks to encompass the entire Bay St. George area. The Women's Council is housed within a comfortable domestic setting that seems to recognize, by its very design, the history that most area women share. Yet at the Women's Centre the public domain of community and the private world of intimate relationships intersect in a way that both respects 'the past' and actively works to change it. This is exemplified by the maintenance of cultural traditions and domestic activities which surround women's traditional roles.

At the centre, seasonal celebrations such as Thanksgiving, Easter and Christmas, are acknowledged with a dinner. In 1993, for example, an Easter dinner followed the work of compiling the quarterly newsletter. There is also a yearly Christmas party in which area residents fill the entire house for an elaborate meal. On these occasions, continuity of women's roles is most apparent in the amount and variety of work that underlies the success of activities, such as the production of the newsletter and the dinners. During the newsletter compilation and Easter dinner, I counted at least 60 hours of work, shared by ten or more women, apart from writing the articles. Christmas took at least 80 woman hours of preparation over three days. However, just as domestic labour is rarely recognized for the amount of energy it entails, so too are women at the centre reluctant to view these preparations as work if this would negate the pleasure and value they derive from them.

Moreover, the celebration of family life is implicit in the way children are easily integrated into the deadline work of compiling a newsletter, for example, by re-arranging the living room to let them watch a video. At the same time, the family as an institution and its concomitant ideal form is challenged by the recognition of the diverse family forms represented here. At Easter, several women arrived with children in tow. Some are single mothers; two others, one of whom works in the evening, bring their children along while husbands work; another babysits two children while their parents work.

The informal atmosphere lends itself to extensive and diverse discussion in which feminist perspectives are injected between a laugh and a story. At Easter, a few women complain that the UI and GST cheques are late. Says one single mother, "Never mind bunnies, I can't even buy groceries!" Stereotypes of single mothers are challenged through rowdy joking and running commentaries on the sexist comments made by local male community leaders. The problem of 'safe sex' is a popular topic. "Hang a condom around your neck—then he'll get the message!" says Joyce, the co-ordinator. The celebrations themselves are devoid of religious overtones; rather, the traditional religious occasion seems to provide the social context for the display of feminist hospitality and the assembly of community residents under what appears to be politically neutral circumstances.

Within this same domestic context, 'the community' enters both at the invitation of the council, and through the work and other outside experiences that members and visitors bring with them. At dinners and over more informal lunches, women pass through on a break from work or meetings. Social workers, counsellors, nurses, and ministers, while maintaining the discretion implicit in their jobs, bring the experiences of other women with them.

The boundaries which distinguish other women in the region from those who participate at the Women's Centre do not neatly correspond to geographic, political or social divisions within the urban-rural enclave of Bay St. George. Like the communities which make-up the region, the Women's Council is a flexible entity which connects women in diverse ways. Although the council itself consists of 12 board members and a paid executive director, former board members remain in close contact. Through their own occupations and participation in various organizations, and through individual liaison, the council has been represented, either formally or individually, in area organizations such as Community Futures, the Anti-Violence Coalition, The Sex Abuse Counselling Service, and the Canada Employment Centre.

Yet the sphere of participants is considerably widened through the operation of the Women's Centre which employs a few women on a part-time and temporary basis, and draws on the services of numerous volunteers. Moreover, it receives an assortment of people who come on a one-time or regular basis to use the council's services including information on health, sexuality, training, and abuse through limited counselling and a resource library. The Women's Shelter, located in the basement apartment, houses women and their children who for numerous reasons require temporary and relatively safe residence. [5]

Equally important is the participation of council members in area-wide events in which a Women's Centre perspective and resources are requested as well as the numerous events they initiate and carry-out in town and in outlying communities. Many council members, who number 350 in total and include women from the entire area, do not visit the centre often but are kept informed of council activities and events in the area and within the national and provincial feminist movement through the quarterly newsletter which is mailed or hand-distributed.

Levelling Hierarchies

It is within this domestic space that social hierarchies within the larger 'community' are mediated. At a surface level, hierarchies of power are mediated by the sense of responsibility for others that women in service occupations seem to have. Moreover, feminist values and ideology, which highlight women's subordination within larger patriarchal structures, seem to reinforce a levelling of social status among women. While those whose occupations do give them power over other residents recognize their privilege, those involved in the centre repeatedly argue that they simply do not feel this as power per se. Rather, they view themselves as also powerless, or having little control within a larger social system. Nonetheless, as feminist studies show, it is one thing to speak of feminist egalitarianism, it is more difficult to achieve this ideal given the everyday pressures of running a feminist organization [6].

At the Bay St. George Women's Centre, social levelling is achieved in subtle, everyday ways that, I would argue, are implicit in the local culture, particularly domestic culture, and are not openly expressed as official rules of behaviour.[7] For example, exclusive, intimate conversation in the living/kitchen area is gently discouraged. Women who make regular appearances, regardless of their social position, are expected to dry dishes, make tea, or lick envelopes. Women who exhibit their distinctiveness as a virtue, or as a sign of their superiority, are cheerfully mocked for "being uppity." At the same time, the specific skills of individual women are noted and encouraged, and all contributions are recognized without priorizing their importance. Three women recount their view of the centre:

> I went to the centre as a volunteer and I had a lot of problems at the time. I done mostly maintenance work—going to the bank and the post office, washing dishes. Everybody chips in and does their part, and each part is given equal credit. You're able to stop by and do something for an hour, or longer if you have the time and there's respect for your circumstances and lack of judgement in a bad way
>
> I used to wonder what they thought about me just dropping in like I did. . . then one day, I dropped by and I asked if there was anything I could do and Joyce (the co-ordinator) said I could bring apple juice, because they always needed that. . . and so I did that.

While women in this region share a certain history of 'womanly' expectations, social identities, family obligations and responsibilities, gender inequalities do not spread evenly through the community, and individual women are, for numerous reasons, differently equipped at a given time to address their own social problems as well as others'. Moreover, this is a diverse group of women, employed and unemployed, single, married, and divorced, with different levels of education that may or may not give them access to social and economic power. At the Women's Centre, there is no sharp distinction made between 'the helpers' and 'the helped.'

At the same time, the Women's Council is not simply a microcosm of the region; nor do its members represent all local social groups. There is lower membership and participation among women who work in the private sector and among older women. This suggests that a knowledge and expression of women's diverse and shared experiences may be fostered in those social arenas which give value and access to the exchange of experience and information such as government sector occupations, and the informal face to face networks that connect women though family and friendship.

Empowering Women in Bay St. George

Members of the Bay St. George Women's Council, like other feminists, struggle in their desire to achieve effective change while maintaining the most valued features of their way of life. I suggest that this Women's Council maintains a delicate and difficult balance between continuity and change because of the varied experiences and perspectives of its members, and a recognition of the social barriers that local women face and the possible solutions they have at hand. This means providing a place—not simply an organization—where women can maintain the many identities which make up their individuality, and feel sufficiently comfortable to consider social and personal change.

Most women I interviewed emphasized that they liked the Women's Centre because they very quickly felt comfortable and "at home" there. "I like it because its relaxed and informal, and you can have a laugh and still know you're doing important work there," said one long-time volunteer.

Martha, the mother of a toddler, describes her first visit to the centre several years before:

> I remember when I first came to the centre. We were in the old centre and there was a big flight of stairs and when I went up, there was Sammy the dog and I said "this is home"... When I found the Women's Centre I found myself... I found my little nook in life; I know wherever I go, I'll always have that as my family... I've never really left the centre. I came back and did a lot of volunteer work.

While some women are comfortable expressing their opinions, others who are unaccustomed to being asked what they think or do, or who feel inhibited, seem to find more than a word or two at the Women's Centre. In fact, they can become quite bossy in this domestic context, as if holding a spoon or wiping a table places them in a situation with which they are only too familiar, and in which their expertise is a given. Some women seem to be able to recount their experiences best between table clearing and gulps of tea. Rarely does one person hold an 'audience' without considerable interruption.

Jennie, an unemployed single mother describes what the centre means for her:

> I never heard tell of the women's movement before... then they had a meeting and there was an election of officers like, and I never went—I figure, well that's not for me right? And when we moved down there to the centre, and I went there I got to know more what a nice atmosphere and everything it was... in the place like... it was I think, its the best thing that ever happened, was for Stephenville to have a place like this. It was really, really comfortable.

It is the sense of comfort that allows Jenny to express her opinions and recount her experiences. Such an atmosphere is crucial when institutional powers and male authority are challenged as they were during the meeting which begins this paper. Unlike many private homes which may protect family secrets of abusive behaviours and tensions, the Women's Centre is a home which confronts publicly a myriad of social problems and inequalities from sexual abuse and family violence to health care. Although there is a profound respect for women's traditional skills and roles, these traditions are not guarded or romanticized as essentially or exclusively female. Moreover, the Women's Centre requires the experience and social power that accompanies women's new social and economic roles.

Conclusion

Feminist practices help women recognize their commonalities, validate their differences and mediate the various hierarchies between women that might fragment their collectivity. At the same time, the ideology of feminism does not spread uniformly through a population or a region. Rather, feminist ideas are absorbed into the life experiences of individual women, and infused through the ideologies of family, church and gender expectations that have historically framed life experience. Although consensus and egalitarian behaviour have long been heralded as key principles of feminist practice, considerable difficulty has been found in actually mediating hierarchies, affirming distinct contributions and maintaining co-operation within a feminist setting. While there is a clear indication that feminist principles inform activities at the Women's Centre, I suggest that this is facilitated, not by disregarding a shared history, but by recognizing and reshaping a way of life in all its dimensions.

Jane, the only woman at the centre to have lived away for some time, commented that she learned some of her feminist ideas in Toronto:

> In Toronto, I was carrying out traditional roles in and out of the home, and working to raise two children. I couldn't do it in Toronto, . . . I had no extended family, no community support. . . and the few friends I had, weren't enough. . . . I needed a place, and it was only here (Stephenville) that I could put my feminist ideas into play. I was looking for an opportunity to find my space and my safety here. . . . I was at a point to demand a place, and in spite of some rigidity at the centre in terms of behaviour, there was also an acceptance of diverse behaviour.

Feminists debate the means by which women might effect social change; they argue about the 'future' of the gender emancipation they envision. While feminist theorists argue the merits of various feminisms that include radical and liberal, such distinctions are not so finely parsed in the everyday activity of a women's centre or the individual evaluations of women. It is important to explore the ways in which feminism as an ideology can both reshape a cultural context, and be absorbed by it. In this way, feminism becomes more than just a crude plan or a language that may be appropriated or superimposed on social relationships that remain unchanged. It becomes a new way of life.

1 Funding for my research was provided by the Social Sciences and Humanities Research Council. Fieldwork research was conducted in Bay St. George from May 1992 to June 1993 and comprised participant observation and extensive interviews with residents, including numerous open-ended life histories. I would like to thank the women of Bay St. George, and the Bay St. George Women's Council whose co-operation and kindness made my research both possible and pleasant. I also thank Dr. Stuart Philpott, Dr. Marilyn Porter, and Dr. Barbara Neis for their helpful comments.

2 For a discussion of women's and men's roles historically see Marilyn Porter, this volume; Hilda Chaulk Murray, *More Then Fifty Per Cent.*

3 see Census of Canada, 1971,1976,1981,1986.

4 The nature and extent of female subordination in Newfoundland needs further research and theoretical elaboration which cannot be undertaken here. Academic studies which focus on economic relationships between men and women must be analysed with more recent studies sponsored by feminist organizations such as the Provincial Advisory Council, and Women's Policy Office, which document a range of abuses from cultural to physical and sexual.

5 This is not, however, a transition house and cannot offer the same kind of full-time security and protection.

6　For a consideration of diverse aspects of this problem, see collected essays in *Women and Social Change* ed. Jeri Dawn Wine,1991; also see Sheila Radford-Hill 'Considering Feminism as a Model for Social Change', 1986 and other collected essays in *Feminist Studies, Critical Studies*, 1986.

7　Research emphasizes the egalitarian nature of outport culture, (Davis, 1981; Faris, 1973; Chiariamonte, 1970; Porter, this volume). Socio-economic hierarchies in Bay St. George are somewhat truncated even in Stephenville itself, in comparison to the larger towns of Corner Brook and Grand Falls, which are viewed by many Newfoundlanders as considerably more status conscious and distinguished by class. An examination of class dynamics and culture in Bay St. George, however, goes beyond the scope of this paper.

The Innu and Militarization of Quebec/Labrador: Will the Silent People Please Stand Up?

Camille Fouillard

Camille Fouillard works with the Social Action Commission in St. John's, Newfoundland, and has worked in community development with the Innu for five years.

WHAT IS THE MILITARY DOING IN LABRADOR/QUEBEC? *At the Women and Development: The Effects of Militarization* conference held in North West River, women testify. One by one, women enter into roles and place themselves on a floor map of Labrador, sharing their knowledge and experiences of the impacts of the military expansion. "I'm a teacher from Port Hope Simpson. I don't know what's going on. I hear only what's in the news. What's all the fuss about?"

"I am a seal hunter's wife from the North Coast. We need country food because the food at the store costs too much. My husband came home with no seals because the jets flew over and scared them. What will we eat?"

"I am a woman from Labrador sitting in her bathroom because this military stuff is scaring the crap out of me. I love Labrador very much, but I'm scared to speak up because of the way business people belittle our opinions. I would be very powerful if I got together with everyone who is scared for our land and our people, and support the Innu."

"I am a letter on its way from the Straits to my son in Ontario. A letter, being sent because there were no jobs here. I am telling him to come home because there's lots of jobs in Labrador now."

"I am a woman and child from an East bloc country. We are the victims that NATO is training to kill."

"I am an Innu child running into the woods, freaked out by the fighter jets. I am a baby miscarried, dead, after a jet flow over my mother in the country."

We are seventy women gathered in the room. We come from all over Labrador, the North and South Coasts, the Straits, the Lake Melville area, and Nitassinan (Innu for "our homeland"), from 5 Quebec Innu communities, from Newfoundland, Nova Scotia, Ontario, the United States and the Philippines. We need this conference. Feelings are high. Tensions fill the air, stay with us and keep us on the edge of our seats. Tears and laughter punctuate our words - words in English and Innu-eimun. At one point, the group process breaks down. It is late afternoon; too many words in English don't exist in Innu-eimun.

"I am a German pilot looking for a fling here. It doesn't matter that I have a wife and children back home."

"I am the security fence they said they would never build."

Millicent Loder welcomes us all to "this beautiful, peaceful, free, still free, country of ours. . . I've lived long enough to know the before and after. I lived at a time when the Inuit and Settler people in the North lived peacefully together, and a time when the Innu and the Settlers around Lake Melville lived together without conflict."

"I am the salmon eggs destroyed by PCBs in our rivers."

"I am the Innu children protesting on the runway."

Emily Flowers, from Happy Valley, comes to me Saturday noon.

"This session didn't go at all the way you wanted, did it?"

"Well, not really."

"You wanted some information like the number of bombing ranges, and stuff like sonic booms, right?"

"Well yea, I think women want to know more about these things and I know there must be a fair bit of information in this room. If shared, it could give us a pretty good picture of what's happening."

"Well, I resent having to learn all those things. The military is not interested in learning about us."

I too am allergic to this information, it pollutes my mind; but I plead that knowledge is power. Maybe though, the group is right and it is enough to know the destruction, the divisions, the fear, the desperation, the unanswered questions.

Bernadette Jaqunos tells us about life in the Philippines with the American Clark and Subic Bases. Prostitution rings. 12-year-old girls infected with syphilis and gonorrhoea, suffering from multiple beatings—a ring maintained to whet the appetite of a U.S. military officer. She tells us of 23,000 "rest and recreation" girls, desperately poor, prostitutes, or according to the U.S. military "little brown fucking machines". A boy shot and killed while scavenging for scrap, mistaken for a wild pig. The military men transferred rather than prosecuted, their crimes committed "while performing their duty". The same U.S. military which is in our province.

"I am the declining fish stocks. The longliners want me, but I'm in the middle of the proposed sea bombing range."

"I am an Innu woman, pregnant, in the Stephenville jail. I left my kids at home. I'm unhappy and upset, but I will go on fighting for our rights."

Who is in control here? The women break up into small groups to discuss, and report back with drawings and theatre. Commanding Officer Engstad, ambition: to become Brigadier General. Ian Strachan, businessman, ambition: to become very rich. Small businesses get fewer bucks than they figured. Different parts of Labrador are stripping pieces off each other. The military wants more and more. There is a lot of sadness and discontent, dreams about having more control and what the people here want for their land.

The women from the Lake Melville area have a plan. We want development that relates to and builds on the cultures here. Development based on renewable resources. You can't take things from the land without putting things back in. We want tourism, adventure packages, bed and breakfast homes, tours on our water-ways. Forestry, wood supply to local markets, furniture manufacturing and wood crafts. Berry picking, jams and pies for tourists and locals. Seal and caribou tanning, leather crafts industry. Fish hatcheries and boat building. Farming, livestock, market gardening and small greenhouses. Recycling industries. Development of minerals such as Labradorite. Small businesses and co-ops. All for local people, controlled by us.

The Innu women add: "Why practice for war? If the military doesn't destroy the land that God put here on earth, the majority of people will survive."

A committee is formed to plan follow-up to the conference. Women, awake, and unite. This is all of our struggle.

Gathering Voices

This book opened with a collage of writings on the First Nations women who lived in Newfoundland and Labrador prior to, and during the early years of European colonization. These women's lives and work were available to us only through the eyes of predominantly male, European observers. During the past few years, some attempts have been made to gather together the writings and thoughts of First Nations women. This work is perhaps most advanced among the Innu. We would like to close this book with excerpts from two recent Innu reports: Mamunitau Staianimuanu: Ntuapatetau Tshetshi Uitshiakuts Stuassiminuts (Gathering Voices: Finding Strength to Help our Children) and Kamamuetimak: Tshentusen- timak Nte Steniunu Utat, Nitshish, Kie Nte Nikan (Gathering Voices: Discovering our Past, Present and Future). The first report, done by The Innu Nation and the Mushuau Innu Band Council, Utshimasits, Ntesinan, was their response to the tragic loss of 6 children in a house fire in Utshimasits (Davis Inlet). This report opens as follows:

> In February, our community lost 6 children in a house fire. This is still a very painful time for us. This is not the first time that our community was struck by tragedy. Everyone here has been touched by tragedy in our lives. Since 1973, we have lost forty-seven people in our community through alcohol-related deaths. In March, the Innu Nation and the Mushuau Innu Band Council decided to hold a People's Inquiry to gather information on why we have had so many tragedies in Utshimasits. We decided it was time we stopped and looked at why these accidents and violent deaths are happening to our people before it happens again. Too many people have died.

The second *Gathering Voices* report was the result of an Innu National Community Research project funded by the Royal Commission on Aboriginal Peoples.[1] It was dedicated:

> *To our elders,*
> in recognition of their wisdom,
> based in the past and the guide to our future.

330

Tshenut (Elders)
by Manimat Hurley

I want to learn more about our History
I am seeking help from you
Please, Do not ignore my plea
It is important at least you share.

Some of the old ways of your life
Turn around and face me and we should speak our minds.
It could take years, months, or many hours
Until I understand.

I am sorry for what has happened
I forgive you for not being able to teach me.
It will take time, I know
But, at least it is a beginning.

Don't be ashamed of our History
you know we are so Rich.
With all the Love and Resources we have.
Let's get off from the chair
and sit on the boughs while we chat.

August 21, 1993.

We Remember

"One time my father got an otter, but there was a man in the camp who was very angry and my father said it would be a long time before he would get another otter because the spirit was upset. It was a long time, years later when he got two otters; he said it was a gift from the animal spirit. Then we had a feast and looked after the bones and made sure no one in the camp got mad. And we shared it. When you kill an animal, you have to share it." Epa, Utshimassiu woman. [GV #2]

"One of the shamans was named Pien. I used to see him using the sweat lodge to dream. The elders would be able to tell young people where the animals were after using the sweat lodge. This is why I believe the elders, especially the women. I was raised in the country and followed the path of my elders." Katinen Pastitshi., Sheshatshiu woman. [GV #2]

Life Was a Lot of Hard Work

"I remember a time when my mother and my grandmother used the caribou skin to make a tent. I heard stories that people used bark for the tents as well. It's really unbelievable how people used to manage long ago. People used to hunt to survive. We never received anything from the government." *Mani An, Sheshatshiu Elder. [GV #2]*

Dependence

"In the old days, families used to travel inside wherever they liked. The leader always made the decision to move. As more families settled in Davis Inlet, the leadership disappeared. The only visible leadership was by the priest or his chosen people. Not that I dislike my grandfather. He was definitely a good leader, but he was taking orders from the priest.

My grandmother was in her 70's when she died and she had a big cross around her neck all the time. This was supplied by the priest. None of her beliefs were visible except for the big cross. It seemed like all her beliefs were buried by this cross." Kiti. [GV #1]

Some of us know that brothers and priests sexually abused boys and girls in this community. This is very hard for us to speak of.

"The brothers that came here teaching did things to us in the bathroom. When we were in school, they used to give us showers and wash our bottoms. We were all girls. They gave teenage girls showers. I was really afraid of these brothers." Gathering Voices Participant. [GV #1]

"When the first houses were constructed in 1967 in Utshimassits, there was a man here, a labourer, who asked the foreman, why there were no basements built? This was one of the promises that was made to us. 'Those will come later,' he was told, and 25 years later we are still waiting." Kiti, Utshimassiu woman. [GV #1]

Pregnant women now have to go out of the community to the hospital for a long time. There used to be midwives and they knew what they were doing. Now it is all changed. Some women wait one or two months for their delivery.

"I waited for a month when I was pregnant and I was really homesick. I didn't know anybody in Goose Bay. I missed my little girl and my husband. When I came home, my little girl didn't want to come to me. She didn't know me. It is really hard for women to be away from their families too long. We have midwives in the community. They can look after the deliveries. Many Innu children were born in the country with Innu midwives. That's all been taken from us too." Epa. [GV #1]

Some of us believe that if social workers have to take children away from their parents, they should place them in the community with families here. They should place them with their relatives. Or, we should have our own group home built in the community. Some of our children are asking for this. We should help our troubled children if they need help. We should stop Social Services from taking our children away. We care about our children.

Social Services also sends our women away to Libra House when they are beaten by their husbands. Most women run away from their husbands when they are drunk because they want to be placed in Libra House. A lot of women end up in hospital when they are beaten up by their husbands. This is an issue we don't agree on. Some of us think the man is the problem. Others think the woman starts the trouble. Some believe Libra House is good for the Protection of the women, and others think this only creates more problems. Many of us feel Social Services and Libra House are not dealing with the real problem when they send the women away.[GV #1]

"Right now I'm living by myself. My husband died years ago. There are a lot of people here in Sheshatshit. Now I never see anybody. It is very difficult to get help from people in Sheshatshit. This hurts me a lot to say this. I find it very difficult how some people don't respect their relatives. They don't give them anything when they are asked. We used to give each other food and visit each other. Elders were given food and they would visit each other. But now when I visit an elder, people laugh at me. They make fun of me and the other elder.

Now young people are spending too much time with a pencil. They should visit the elders and ask questions. If only young people now could just take the words from the elders. The children know everything in English, yet they don't know the traditional words. Here I am trying to teach them the words that I know, giving them advice, and yet every time they laugh at me. I talk to my kids. They won't listen to my advice. I have a foster child who is a boy, and I tell him a lot of things of what I know but he just laughs at me. His grandfather died but his spirit is still living. I tell him a lot of things every single day, but he doesn't seem to listen to me any more.

I don't work as hard as I used to, just slowly now, I am very tired when I give advice to my grandkids. Some of them don't listen to me. Only one grandchild comes to me and I give good advice to her. She told me she should have listened to my advice about her marriage. If she had, she would not be where she is today. I am not laughing at my grandchildren. Even if I gave her advice and she didn't listen, she learned from her mistakes." Mani Matinen Mishen, Sheshatshiu community workshop. [GV #1]

Alcohol and Substance Abuse: A Personal Story

"When we came to live in the community, my parents started drinking. It was really bad. It hurt everybody in the family. My sisters and I started drinking too. There was a lot of violence. When we were in the country, we used to listen to my parents all the time when they wanted us to do something. But in the community, we never listened to them.

My parents started drinking because there was nothing to do; there were no jobs in the community. But when I was really young, we would be out in the country and come back to the community. My father had a job with the priest working on the houses. Those days were good even if we were in the community. A lot of people were always helping one another. Men would be out hunting together. They would be playing checkers or cards all night. Women used to do things together too to help one another. Instead of going to home brew, people were always having meals together. The women would make a big pot of food, people would help themselves. There would be a big pot of tea. This would happen on the weekends, rather than when we were in school.

As I got older, I didn't see this happening much. There was more drinking. Now, women are fighting one another. Women used to tell their girls not to do stuff, but now they just let things go. A lot of women are drinking with their husbands too.

When I was young, my dad would drink but my mother was always with us. When she started drinking it got really bad. We were left by ourselves, we had to look after ourselves. In the mornings when it was school, we would sleep in. There would be no meals on for us. They would be drinking very early.

My parents drinking would really hurt me. I always felt like my parents didn't want me. I felt like they didn't love us when they turned to booze. It still hurts.

When they were in the country when we were getting older, they used to drink in the country too. When we knew we were getting ready to go, we would run away. We didn't want to go because of the booze. We would walk back to the community. We would have to do all the work they would tell us. I didn't want to be around them when they were drinking. They would stay up all night.

We always had to try to make them happy and we thought they would stop drinking if we listened. But even when we listened to them they wouldn't stop drinking. We would have to cook the meals. They would get us up in the middle of the night telling us to cook meals. When my parents would be out drinking, my older sister looked after us. She was like a mother. She would cook meals and do the laundry. My dad used to hit us when he would get really mad. My other sister was the hard case and she would fight my parents.

They would want us to get water to make their home brew. We used to help them. They would show us how and we used to make it for them. It's like enabling, that's what my sisters and I were doing. To make them happy, we had to do it.

When my parents were drinking, we didn't want to stay home. We would go to my aunt's house and spend time there. Then we started to act up. We were drinking; we missed a lot of school. We started sniffing gas. There was nothing for us to do in the community.

The home brew bucket was more important to my parents than the children. They would take it with them when they went out in the country. But when I was little, there was no home brew, just as I got older." Utshimassiu woman. [GV #1]

I used to have a problem with drinking before. I gave it up long ago now. I realized I had a problem with alcoholism and that is the reason I have given it up. Sometimes people offer me a drink, but I don't take it. When I say no, they say, "Who are you? What kind of a person are you? Are you a saint? I tell them no. But I did give it up because of God." Mani Matinen Mishen, Sheshatshiu elder.[GV #1]

Sexual abuse is another reason people drink. Disclosures have been made in our communities and there will be more. We don't know how to deal with this and many of us need healing. It's not only sexual abuse, but physical and mental abuse too. Victims are living with a lot of pain and we know the abusers are sick. Many of us don't believe the court system is the way to deal with this problem. It is not safe for victims and they are not winning. Abusers are not getting helped, but we have not developed another way to help people who are dealing with these problems. This has created extra stress and conflict in our communities. [GV # 1]

Healing

"In the summer, we organized a women's camp to learn about the culture. We had a healing circle there too and a sweat lodge. We started working together and there was a lot of communicating there. We plan to have another one next summer again. The women started getting together Christmas presents for the kids. Every month this year, the women gathered together and had birthday parties, baby showers, just to get together.

"Today I see half of the community has quit drinking. Sobriety is very high here. Only forty adults maybe and youth are still drinking. People recognize how alcohol has affected the community. They now have AA to go to. They see support from other sober people. They are realizing that alcohol is no good for them. It is just ruining their lives, their health and their families." Nupi Utshimassiu Alcohol Program worker. [GV #1]

"We have dealt with tragedies in this community. When the fire happened and the children died, people came together to talk about problems and out of this came Gathering Voices. *When the six children were found sniffing in January, we put together Hearing the Voices, a seven-point plan of what was needed to deal with that crisis. People came together again to find the solutions needed. The other tragedy we have been faced with is the disclosures being made about sexual abuse.*

"There are so many problems and issues for us to be dealing with. Even a small issue is major for some people. Like getting water is still a major problem. It is an issue that still needs to be dealt with in the community. We are taking steps to correct some of these problems. We have been discussing these issues at committee meetings; we've been making the right choices, finding solutions." Kiti, Utshimassiu woman. [GV #1]

Taking Control of Our Lives

"As Innu, we know more about the country and about our old people that died long ago when we are out there. The old people talked about the people who used to live there a long time ago, what their names were and what they did in the country. I don't think we will lose our culture because the young people are learning about their culture, like my sons Aaron and Simeon. They are interested in learning about it. The young people like myself and my husband are teaching our kids and they can teach their kids, and their kids, and so on. That way it won't disappear. I don't like speaking English." Kitinish, Utshimassiu woman. [GV #1]

"When I was growing up my father used to send us to school instead of going to the country. Mostly since I've been an adult I have been working. I don't really know what it's like in the country, so I'm not sure what I would feel like out there. I'm afraid I might get bored. But I think people in the country are more happy. They seem to enjoy doing things out there that they cannot do in Davis Inlet, like tanning caribou hide. People say the kids listen a lot more. They quiet down and don't act up like they do here in the village." Katinin, Utshimassiu woman. [GV #1]

"This is Innu land and sometimes now the governments or the white agencies just go ahead and do things without letting the Innu know. I think they should let the Innu know. I want them to do this because when I am gone, I want my grandchildren and their children to use the land. This is Innu land," Mani Ann Selma, Sheshatshiu elder. [GV #1]

"We are now at a very critical stage in the community's and in people's lives. We are seeing people come together to find solutions, make the right choices and changes for our children and future generations. We are facing up to and dealing with the issues and problems at hand. We will become a model for other Native communities across Canada that have similar problems to us. We will be able to show other people how we have dealt with our problems." Kiti, Utshimassiu woman. [GV #1]

---

[1] These reports are being published in book form as *Gathering Voices: Finding Strength to Help Our Children*, ed. Camille Fouillard, Douglas & McIntyre, Vancouver, 1995.

References

Primary Sources-Archival
CENTRE FOR NEWFOUNDLAND STUDIES (CNS)
MEMORIAL UNIVERSITY

Acts of the Honourable Commission of Government of Newfoundland, 1942 and 1944 (St. John's).

Canada Employment Centre (Stephenville) 1983. 'Report on Youth Survey.'

Canada and Newfoundland 1953. Newfoundland Fisheries Development Committee Report. St. John's.

Census of Newfoundland and Labrador, 1911, 1921, 1935, 1945.

Census of Canada. 1991. Catalogue 93-311. Dwellings and Households the Nation.

Educational Planning and Design Associates, 1994. *Women of the Fishery.*

The Evening Telegram.

Papers of the Newfoundland and Labrador Women's Institutes (NLWI):

Executive Committee Minutes:
>   Book II August 1936 - April 1938
>   Book III May 1938 - February 1942

Trustee Minutes:

1935-47 *Trustee Minute Book*

Annual General Meeting (AGM) Minutes:

Book I, 1937-64 *Annual Meeting Minutes*, Volume 1.

Annual Reports:

1936-60, *Annual Reports.*

Newfoundland and Labrador Women's Institutes (NLWI) ~Correspondence:

1937-64, "Historical Information Dealing/Relating to Jubilee Guilds Institute".

Biographies of Past Presidents.

1936 forward

Proceedings of the Newfoundland House of Assembly 1925, 1926, 1929, 1930. St. John's.

Report of the Findings of the Royal Commission of 1922 in *The Liberal Press*, 16 March 1929.

NATIONAL ARCHIVES OF CANADA (NAC)
Papers of Charles A. McGrath, 1933. Microfilm H1419-20-21.

PROVINCIAL ARCHIVES OF NEWFOUNDLAND AND LABRADOR (PANL)
British Empire Service League. MG 617, files #1, 2, 3/3A.

Commission Department of Natural Resources, GN 31/2 file # 318, Volume I, Jubilee Guilds file "Jubilee Guilds of Newfoundland, Outport Organization" GN 31/3A, file #R116

"Jubilee Guilds of Newfoundland."

"The Jubilee Guilds of Newfoundland, Organization of the Guilds." file C10/11

"Co-operative Women's Organization."

Newfoundland Board of Trade, P8/B/11, Box 11, File 13.

Eric Ellis Papers, PN55, Box 1.

Executive Council, GN9/1, Minute Books, Minutes of Commission of Government, 4 September 1933, #633.

OTHER

Canada Employment Centre (Stephenville). 1992. 'Labour Force Analysis'

Canada Employment Centre (Stephenville). 1987. 'Youth Survey Follow-up', 1987

Employment and Immigration Canada, n.d. "Invest in your own future" Ottawa: EIC.

Seventh Census of Canada, 1931.

Sixth Census of Canada, 1921.

Statistics Canada. 1988. Population and Dwelling Characteristics -Census Divisions and Sub-divisions. Profiles. Newfoundland:

Statistics Canada 1982 "Family Income, 1982", # 13-208."Income Distribution, 1982", # 13-206

Statistics Canada. 1993. "Violence Against Women Survey", *The Daily*, Thursday Nov. 18.

Secondary Sources:

Abbott, Walter M., S.J. (ed) 1966. *The Documents of Vatican II*. New York: Guild Press.

Acheson, James M. 1981. "Anthropology of Fishing." *Annual Review of Sociology* 10:275-316.

Alcoff, Linda 1988. "Cultural Feminism Versus Post-Structuralism: The Identity Crisis in Feminist Theory." *Signs* 13: 405-436.

Alexander, D. 1976. "Newfoundland's Traditional Economy and Development to 1934." *Acadiensis*, 5: 56-78.

Alexander, D. 1977. *The Decay of Trade*. St. John's: ISER.

Allison, C., S. Jacobs, M. Porter 1989. *Winds of Change: Women in Northwest Commercial Fishing*. Seattle: University of Washington Press.

Alonso, Ana Maria 1988. "The Effects of Truth: Re-Presentations of the Past and the Imagining of Community." *Journal of Historical Sociology* 1 (1): 33-57.

Andersen, R. and Wadel, C. 1972. *North Atlantic Fishermen*. St. John's: ISER.

Anderson, Karen L. 1991. *Chain her by One Foot: The Subjugation of Women in Seventeenth-Century New France*. London: Routledge.

Andrews, Ray 1969. "The Role of Women in the Port de Grave Fishery in 1969." Unpublished Manuscript, Memorial University.

Anger, Dorothy, C. McGrath, S. Pottle 1986. Women and Work in Newfoundland. Background Report to the Royal Commission on Employment and Unemployment. St. John's: Queen's Printer.

Anger, Dorothy 1988. *Novwa' mkisk (Where the Sand Blows...): Vignettes of Bay St. George Micmacs*. Port au Port East: Bay St. George Regional Indian Band Council.

Anonymous 1975. *Alluring Labrador: Labrador Today with the Past in Hand*. Happy Valley: Them Days.

Antler, Ellen 1977. "Women's Work in Newfoundland Fishing Families." *Atlantis*, 2(2): 106-113.

Antler, E. 1981. Fisherman, Fisherwoman, Rural Proletariat: Capitalist Commodity Production in the Newfoundland Fishery. Unpublished Ph.D. dissertation, University of Connecticut.

Antler, E., Faris J. 1979. "Adaptation to Changes in Technology and Government Policy: A Newfoundland Example." *North Atlantic Maritime Cultures* Raoul Andersen (ed). Mouton: the Hague.

Armitage, Peter 1990. Land Use and Occupancy among the Innu of Utshimassit and Sheshatshit. Prepared for the Innu Nation, July.

Armitage, Peter 1991. *The Innu (the Montagnais-Naskapi)*. New York: Chelsea House Publishers.

Armitage, Peter 1992. "Religious Ideology among the Innu of Eastern Quebec and Labrador." *Religiologiques* 6: 64-110.

Armstrong, Pat, Hugh Armstrong 1984. *The Double Ghetto: Canadian Women and Their Segregated Work*. Toronto: McClelland and Stewart.

338

Armstrong, Pat, Hugh Armstrong 1987. "Beyond Sexless Class and Classless Sex," in *The Politics of Diversity* R. Hamilton and M. Barrett (eds). London: Verso. pp. 208-40.

Asad, Talal 1983. "Anthropological Conceptions of Religion: Reflections on Geertz." *Man* (N.S.) 18: 237-59.

Assheton-Smith, Marilyn 1965. "Organization of a Rural Community." Unpublished paper, University of Minnesota.

Assheton-Smith, Marilyn 1973. "Women and Politics in Western Canada: A Socio-Political Study." Paper presented at the Western Association of Sociology and Anthropology, Banff.

Awareness for Women in the Fishery Report 1984. Sydney, Cape Breton.

Barrett, Gene, A. Davis 1984. "Floundering in Troubled Waters: The Political Economy of the Atlantic Fishery and the Task Force on Atlantic Fisheries." *Journal of Canadian Studies* 19:108-124.

Barrett, Michelle, M. McIntosh 1980. "The Family Wage: Some Problems for Socialists and Feminists." *Capital and Class*, 2 (Summer): 51-72.

Bartky, Sandra Lee 1988. "Foucault, Femininity, and the Modernization of Patriarchal Power." *Feminism and Foucault: Reflections on Resistance.* Irene Diamond and Lee Quinby (eds). Boston: Northeastern University Press.

Bates, Stewart 1944. Report on the Canadian Atlantic Sea-Fishery. Halifax: Department of Trade and Industry.

Batten, E., D. Gray, C. Hallett, A. Lewis, J. Lewis 1974. *Working Women in Newfoundland.*

Ben-Dor, Shmuel 1966. *Makkovik: Eskimos and Settlers in a Labrador Community: A Contrastive Study in Adaptation.* St. John's: ISER.

Benhabib, Seyla, Drucilla Cornell. 1990. "Introduction: Beyond the Politics of Gender." *Feminism as Critique* Seyla Benhabib and Drucilla Cornell (eds). Minneapolis: University of Minnesota Press.

Benoit, Cecilia 1981. The Poverty of Mothering. Unpublished M.A. dissertation, Memorial University.

Benoit, Cecilia 1990. "Mothering in a Newfoundland Community, 1900-1940." *Delivering Motherhood* K. Arnup, A. Levesque, R. Roach Pierson (eds). London: Routledge pp. 173-189.

Benoit, Cecilia 1991. *Midwives in Passage: The Modernisation of Maternity Care.* St. John's: ISER.

Bluestone, Barry, Bennett Harrison 1982. *The Deindustrialization of America.* New York: Basic.

Bodenhorn, Barbara 1990. "I'm Not the Great Hunter, My Wife Is" Inupiat and Anthropological Models of Gender." *Inuit Studies* 14(1-2): 55-74.

Bolster, M. Angela, R.S.M 1990. *Catherine McAuley: Venerable for Mercy.* Dublin: Dominican Publications.

Boserup, Ester 1970. *Women's Role in Economic Development.* London: Allen and Unwin.

Bossen, Laurel 1975. "Women in Modernizing Societies." *American Ethnologist* 2(4):587-601.

Brantenburg, Anne 1977. "The Marginal School and the Children of Nain." *The White Arctic: Anthropological Essays on Tutelage and Ethnicity* Robert Paine (ed). St. John's: ISER.

Brice-Bennett, Carol 1981. Two Opinions: Inuit and Moravian Missionaries in Labrador 1804-1860. Unpublished M.A. dissertation, Memorial University.

Briggs, Jean 1974. "Eskimo Women: Makers of Men." *Many Sisters: Women in Cross-Cultural Perspective* Carolyn J. Matthiasson (ed). New York: The Free Press.

Briskin, Linda 1991. "Feminist Practice: A New Approach to Evaluating Feminist Strategy." *Women and Social Change* Jeri Dawn Wine and Janet Ristock (eds). Toronto: James Lorimer and Company.

Brox, Ottar 1969. *The Maintenance of Economic Dualism in Newfoundland.* St. John's: ISER.

339

Budgell, Richard 1992. "Beothuks and the Newfoundland Mind." *Newfoundland Studies* 8(1): 15-33.

Burman, Patrick 1991. "Living and Theorizing the New Terms for Human Agency." Paper presented at the Annual Meeting of the Canadian Sociology and Anthropology Association, Kingston, June.

Burnham, Dorothy K. 1992. *To Please the Caribou: Painted Caribou-Skin Coats worn by the Naskapi, Montagnais, and Cree Hunters of the Quebec-Labrador Peninsula.* Toronto: Royal Ontario Museum.

Burstyn, Varda 1983. "Masculine Dominance and the State." *The Socialist Register* pp. 45-89.

Buss, Terry, F. Stevens Redburn 1983. *Shutdown at Youngstown Public Policy for Mass Unemployment.* Albany: SUNY Press.

Butler, Judith 1990. *Gender Trouble: Feminism and the Subversion of Identity.* New York: Routledge.

Buvinic, Mayra 1984. "Projects for Women in the Third World: Explaining Their Misbehavior." Prepared for the Office of Women in Development, US Agency for International Development. Washington, D.C.: International Center for Research on Women.

Byrne, Lavinia 1988. *Women Before God.* London: SPCK.

Cadigan, Sean 1991. Economic and Social Relations of Production in the Northeast-Coast of Newfoundland, with Special Reference to Conception Bay 1785-1855. Unpublished Ph.D. dissertation, Memorial University.

Caine, Barbara, E.A. Grosz, M. de Lepervanche (eds) 1988. *Crossing Boundaries: Feminisms and the Critique of Knowledges.* Sydney: Allen Unwin.

Callender, Claire 1987. "Women and the Redundancy Process: A Case Study." *Redundancy, Layoffs and Plant Closures Their Character, Causes and Consequences* Raymond M. Lee (ed). London: Croom Helm, pp. 141-180.

Campbell-Jones, Suzanne 1979. *In Habit: An Anthropological Study of Working Nuns.* Boston: Faber & Faber.

Canadian Conference of Catholic Bishops 1990. "Workshops on Inclusive Language". Ottawa: Publications Service, Canadian Conference of Catholic Bishops.

Carroll, Berenice A. 1979. "Political Science, Part I: American Politics and Political Behavior." *Signs,* 5(2): 289-306.

Cashin, Richard 1990. "Campaign for Survival." St. John's: Fishermen, Food and Allied Workers Union.

Cell, G.T. 1972. *Newfoundland Discovered: English Attempts at Colonization, 1610-1630.* London: Hakluyt Society.

Chamberlain, M. 1977. *Fenwomen.* London: Virago.

Chamberlin, J.E. 1975. *The Harrowing of Eden: White Attitudes Toward Native Americans.* New York: Seabury Press.

Charest, Paul 1973. "Cultural Ecology of the North Shore of the Gulf of St. Lawrence." *Communities and Culture in French Canada* Gerald Gold and Marc-Adelard Tremblay (eds). Toronto: Holt, Rinehart and Winston, pp. 11-50.

Chiarmonte, Louis 1970. *Craftsman-Client Contracts.* St. John's: ISER.

Christiansen-Ruffman, Linda 1980. "Women as Persons in Atlantic Canadian Communities." *Resources for Feminist Research,* (Special Publication No. 8): 55-57.

Christiansen-Ruffman, L. 1983. "Women's Political Culture and Feminism in Canada." Unpublished paper.

Christiansen-Ruffman, L. 1987. "Wealth Re-Examined: Toward a Feminist Analysis of Women's Development Projects in Canada and in the Third World." *Women in International Development Publication Series.* East Lansing: Michigan State University.

340

Christiansen-Ruffman, L. 1989. "Women and Development in Canada." *Women and Development in Africa: Comparative Perspectives.* Jane Parpart (ed). Lanham, MD: University Press of America.

Christiansen-Ruffman, L. 1989b. "Inherited Biases Within Feminism: The "Patricentric Syndrome" and the "Either/Or Syndrome" in Sociology." *Feminism: From Pressure to Politics* Angela Miles and Geraldine Finn (eds). Montreal: Black Rose Books.

Christiansen-Ruffman, L. 1990. "On the Contradictions of State-Sponsored Participation: A Case Study of the Community Employment Strategy Program in Labrador, Nova Scotia and Prince Edward Island." *Community Organization and the Canadian State* Roxana Ng, G. Walker, J. Muller (eds). Toronto: Garamond, pp. 85-107.

Christiansen-Ruffman, L. forthcoming. "Women's Conceptions of the Political: Three Canadian Women's Organizations." *Feminist Organizations: Harvest of the New Women's Movement* Myra Marx Ferree and Patricia Yancey Martin (eds). Philadelphia: Temple University Press.

Christiansen-Ruffman, L., L. Brown 1985. "Women's Community Work: A Third Part of the Puzzle." Paper presented at the conference "Women and the Invisible Economy" Concordia University, February.

Christiansen-Ruffman, Linda, R. Hafter, H. Ralston, W. Katz, F. Chao 1975. "Women's Concerns About the Quality of Life in the Halifax Metropolitan Area." prepared for Ministry of State for Urban Affairs. Halifax: Saint Mary's University.

Clark, Richard 1951. Newfoundland 1934-1949 - A Study of the Commission of Government and Confederation with Canada. Unpublished Ph.D. dissertation, University of California, Los Angeles.

Clear, Catriona 1987. *Nuns in Nineteenth Century Ireland.* Dublin: Gill and MacMillan.

Clement, Wallace 1986. *The Struggle to Organize: Resistance in Canada's Fishery.* Toronto: McClelland and Stewart.

Cohen, Marcy 1992. "A New Framework for Regulating Training Policy: the Implications for Progressive Trade Unionists and Social Activists in Canada." Unpublished paper, Toronto, OISE.

Cohen, M, 1991. "Reflections on Past Research—A Feminist Post-Structuralist Reading of the Deskilling Debate." Unpublished paper, Toronto, OISE.

Cole, Sally 1991. *Women of the Praia: Work and Lives in a Portuguese Coastal Community.* Princeton: Princeton University Press.

Connelly, Pat, M. MacDonald 1991-92. "The Impact of State Policy on Women's Work in the Fishery." *Journal of Canadian Studies,* 4: 18-32.

Connelly, P. 1978. *Last Hired, First Fired: Women and the Canadian Work Force.* Toronto: The Women's Press.

Crantz, David 1820. "Narrative of the First Settlement made by the United Brethren on the Coast of Labrador with a brief view of the Progress of the Mission." *The History of Greenland* 2: Appendix. London: Longman, Rees, Orme and Brown.

Crowley, Terry 1986. "The Origins of Continuing Education for Women, The Ontario Women's Institutes." *Canadian Woman Studies/Les Cahiers De La Femme,* 7 (3): 78-81.

Cullum, Linda, M. Baird, C. Penney 1993. "Women and Law in Newfoundland from Early Settlement to the Twentieth Century." *Pursuing Equality: Historical Perspectives on Women in Newfoundland and Labrador* Linda Kealey (ed). St. John's: ISER, pp. 66-162.

Dalton, Mary 1992. "Shadow Indians: The Beothuk Motif in Newfoundland Literature." *Newfoundland Studies* 8(2): 135-146.

Danylewycz, Marta 1987. *Taking the Veil: An Alternative to Marriage, Motherhood, and Spinsterhood in Quebec, 1840-1920.* Paul-André Linteau, A. Prentice, W. Westfall (eds). Toronto: McClelland and Stewart.

Davies, Bronwyn, Rom Harre 1990. "Positioning: The Discursive Production of Selves." *Journal for the Theory of Social Behaviour*, 20 (1): 43-63.

Davis, Dona Lee 1979. "Social Structure, Sex Roles and Female Associations in a Newfoundland Fishing Village." Paper presented at the CESCE Meetings, Banff, February.

Davis, D. L. 1983. "The Family and Social Change in the Newfoundland Outport." *Culture* 3(1): 19-31.

Davis, D. L. 1983a. *Blood and Nerves: An Ethnographic Focus on Menopause*. St. John's: ISER.

Davis, D. L. 1986. "Occupational Community and Fishermen's Wives in a Newfoundland Fishing Village." *Anthropological Quarterly*, 59(3): 129-142.

Davis, D. L. 1988. "Shore Skippers and Grass Widows": Active and Passive Women's Roles in a Newfoundland Fishery." *To Work and to Weep: Women in Fishing Economies* Janet Nadel-Klein, D.L. Davis (eds). St. John's: ISER.

DAWN, 1985. *Development, Crises and Alternative Visions: Third World Women's Perspectives* Gita Sen (ed). Monthly Review Press.

de Lauretis, Teresa 1986. "Feminist Studies/Critical Studies: Issues, Terms, Contexts." *Feminist Studies/Critical Studies* Teresa de Lauretis (ed). Bloomington: Indiana University Press.

Decks Awash 1986. *Labrador Straits Communities* 15 (5).

Demmler-Kane, Jean 1980. Multiple Migration and the Social Participation of Married Women. Unpublished Ph.D dissertation, McMaster University.

Dewitt, Robert L. 1969. *Public Policy and Community Protest: The Fogo Case*. St. John's: ISER.

di Leonardo, Micaela. 1991. "Introduction: Gender, Culture, and Political Economy, Feminist Anthropology in Historical Perspective." *Gender at the Crossroads of Knowledge: Feminist Anthropology in the Postmodern Era* Micaela di Leonardo (ed). Berkeley: University of California Press.

Diack, Lesley 1964. *Labrador Nurse*. London: Gollancz.

Dillon, L. 1983. Black Diamond Bay: A Rural Community in Newfoundland unpublished M.A. dissertation, Memorial University.

Dinn, Sister Mary James 1975. *Foundation of the Presentation Congregation in Newfoundland*. St. John's: Presentation Sisters of Newfoundland.

Duley, Margot 1993. "'The Radius of Her Influence for Good': The Rise and Triumph of the Women's Suffrage Movement in Newfoundland, 1909-1925, with Associated Documents." *Pursuing Equality: Historical Perspectives on Women in Newfoundland and Labrador* Linda Kealey (ed). St. John's: ISER. Books.

Dumont, Micheline 1992. "The Origins of the Women's Movement in Quebec." *Challenging Times: The Women's Movement in Canada and the United States* Constance Backhouse, David Flaherty (eds). Montreal and Kingston: McGill-Queen's University Press.

Ebaugh, Helen Rose Fuchs 1993. *Women in the Vanishing Cloister: Organizational Decline in Catholic Religious Orders in the United States*. New Brunswick, N.J.: Rutgers University Press.

Emmett I. 1964. *A North Wales Parish*. London: Routledge.

Fardy, B.D. 1988. *Demasduit Native Newfoundlander*. St. John's: Creative Publishers.

Faris, James 1972. *Cat Harbour: A Newfoundland Fishing Settlement*. St. John's: ISER.

Farrell, Susan A. 1991. "'It's Our Church Too!': Women's Position in the Catholic Church Today." *The Social Construction of Gender* Judith Lorber, Susan A. Farrell (eds). London: Sage Publications.

Felt, Larry 1987. *Take the 'Bloods of Bitches' to the Gallows: Culture and Structural Constraints Upon Interpersonal Violence in Rural Newfoundland*. St. John's: ISER.

342

Feltham, F. 1968. *White and Blue Collars in a Mill Shutdown*. Ithaca, New York: Cornell University Press.

Ferris, J.S., C. G. Plourde 1982. "Labour Mobility, Seasonal Unemployment Insurance, and the Newfoundland Inshore Fishery." *Canadian Journal of Economics* 15(3): 426-441.

Firestone, Melvin 1967. *Brothers and Rivals: Patrilocality in Savage Cove*. St. John's: ISER.

Fishery Research Group 1986. *The Social Impact of Technological Change in Newfoundland's Deepsea Fishery*. St. John's: ISER.

Fishery Products International 1990. *Fishery Products International Annual Report 1989*. St. John's: FPI.

Flynn, J. 1937. "The Catholic Church in Newfoundland." *The Book of Newfoundland, Vol. III* J.R. Smallwood (ed). St. John's.

Fogo Island Co-operative Society, Ltd. 1982. "Submission to Task Force on Atlantic Fisheries" Seldom, Newfoundland (April 30).

Forestell, Nancy, Jesse Chisolm 1988. "Working Class Women as Wage Earners in St. John's, Newfoundland, 1890-1921." *Feminist Research: Prospect and Retrospect* Peta Tancred-Sheriff (ed). Montreal: McGill Queen's.

Forestell, N. 1987. Women's Paid Labour in St. John's Between the Two World Wars. Unpublished M.A. dissertation, Memorial University.

Foucault, Michel 1979. *Discipline and Punish: The Birth of the Prison*. Alan Sheridan (trans.). New York: Vintage Books.

Fouillard, Camille 1990. Identification of Major Deficiencies with Regard to Women in the Environmental Impact Statement on Military Flying Activities in Labrador and Quebec. Report prepared for the National Action Committee on the Status of Women and Canadian Voice of Women for Peace.

Francis, Daniel 1992. *The Imaginary Indian: The Image of the Indian in Canadian Culture*. Vancouver: Arsenal Pulp Press.

Franco, Jean 1989. *Plotting Women: Gender and Representation in Mexico*. New York: Columbia University Press.

Frankenberg R. 1966. *Communities in Britain*. Harmondsworth: Penguin.

Gardiner, Jean 1977. "Women in the Labour Process and Class Structure." *Class and Class Structure* A. Hunt (ed). London, pp. 22-48.

Gersuny, Carl and John J. Poggie Jr. 1974. "A Fishermen's Cooperative: Open System Theory Applied." *Maritime Studies and Management* 1: 215-222.

Gillespie, Bill 1986. *A Class Act: An Illustrated History of the Labour Movement in Newfoundland and Labrador*. St. John's: The Newfoundland and Labrador Federation of Labour.

Goode, William 1971. "Civil and Social Rights of Women." *The Other Half: Roads to Women's Equality* C. Epstein, W. Goode (eds). Englewood Cliffs: Prentice-Hall, pp. 21-39.

Government of Newfoundland and Labrador 1985. *Historical Statistics of Newfoundland and Labrador, Vol 2*. St. John's: Department of Public Works and Services.

Grant-Head, C. 1976. *Eighteenth Century Newfoundland*. Toronto: University of Toronto Press.

Grayson, J. Paul 1986. "Plant Closures and Political Despair." *Canadian Review of Sociology and Anthropology* 23(3): 331-349.

Gregory, Ann 1987. Study of the Impact of a Household Based Support Programme Upon Women in Newfoundland and Labrador. St. John's: Women's Policy Office, Government of Newfoundland and Labrador.

Grieco, Margaret 1981. "The Shaping of a Work Force: A Critique of the Affluent Worker Study." *The International Journal of Sociology and Social Policy 1(1)*.

Guemple, Lee 1986. "Men and Women, Husbands and Wives: The Role of Gender in Traditional Inuit Society" *Inuit Studies*, 10(1-2): 9-24.

Halton, J. M. Harvey 1883. *Newfoundland: The Oldest British Colony*. London.

Hamilton, Sylvia 1993. "The Women at the Well: African Baptist Women Organize." *Feminist Political Mobilizing in Contemporary Canada* Linda Carty (ed). Toronto: Women's Press, pp. 189-203.

Handcock, W. Gordon 1977. "English Migration to Newfoundland." *The Peopling of Newfoundland* John Mannion (ed). St. John's: ISER.

Handcock, W. G. 1989. *So longe as there comes noe women: Origins of English Settlement in Newfoundland*. St. John's: Breakwater.

Hansen, Gary B. 1988. "Layoffs, Plant Closings, and Worker Displacement in America: Serious Problems that Need a National Solution." *Journal of Social Issues* 44(4): 153-171.

Hardon, John A., S.J. 1980. *Modern Catholic Dictionary*. Garden City, N.Y.: Doubleday and Company.

Hayden, Dolores 1981. *The Grand Domestic Revolution: A History of Feminist Designs for American Homes, Neighbourhoods, and Cities*. Cambridge: MIT Press.

Hayden, D. 1984. *Redesigning the American Dream: The Future of Housing, Work and Family Life*. Don Mills: Stoddart.

Henriksen, Georg 1973. *Hunters in the Barrens: The Naskapi on the Edge of the Whiteman's World*. St. John's: ISER.

Hill, Robert 1983. *The Meaning of Work and the Reality of Unemployment in the Newfoundland Context*. St.John's: Community Services Council.

Hoagland, Sarah Lucia 1988. *Lesbian Ethics: Toward New Value*. Palo Alto: Institute of Lesbian Studies.

Hogan, Sister M. Williamina 1986. *Pathways of Mercy: History of the Foundation of the Sisters of Mercy in Newfoundland 1842-1984*. St. John's: Harry Cuff Publications.

Hogan, Gail 1983. "Female Labour in the Labrador Floater Fishery." Unpublished paper, Maritime History Group, Memorial University.

Howell, Colin, R. J. Twomey (eds) 1991. *Jack Tar in History: Essays in the History of Maritime Life and Labour*. Fredericton: Acadiensis Press.

Howley, The Very Reverend M.F., D.D. 1979. *Ecclesiastical History of Newfoundland*. Ontario: Mika Publishing [first published: 1888].

Howley, J.P. 1974. *The Beothucks or Red Indians: The Aboriginal Inhabitants of Newfoundland*. Toronto: Coles.

Hubbard, Mina 1983. *A Woman's Way Through Unknown Labrador*. St. John's: Breakwater.

Hussey, Greta 1987. *Our Life on Lears Room, Labrador*. St John's: privately printed.

Inglis, Gordon 1985. *More than Just a Union: The Story of the NFFAWU*. St. John's: Jesperson.

Innu Nation Community Research Project 1993. *Gathering Voices: Discovering our Past, Present and Future*. Report Funded by the Royal Commission on Aboriginal Peoples, Nitassinan.

Innu Nation and the Mushuau Innu Band Council 1992. *Gathering Voices: Finding Strength to Help our Children*. Report of the People's Inquiry, Utshimasits, Nitassinan.

Iverson, Noel, D.R. Matthews 1968. *Communities in Decline: An Examination of Household Resettlement in Newfoundland*. St. John's: ISER.

Jackson, Nancy 1989. "Training for Workers, not for Bosses." *It's Our Own Knowledge: Labour, Public Education and Skills Training*. Toronto: Our Schools/Our Selves Educational Foundation and Garamond Press, pp.81-97.

Jaquette J.S. 1974. *Women in Politics*. New York: Wiley.

John Paul II 1988. Dignity and Vocation of Women. *Apostolic Letter Mulieris Dignitatem of the*

Supreme Pontiff on the Occasion of the Marian Year, Vatican (trans.). Sherbrooke: Editions Paulines.

Kaplan, Temma 1982. "Female Consciousness and Collective Action: The Case of Barcelona, 1910-1918." *Signs* 7(3): 545-566.

Kaplan, Temma 1990. "Community and Resistance in Women's Political Cultures." *Dialetical Anthropology* 15: 259-267.

Kealey, Linda (ed) 1993. *Pursuing Equality: Historical Perspectives on Women in Newfoundland and Labrador.* St. John's: ISER.

Kennedy, John C. 1982. *Holding the Line: Ethnic Boundaries in a Northern Labrador Community.* St. John's: ISER.

Kessler-Harris, Alice 1976. "Women's Work and Economic Crisis: Some Lessons of the Great Depression." *Review of Radical Political Economics*, 8: 73-97.

Kessler-Harris, A. 1982. *Out to Work: A History of Wage-Earning Women in the United States.* New York.

Kirby, Michael J. 1984. Restructuring the Atlantic Fishery: A Case Study in Business-Government Relations. York University.

Knight, Dennis 1993. Final Report Southern Avalon (Trepassey Plant) Industrial Adjustment Committee. St. John's: Employment and Immigration Canada.

Kome, Penney 1983. *The Taking of Twenty-Eight: Women Challenge the Constitution.* Toronto: Women's Press.

Kondo, Dorinne K. 1990. *Crafting Selves: Power, Gender and Discourses of Identity in a Japanese Workplace.* Chicago: University of Chicago Press.

Krahn, Harvey, J. Gartrell, L. Larson 1981. "The Quality of Family Life in a Resource Community." *Canadian Journal of Sociology*, 6(3).

Ilcan, Suzan 1985. "The Position of Women in the Nova Scotia Secondary Fishing Industry: A Community-Based Study." Working paper no. 8-85, Gorsebrook Research Institute, Saint Mary's University, Halifax.

Land, Hilary 1980. "The Family Wage." *Feminist Review*, 6: 55-77.

Larkin, Maureen 1990. "State Policy and Survival Strategies in P.E.I. Lobster Fishing Households." *From the Margin to the Centre: Proceedings of the 25th Anniversary Meeting of the Atlantic Association of Sociologists and Anthropologists* Janet Burns, G. Pool and C. McCormick (eds). Saint John: University of New Brunswick.

Lather, Patti 1991. *Getting Smart: Feminist Research and Pedagogy With/in the Postmodern.* New York: Routledge.

Leddy, Mary Jo, Bishop Remi de Roo, D. Roche 1992. *In the Eye of the Catholic Storm: The Church Since Vatican II.* Toronto: Harper Perennial, Harper Collins.

Leyton, Elliott 1975. *Dying Hard: The Ravages of Industrial Carnage.* Toronto: McClelland and Stewart.

Light, B., Prentice, A. 1980, *Pioneer and Gentlewomen of British North America, 1713-1867.* Toronto: University of Toronto Press.

Little, Linda 1984. Plebeian Collective Action in Harbour Grace and Carbonear, Newfoundland, 1830-1840. Unpublished M.A. dissertation, Memorial University.

Lummis, Trevor 1985. *Occupation and Society: The East Anglian Fishermen 1880-1914.* Cambridge: Cambridge University Press.

Luxton, Meg 1980. *More Than a Labour of Love: Three Generations of Women's Work in the Home.* Toronto: The Woman's Press.

Luxton, M. 1990. "Two Hands for the Clock: Changing Patterns in the Gendered Division of Labour." *Through the Kitchen Window: The Politics of Home and Family* Meg Luxton, H. Rosenberg, S. Arat-Koc (eds). Toronto: Garamond Press.

Luxton, M. 1990a. "From Ladies Auxiliaries to Wives Committees." *Through the Kitchen Window* Meg Luxton, H. Rosenberg, S. Arat-Koc (eds). Toronto: Garamond Press.

MacDonald, Martha, P. Connelly 1989. "Class and Gender in Fishing Communities in Nova Scotia." *Studies in Political Economy*, 30: 61-86.

Mackintosh, Maureen 1977. "Reproduction and Patriarchy." *Capital and Class*, 2.

Maida, Carl, N. S. Gordon, N. L. Farberow 1989. *The Crisis of Competence: Transitional Stress and the Displaced Worker.* New York: Brunner/Mazel Psychosocial Stress Series No.16.

Mailhot, José 1984. "Beyond Everyone's Horizon Stand the Naskapi." *Ethnohistory*, 33(4): 384-418.

Mannion, John (ed) 1977. *The Peopling of Newfoundland.* St. John's: ISER.

Marchak, Patricia 1976. "Women in Corporate and Marginal Employment Situations in Hinterland Forestry Towns in British Columbia." Paper presented to the Conference: Research on Women: Current Projects and Future Directions, Mount St. Vincent University, Halifax.

Margolis, Diane R. 1979. "The Invisible Hands: Sex Roles and the Division of Labor in Two Local Political Parties." *Social Problems* 26 (3): 314-324.

Marshall, Ingeborg C.L. 1989. *Reports and Letters by George Christopher Pulling Relating to the Beothuk Indians of Newfoundland.* St. John's: Breakwater.

Martin, Kent 1979. "Play by the Rules or Don't Play at All: Space Division and Resource Allocation in a Rural Newfoundland Fishing Community." *North Atlantic Maritime Cultures* Raoul Andersen (ed). the Hague: Mouton.

Martin-Matthews, Anne 1977. Wives' Experiences of Relocation: Status Passage and the Moving Career. Unpublished Ph.D. dissertation, McMaster University.

Martin-Matthews, Anne 1980. "The Newfoundland Migrant Wife." *People, Power and Process* A. Himelfarb, J. Richardson, (eds). Toronto: University of Toronto Press.

Matthews, D. Ralph 1976. *'There's No Better Place than Here': Social Change in Three Newfoundland Communities.* Toronto: Peter Martin Associates.

Matthews, D. R. 1993. *Controlling Common Property: Regulating Canada's Eash Coast Fishery.* Toronto: University of Toronto Press.

McCay, Bonnie J. 1976. 'Appropriate Technology' and Coastal Fishermen of Newfoundland. Unpublished Ph.D. dissertation, Columbia University.

McCay, B. 1978. "Systems Ecology, People Ecology, and the Anthropology of Fishing Communities." *Human Ecology* 6(4): 397-427.

McCay, B. 1979. "'Fish is Scarce': Fisheries Modernization on Fogo Island." *North Atlantic Maritime Cultures* Raoul Andersen (ed). The Hague: Mouton.

McCay, B. 1980. "A Fishermen's Co-operative, Limited: Indigenous Resource Management in a Complex Society." *Anthropological Quarterly* 53(1): 29-38.

McCormack, Sister Mary Basil, S.M. 1955. The Educational Works of the Sisters of Mercy in Newfoundland: 1845-1955. Unpublished M.A. dissertation, Catholic University of America.

McGrath, Carmelita 1990. "Ethnography of Southeast Bight." Women and Economic Life in Newfoundland: Three Case Studies Marilyn Porter (ed). A report on project #482-87-0005 funded by SSHRC, Women and Work Strategic Grants.

McLintock, A.H. 1941. *The Establishment of Constitutional Government in Newfoundland, 1783-1832.* London: Longmans, Green & Co., Ltd.

McQuaig, Linda 1991. *The Quick and the Dead: Brian Mulroney, Big Business and the Seduction of Canada.* Toronto: Ryerson.

Meillassoux, Claude 1975. *Maidens, Meal and Money.* Cambridge: Cambridge University Press.

Metzgar, Jack 1980. "Plant Shutdowns and Worker Response: The Case of Johnston, Pa." *Socialist Review*, 53 10(5): 9-49.

346

Michael, Lorraine 1991. "How I Lost Faith in the Church."*Toronto Star*, March 9.

Miles, Angela 1991. "Reflections on Integrative Feminism and Rural Women."*Women and Social Change* Jeri Dawn Wine, Janice Ristock (eds). Toronto: James Lorimer.

Mills J. 1978. "Women in the Labour and Conservative Parties." paper presented at PSA Conference.

Ministers Valcourt/ Wilson, n.d.. An Agenda for Prosperity. Ottawa: Employment and Immigration Canada.

Mohanty, Chandra Talpade 1992. "Feminist Encounters: Locating the Politics of Experience." *Destabilizing Theory: Contemporary Feminist Debates* Michelle Barrett, A. Phillips (eds). Stanford: Stanford University Press.

Morgan, Bernice 1992. *Random Passage.* St. John's: Breakwater Books.

Muir, Margaret 1977. "Professional Women and Network Maintenance in a French and an English Canadian Fishing Village."*Atlantis*, 2(2) Part II: 45-56.

Murray, Hilda 1979. *More Than 50%: A Woman's Life in a Newfoundland Outport, 1900-1950.* St. John's: Breakwater Books.

Nadel-Klein, Janet, D.L. Davis (eds) 1988. *To Work and to Weep: Women in Fishing Economies.* St. John's: ISER.

National Film Board of Canada (NFB) 1979. *No Life for a Woman.* produced and directed by Bonnie Kreps.

Neary, Peter 1988. *Newfoundland in the North Atlantic World, 1929-1949.* Kingston: McGill-Queens.

Neis, Barbara 1994. "Occupational Health and Safety of Women Working in Fish and Crab Processing in Newfoundland and Labrador,"*Chronic Diseases in Canada* 15(1): 6-11.

Neis, Barbara, Susan Williams 1993. *Occupational Stress and Repetitive Strain Injuries: Research Review and Pilot Study.* Report No. 8. St. John's: ISER.

Nemec Tom 1971. "I fish with My Brother." *North Atlantic Maritime Cultures* Raoul Andersen (ed). the Hague: Mouton.

Nevitt, Joyce 1978. *White Caps and Black Bands: Nursing in Newfoundland to 1934.* St. John's: Jesperson.

Newfoundland Department of Economic Development, A.R.D.A. 1964. Stephenville and the Port au Port Peninsula: a preliminary statement on the problems and possibilities of the newly designated A.R.D.A. study region. St.John's.

Newfoundland and Labrador, Government 1974. Report of the Royal Commission on Labrador, esp. Vol. V Status of Women. St. John's: Queen's Printer.

Newfoundland and Labrador, Government 1986. *Building on Our Strengths: Report of the Royal Commission on Employment and Unemployment.* St. John's: Queen's Printer.

Newfoundland Fisheries Commission 1963. Report and Recommendations of the Newfoundland Fisheries Commission to the Government of Newfoundland, April, St. John's.

Nicholson, Linda 1986. "Feminism and Marx: Integrating Kinship with the economic."*Feminism as Critique* Seyla Benhabib, Drucilla Cornell (eds). Minneapolis: University of Minnesota Press.

Oakley Ann, J. Mitchell (eds) 1967. *The Rights and Wrongs of Women.* Harmondsworth: Penguin.

O'Neill, Paul 1980. "Jezebels and the Just: Women in Newfoundland 1500-1800." Lecture presented to the Newfoundland Historical Society, April 17.

Oosten, Jaarich G. 1986. "Male and Female in Inuit Shamanism."*Inuit Studies*, 10(1-2): 115-131.

Orbach, M.K., J. R. Maiolo (eds) 1982. *Modernization and Marine Fisheries Policy.* Ann Arbor: Ann Arbor Science.

Orbach, M. 1977. *Hunters, Seamen and Entrepreneurs.* Berkely: University of California Press.

Organization for Economic Co-operation and Development 1983. *Positive Adjustment Policies Managing Structural Change*. Paris: OECD.

Overton, James 1988. "Public Relief and Social unrest in Newfoundland in the 1930s: An Evaluation of Piven and Cloward." *Class, Gender and Region: Essays in Canadian Historical Sociology* G.S. Kealey (ed). St. John's: Canadian Committee on Labour History.

Overton, J. 1990. "Economic Crisis and the End of Democracy: Politics in Newfoundland During the Great Depression." *Labour/Le Travail*, 26: 85-124.

Palmer, Craig 1991. "Growing Female Roots in Patrilocal Soil: Female Property Rights and the Flexibility Needed to Survive a Failing Fishery." *Living on the Edge* Peter Sinclair, L. Felt (eds). St. John's: ISER.

Parr, Joy 1990. *The Gender of Breadwinners: Women, Men and Change in Two Industrial Towns, 1880-1950*. Toronto: University of Toronto Press.

Parsons, Linda 1987. Passing the Time: The Lives of Women in a Northern Industrial Town. Unpublished M.A dissertation, Memorial University.

Pastore, Ralph T. 1978. *Newfoundland Micmacs: A History of their Traditional Life*. St. John's: Newfoundland Historical Society Pamphlet No. 5.

Pastore, R. T. 1992. *Shanawdithit's People: The Archaeology of the Beothuks*. St. John's: Breakwater.

Patey, Nina n.d. "Perceptions of the Involvement of Women in the Labrador Fishery." Unpublished Paper, Maritime History Group, Memorial University.

Penney, Sister Mary Paula, R.S.M. 1980. A Study of the Contributions of Three Religious Congregations to the Growth of Education in the Province of Newfoundland. Unpublished Ph.D. dissertation, Boston College.

Pocius, Gerald L. 1991. *A Place to Belong: Community Order and Everyday Space in Calvert, Newfoundland* Montreal: McGill-Queen's.

Pocius, G. L. 1979. "Hooked rugs in Newfoundland: the Representation of Social Structure in Design." *Journal of American Folklore*, 92: 273-84.

Pope, Peter 1992. The South Avalon Planters, 1630 to 1700: Residence, Labour, Demand and Exchange in Seventeenth-Century Newfoundland. Unpublished Ph.D. dissertation, Memorial University.

Porter, Helen, 1988. *January, February, June or July*. St. John's: Breakwater.

Porter, Marilyn 1982. *Home, Work and Class Consciousness*. Manchester: Manchester University Press.

Porter, M. 1983. "Women and Old Boats: The Sexual Division of Labour in a Newfoundland Outport." *Public and Private: Gender and Society* E. Garmarnikow et.al. (eds). London: Heinneman.

Porter, M. 1985. "'The Tangly Bunch': Outport Women of the Avalon Peninsula." *Newfoundland Studies* 1: 77-90.

Porter, M. 1987. "Peripheral Women: Towards a Feminist Analysis of the Atlantic Region." *Studies in Political Economy* 23:41-72

Porter, M. 1988. "Mothers and Daughters: Women's Life Stories in Grand Bank, Newfoundland." *Women's Studies International Forum*, 11.

Porter, M. 1991. "Time, The Life Course and Work in Women's Lives." *Women's Studies International Forum*, 14(1-2): 1-13.

Porter, M. 1993. *Place and Persistence in the Lives of Newfoundland Women*. Aldershot: Avebury.

Porter, Marilyn, B. Brown, E. Dettmer, C. McGrath 1990. Women and Economic Life in Newfoundland: Three Case Studies. A report on project #482-87-0005 funded by SSHRC, Women and Work Strategic Grants.

348

Quinonez, Lora Ann, CDP, M. D. Turner 1992. *The Transformation of American Catholic Sisters*. Philadelphia: Temple University Press.

Reddin, Estelle 1991. "Organizing in a Small Community - Prince Edward Island." *Women and Social Change* Jeri Dawn Wine, Janice Ristock (eds). Toronto: James Lorimer.

Rendel, M. (ed) 1981. *Women, Power and Political Systems*. London: Croom Helm.

Report of the Task Force on the Atlantic Fishery, 1983. *Navigating Troubled Waters: A New Policy for the Atlantic Fisheries*. Ottawa: Minister of Supply and Services.

Richard, Agnes M. 1989. *Threads of Gold, Newfoundland and Labrador Jubilee Guilds and Women's Institutes*. St. John's: Creative Publishers.

Richardson, Gerald 1940. *Report of the Co-operative Division of the Department of Agriculture and Rural Reconstruction*. St. John's.

Riley, Denise 1988. *"Am I That Name?": Feminism and the Category of 'Women' in History*. Minneapolis: University of Minnesota Press.

Ristock, Janice 1991. "Feminist Collectives: The Struggles and Contradictions in our Quest for a Uniquely Feminist Structure." *Women and Social Change* Jeri Dawn Wine, Janice Ristock (eds). Toronto: James Lorimer.

Roberts, Elizabeth 1984. *A Woman's Place: An Oral History of Working-Class Women, 1890-1940*. London.

Rogers S.C. 1978. "Woman's Place: a critical review of anthropological theory." *Comparative Studies in Society and History*, 20.

Rosaldo Michelle Z. 1974. "Women, Culture and Society. *Women, Culture and Society* Michelle Z. Rosaldo, L. Lamphere (eds). Stanford: Stanford University Press.

Rose, Hilary 1985. "Securing Social Citizenship." *New Socialist* 25 (March).

Rosen, Ellen Israel 1987. *Bitter Choices: Blue-Collar Women in and out of Work*. Chicago: University of Chicago Press.

Rosenberg, Harriet 1990. "The Kitchen and the Multinational Corporation." *Through the Kitchen Window* Meg Luxton, H. Rosenberg, S. Arat-Koc (eds). Toronto: Garamond Press.

Rowbotham, Sheila, L. Segal, H. Wainwright 1979. *Beyond the Fragments: Feminism and the Making of Socialism*. London: Merlin.

Rowe, Andy Consulting Economists 1991. Effect of the Crisis in the Newfoundland Fishery on Women Who Work in the Industry. St. John's: Women's Policy Office.

Rowe, Frederick W. 1977. *Extinction: The Beothuks of Newfoundland*. Toronto: McGraw-Hill Ryerson.

Sanday, P. 1974. "Female Status in the Public Domain." *Woman Culture and Society* Rosaldo and Lamphere (eds). Stanford: Stanford University Press.

Scharf, Lois 1980. *To Work or to Wed: Female Employment, Feminism, and the Great Depression*. Westport, Conn..

Scheffel, David 1980. The Demographic Consequences of European Contact with Labrador Inuit, 1800-1919. Unpublished M.A. dissertation, Memorial University.

Schneiders, Sandra M., I.H.M. 1991. "Beyond Patching: Faith and Feminism in the Catholic Church." *The Anthony Jordan Lecture 1990, Newman Theological College, Edmonton*. New York: Paulist Press.

Scott, Joan 1988. "Deconstructing Equality-Versus-Difference: or, the Uses of Poststructuralist Theory for Feminists." *Feminist Studies* 14(1): 33-50.

Scott, J. 1988. *Gender and the Politics of History*. New York: Columbia University Press.

Sealy, Nanciellen 1976. "Women's Work and Worth in an Acadian Maritime village." Paper delivered at the conference: Research on Women: Current Projects and Future Directions, Mount St. Vincent University, Halifax.

Seaman's Institute Administration Changes 1926. *Among the Deep Sea Fishers*, 29 (April).

Sheehan, Nancy M. 1986. "Women's Organizations and Educational Issues." *Canadian Woman Studies/Les Cahiers de la Femme*, 7 (3): 90-94.

Sheppard, Manson H. 1972. "A Brief History of the Fogo Island Shipbuilding and Producers Cooperative." Student paper (Department of Geography) in Centre for Newfoundland Studies, Memorial Univ.

Sider, Gerald 1980. "The Ties that Bind: Culture and Agriculture, Property and Propriety in the Newfoundland Village Fishery." *Social History* 5(1): 1-39.

Sievers, Sharon L. 1981. "Feminist Criticism in Japanese Politics in the 1880's: The Experience of Kishida Toshiko." *Signs*, 6(4): 602-616.

Sinclair, Peter 1985. *From Traps to Draggers: Domestic Commodity Production in Northwest Newfoundland, 1850-1982*. St. John's: ISER.

Sinclair, P. 1987. *State Intervention and the Newfoundland Fisheries*. Aldershot: Avebury.

Sinclair, P. and L. Felt. 1994, forthcoming. "Coming Back: Return Migration to Newfoundland's Great Northern Peninsula." *Newfoundland Studies*.

Sisters of the Presentation of the Blessed Virgin Mary 1958. Constitutions of the Congregation of the Sisters of the Presentation of the Blessed Virgin Mary. St. John's: Presentation Sisters of Newfoundland.

Sisters of Mercy 1954. Revised Constitutions of the Congregation of the Sisters of Mercy of Newfoundland. St. John's: Patrick J Skinner, C.J.M., Archbishop of St. John's.

Slote, A. 1969. *Termination: The Closing of Baker Plant*. New York: Bobbs-Merrill.

Smith, Dorothy E. 1987. *Everyday World As Problematic: A Feminist Sociology*. Toronto: University of Toronto.

Smith-Rosenberg, Carroll 1975. "The Female World of Love and Ritual: Relations Between Women in Nineteenth Century America." *Signs*, 1 (1): 1-29.

Snell, James G. 1993. "The Newfoundland Old Age Pension Programme, 1911-1949." *Acadiensis*, 23(1): 86-109.

Stack, Carol B., L. M. Burton 1993. "Kinscripts." *Journal of Comparative Family Studies*, 14(2).

Statistics Canada 1983. *Newfoundland and Labrador 400 Years Later: A Statistical Portrait*. St. John's.

Stern, James 1971. "Consequences of a Plant Closure." *The Journal of Human Resources*, 7(1): 3-25.

Steffler, John 1992. *The Afterlife of George Cartwright*. Toronto: McClelland and Stewart.

Stellman, Jean, S. Daum 1973. *Work is Dangerous to Your Health*. New York: Vintage Books.

Stevenson, Nicola 1990. "A Follow-Up Study of Women in a Northern Industrial Town." Unpublished paper, Memorial University.

Stewart, Kathleen 1991. "On the Politics of Cultural Theory: A Case for 'Contaminated' Cultural Critique." *Social Research*, 58 (9): 395-412.

Stiles, R. Geoffrey 1972. "Fishermen, Wives and Radios: Aspects of communication in a Newfoundland fishing community." *North Atlantic Fishermen* Raoul Andersen, C. Wadel (eds). St John's: ISER.

Stiles, R. G. 1979. "Labor Recruitment and the Family Crew in Newfoundland." *North Atlantic Maritime Cultures* R. Andersen (ed). the Hague: Mouton.

Straus, Richard 1967. "The Americans Come to Newfoundland." *The Book of Newfoundland*. St. John's: Newfoundland Publishers, pp. 555-560.

Szala, K.K. 1978. Clean Women and Quiet Men: Courtship and Marriage in a Newfoundland Fishing Village. Unpublished M.A. dissertation, Memorial University.

350

Szwed J. 1966. *Private Cultures and Public Imagery*. St. John's: ISER.

Taylor, J. Garth 1974. *Labrador Eskimo Settlements of the Early Contact Period*. National Museum of Canada Publication in *Ethnology* 9, Ottawa.

The Annual Report of the Seaman's Institute 1921. *Among the Deep Sea Fishers*, 24, (October).

The Sisters of Mercy and the Presentation Sisters, St. John's. 1990. "Brief." The Report of the Archdiocesan Commission of Enquiry into the Sexual Abuse of Children by Members of the Clergy, Volume II Background Studies and Briefs. St. John's: Archdiocese of St. John's.

Thompson, Paul, T. Wailey, T. Lummis 1983. *Living the Fishing*. London: Routledge and Kegan Paul.

Thompson, P. 1979. Paper presented to ASA Symposium on "Women in Fishing Economies"

Thompson, F. 1939. *Lark Rise to Candleford*. Oxford: Oxford University Press.

Thornton, Patricia 1985. "The Problem of Out-Migration from Atlantic Canada, 1871-1921." *Acadiensis*, 15(1): 3-33.

Tuck, James A. 1976. *Newfoundland and Labrador Prehistory*. Ottawa: National Museum of Man.

Tuck, J. A., R. T. Pastore 1985. "A Nice Place to Visit, but...Prehistoric Human Extinctions on the Island of Newfoundland." *Canadian Journal of Archaeology* 9(1): 69-79.

Tunstall, J. 1962. *The Fishermen*. London: MacGibbon Kee.

Upton, L.F.S. 1978. "The Beothucks: Questions and Answers." *Acadiensis* 8(2): 150-155.

Valverde, Mariana 1991. *The Age of Light, Soap, and Water: Moral Reform in English Canada, 1881-1925*. Toronto: McClelland and Stewart.

Vickers, Jill McCalla. "Where Are the Women in Canadian Politics?" *Atlantis* 3(2), Part II, 1978: 40-51.

Wadel, Cato 1969a. *Marginal Adaptations and Modernization in Newfoundland*. St. John's: ISER.

Wadel, C. 1969b. Communities and Committees: Community Development and The Enlargement of the Sense of Community on Fogo Island, Newfoundland. St. John's: Extension Service, Memorial University.

Walsh, T.J. 1980. *Nano Nagle and the Presentation Sisters*. Monastrevan, Ireland: Presentation Generalate [first published 1959].

Ware, S. 1982. *Holding Their Own: American Women in the 1930s*. Boston.

Washburne, Heluiz C. and Anauta 1940. *Land of the Good Shadows: The Life Story of Anauta, an Eskimo Woman*. New York: John Day Co.

Weaver, Mary Jo 1986. *New Catholic Women: A Contemporary Challenge to Traditional Religious Authority*. San Francisco: Harper and Row Publishers.

Weedon, Chris 1987. *Feminist Practice and Poststructuralist Theory*. Oxford: Basil Blackwell.

Weir, Lorna 1986. Sexual Rule, Sexual Politics: Studies in the Medicalization of Sexual Danger, 1830-1930. Unpublished Ph.D. dissertation, York University.

Whitaker, Robin 1993. Staying Faithful: Challenges to Newfoundland Convents. Unpublished M.A. dissertation, York University.

White, Linda 1991. The General Hospital of Nursing, St. John's, Newfoundland, 1903-1930. Unpublished M.A. dissertation, Memorial University.

Whitehead, A. 1976. "Sexual Antagonism in Herefordshire." *Dependence and Exploitation in Work and Marriage* Barker and Allen (eds). London: Longmans.

Will, Gavin 1992. "Church in a State." *This Magazine*, 26 (5): 11-12.

Williams, Raymond 1976. *Keywords*. London: Fontana.

Wilson, W. 1966. *Newfoundland and its Missionaries*. Cambridge Mass.: Dakin and Metcalfe.

Wilson, S.J. 1982. *Women, the Family and the Economy*. Toronto: McGraw-Hill Ryerson.

Winter, Keith 1975. *Shananditti: The Last of the Beothucks*. Vancouver: J.J. Douglas.

Wittberg, Patricia 1989. "Feminist Consciousness Among American Nuns: Patterns of Ideological Diffusion." *Women's Studies International Forum*, 12 (5): 529-537.

Women's Institute Project 1977. Report on the Women's Institute in Labrador Straits. Capstan Island, Labrador.

Women's Reference Group 1992. Draft Women's Agenda for Training. Toronto: Canadian Labour Force Development Board.

Women's Unemployment Study Group 1983. *Not for Nothing: Women, Work and Unemployment in Newfoundland and Labrador*. St. John's.

Yetman, Lori, 1990. Sex as Power: Stories as Memories, unpublished M.A. dissertation, Memorial University.

Zulaika, J. 1981. *Terra Nova: The Ethos and Luck of Deepsea Fishermen*. St. John's: ISER.

Contributors

Cecilia Benoit is the author of *Midwives in Passage* and currently teaches Sociology at the University of Victoria.

Isobel Brown is a writer. Her experience as a war bride was the basis for her award winning personal narrative, "Two Photographs," included in this book.

Roberta Buchanan's work includes poetry, drama and criticism. She currently teaches in the Department of English at Memorial University.

Sean Cadigan holds a post doctoral fellowship in History at Memorial University and is currently researching the turn of the century history of Cape Bonavista communities.

Jaya Chauhan specializes in the area of women and science. She currently resides in Edmonton, Alberta.

Linda Christiansen-Ruffman actively promotes research on gender issues both regionally and internationally. She currently teaches Sociology at St. Mary's University.

Linda Cullum was a contributor to *Pursuing Equality* and is currently a doctoral student at the Ontario Institute for Studies in Education.

Mary Dalton is the author of two books of poetry *The Time of Icicles* (Breakwater, 1989) and *Allowing the Light* (Breakwater, 1993). She teaches in the Department of English at Memorial University.

Dona Davis is the author of *Blood and Nerves* and co-editor of *To Work and to Weep*. She currently teaches at the University of South Dakota.

Elke Dettmer is a folklorist and was a researcher on the *Women's Economic Lives* project. She lives in Pouch Cove.

Nancy Forestell is currently teaching in the Department of History, St. Francis Xavier University.

Camille Fouillard is a journalist, writer, and recent prize winner in the Writers' Union of Canada 1994 Short Prose Competition for Developing Writers.

Glynys George is a doctoral student in Anthropology at the University of Toronto. She did her field work in Stephenville.

Noreen Golfman is still a board member with CARAL (Canadian Abortion Rights Action League). She teaches in the Department of English and in Women's Studies at Memorial.

Anne Hart's work includes poems, short stories and two books, *The Life and Times of Miss Jane Marple* (Dodd Mead, 1985) and *The Life and Times of Hercule Poirot* (Putnam's, 1990). She is head of the Centre for Newfoundland Studies at Memorial University.

Greta Hussey has spent most of her life in Port de Grave, with the exception of summers in Southern Labrador from 1923-1942, on which her book, *Our Life on Lears Room*, is based. In recent years, she has demonstrated crafts in Newfoundland and across Canada.

Bonnie McCay is an internationally-recognized expert on fishery related issues. She has been researching the Fogo Island fishery for almost 20 years. Bonnie currently teaches at Rutgers University.

Carmelita McGrath is a writer and editor who has also worked in research and education. Her books are *Poems on Land and on Water* (Killick Press, 1992) and *Walking to Shenak* (fiction, Killick Press, 1994).

Lorraine Michael is alive and well and living in Toronto. She continues to work on women's and social justice issues with the Ecumenical Coalition for Economic Justice.

Bernice Morgan is a writer who has explored the past and present lives of women in Newfoundland in her novels *Random Passage* (Breakwater, 1992) and *Waiting for Time* (Breakwater, 1994).

Barbara Neis teaches Sociology and Women's Studies at Memorial University and is currently researching the demise of the Newfoundland and Labrador fisheries.

Linda Parsons currently teaches in the Department of Sociology at Memorial University.

Evie Plaice is the author of *The Native Game* and is currently teaching anthropology at the University of Natal.

Helen Porter is the author of *Below the Bridge* (Breakwater, 1980), the novel *January, February, June or July* (Breakwater, 1988) and the fiction collection *A Long and Lonely Ride* (Breakwater, 1991) from which the story in this collection is taken.

Marilyn Porter teaches Sociology and Women's Studies at Memorial. After ten years studying aspects of women's lives in Newfoundland she is extending her interests to women in other parts of the world.

Jane Robinson recently completed her Masters degree at the Ontario Institute for Studies in Education. She lives in Pouch Cove and has continued her involvement with research related to women's issues in the province.

Virginia Ryan is a writer in St. John's. She has published in *TickleAce* and *Canadian Fiction Magazine*, the publication where the story "Mary Conway" in this collection originally appeared.

Victoria Silk has been displaced by the fishery crisis. She currently works for the Justice Institute in Vancouver.

Robin Whitaker is currently completing her doctorate in Anthropology at the University of Santa Cruz, Santa Cruz, California.

Miriam Wright is currently researching provincial fisheries policy in the post World War II period in the doctoral program at Memorial University.